RHETORIC and COMPOSITION

a sourcebook for teachers

HAYDEN ENGLISH LANGUAGE SERIES

Robert W. Boynton — Consulting Editor

Former Principal, Senior High School
and Chairman, English Department
Germantown Friends School

GRAMMAR BASICS: A Reading/Writing Approach (Second Ed.)
Jean Malmstrom

LANGUAGE IN SOCIETY (Second Ed.)
Jean Malmstrom

WORDS, WORDS, WORDS
Vocabularies and Dictionaries (Second Ed.)
Richard R. Lodwig and Eugene F. Barrett

WRITING TO BE READ (Second Ed.)
Ken Macrorie

TELLING WRITING (Second Ed.)
Ken Macrorie

ENGLISH I and II: A Contemporary Approach
R. W. Boynton, Ruby K. Johnson, and Ruth E. Reeves

EXERCISES IN READING AND WRITING
Alexandra Davis and O. B. Davis

COMPOSING: Writing as a Self-Creating Process
William E. Coles, Jr.

THE IMPACT OF MASS MEDIA
Pearl G. Aldrich

RHETORIC and COMPOSITION: A Sourcebook for Teachers
Richard L. Graves

FORMING/THINKING/WRITING: The Composing Imagination
Ann E. Berthoff

RHETORIC and COMPOSITION

a sourcebook for teachers

RICHARD L. GRAVES

Professor of English Education
Auburn University

HAYDEN BOOK COMPANY, INC.
Rochelle Park, New Jersey

Library of Congress Cataloging in Publication Data

Main entry under title:

Rhetoric and composition.

(Hayden English language series)
1. English language—Study and teaching. 2. English language—Rhetoric. I. Graves, Richard Layton, date
PE1065.R48 808'.042 76-13016
ISBN 0-8104-5984-1

Printed in the United States of America

3	4	5	6	7	8	9	PRINTING
78	79	80	81	82	83	84	YEAR

Preface

Rhetoric and Composition: A Sourcebook for Teachers is intended for practicing and prospective teachers—from elementary school to graduate school—who are (or will be) involved in the most challenging task in the educational enterprise, helping others learn how to write. The book has grown out of my belief that the best single source of help in this area lies in certain articles which have appeared in recent years in the professional literature. Of the greatest help are those journals whose chief audience is English teachers, and those authors who are experienced practitioners. This book reflects the conviction that most teachers, given the opportunity to study these articles with care, will have the wisdom and initiative to translate them into effective classroom practice.

Although *Rhetoric and Composition* has no single unifying theme, it does include three major strands or undercurrents, three prevailing beliefs about the practice and teaching of writing. It is important to recognize that their presence in this text is merely representative of their life in the broader profession.

The first underlying belief is that writing is a difficult though satisfying experience. Like other creative activity, it includes both spiritual agony and exhilaration. Good writing demands rigorous self-discipline and brings a deep sense of satisfaction and accomplishment. In the past, unfortunately, this attitude has not always prevailed. It has been more customary for teachers to view writing as a necessary drudgery, as something that must be endured but never can be perfected and enjoyed. But now fresh winds are blowing, and attitudes seem to be changing. More attention is being given to the *act* of writing, the process of beginning with a hunch, turning the hunch into a respectable thesis, marshaling evidence and related material, ordering the parts into a logical pattern, revising and recasting and rereading. In all this the writer's goal is not to dazzle his audience but to say what he believes is true. In the very process the writer comes to know his subject and, more important, to comprehend more fully his own stance toward it.

A second widely held belief is that current practice in teaching composition in our schools is in a shambles. James R. Squire, former executive secretary of NCTE, has used the word "chaos" to describe the situation. "Writing," he has said, "is the disgrace of American education. . . . In no other area of elementary, secondary, and college English education is our need so great."

The public has good reason to wonder why after twelve years of education, after several thousand hours spent in the classroom studying English, so many young people graduate from high school still unable to write a good sentence or compose a coherent paragraph. One thing the public may not realize is that English teachers see themselves primarily as teachers of literature, not composition, and as a consequence most class time is spent studying literature. This arrangement seems natural to English teachers, for most of their professional preparation consists of course work in British and American literature. Furthermore, the schools are not well organized for teaching composition. Much value is placed on group work and socialization but very little on individual privacy. The school day is divided into hourly segments, but the composing process often requires long stretches of uninterrupted time. Even if time were available, many teachers remain uninformed about how to teach writing and often confuse paper-marking with teaching. When asked about the proportion of time devoted to composition, some of the participants in the Squire-Applebee study unwittingly confessed that current class (and paper) loads prevented any more attention to composition. The researchers concluded that "For most teachers, correcting papers is synonymous with teaching writing."

If teachers lack knowledge of specific skills and strategies for teaching writing, part of the fault must lie in the educational theory that has been dominant in American schools during the twentieth century. The following statements, taken from a chapter on teaching composition in a popular language arts curriculum textbook of the 1950s, illustrate the kind of banal generalization that has too long afflicted teacher education:

> *Proficiency in language skill varies greatly from youngster to youngster.*
>
> *Speech and writing alike find their motivation in daily experiences both inside and outside the school, and range in content from the purely personal to international affairs.*
>
> *Writing, despite its resemblance to speech, makes peculiar demands.*
>
> *By the time students reach the junior high school they are interested in expressing their opinions.*
>
> *The student who has learned to consider his audience will find little difficulty in understanding the format of the business letter.*
>
> *Young people need now to understand the importance of reporting little details in family life, the humorous or pathetic incident, bits of conversation, beliefs, and personal feelings.*

Near the end of the twenty-six page chapter is a revealing comment:

> *Space will not permit a comprehensive discussion of the technical skills involved in writing.*

The situation at the college level is little better. Most tenured English professors teach literature, and composition is left, in Richard M. Weaver's words, to "beginners, part-time teachers, graduate students, faculty wives, and various fringe people." In freshman composition it is routine to expect a continuous turnover of teaching assistants whose primary interest is literature. One could not design a better system for insulating senior professors from undergraduate students.

A third belief is that the means for making a significant improvement in teaching and learning composition are now within reach. Ross Winterowd of the University of Southern California has noted the impact of recent advances in our understanding of syntactic growth:

> At the level of syntax, we are beginning to get theories and materials—such as those of Francis Christensen and John Mellon—that enable the teacher to be of significant help in the student's quest for the ability to put idea within idea within idea. . . . That is, for the first time, we now have the means actually to help students systematically attain syntactic fluency, and surely that fluency is one of the significant intellectual accomplishments.

The same might also be said of other composition concerns. The past decade has seen remarkable developments in such areas as the understanding of peer influences in writing, the understanding of the structure of the paragraph and other units "beyond the sentence," and the uses of the electronic media for communal authorship. Interest in classical rhetoric grows stronger each year and now verges on creating something of a renaissance within the profession. All these developments, plus the existing framework of mandatory public education, inspire new hope for achieving widespread literacy in written expression.

I want to express my sincere appreciation to those who have granted permission for their work to appear here. Their writings have contributed much to my own professional growth, and it is my hope that through wider dissemination their sphere of influence will be enlarged. I also wish to thank Donna Mitchell and her staff in the Secretarial Services Center, who worked faithfully on portions of the manuscript, and Robert W. Boynton, English editor at Hayden, whose comments and suggestions have improved the quality of this book. Special thanks go to my wife, Eloise, whose encouragement and understanding have been constant.

Auburn, Alabama R.L.G.

Contents

Part One

Introduction

"*. . . Except he come to composition, a man remains un-put-together, more than usually troubled by the feuds within, and therefore a little more addicted to those without.*"

ROBERT B. HEILMAN

In this section the reader is introduced to the idea that though writing is a worthwhile and rewarding activity, current practice in teaching writing can best be described as a Wasteland. In "Writing as a Way of Knowing," James M. McCrimmon convincingly explains the value of writing, not only for those who might benefit from the reading but for the writer himself. (McCrimmon's work originally appeared in the NCTE Distinguished Lecture Series for 1970.) The decline of competence in written expression is shown next, first in Squire's and Applebee's thorough and systematic survey of current practice in the high schools, and then in Richard M. Weaver's prophetic analysis of the situation in higher education and the teaching profession at large.

A graduate student once remarked that he had "finished" his research and all that remained was to "write it up." Such a view, according to McCrimmon, is wrong, for in the writing process the researcher really discovers what he has found. It is not the raw data, the statistics, or even the research design which is most important, but the interpretation of one's findings, the determination of their meaning for human experience. Thus seen, the act of writing becomes a search to discover the precise language to convey one's meaning. As McCrimmon says so eloquently, it is a way of knowing as well as a way of telling.

In his discussion of prewriting, McCrimmon also reminds us that careful observation has long been a hallmark of great teachers, and that it is an equally necessary trait for becoming a skilled writer. If we could encourage students to examine their thinking and their early drafts in the same way, say, that Louis Agassiz required his students to examine zoological specimens, or that George Washington Carver meticulously studied common vegetables and nuts, then the quality of student writing would show a marked improvement. McCrimmon calls this kind of close observation "the best cure I know for the generality and incompleteness of student writing."

These viewpoints, though, have not gained wide acceptance in the public schools, where the grading of papers remains synonymous with teaching composition. Most English teachers recognize the rampant inconsistencies in evaluating student papers, but surprisingly few seem to realize or care that such inconsistencies represent a gross injustice against a vast number of young people. If the same level of evaluation existed in other professions (the medical profession, for example), the public would rise up in moral indignation and demand an accounting. As a protest against the current arbitrary and unfair practice, no articles on evaluation appear in this text. Rather, the emphasis throughout is on *teaching and learning composition.* In my opinion the time is at hand for a wholly new approach to evaluating student writing, one which has as its starting point *what has been taught*, not the subjective and sometimes whimsical opinions of the teacher.

Richard M. Weaver's essay completes the picture. A look at the college and university composition curriculum reveals why public school teachers feel insecure about teaching composition and consequently why writing ability in general remains at such a low ebb. At the freshman level, graduate students man the composition classes, and in the upper division either literature specialists or those that Weaver calls "fringe people" hold forth. There are some notable exceptions, but by and large this system, multiplied in the many schools throughout the land and operating over a long period of time, has spawned a failure of national proportions.

Not all readers will agree with the order of Weaver's hierarchy, one which gives preeminence to definition and predication, but it is an argument which deserves careful reading. Despite his concern over the decline of rhetoric, Weaver's central thesis is optimistic. His ultimate purpose is to rekindle interest in things rhetorical and to discover ways of promoting compositional skills. And this, I submit, is the concern of all teachers of writing.

Writing as a Way of Knowing

JAMES M. McCRIMMON

I

Traditionally, the teaching of composition is slanted toward the needs of the reader. Students write for a reader, and the effectiveness of their work is usually judged by the ease and clarity with which the reader understands what is written.

This traditional concern with making the message clear to the reader emphasizes writing as a way of telling. The controlling assumption is that the writer has something to say to a reader and must choose the best way of saying it. In this assumption the writer knows and is willing to tell; the reader does not know but is willing, or can be induced, to learn. The study of composition in the schools, then, is largely concerned with mastering efficient techniques for telling. Thus, however much composition texts may vary, they have a common core of instruction dealing with the organization of material, the development of paragraphs, the construction of various types of sentences, the choice of appropriate diction, and the conventions of standard usage. When writing is considered as a way of telling, proficiency in these skills constitutes the goals of instruction.

These goals need no apology. If they are achieved, the young writer knows how to organize and present his material, and in a world that depends heavily on effective communication, this is a solid accomplishment. But . . . I am concerned with a different view of the writing process, with writing as a way of knowing, not of knowing in order to be able to tell others, but of knowing for self-understanding. I am concerned with the kind of insights a writer gets of his subject during the writing process, in which process I include both the planning and the writing of the paper.

The notion that a writer learns about his subject by writing about it doesn't quite make sense in the traditional view. It is likely to remind us of the student who complained to his instructor, "How can I tell what I mean

The Promise of English: NCTE 1970 Distinguished Lectures (Urbana, Illinois: National Council of Teachers of English, 1970), pp. 115–130.

until I see what I've written?" And that seems like a classic example of putting the cart before the horse, until we find distinguished writers saying the same thing in more sophisticated language. Listen to this comment by C. Day Lewis about his own writing:

> I do not sit down at my desk to put into verse something that is already clear in my mind. If it were clear in my mind, I should have no incentive or need to write about it, for I am an explorer, not a journalist, a propagandist, or a statistician. . . . The theme of a poem is the meaning of its subject matter for me. When I have discovered the meaning *to me* of the various fragments of experience which are constellating in my mind, I have begun to make sense of such experience and to realize a pattern in it; and often I have gone some way with the poem before I am able to grasp the theme which lies hidden in the material that has accumulated.[1]

Obviously there are great differences between a British poet laureate writing a poem and an average student writing a composition, but I suggest that the two situations have enough in common to make the Lewis quotation useful to us as teachers. The common element is the writer's need to understand his own private, and therefore original, view of the subject, to shape discrete impressions into a pattern which he can identify as his personal interpretation of the subject. The recognition of this pattern allows him to fit what Lewis calls the "constellating fragments" into a cognitive structure. By finding a unifying relation among the fragments the writer learns what they mean to him.

We use various names for this unifying relation. Lewis calls it a "theme," a painter or musician might call it a "motif," a journalist could call it an "angle." I prefer to consider it here as the *real* subject in contrast to the *nominal* subject. It is what the writing is really about, what it has to say. The nominal subject indicates no content. It is merely a topic to be explored, say, Chicago or Main Street. The real subject is what Sandburg sees in his "Chicago" or what Sinclair Lewis sees in his *Main Street.* What they see, and therefore what they say, is an interpretation of what the place means to them. This interpretation has to be discovered sometime during the writing process, and part of the function of the writing is to lead to that discovery.

We get a commoner illustration of the evolution of a real subject if we shift from writing to speaking. We all know that in any serious conversation on an important topic our view of the subject changes as we move through the conversation. Some lines of thought peter out; others open up and suggest ideas not previously thought of, and what we end with may be a considerably different view of the subject that we had at the beginning. In retrospect we seem to have been groping toward an understanding that was

[1] "The Making of a Poem," *Saturday Evening Post*, 234 (January 21, 1961), p. 19.

unknown or only dimly foreseen when the conversation started. Perhaps the noblest example of this process is the dialectic of a Platonic dialogue which transcends the limitations of the opening statements and discovers what Plato called the "truth."

A similar kind of inquiry goes on as we write. The process of writing is a process of making choices. Often the writer does not know at the beginning what choices he will make, or even what his choices are; but each fresh choice tends to dictate those that follow, and gradually a pattern begins to emerge and the constellating fragments fall into place just as they did in C. Day Lewis' poem. But, unlike speaking, the choices in writing are made in secret. Except on rare occasions when a reader can compare the first draft with the final version, he does not overhear the internal debate that went on in the writer's mind. All he sees is the finished product, and all the writer's conflicts have presumably been resolved before that product was submitted to the reader.

Usually, but not always. Recently I read a student paper which gave me a kind of X-ray picture of the writer's thinking as he rejected what he was saying, reversed himself, and destroyed the unity of his essay by discovering his real position. I had asked each member of the class to play the role of final judge in an essay contest. Each student was given the same three essays and was told that a screening committee had chosen these as the three best essays out of all those written by freshmen during the term. My students were to choose the best and next best of the three essays as winner and runner-up in a freshman essay contest. They had two hours in which to study the essays and write their judgments.

This particular student began his paper by saying that although he felt that one essay had the most interesting and the most mature content, he had to reject it because of a syntactic weakness. He then proceeded to explain the reasons for his first and second choices. But just as he had apparently finished his judgment he added another paragraph in which he reversed himself and awarded first place to the essay he had originally rejected. His explanation was that he found himself becoming increasingly dissatisfied with his decisions and that he now felt that he had overestimated the significance of what he thought was awkwardness in one long, involved sentence of the rejected essay and had consequently underrated the paper as a whole.

Perhaps we might think that he should have made up his mind before he began to write his judgment, but the fact is that he *had* made up his mind. He wrote what he intended to write and in writing discovered he was wrong. He had started with the assumption that syntactic correctness was a major criterion and that it must dominate his judgment, but in the process of trying to support his judgment he found it insupportable. If he had had time he would probably have rewritten his paper to conceal his change of mind. But in a situation that did not permit rewriting he had to choose between consistency and honesty. In my opinion he made the right choice.

I have chosen a very simple illustration of writing as a discovery process. Any editor could provide more complex examples of a writer who learned what he wanted to say through a series of rough drafts that groped toward his final view of the subject. This is especially true of fiction. The testimony of short story writers, novelists, and dramatists shows that during the writing a character will outgrow the author's original conception of him and begin to force changes in the plot, much as the characters in Pirandello's *Six Characters in Search of an Author* gradually took over the play from the manager. But it is also true of exposition. I have seen a memorandum by Wayne Booth, the author of *Rhetoric of Fiction*, showing the five-year evolution of that book, as he moved from the intent to write an essay refuting certain critical errors to a history of narration and finally to a rhetoric of fiction. Booth's concept of his subject grew with his writing about it, and it was only after he had written a 2500-page manuscript that he saw what he wanted to do in his 500-page book. At no time was Booth's problem one of trying to say clearly what he knew. Quite the opposite, he was trying to know clearly what to say. He was trying to find his real subject.

The tools that a writer uses to explore his subject are words. He is continually concerned with finding the words that most accurately record his impressions of the subject. But since the words he uses will help determine these impressions, he is in a constant process of trying to equate words with concepts and attitudes. Even at a time when he is not sure what precisely he wants to say he must understand the implications of the statements he makes so that he can see in what direction his writing is taking him. John Ciardi calls this procedure a groping for words that are intuitively recognized as right when they are discovered. In other words, the writer may not know precisely what he wants to say, but he recognizes an accurate statement of his meaning when he makes it.

In all this search for the right words young writers especially must be on guard against two kinds of corruption—vagueness and artificiality. At this point I am concerned with vagueness not as an offense against the reader, which it also is, but as an offense against the writer himself, or rather against the discipline of writing. Every instance of vagueness is a sign that the writer has settled for a superficial view of his subject by glossing over details that need to be investigated closely. Artificiality, which is often a major cause of vagueness, is a sign that the writer is more concerned with impressing readers with what he imagines to be stylistic virtuosity than in improving his knowledge of the subject. If writing is a way of learning, vagueness and artificiality are cardinal sins, perhaps the only cardinal sins in composition.

II

The practical difference between viewing writing as a way of knowing and viewing it as a way of telling is that the first view emphasizes the quality of what is presented and the second emphasizes the quality of the presentation. The classroom terms that come closest to naming this contrast are "content" and "style." These are not mutually exclusive terms, for content and style are so interrelated that it is often impossible to discuss either except in relation to the other. But they are pedagogically useful terms and, with a necessary expansion of the meaning of "content," they will serve to introduce a contrast of emphases in the practical conduct of a composition course.

We often use the word "content" to refer to the information provided about the subject, to what is sometimes called the "message." In this sense "content" refers to the writer's materials: the events he is relating, the objects he is describing, the contrasts and distinctions he is drawing, and the explanations and arguments he uses. But this sense is too limited for my purposes. As I am using "content" here it refers not only to the materials but also to the reason for using these materials—that is, the theme or controlling image that determines what kinds of things the author has to say about his subject. For example, the controlling image of Keats' "On First Looking into Chapman's Homer" is the theme of discovery, and that theme requires that everything that Keats has to say about his reactions to Chapman's Homer must develop that discovery image. In this larger sense "content" is a synonym for what classical rhetoric called "invention." It refers to the writer's unique conception of his subject, to what I earlier called his real subject.

I hope it will be clear that, in saying that writing as a way of telling is chiefly concerned with style and that writing as a way of knowing is chiefly concerned with content or invention, I am talking about two complementary ways of looking at writing. There is no possibility of accepting one view and rejecting the other, since both are necessary in the teaching of composition. But there is a practical question of how we distribute the emphasis in our teaching. That is a basic question, since the emphasis defines the nature and conduct of the course, and therefore our professional image.

I think there is no doubt that the prevailing emphasis in a conventional composition course is on style, and often attention to style never rises above the level of usage. This is especially true in high schools. In *High School English Instruction Today*, which is a report of a study of more than a hundred schools conducted jointly by NCTE and the University of Illinois, James Squire and Roger Applebee report that

> The great bulk of comments and corrections found on student papers have to do with correcting faults in spelling, sentence structure, and mechanics—with proofreading rather than teaching. Moreover the majority of revisions by students are directed toward these matters to the exclusion of such elements as organization, logic, or even content.

And, as Albert Kitzhaber has pointed out, the situation is often only relatively better in colleges.

This emphasis on usage is a source of concern in the profession. Social pressures and college entrance requirements demand that high school graduates should have a reasonable mastery of the conventions of the standard English dialect; but linguistic habits are deeply rooted and often cannot be satisfactorily changed within the limited context of the school curriculum. This is especially true of underprivileged students, for whom the standard dialect is sometimes a foreign language. And this difficulty is increased by the fiction, maintained by many teachers and textbooks, that certain usages which are common in the speech of educated people, including English teachers, are not acceptable as "correct English." Students are literally expected to be more correct than the editors of Webster's Dictionary.

Under these conditions the teaching of usage is often a labor of Sisyphus: the time and effort expended by the teacher is out of proportion to the results obtained. Yet, by a curious kind of compensation, the greater the failure to change the student's native dialect, the more that failure is used to justify a still greater effort, until the teaching of composition is reduced to a series of proofreading exercises.

This overemphasis on usage has been condemned by linguists, rhetoricians, and teachers high in the councils of NCTE. For nearly half a century Mencken, Bloomfield, Fries, and I. A. Richards, to name only the best-known critics, have denounced the doctrine of "correctness" as unsound in theory and stultifying in practice, and some more recent critics have suggested that the only way to avoid excessive attention to usage is to stop teaching it altogether in the schools. More moderate critics, such as Robert Pooley, have urged that what is needed is a more realistic and selective approach to the teaching of usage. But there is little evidence that these criticisms have had much influence on classroom practices.

Of course, the decision about what usage to teach and how much time to spend on it will finally be made by individual teachers. Whether they follow the evidence and the weight of authoritative opinion or their own personal preferences is a decision only they can make. But I think it not unreasonable to suggest that usage is a very small part of the total composition process and that that fact should be taken into account in the composition classroom.

The study of style could be a valuable approach to improvement of student writing if style were considered in relation to the writer's attitudes toward his subject and his audience, as Walker Gibson believes; or better still, if we followed Richard E. Young and Alton L. Becker, who define style as follows:

> A writer's style, we believe, is the characteristic route he takes through all the choices presented in both the prewriting and writing stages. It is the manifestation of his conception of his topic, modified by his audience, situation, and intention—what we might call his "universe of discourse."

This is the most comprehensive concept of style I know. It subsumes everything under style, and so defines style as the whole art of discourse. Obviously if this were what we were teaching in the schools as style, there would be no reason for contrasting content and style, since the content of a paper would be part of its style. If we followed the Young-Becker definition we would be teaching style all the time, because there would be nothing else to teach.

With the possible exception of argument, composition teachers have tended to slight instruction in content. The Squire-Applebee report points out that the prevailing pattern of instruction in the schools visited was to say little or nothing about assignments until after the papers had been written and then to comment only on style. The inference to be made from this procedure is that these teachers believe that establishing the content of a paper is entirely the student's responsibility and that there is little the teacher can do about it.

There is, of course, something we can do about improving the content of student writing, and the best teachers have been doing it ever since Aristotle. We can, at the very least, show by our comments on student papers that we are concerned about the content and value it. Since students are always trying to guess what the teacher wants in a paper they will soon infer that he likes good content, and they may try to give it to him. At least they will have to give up the negative concept that good writing is writing which has no errors.

But we can do more than that. One of the most satisfying contributions of the new rhetorics is their reemphasis on invention through attention to prewriting—that is, to that part of the composition process that precedes the writing of the first draft. Let me briefly suggest three practical techniques for prewriting.

The simplest method, especially suited for junior and senior high school classes, is for the teacher and students to talk out the potential content of an assignment before any student begins to write. The students are given a subject and are asked to suggest pertinent materials. These suggestions are written on the board. If a suggestion is vague, it can be clarified by discussion. If it is too comprehensive, the class can be asked to break it down into more specific items. As the material accumulates it becomes more than any student could use, so the process of purposeful selection emerges, and with it an appropriate grouping or outlining of the selected content. When all this is done, each student takes whatever view of the subject he prefers and uses the appropriate content to develop that view.

Of course this method can be used only when the class is working on a common subject. When each student is writing on his own subject, he will have to do his own prewriting. But if he is familiar with this procedure through repeated experience with it in the classroom, he will have a way of getting started and can thus minimize the pencil-chewing stage when he is waiting for inspiration to strike. And the teacher can, if he wishes, consult with students on their prewriting plans, as he sometimes now does with outlines. The difference between the outline and the prewriting is that the outline shows only the structure of a projected paper; the prewriting shows both the structure and the content.

One advantage of such class exercises on prewriting is that not all prewriting has to be followed up with writing, since if the purpose of the exercise is to give students experience establishing the potential content of a paper, that object has been achieved once the prewriting is finished. Students can thus prewrite more papers than they have time to write, and teaching is not limited to what the teacher has time to grade. What the procedure does is to increase the amount of experience students have with thinking out the content of a composition without increasing the grading time. And for papers that are to be graded, it allows the teacher and the student to handle problems of content *before* the paper is written.

When, as in this procedure, learning takes the form of discussion rather than lecture or teacher-directed demonstration, both the attitude of the students and the quality of their writing improve. What students need, more than explicit instruction about writing, is the opportunity to explore a subject before and after it is developed into an essay. They need to do a lot of talking about writing and to make up their minds about how their work can be improved, and this talk is most profitable when it is removed from the pressure of grades. There is no good reason why everything a student writes should be graded, but there is a good reason why a student should have the opportunity of having his work read by others—preferably by more than one person—and hearing it discussed. James Moffett in his *Teaching the Universe of Discourse*, a book which in my opinion opens up a whole new view of what teaching could be like in a student-centered curriculum, makes a strong case for small group conferences in which students write for their peers and have their work evaluated by them. I have seen Moffett's suggestions worked out in college classrooms and I am impressed by the results.

A second kind of prewriting, one especially suited to college classes, stresses observation and inferences drawn from observation as the means of getting a detailed knowledge of the subject. It is surprising that, for all our talk about the importance of careful observation to a writer, so little time is given to it in the English curriculum. The only time I was ever asked to combine observation and writing in a composition was when, as a graduate student at Northwestern, I took a course in prosody from Lew Sarrett. Sarrett asked each member of the class to select some object, not too complex an object, and to spend not less than thirty minutes studying it with a view to writing about it. During the first ten minutes we were to examine the object carefully, noting everything we saw in it: its size, shape, contour, texture, color, function, anything that would give us a fuller knowledge of the object. Next we were to spend about ten minutes inviting in a relaxed way whatever associations the object suggested to us. Then we were to look at the object metaphorically. When all this was done we were to write a piece of verse or prose suggested by our total experience with the object. That was nearly forty years ago, but I remember the assignment as the best lesson on invention I ever received as a student.

Some modification of that assignment is the best cure I know for the generality and incompleteness of student writing. Most students start to write about a subject without any serious exploration of it, and because they have only a general knowledge of the subject they can give it only a shallow treatment. Usually we complain that their writing is vague and that they should choose more concrete diction. But often the diction is a symptom, not a cause. What they need is not a bigger vocabulary but more knowledge of how they see the subject. They are not likely to get that kind of knowledge in a dictionary or a thesaurus. Their best remedy is a closer look at the subject.

Close observation of details is a prerequisite for much of the expository writing a student does in high school and college. It is important in description, in definition, in classification, in reports of events and processes. It is especially important in any writing which requires the writer to infer a conclusion from his observations, as in contrasts, causal analyses, criticisms, and arguments. In view of its importance it would seem to merit a more prominent place in the curriculum than it usually gets.

The third kind of prewriting procedure I want to mention is one suggested by Kenneth Pike and his associates at the University of Michigan. Pike's theory is that any subject can be adequately defined or described only if it is approached from three points of view, which he calls "particle," "wave," and "field." From the particle view we get a knowledge of the elements of the subject, say, individual lines or sentences or metaphors or stanzas in a poem. From the wave view we get knowledge of the interrelation among the parts or particles—for example, the metrical pattern of a poem and the flow of the theme through that pattern. From the field view we get a knowledge of the poem as a whole in the various contexts in which it can occur.

The core of Pike's trimodal analysis is close observation of the subject, so that it could be described as a system for guiding observation. It gives the student a methodical procedure for studying his subject which emphasizes the personal nature of observation and so invites the student to define the subject by his personal insights of it. In its present state Pike's system would be a bit difficult for high school students, but at the college level it can be used effectively both for the interpretation of poetry and for the prewriting of an essay.

These three prewriting procedures are systems for helping a writer to explore his subject to see what can be said about it. Since each system will yield more knowledge than can be incorporated in a single paper, all of them impose on the writer the necessity of defining the subject in terms of his dominant interest in it. Of all the things that he could say he must choose the theme that identifies his own unique view. Thus the three roads all lead back to C. Day Lewis' problem of deciding what the subject means to him. In my judgment, this is the controlling decision in composition, out of which decisions about structure and style emerge. This, of course, is equivalent to saying that arrangement and style are consequences of invention, and that the way of telling is dependent on the way of knowing.

But whether we emphasize style or invention will make little difference unless the classroom provides an environment that encourages learning. The teacher-dominated, overly directed classroom does not provide such an environment. Students, especially modern students, cannot write effectively in a situation in which what they are to write and how they are to write it are prescribed by a teacher or a textbook. If they are going to mature as writers they must be free to make up their own minds about what they want to do and how they want to do it. This is not to say that their choices cannot be questioned. Young writers especially need the corrective influence of the feedback of an audience, whether that audience is a teacher or a peer group. But the criticism is most helpful when it consists of constructive suggestions of alternatives, and best of all when both the writer and his critics can engage in a free discussion of the consequences of making one choice rather than another in relation to the whole context of the paper. This kind of discussion requires a democratic attitude in the classroom. It cannot be maintained if all the wisdom and all the authority are presumed to be on one side of the desk.

The Teaching of Composition

JAMES R. SQUIRE and ROGER K. APPLEBEE

Certainly the component of English which is the most elusive and difficult to assess is the teaching of composition, and observers faced many problems in trying to characterize individual programs. Although corrected class sets of papers were usually made available to visitors during their one- or two-day stay, and although these papers were solicited with the understanding that they would be typical efforts of students, there is reason to believe that in a number of instances the papers had been hand-picked to show both students and teachers to their best advantage. Observers were also hampered by limitations of time and could not always read all of the papers at hand. Nevertheless, these papers, supplemented by interviews with students and teachers, afforded direct knowledge about the program; indirect data concerning the frequency of writing and the emphasis and point of view in writing instruction came from questionnaires.

The most discouraging conclusion which the project staff reached concerning instruction in writing is that there is simply very little of it. On the basis of classroom observation, teachers at all levels in all schools combined spent only 15.7 percent of their class time emphasizing composition. There was slight variation among grade levels and even less between those groups considered terminal and those labeled college preparatory, but the relatively small incidence of teaching directed to writing improvement came as a surprise to observers. Moreover, the bulk of the instruction during the 15.7 percent of total class time devoted to writing was instruction *after* the fact—after papers had been written.

The primary process of writing instruction consists of having students write compositions followed by teacher "correction" and the subsequent return of compositions—in many cases to be read by students and revised. This is a time-honored system that will doubtless continue to carry much of

---

"The Teaching of Composition" appears as Chapter 6 in *High School English Instruction Today* (New York: Appleton, 1968), pp. 121–138. This book is based on a survey of English programs in 158 high schools in 45 different states.

the weight of instruction, but it is a tenuous chain of action and reaction which, like the chain letters of two decades or so ago, can be useful only if all links follow in orderly progression. From the observation of project visitors the chain is seldom continuous; and the result of these efforts is, at best, a fragmentary approach to the writing process.

The Correction and Annotation of Papers

A sampling of thousands of papers that had presumably gone through the complete cycle revealed one third that had not been revised in any way, another third with gross errors of spelling and usage corrected. Only in about 12 percent of the high schools had most students revised their writing completely in response to teacher "correction." There was no way to determine statistically, of course, how effective this process was either with the minority of students who revised or with the vast majority who did not. In spite of the lack of empirical knowledge, however, there can be little doubt that those students who are forced to think back through their first writing and then rework the original into something better must gain in fluency and precision.[1]

For most teachers, correcting papers is synonymous with teaching writing. To a question posed during the interview with entire English departments about the proportion of teaching time or emphasis on composition, the most typical response was that more time and emphasis on composition were impossible with existing class loads. In other words, there was simply not time to correct more papers than were currently being produced. According to individual questionnaires, teachers spend an average of nine to twelve hours weekly reading and correcting papers, a sizable proportion of time considering their other professional obligations. Similarly, students report that they submit an average of one theme a week, with able senior students tending to write more frequently and tenth grade students somewhat less often. It is difficult to imagine how this enormous paper load might be increased and still have any significance for either student or teacher.

The average English teacher in these schools meets about 130 pupils daily. If he spends as much as 8.6 minutes in annotating each theme—the average number of minutes which Dusel reported required "to teach writing and thinking,"[2] then eighteen hours weekly would be required for paper correction alone. When it is realized that the average number of pupils per teacher nationally is about 150,[3] and that some teachers, even in this

[1] Richard Braddock, Richard Lloyd-Jones, and Lowell Schoer, *Research in Written Composition* (Champaign, Ill., National Council of Teachers of English, 1963), pp. 35–36.

[2] William J. Dusel, "Determining an Efficient Teaching Load in English," *Illinois English Bulletin*, 43: 1 (October 1955).

[3] Committee on National Interest, *The National Interest and the Teaching of English* (Champaign, Ill., National Council of Teachers of English, 1961), pp. 98–99.

sampling, are expected to teach writing to as many as 200 pupils in six different classes, it would be irresponsible criticism to assert they are not doing justice to one of the main elements of English instruction. The simple fact is that they cannot.

One method for reducing the paper load of classroom teachers is to employ lay readers, a practice being followed in a significant number of high schools across the country.[4] Among those schools participating in the National Study, 20 percent indicated that readers were used to one degree or another. In larger districts, they are usually assigned to schools after they have satisfied certain requisites, including the successful completion of a qualifying examination. In the case of schools in smaller, more autonomous districts, readers are employed directly on the basis of personal contact and previous experience; more often than not they are former teachers in the respective schools.

It would be impractical to assume that outside readers could upgrade a school's writing program merely by increasing the frequency of writing, and, indeed, no direct relationship between the frequency or quantity of student writing and the use of readers was found. What readers can do is relieve the laborious burden of correction to allow more time for the *teaching* of writing. If classroom teachers must spend ten or more hours a week reading papers, they have substantially less time to prepare thoughtful and purposeful lessons. No doubt this demand has much to do with the sometimes superficial marking that observers noticed on sets of papers.

Lay reader programs differ in a number of respects. In some, readers always remain behind the scenes, in a few instances transacting most of the paper exchange through the mail; in others, readers are required to visit classes when writing assignments are made, or even to hold conferences with students. Rarely do readers grade and correct more than a minority of student papers, and usually teachers review grading by sampling a number of papers from each set marked by a reader. In some programs, notably in the so-called Rutgers Plan,[5] graders are assigned to specific teachers and classes—i.e., those classes following the Rutgers Plan in other respects. Less structured programs allow several teachers to call upon a reader as they require.

Interviews with students who have had experience with theme readers revealed mixed reactions. Interestingly, some students are delighted with the notion that an "outsider," someone who doesn't know them, will read their papers and pass judgment from what they believe to be a more objective point of view. Other students prefer the more intimate touch and

---

[4] A good discussion of such programs appears in Virginia Burke, *The Lay Reader Program: Background and Procedures* (Milwaukee, Wisc., Wisconsin Council of Teachers of English, 1961).
[5] Paul Diederich, "The Rutgers Plan for Cutting Class Size in Two," *English Journal*, XLIV (April 1960), pp. 229–236, 266.

object to their work being read by anyone other than the teacher. It is fair to say that, in general, student response to the employment of theme readers is negative, but not overwhelmingly so.

Teachers, too, are as a whole ambivalent in their attitudes toward a lay reader program, though, for a sizable portion of the teaching community, feelings run very high. Ten percent feel lay readers are detrimental, 8 percent that they are absolutely essential, and the majority that they are of only minor importance. During department interviews, the subject of lay readers arose with some regularity in response to the question of how departments might spend a sum of money added to their department's budget, but it was ranked after such items as recordings, overhead projectors, supplementary books, and clerical help. It is clear that most teachers do not view the establishment of lay reader programs with any great urgency; indeed, most are quite emphatic in stating that funds would be better spent in reducing the number of students per teacher.

Clearly, lay readers do not provide a panacea for a poor writing program, though they can make a good one better, and reports from project observers make possible a number of generalizations about successful programs. The best enlist the services of very able readers who write well themselves, can recognize problems that others may have, and are able to translate their analyses into terms which high school students can comprehend. Frequently, though not always, such people were themselves English teachers. These readers work on a regular basis with one or two teachers, observing some classes to become more familiar with the capabilities of the students and the teaching methods used. In the best programs the reader is more than a proofreader, encouraging and commenting on good efforts as well as pointing to errors in mechanics and usage. To this end, a series of conferences with students as well as the teacher can greatly enhance the effectiveness of the reader. No matter how well structured the lay reader program may be, however, the teacher must still teach writing. To foist onto others the burden of reading and correcting without accepting the responsibility for continuous instruction would be to renege on the contract implicit in the provision of readers.

The reports of project observers make clear that individual English departments must give more thought to their objectives and practices in the teaching of student writing. Much that was seen suggested little more than mechanical activity: assignments manufactured to suit the time of year, compositions of cryptic symbols relating to the mechanics of writing rather than to its substance. Department chairmen did report, when asked about instruction in writing, that the element of primary importance was organization of ideas followed by clear thinking or logic. These concerns rated well ahead of such matters as diction, style, or originality and somewhat ahead of the more pedestrian "correct" mechanics and usage. Similarly, when asked to give priority to criteria for evaluating student writing, chairmen considered clarity of thought and organization, appropriate development, and sentence structure, in that order, to be of greatest importance. Yet these conditions simply do not obtain even in these schools. In reviewing student assignments made available to them, observers noted that two thirds of the papers were corrected from a negative point of view involving only correcting faults and assigning grades. In only 17 percent of the schools could they say that comments were designed to teach writing and thinking—the avowed purpose of the whole cycle of writing, correcting, and revising. If there is little instruction in these important matters by way of teacher comments on individual papers, and none at all in the classroom, where are students to learn about them?

The Focus of Instruction

One source of instruction, of course, is the occasional or systematic use of textbooks. Figure 1 shows, however, that less than a third of the teachers interviewed indicated that they regularly made use of such texts; even fewer responded favorably to traditional workbooks used to provide drill in grammar and usage. From statistically less solid ground, project observers reported that they seldom saw composition texts in use, although they were often in evidence; most schools lend or rent such books to students or ask students to purchase them. If composition texts are, in fact, as little used on the national scale as they were in the project sample (and there is no reason to assume any great difference), the issue is raised of the considerable public expense versus the slight instructional value of the books. One problem in this regard is that texts frequently must be purchased from lists compiled by local school boards or state authorities, a requirement that can force a teacher to use a book he feels to be inferior to one he might have chosen himself. Significantly, however, less than 10 percent of these teachers who indicated disaffection for the composition-grammar books which were authorized would or could suggest other titles. In large measure this may reflect the failure of commercial publishers to offer materials appreciably different in content or approach from those the teachers already have available.[6]

A content analysis of fourteen sets of composition-grammar textbooks by James Lynch and Bertrand Evans[7] several years ago reveals an interesting parallel between the emphasis found on instruction in composition in the National Study and the proportion of instructional material as evidenced by the number of pages given to composition and rhetoric in the texts. Over twice as many pages dealt with matters of grammar, usage, and mechanics in these books than showed any emphasis on units larger than the sentence. In view of this surprisingly small attention to writing in the

[6] Within the last few years, however, several companies have offered texts that are different with respect to their viewpoint concerning language and the emphasis given to instruction in writing.

[7] James J. Lynch and Bertrand Evans, *High School English Textbooks: A Critical Examination* (Boston, Mass., Little, Brown and Co., 1963).

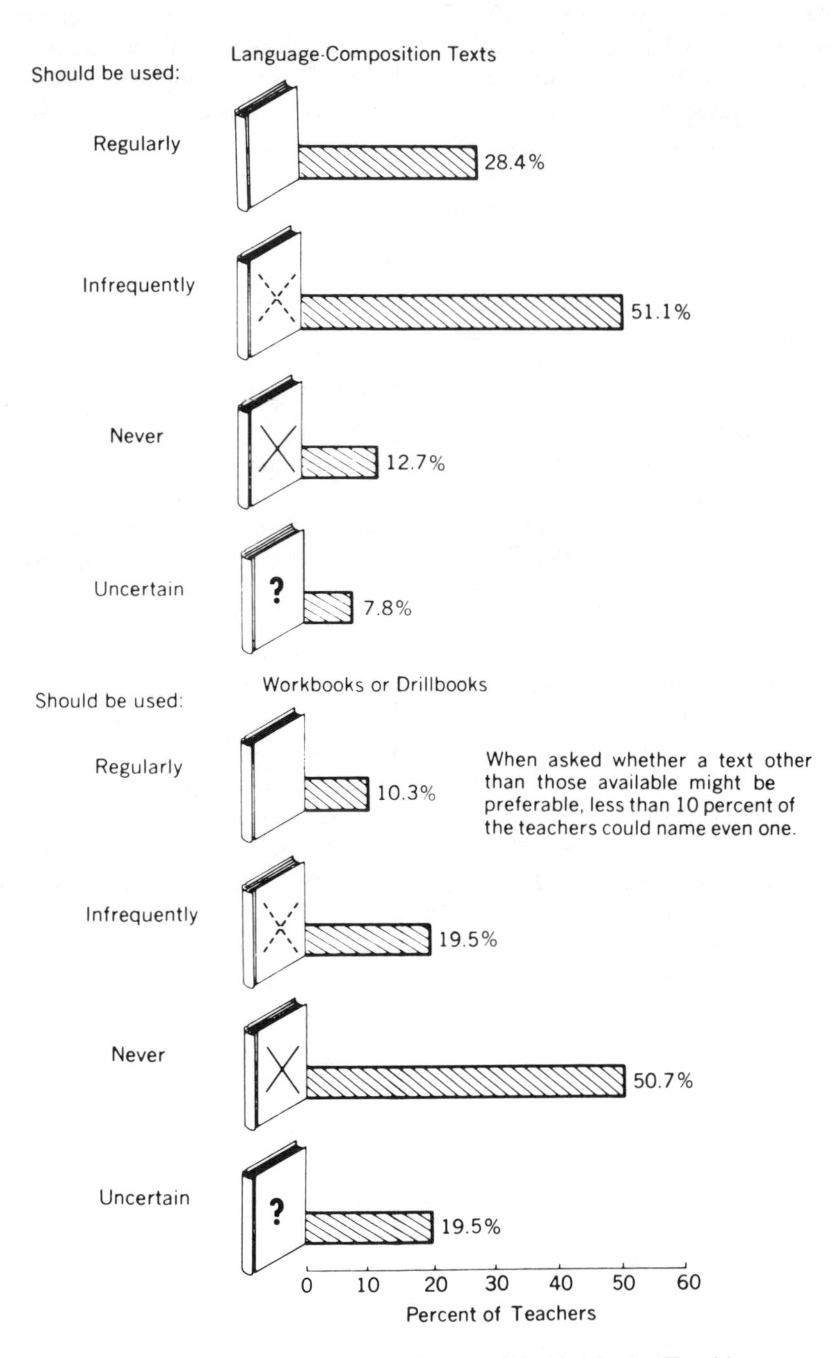

Fig. 1. The Value of Textbooks and Workbooks in Teaching Composition and Language (interview responses of 370 teachers).

composition texts, one almost wonders whether the lack of classroom instruction in writing reported by observers was somehow a reflection of the quantity of treatment in available textbooks. Similarly, the whole mode of teacher correction mirrors the rationale implied in the textbooks: about two thirds to the problems of grammar-mechanics-usage and a much less significant proportion to the rhetoric, the development and organization, of writing. Although department chairmen and well-meaning English teachers feel that the latter are of greater value, these matters are clearly not receiving the priority they deserve.

Lynch and Evans also bewail the lack of any real differentiation in the approaches which these textbooks take at successive stages of composition instruction. A given series will typically list essentially the same topics for each of the four years of high school, topics more often than not concentrating on experiences or ideas assumed to be very close to the students' immediate concerns rather than on literary experiences. While a glance through almost any of these series would corroborate these assertions, one must also note that at least twice as many of the papers reviewed by project observers were based on literature as on all other subjects combined, including personal experiences, the social sciences generally, and imaginative topics involving creative writing. Although no absolute data were tabulated in this regard, teachers themselves generally indicated that a good writing program should allow for diverse writing experiences, including exposition, argumentation, description, and narration, but that literature should "very often" serve to stimulate such writing.

From time to time, high school programs have been criticized for allowing a disproportion of creative writing to more formal and academically respectable assignments in exposition. Indeed, some critics would, in Procrustean fashion, lop off all imaginative writing as extraneous to the legitimate concern of the high school, insisting that appropriate expository assignments based on literature will offer enough to feed the creative impulses of the students. From the point of view of project staff and observers, however, this position is for a number of reasons untenable. Among papers given to observers for review, for example, there were far fewer instances of creative writing than of any other kind. In descending order of frequency, students wrote on: (1) literary topics, (2) subjects close to their own experience, (3) nonliterary subjects requiring special information, and (4) topics classified as "creative writing." Perhaps as a direct result of the rigid assignments and mechanical instruction that characterize so much composition teaching, two thirds of the sixty advanced twelfth grade classes which indicated they would like to see an improved composition program specified more creative writing, an emphasis reflected too in the enthusiasm of students enrolled in such classes. In the opinion of the project staff, the occasional experience of creating a poem or story can carry a number of extrinsic dividends. The opportunity to create something even remotely literary may not turn the student into an artist, but it should help him develop an appreciation of the distinctions between the language and conventions of literature and the language and conventions of his own immediate world. While the project staff does not recommend sudden, wholesale, and capricious efforts, it does feel that the occasional assignment in the area known as creative writing can be of significant value. Whether the note of protest against creative writing and the emphasis on expository themes by committees of the NCTE and the CEEB Commission on English has changed a previously distorted pattern, or whether such writing has never been overly emphasized in the better schools of the country, the National Study reveals no need for a radical shift in the *kinds* of writing being asked of students in most of the cooperating high schools.

Continuity and Sequence

As suggested above, most of the time and attention devoted to composition entails an *analysis* (whether superficial or comprehensive) of the finished product. With few exceptions, any concerted efforts of English departments have been directed to setting standards for grading or for establishing requirements for student writing in terms of numbers of words or assignments. Although courses of study proclaim worthy enough objectives relating to "improving abilities" or "increasing writing skills," the project staff found little thought or effort given to *how* a student's writing ability can be improved. As a result of this lack of focus on the *process* or *sequence* of writing, the writing experience of students in most programs suffers from either redundancy or fragmentation. Students are therefore inclined to view the program in composition as a disconnected series of activities, and they can scarcely be blamed if, faced with the same topics, they write in the same ways they have found successful before. If growth and improvement are to be expected from the students, they must be built into the program itself.

One method of encouraging continuity and progression in the individual classroom is to use cumulative folders or notebooks to contain all of the consequential pieces that a student writes. Teachers in the cooperating schools were generally in favor of this practice, as it gave them an opportunity to observe student progress throughout the year. Some departments had gone even further, preserving selected writings over a three- or four-year period to add some measure of continuity to the program as a whole. In either case, this procedure, while providing an important perspective on the growth of the individual student, is at best a roundabout method of ensuring sequence and continuity within the writing program of a school.

Perhaps as a result of the currently popular theory of the spiral curriculum, a number of schools have written new courses of study, frequently called "sequential guides" to composition. Inherent in the design of these programs is the principle that the important skills of writing are developed incrementally. This does not imply that the ninth grade students learn all there is to know about constructing sentences; tenth grade students, the paragraph; and juniors, a multiparagraph composition. Instead, a typical guide provides from twenty to fifty writing experiences for each grade level, from which some twelve to twenty will be chosen by the individual teacher on the basis of the needs and capabilities of his class. At all levels students are required to write narration, description, exposition, and argumentation, though in the ninth grade there is likely to be a greater emphasis on narration and description, and in the twelfth, greater concern with more complex and subtle forms of exposition and argumentation. Many of these assignments are clearly related to the literature taught at particular grade levels, and at times students are asked to emulate the style of an author—to write "in the manner of" John Buchan or E. B. White, for example, while developing a personal essay. Sequential composition guides differ in the extent to which they include other apparatus: standards for grading, a style sheet for students, a glossary of technical terms. Some contain explicit instructions to teachers and list questions to direct the class discussion preceding the writing experience; others depend on the teacher and the general context of each course to motivate the sequential assignments. With the shortcomings of composition textbooks as noted above, it is important that high school departments focus in some manner on the essential problems of sequence and continuity in the writing program. Merely to determine how many compositions should be required at each grade level begs the critical questions involved.

The Term Paper

The high school research or term paper is a fairly well-entrenched requirement in many English programs. About 71.7 percent of the teachers in the Study schools support a requirement for at least one such paper in every student's high school career. Although there is no discernible pattern for such papers, ranging as they do among subjects in literature, history, politics, science, and current events and varying in depth and scope, the tradition is somehow maintained that college-bound students should be submitted to the process of gathering information, taking notes, and preparing a paper of anywhere from five to fifty pages. For some time the value of this process has been questioned by many high school teachers and college English instructors on the grounds that such writing is frequently a waste of time—time that might more profitably be spent on other aspects of composition or on the study of literature and language. Such writing, it is claimed, is in no sense *research* and more often than not results in both plagiarism of source material and unfortunate superficiality: teachers are prone to emphasize the mechanical aspects of taking notes, preparing footnotes, and compiling bibliographies to the exclusion of processes of thought or logical development; topics are usually unrelated to any other aspect of English, often turning to the trivial or transitory; few high schools have libraries adequate for such research.

These arguments are countered by individuals who feel that it *is* profitable for a student to pursue a subject in depth and to sustain his best writing efforts in an extended paper. In the process, it is assumed, he will learn much about the library and about using source material. Furthermore, the term paper advocates state, other academic departments both expect students to know the proper form and procedure for writing a long source paper and regard the English class as the appropriate place for such instruction. Supporters also claim that former students return from college to tell them how useful this instruction has been in their beginning college course, to some extent refuting the frequent argument that college departments of English do not expect freshmen to know how to write term papers and, in fact, would prefer that incoming students be taught other things instead.

The most profitable means of resolving this dilemma is to inquire to what extent the research paper helps students become more able writers in the whole scheme of individual composition programs. Only from this perspective can individual teachers and departments satisfactorily determine whether their efforts at instruction as well as their students' long labors offer an efficient vehicle for writing improvement. Though such a perspective was of its very nature not available to the members of the National Study, their observations do allow a number of inferences about the general practice of requiring long source papers of high school students.

Individually, many observers read some long papers that would suggest the manifest worth of such assignments. Selected samples showed that a number of high school students are capable of writing sustained, coherent, and comprehensive papers. In contrast to these samples, of course, were many others that suffered from all of the ills of bad writing and dishonest thinking imaginable, compounded in these respects by the demand for length. Unless the long paper evolves from other written assignments over a period of years, and unless the subject matter of these efforts has some relationship to English (or else some immediacy to related disciplines), observers feel that the instructional time might better be spent on other writing. The crash programs which they occasionally witnessed, where students were thrown into the school library and asked to produce twenty pages of prose in two weeks, are not worthwhile educational pursuits; nor is mere instruction on the formal aspects of note-taking, footnoting, and manuscript form valuable *per se.* Unless the whole enterprise grows from roots which have already been nourished by other work *in English,* it is the critics rather than the supporters of long source papers who must be heeded. To consider instruction on the long paper as a necessary end in itself, as a service function to other high school departments, or as an assumed college requirement makes the task unrewarding and the practice unsound.

Approaches to Writing

In a small number of participating schools, schoolwide "composition days" have been established, allowing for infrequent but planned occasions when all students write compositions of specified length and type. Teams of readers assess the strengths and limitations of all of these efforts, lending an objective measure to pupil improvement and a positive touchstone to the tenor of the writing program. The most worthwhile by-product of this enterprise is that it focuses attention on this important component of English and, in spite of the mechanical aspects, motivates students to improve their work. Too often, from the observation of visitors to schools, English departments are willing to relinquish the essay in final examinations in favor of the more easily corrected objective question. Whether or not these tests are a valid measure of other aspects of the English program, they neither measure a student's composing ability nor motivate him to improve. Such a device as the schoolwide "composition day" can mitigate some of the shortcomings of the final objective test in English by asserting once again the importance of the act of writing.

Another promising procedure in the teaching of composition is the pupil-teacher conference. In department interviews, teachers conceded that systematic discussion with individual students about their writing would indeed be beneficial. They also pointed, however, to heavy class loads, obligations to police corridors or locker rooms, and "extracurricular" assignments that curtail after-school conferences. At one school this problem was circumvented by naming two additional English teachers as "composition teachers" whose sole function was to teach students singly or in pairs in frequent tutorial sessions. In addition to their regular English classes, the majority of students in two grade levels were assigned to one or the other of these teachers for one conference a week over the entire year. Administrators and teachers at this school were convinced enough of the worth of this program to continue it beyond the experimental phase. In view of the value placed on these face-to-face encounters, teachers might well look more closely at methods to institute conferences on a more frequent basis than obtains at present, even at the expense of other class activities. To be effective, of course, it is incumbent upon teachers to recognize that techniques different from those used in teaching a class are open to them in tutorial sessions. A conference presents an opportunity for the teacher to reach even the most reluctant writer and to come to grips with more salient problems than those implied in "correctness."

Observers watched numerous sets of papers being returned to students during class sessions, but they were struck by the very few times that teachers took advantage of these occasions to teach some facet of writing. Some teachers had prepared lists of "common errors" that were written on the board or reproduced for class correction, but very few took the time to reproduce or analyze an entire paragraph or theme in this fashion. Significantly, even fewer teachers used opaque or overhead projectors to facilitate a common study of the larger aspects of composition, those very elements of organization, logic, and development which claimed high priorities on their questionnaires. In the judgment of observers, such direct instruction can fill an unfortunate void in the whole effort of teaching writing in the schools. Another neglected source of practical instruction is the practice of having students read each other's papers. At the least, such a device can lead to superficial improvements in usage and mechanics; at best it contributes to an overall development of style. Students with a clear notion of audience and a more immediate sense of purpose will write with a clarity and conviction usually lacking when they know that only the teacher will read their work.

A number of programs throughout the country use models to help students achieve a better sense of direction and form in their writing. Particularly those schools with sequential programs have employed literary models (and occasionally student efforts) to suggest patterns that students can emulate. Though there is the built-in hazard that students will ape the original too closely or will consider it too far above their own abilities, the judicious use of models is a positive and valuable device in teaching students to write better. Similarly, it is often valuable for the teacher himself to write an assignment that he has given to a class and then to use his own paper as a model for demonstration. Obviously discretion is necessary, but as an added dividend teachers are made aware of some of the problems and pitfalls that they are prone to overlook when they merely correct the errors of others.

Summary

Needless to say, there are many qualitative differences among the various composition programs. Some committed departments are involved in continuous efforts to improve instruction in writing by a number of methods, whereas others make no concerted effort to create cohesive, schoolwide programs, allowing individual teachers their own frequently haphazard approaches. Optimistically, in observer reports of general strengths, programs in composition were cited fifty times, second only to teaching staff in frequency of comment. On the other hand, inadequate programs in composition were cited forty-one times, ranking seventh among general weaknesses of English programs.

When teachers were asked to indicate on questionnaires the aspect of English in which they felt most deficient, composition outranked all others (including literature, language, reading, and speech) by a considerable margin. Approximately 25 percent of the teachers surveyed reported taking a course in advanced composition since they began teaching, and a solid 82 percent revealed that such a college course would be of "some" or "great" importance to them. These figures suggest commitment and a professional need that is not always met, but the newly established NDEA Institutes, many of which offer a composition component or, failing that, oblique instruction in the teaching of writing through their workshops, allow a note of optimism. Furthermore, changing certification requirements are beginning to prompt a noticeable addition of new writing courses to the offerings of colleges and universities.

In spite of the evidence of considerable writing activity in most English classes, observation reveals that there is very little effort directed to *instruction* in writing. For one reason or another, teachers depend heavily on the process of correction and revision to improve student composition. Skillful teachers with enough time to make the process significant and enough patience to complete the cycle through revision are able to promote student achievement, not only in mechanical "correctness" but also in rhetorical power and stylistic flavor. Where the conditions of skill and time are not present, however, instruction through correction is extremely limited.

While teachers are generally conscientious in assigning and grading many sets of papers, there is a clear lack of consistent and progressive instruction in writing. After observing a large number of high school English classes, one can easily get the impression that compositions are often assigned in lieu of any ordered classroom instruction, as though mere practice were all that was needed. The project staff is convinced that the quality of the writing assignments, the care taken by the teacher in correcting the paper, and the continuing dialogue between writer and reader are of greater importance than the frequency of writing. Moreover, unless these qualities are an integral part of the writing program, it is distinctly possible that frequent but routine writing assignments will inspire little more than trivial efforts that promote no growth whatsoever in writing ability.

To add confusion to neglect, teachers are in no clear agreement about methods and priorities in teaching students to write. The responses of students and teachers to a check list of concepts which might be taught at various levels indicate clearly that concepts related to rhetoric and composition are only inconsistently presented; some are overtaught, some not taught at all. Although a good deal of research has been undertaken on the teaching of writing, few of the findings are easily translatable to classroom technique. Indeed, some results appear at least superficially to be in conflict with the claims of other investigations. As indicated in the Braddock report, there remains a manifest need for more controlled research in a number of basic areas related to the teaching of composition.[8]

[8] Richard Braddock *et al., op. cit.* See especially Chapter 3, "The State of Knowledge about Composition," pp. 29–53.

Confusion about conflicting ideas and ignorance of research, however, provide no rationalization for an inadequate composition program. Teachers cannot wait in expectation of the seminal study on the teaching of writing; they can combine knowledge, experience, and intuition to develop meaningful programs of writing in the high school. To take the position (as some individual teachers have) that writing "cannot be taught," or that the process is too mysterious for words, or that it has no more sequence and content than a bag of tricks, is strangely inconsistent with the general pattern of educational philosophy in our time.

Language Is Sermonic

RICHARD M. WEAVER

Our age has witnessed the decline of a number of subjects that once enjoyed prestige and general esteem, but no subject, I believe, has suffered more amazingly in this respect than rhetoric. When one recalls that a century ago rhetoric was regarded as the most important humanistic discipline taught in our colleges—when one recalls this fact and contrasts it with the very different situation prevailing today—he is forced to see that a great shift of valuation has taken place. In those days, in the not-so-distant Nineteenth Century, to be a professor of rhetoric, one had to be *somebody.* This was a teaching task that was thought to call for ample and varied resources, and it was recognized as addressing itself to the most important of all ends, the persuading of human beings to adopt right attitudes and act in response to them. That was no assignment for the plodding sort of professor. That sort of teacher might do a middling job with subject matter courses, where the main object is to impart information, but the teacher of rhetoric had to be a person of gifts and imagination who could illustrate, as the need arose, how to make words even in prose take on wings. I remind you of the chairs of rhetoric that still survive in title in some of our older universities. And I should add, to develop the full picture, that literature was then viewed as a subject which practically anyone could teach. No special gift, other than perhaps industry, was needed to relate facts about authors and periods. That was held to be rather pedestrian work. But the instructor in rhetoric was expected to be a man of stature. Today, I scarcely need point out, the situation has been exactly reversed. Today it is the teacher of literature who passes through a long period of training, who is supposed to possess the mysteries of a learned craft, and who is placed by his very speciality on a height of eminence. His knowledge of the intricacies of Shakespeare or Keats or Joyce and his sophistication in the critical doctrines that have been developed bring him the esteem of the academy. We must recognize in all fairness that the elaboration of critical techniques and special approaches has made the

Dimensions of Rhetorical Scholarship, ed. Roger E. Nebergall (Norman, Oklahoma: Department of Speech, University of Oklahoma, 1963), pp. 49–63. Reprinted by permission of the editor.

teaching of literature a somewhat more demanding profession, although some think that it has gone in that direction beyond the point of diminishing returns. Still, this is not enough to account for the relegation of rhetoric. The change has gone so far that now it is discouraging to survey the handling of this study in our colleges and universities. With a few honorable exceptions it is given to just about anybody who will take it. The "inferior, unlearned, mechanical, merely instrumental members of the profession"—to recall a phrase of a great master of rhetoric, Edmund Burke—have in their keeping what was once assigned to the leaders. Beginners, part-time teachers, graduate students, faculty wives, and various fringe people, are now the instructional staff of an art which was once supposed to require outstanding gifts and mature experience. (We must note that at the same time the course itself has been allowed to decline from one dealing philosophically with the problems of expression to one which tries to bring below-par students up to the level of accepted usage.) Indeed, the wheel of fortune would seem to have turned for rhetoric; what was once at the top is now at the bottom, and because of its low estate, people begin to wonder on what terms it can survive at all. . . .

Under the force of . . . narrow [scientific] reasoning, it was natural that rhetoric should pass from a status in which it was regarded as of questionable worth to a still lower one in which it was positively condemned. For the most obvious truth about rhetoric is that its object is the whole man. It presents its arguments first to the rational part of man, because rhetorical discourses, if they are honestly conceived, always have a basis in reasoning. Logical argument is the plot, as it were, of any speech or composition that is designed to persuade. Yet it is the very characterizing feature of rhetoric that it goes beyond this and appeals to other parts of man's constitution, especially to his nature as a pathetic being, that is, a being feeling and suffering. A speech intended to persuade achieves little unless it takes into account how men are reacting subjectively to their hopes and fears and their special circumstances. The fact that Aristotle devotes a large proportion of his *Rhetoric* to how men feel about different situations and actions is an evidence of how prominently these considerations bulked even in the eyes of a master theorist.

Yet there is one further fact, more decisive than any of these, to prove that rhetoric is addressed to man in his humanity. Every speech which is designed to move is directed to a special audience in its unique situation. (We could not except even those radio appeals to "the world." Their audience has a unique place in time.) Here is but a way of pointing out that rhetoric is intended for historical man, or for man as conditioned by history. It is part of the *conditio humana* that we live at particular times and in particular places. These are productive of special or unique urgencies, which the speaker has got to recognize and to estimate. Hence, just as man from the point of view of rhetoric is not purely a thinking machine, or a mere seat of rationality, so he is not a creature abstracted from time and place. If science deals with the abstract and the universal, rhetoric is near the other end, dealing in significant part with the particular and the concrete. It would be the height of wishful thinking to say that this ought not be so. As long as man is born into history, he will be feeling and responding to historical pressures. All of these reasons combine to show why rhetoric should be considered the most humanistic of the humanities. It is directed to that part of our being which is not merely rational, for it supplements the rational approach. And it is directed to individual men in their individual situations, so that by the very definitions of the terms here involved, it takes into account what science deliberately, to satisfy its own purposes, leaves out. There is consequently no need for wonder that, in an age that has been influenced to distrust and disregard what is characteristically human, rhetoric should be a prime target of attack. If it is a weakness to harbor feelings, and if furthermore it is a weakness to be caught up in historical situations, then rhetoric is construable as a dealer in weaknesses. That man is in this condition religion, philosophy, and literature have been teaching for thousands of years. Criticism of it from the standpoint of a scientistic Utopia is the new departure.

. . . Rhetoric has a relationship to the world which logic does not have and which forces the rhetorician to keep his eye upon reality as well as upon the character and situation of his audience. The truth of this is seen when we begin to examine the nature of the traditional "topics." The topics were first formulated by Aristotle and were later treated also by Cicero and Quintilian and by many subsequent writers on the subject of persuasion. They are a set of "places" or "regions" where one can go to find the substance for persuasive argument. Cicero defines a topic as "the seat of an argument." In function they are sources of content for speeches that are designed to influence. Aristotle listed a considerable number of them, but for our purposes they can be categorized very broadly. In reading or interpreting the world of reality, we make use of four very general ideas. The first three are usually expressed, in the language of philosophy, as being, cause, and relationship. The fourth, which stands apart from these because it is an external source, is testimony and authority.

One way to interpret a subject is to define its nature—to describe the fixed features of its being. Definition is an attempt to capture essence. When we speak of the nature of a thing, we speak of something we expect to persist. Definitions accordingly deal with fundamental and unchanging properties.

Another way to interpret a subject is to place it in a cause-and-effect relationship. The process of interpretation is then to affirm it as the cause of some effect or as the effect of some cause. And the attitudes of those who are listening will be affected according to whether or not they agree with our cause-and-effect analysis.

A third way to interpret a subject is in terms of relationships of similarity and dissimilarity. We say that it is like something which we know in fuller detail, or that it is unlike that thing in important respects. From such a comparison conclusions regarding the subject itself can be drawn. This is a very common form of argument, by which probabilities can be established. And since probabilities are all we have to go on in many questions of this life, it must be accounted a usable means of persuasion.

The fourth category, the one removed from the others by the fact of its being an external source, deals not with the evidence directly but accepts it on the credit of testimony or authority. If we are not in position to see or examine, but can procure the deposition of some one who is, the deposition may become the substance of our argument. We can slip it into a syllogism just as we would a defined term. The same is true of general statements which come from quarters of great authority or prestige. If a proposition is backed by some weighty authority, like the Bible, or can be associated with a great name, people may be expected to respond to it in accordance with the veneration they have for these sources. In this way evidence coming from the outside is used to influence attitudes or conduct.

Now we see that in all these cases the listener is being asked not simply to follow a valid reasoning form but to respond to some presentation of reality. He is being asked to agree with the speaker's interpretation of the world that is. If the definition being offered is a true one, he is expected to recognize this and to say, at least inwardly, "Yes, that is the way the thing is." If the exposition of cause-and-effect relationship is true, he may be expected to concur that X is the cause of such a consequence or that such a consequence has its cause in X. And according to whether this is a good or a bad cause or a good or a bad consequence, he is disposed to preserve or remove the cause, and so on. If he is impressed with the similarity drawn between two things, he is as a result more likely to accept a policy which involves treating something in the same way in which its analogue is treated. He has been influenced by a relationship of comparability. And finally, if he has been confronted with testimony or authority from sources he respects, he will receive this as a reliable, if secondary kind of information about reality. In these four ways he has been persuaded to read the world as the speaker reads it.

At this point, however, I must anticipate an objection. The retort might be made: "These are extremely formal categories you are enumerating. I fail to see how they are any less general or less indifferently applicable than the formal categories of logic. After all, definitions and so on can be offered of anything. You still have not succeeded in making rhetoric a substantive study."

In replying, I must turn here to what should be called the office of rhetoric. Rhetoric seen in the whole conspectus of its function is an art of emphasis embodying an order of desire. Rhetoric is advisory; it has the office of advising men with reference to an independent order of goods and with reference to their particular situation as it relates to these. The honest rhetorician therefore has two things in mind: a vision of how matters should go ideally and ethically and a consideration of the special circumstances of his auditors. Toward both of these he has a responsibility.

I shall take up first how his responsibility to the order of the goods or to the hierarchy of realities may determine his use of the topics.

When we think of rhetoric as one of the arts of civil society (and it must be a free society, since the scope of rhetoric is limited and the employment of it constrained under a despotism) we see that the rhetorician is faced with a choice of means in appealing to those whom he can prevail upon to listen to him. If he is at all philosophical, it must occur to him to ask whether there is a standard by which the sources of persuasion can be ranked. In a phrase, is there a preferred order of them, so that, in a scale of ethics, it is nobler to make use of one sort of appeal than another? This is of course a question independent of circumstantial matters, yet a fundamental one. We all react to some rhetoric as "untruthful" or "unfair" or "cheap," and this very feeling is evidence of the truth that it is possible to use a better or a worse style of appeal. What is the measure of the better style? Obviously this question cannot be answered at all in the absence of some conviction about the nature and destiny of man. Rhetoric inevitably impinges upon morality and politics; and if it is one of the means by which we endeavor to improve the character and the lot of men, we have to think of its methods and sources in relation to a scheme of values.

To focus the problem a little more sharply, when one is asking men to cooperate with him in thinking this or doing that, when is he asking in the name of the highest reality, which is the same as saying, when is he asking in the name of their highest good?

Naturally, when the speaker replies to this question, he is going to express his philosophy, or more precisely, his metaphysics. My personal reply would be that he is making the highest order of appeal when he is basing his case on definition or the nature of the thing. I confess that this goes back to a very primitive metaphysics, which holds that the highest reality is being, not becoming. It is a quasi-religious metaphysics, if you will, because it ascribes to the highest reality qualities of stasis, immutability, eternal perdurance—qualities that in Western civilization are usually expressed in the language of theism. That which is perfect does not change; that which has to change is less perfect. Therefore if it is possible to determine unchanging essences or qualities and to speak in terms of these, one is appealing to what is most real in so doing. From another point of view, this is but getting people to see what is most permanent in existence, or what transcends the world of change and accident. The realm of essence is the realm above the flux of phenomena, and definitions are of essences and genera.

I may have expressed this view in somewhat abstruse language in order to place it philosophically, yet the practice I am referring to is everyday enough, as a simple illustration will make plain. If a speaker should define man as a creature with an indefeasible right to freedom and should upon this base an argument that a certain man or group of men are entitled to freedom, he would be arguing from definition. Freedom is an unchanging attribute of his subject; it can accordingly be predicated of whatever falls within the genus man. Stipulative definitions are of the ideal, and in this fact lies the reason for placing them at the top of the hierarchy. If the real progress of man is toward knowledge of ideal truth, it follows that this is an appeal to his highest capacity—his capacity to apprehend what exists absolutely.

The next ranking I offer tentatively, but it seems to me to be relationship or similitude and its subvarieties. I have a consistent impression that the broad resource of analogy, metaphor, and figuration is favored by those of a poetic and imaginative cast of mind. We make use of analogy or comparison when the available knowledge of the subject permits only probable proof. Analogy is reasoning from something we know to something we do not know in one step; hence there is no universal ground for predication. Yet behind every analogy lurks the possibility of a general term. The general term is never established as such, for that would change the argument to one of deductive reasoning with a universal or distributed middle. The user of analogy is hinting at an essence which cannot at the moment be produced. Or, he may be using an indirect approach for reason of tact; analogies not infrequently do lead to generalizations; and he may be employing this approach because he is respectful of his audience and desires them to use their insight.

I mentioned a moment earlier that this type of argument seems to be preferred by those of a poetic or non-literal sort of mind. That fact suggests yet another possibility, which I offer still more diffidently, asking your indulgence if it seems to border on the whimsical. The explanation would be that the cosmos *is* one vast system of analogy, so that our profoundest intuitions of it are made in the form of comparisons. To affirm that something is like something else is to begin to talk about the unitariness of creation. Everything is like everything else somehow, so that we have a ladder of similitude mounting up to the final oneness—to something like a unity in godhead. Furthermore, there is about this source of argument a kind of decent reticence, a recognition of the unknown along with the known. There is a recognition that the unknown may be continuous with the known, so that man is moving about in a world only partly realized, yet real in all its parts. This is the mood of poetry and mystery, but further adumbration of it I leave to those more gifted than I.

Cause and effect appears in this scale to be a less exalted source of argument, though we all have to use it because we are historical men. Here I must recall the metaphysical ground of this organization and point out that it operates in the realm of becoming. Causes are causes having effect and effects are resulting from causes. To associate this source of argument with its habitual users, I must note that it is heard most commonly from those who are characteristically pragmatic in their way of thinking. It is not unusual today to find a lengthy piece of journalism or an entire political speech which is nothing but a series of arguments from consequence—completely devoid of reference to principle or defined ideas. We rightly recognize these as sensational types of appeal. Those who are partial to arguments based on effect are under a temptation to play too much upon the fears of their audience by stressing the awful nature of some consequence or by exaggerating the power of some cause. Modern advertising is prolific in this kind of abuse. There is likewise a tempation to appeal to prudential considerations only in a passage where things are featured as happening or threatening to happen.

An even less admirable subvariety of this source is the appeal to circumstance, which is the least philosophical of all the topics of argument. Circumstance is an allowable source when we don't know anything else to plead, in which cases we say, "There is nothing else to be done about it." Of all the arguments, it admits of the least perspicaciousness. An example of this which we hear nowadays with great regularity is: "We must adapt ourselves to a fast-changing world." This is pure argument from circumstance. It does not pretend, even, to offer a cause-and-effect explanation. If it did, the first part would tell us why we must adapt ourselves to a fast-changing world; and the second would tell us the result of our doing so. The usually heard formulation does neither. Such argument is preeminently lacking in understanding or what the Greeks called *dianoia.* It simply cites a brute circumstance and says, "Step lively." Actually, this argument amounts to a surrender of reason. Maybe it expresses an instinctive feeling that in this situation reason is powerless. Either you change fast or you get crushed. But surely it would be a counsel of desperation to try only this argument in a world suffering from aimlessness and threatened with destruction.

Generally speaking, cause and effect is a lower-order source of argument because it deals in the realm of the phenomenal, and the phenomenal is easily converted into the sensational. Sensational excitements always run the risk of arousing those excesses which we deplore as sentimentality or brutality.

Arguments based on testimony and authority, utilizing external sources, have to be judged in a different way. Actually, they are the other sources seen through other eyes. The question of their ranking involves the more general question of the status of authority. Today there is a widespread notion that all authority is presumptuous. ("Authority is authoritarian" seems to be the root idea); consequently it is held improper to try to influence anyone by the prestige of great names or of sanctioned pronouncements. This is a presumption itself, by which every man is presumed to be his own competent judge in all matters. But since that is a manifest impossibility, and is becoming a greater impossibility all the time, as the world piles up bodies of specialized knowledge which no one person can hope to command, arguments based on authority are certainly not going to disappear. The sound maxim is that an argument based on authority is as good as the authority. What we should hope for is a new and discriminating attitude toward what is authoritative, and I would like to see some source recognized as having moral authority. This hope will have to wait upon the recovery of a more stable order of values and the re-recognition of qualities in persons. Speaking most generally, arguments from authority are ethically good when they are deferential toward real hierarchy.

With that we may sum up the rhetorical speaker's obligation toward the ideal, apart from particular determinations. If one accepts the possibility of this or any other ranking, one has to concede that rhetoric is not merely formal; it is realistic. It is not a playing with counters; its impulses come from insights into actuality. Its topic matter is existential, not hypothetical. It involves more than mere demonstration because it involves choice. Its assertions have ontological claims.

Now I return to the second responsibility, which is imposed by the fact that the rhetorician is concerned with definite questions. These are questions having histories, and history is always concrete. This means that the speaker or writer has got to have a rhetorical perception of what his audience needs or will receive or respond to. He takes into account the reality of man's composite being and his tendency to be swayed by sentiment. He estimates the pressures of the particular situation in which his auditors are found. In the eyes of those who look sourly upon the art, he is a man probing for weaknesses which he means to exploit.

But here we must recur to the principle that rhetoric comprehensively considered is an art of emphasis. The definite situation confronts him with a second standard of choice. In view of the receptivity of his audience, which of the topics shall he choose to stress, and how? If he concludes that definition should be the appeal, he tries to express the nature of the thing in a compelling way. If he feels that a cause-and-effect demonstration would stand the greatest chance to impress, he tries to make this linkage so manifest that his hearers will see an inevitability in it. And so on with the other topics, which will be so emphasized or magnified as to produce the response of assent.

Along with this process of amplification, the ancients recognized two qualities of rhetorical discourse which have the effect of impressing an audience with the reality or urgency of a topic. In Greek these appear as *energia* and *enargia,* both of which may be translated "actuality," though the first has to do with liveliness or animation of action and the second with vividness of scene. The speaker now indulges in actualization to make what he is narrating or describing present to the minds' eyes of his hearers.

The practice itself has given rise to a good deal of misunderstanding, which it would be well to remove. We know that one of the conventional criticisms of rhetoric is that the practitioner of it takes advantage of his hearers by playing upon their feelings and imaginations. He overstresses the importance of his topics by puffing them up, dwelling on them in great detail, using an excess of imagery or of modifiers evoking the senses, and so on. He goes beyond what is fair, the critics often allege, by this actualization of a scene about which the audience ought to be thinking rationally. . . . There are those who object on general grounds to this sort of dramatization; it is too affecting to the emotions. Beyond a doubt, whenever the rhetorician actualizes an event in this manner, he is making it mean something to the emotional part of us, but that part is involved whenever we are deliberating about goodness and badness. On this subject there is a very wise reminder in Bishop Whately's *Elements of Rhetoric*: "When feelings are strongly excited, they are not necessarily over-excited; it may be that they are only brought to the state which the occasion fully justifies, or even that they fall short of this." . . . Our attitude toward what is just or right or noble and their opposites is not a bloodless calculation, but a feeling for and against. As Whately indicates, the speaker who arouses feeling may only be arousing it to the right pitch and channeling it in the right direction.

To reaffirm the general contention: the rhetorician who practices "amplification" is not thereby misleading his audience, because we are all men of limited capacity and sensitivity and imagination. We all need to have things pointed out to us, things stressed in our interest. The very task of the rhetorician is to determine what feature of a question is most exigent and to use the power of language to make it appear so. A speaker who dwells insistently upon some aspect of a case may no more be hoodwinking me than a policeman or a doctor when he advises against a certain course of action by pointing out its nature or its consequences. He *should* be in a position to know somewhat better than I do.

It is strongly to be suspected that this charge against rhetoric comes not only from the distorted image that makes man a merely rationalistic being, but also from the dogma of an uncritical equalitarianism. The notion of equality has insinuated itself so far that it appears sometimes as a feeling, to which I would apply the name "sentimental plebeianism," that no man is better or wiser than another, and hence that it is usurpation for one person to undertake to instruct or admonish another. This preposterous (and we could add, wholly unscientific judgment, since our differences are manifold and provable) is propagated in subtle ways by our institutions of publicity and the perverse art of demagogic politics. Common sense replies that any individual who advises a friend or speaks up in [a] meeting is exercising a kind of leadership, which may be justified by superior virtue, knowledge, or personal insight.

The fact that leadership is a human necessity is proof that rhetoric as the attempt through language to make one's point of view prevail grows out of the nature of man. It is not a reflection of any past phase of social development, or any social institution, or any fashion, or any passing vice. When all factors have been considered, it will be seen that men are born rhetoricians, though some are born small ones and others greater, and some cultivate the native gift by study and training, whereas some neglect it. Men are such because they are born into history, with an endowment of passion and a sense of the *ought*. There is ever some discrepancy, however slight, between the situation man is in and the situation he would like to realize. His life is therefore characterized by movement toward goals. It is largely the power of rhetoric which influences and governs that movement.

For the same set of reasons, rhetoric is cognate with language. Ever since I first heard the idea mentioned seriously it impressed me as impossible and even ridiculous that the utterances of men could be neutral. Such study as I have been able to give the subject over the years has confirmed that feeling and has led me to believe that what is sometimes held up as a desideratum—expression purged of all tendency—rests upon an initial misconception of the nature of language.

The condition essential to see is that every use of speech, oral and written, exhibits an attitude, and an attitude implies an act. "Thy speech bewrayeth thee" is aphoristically true if we take it as saying, "Your speech reveals your disposition," first by what you choose to say, then by the amount you decide to say, and so on down through the resources of linguistic elaboration and intonation. All rhetoric is a rhetoric of motives, as Kenneth Burke saw fit to indicate in the title of his book. At the low end of the scale, one may be doing nothing more than making sounds to expres exuberance. But if at the other end one sits down to compose a *Critique of the Pure Reason*, one has the motive of refuting other philosophers' account of the constitution of being, and of substituting one's own, for an interest which may be universal, but which nonetheless proceeds from the will to alter something.

Does this mean that it is impossible to be objective about anything? Does it mean that one is "rhetorical" in declaring that a straight line is the shortest distance between two points? Not in the sense in which the objection is usually raised. There are degrees of objectivity, and there are various disciplines which have their own rules for expressing their laws or their content in the most effective manner for their purpose. But even this expression can be seen as enclosed in a rhetorical intention. Put in another way, an utterance is capable of rhetorical function and aspect. If one looks widely enough, one can discover its rhetorical dimension, to put it in still another way. The scientist has some interest in setting forth the formulation of some recurrent feature of the physical world, although his own sense of motive may be lost in a general feeling that science is a good thing because it helps progress along.

In short, as long as man is a creature responding to purpose, his linguistic expression will be a carrier of tendency. Where the modern semanticists got off on the wrong foot in their effort to refurbish language lay in the curious supposition that language could and should be outwardly determined. They were positivists operating in the linguistic field. Yet if there is anything that is going to keep on defying positivistic correlation, it is this subjectively born, intimate, and value-laden vehicle which we call language. Language is a system of imputation, by which values and precepts are first framed in the mind and then are imputed to things. This is not an irresponsible imputation; it does not imply, say, that no two people can look at the same clock face and report the same time. The qualities or properties have to be in the things, but they are not in the things in the form in which they are framed by the mind. This much I think we can learn from the great realist-nominalist controversy of the Middle Ages and from the little that contemporary semantics has been able to add to our knowledge. Language was created by the imagination for the purposes of man, but it may have objective reference—just how we cannot say until we are in possession of a more complete metaphysics and epistemology.

Now a system of imputation involves the use of predicates, as when we say, "Sugar is sweet" or "Business is good." Modern positivism and relativism, however, have gone virtually to the point of denying the validity of all conceptual predication. Occasionally at Chicago I purposely needle a class by expressing a general concept in a casual way, whereupon usually I am sternly reminded by some member brought up in the best relativist tradition that "You can't generalize that way." The same view can be encountered in eminent quarters. Justice Oliver Wendell Holmes was fond of saying that the chief end of man is to frame general propositions and that no general proposition is worth a damn. In the first of these general propositions the Justice was right, in the sense that men cannot get along without categorizing their apprehensions of reality. In the second he was wrong because, although a great jurist, he was not philosopher enough to think the matter through. Positivism and relativism may have rendered a certain service as devil's advocates if they have caused us to be more careful about our concepts and our predicates, yet their position in net form is untenable. The battle against general propositions was lost from the beginning, for just as surely as man is a symbol-using animal (and a symbol transcends the thing symbolized) he is a classifying animal. The morality lies in the application of the predicate.

Language, which is thus predicative, is for the same cause sermonic. We are all of us preachers in private or public capacities. We have no sooner uttered words than we have given impulse to other people to look at the world, or some small part of it, in our way. Thus caught up in a great web of inter-communication and inter-influence, we speak as rhetoricians affecting one another for good or ill. That is why I must agree with Quintilian that the true orator is the good man, skilled in speaking—good in his formed character and right in his ethical philosophy. When to this he adds fertility in invention and skill in the arts of language, he is entitled to that leadership which tradition accords him.

If rhetoric is to be saved from the neglect and even the disrepute which I was deploring at the beginning of this lecture, these primary truths will have to be recovered until they are a part of our active consciousness. They are, in summation, that man is not nor ever can be nor ever should be a depersonalized thinking machine. His feeling is the activity in him most closely related to what used to be called his soul. To appeal to his feeling therefore is not necessarily an insult; it can be a way to honor him, by recognizing him in the fulness of his being. Even in those situations where the appeal is a kind of strategy, it but recognizes that men—all men—are historically conditioned.

Rhetoric must be viewed formally as operating at that point where literature and politics meet, or where literary values and political urgencies can be brought together. The rhetorician makes use of the moving power of literary presentation to induce in his hearers an attitude or decision which is political in the very broadest sense. Perhaps this explains why the successful user of rhetoric is sometimes in bad grace with both camps. For the literary people he is too "practical"; and for the more practical political people he is too "flowery." But there is nothing illegitimate about what he undertakes to do, any more than it would be illegitimate to make use of the timeless principles of aesthetics in the constructing of a public building. Finally, we must never lose sight of the order of values as the ultimate sanction of rhetoric. No one can live a life of direction and purpose without some scheme of values. As rhetoric confronts us with choices involving values, the rhetorician is a preacher to us, noble if he tries to direct our passion toward noble ends and base if he uses our passion to confuse and degrade us. Since all utterance influences us in one or the other of these directions, it is important that the direction be the right one, and it is better if this lay preacher is a master of his art.

Part Two

Motivating Student Writing

> *My first impetus to write came from a sixth grade English teacher who filled us with feeling that writing was a good thing to do and that there was something noble about the English language.*
>
> ANONYMOUS

"Motivation" is a deceptive sort of word which can be interpreted in several ways. One teacher, for example, may say, "We need to *motivate* our students to write better." This teacher is probably thinking of the wide range of abilities which exist at any one grade level, and of the continuing need to stress the positive aspects of composition. More than likely this teacher has in mind certain curriculum activities designed to stimulate greater interest in the writing process. Another teacher may say, "Our students do not write better because they are not *motivated*," and mean something quite different. The second teacher seems to believe that the students' failure is their own fault and not much can be done about it. The source of the failure, it is implied, can probably be traced back to parents who have not provided the "right" training. Underlying the second statement is the false assumption that *wanting* to do anything is all that is necessary for doing it. If this were true, one could become a millionaire, a television celebrity, or the fullback of the Cleveland Browns merely by wanting to. This brand of fatalism has a destructive impact on students' self-concept and on their understanding of the composing process.

But as sincere as the first teacher is, this teacher too may err in believing that motivation alone will solve the problem. Some authorities seem to believe that since human beings learn to talk at an early age, we all have within us the technical competence necessary for producing good writing. Therefore the teacher's main task is to discover ways to inspire or motivate young people to release this latent energy—ways such as going on a field trip, participating in a discussion, playing a role, viewing a film, or perhaps just practicing a lot. The problem with this view is that there are many conventions in written expression which do not normally occur in everyday speech—punctuation, balance and parallelism, sentence forms such as the loose or periodic, and various organizational patterns, to name a few. Motivation is important, but motivation alone is not enough.

What then is the role of motivation? The writing teacher's first task, clearly, is to get his students "into" writing, to bring them to the point of wanting to write. Both Jean Pumphrey and Ken Macrorie offer some specific suggestions for doing this. One indication of the success of Pumphrey's "five-minute write-in" technique is revealed in a conversation with a student:

> At one point I asked a student if the five-minute write-ins were helping him. "No," he replied, "I want to keep writing."

Precisely! If our students "want to keep writing," we can pretty well assume they are motivated. But motivation should not be restricted to the beginning of the school year; it should be of continuing concern throughout the year. Writing is a demanding experience, and in the heat of the struggle the novice may become discouraged or be tempted to compromise for something less than his best. The wise teacher will be alert to such moments, always ready to assist as the individual case may require.

In his essay "Creative Expression in Great Britain," John Dixon explains how an experiential approach works in a nation with a long tradition of high and sometimes rigid academic standards. In combining close observation with personal experience, this approach will likely bring to mind the educational philosophy of John Dewey. Stephen Judy ("On Clock Watching and Composing") also advocates getting students "outside the school-and-books environment" as a means of motivating composition. Judy argues that the writing of typical ninth-graders contains cogent ideas but remains "inarticulate" and "incomplete." The reason for this, he concludes, lies in the students' "lack of audience consciousness or audience sensitivity." Most readers will grant Judy's analysis, but some may want to argue with his conclusions.

The concluding essay in this section has all the grace and good sense that only a writer could bring to the teaching of writing. Donald Murray, who is both teacher and writer, believes that we should involve our students in the "demanding, intellectual process" of writing. "How do you motivate your students to pass through this process?" he asks. The answer is clear: Let them write. Let each student find his own subject and discover his own stance. Let the only textbook be the students' writing.

In one sentence Murray captures the essence of what many believe to be the primary goal of the composition curriculum. "We have to respect the student, not for his product, not for the paper we call literature by giving it a grade, but for the search for truth in which he is engaged." Involvement in the search for truth may indeed be the most powerful motivational device available to us.

Teaching English Composition as a Creative Art

JEAN PUMPHREY

If someone came up to you and said, "Go develop a sense of humor," I suppose you'd laugh if you had one, and go into a deeper depression if you didn't. This, I submit, is what happens all too often in the teaching of English composition. So much of what we say to students really amounts to "go write a good theme," and those who can, do; those who can't get depressed, frequently to the point of dropping out.

Even as there is too little meaningful teacher involvement in the process of writing, there is all too often too much involvement of the wrong kind. I think most teachers of composition will recognize the writing style which follows:

> Each separate society is different from one another in their own way as individuals differ from each other. Every society is conditioned around what the people make it to be. The more people contained in a given area, the bigger the society and the greater the norms. And when you have these norms you can only do what is accepted by the people (who, of course, made up the norms) and if you violate the social expectations, you run into conflict.

If I seem to give too much credit to the author of this statement when I refer to her "style," I do not intend to. Credit must go to her teachers. I submit that no one writes this way naturally. Such a style of writing has to be learned. Few of us would like to think that this is what we're teaching, but when we stand outside the process, pushing the student too quickly into communicative language, leaping past the expressive function of language, I believe we are, unwittingly, teaching the style we then sit back and criticize.

Each fall we stagger under the barrage of such language from freshman college students. In an attempt to unscramble the student from such impossible "textbookeze," some may resort to a handbook, assuming the student is not ready for "great ideas" and must return to "go." Others may plead with or otherwise exhort the student to write in his own voice, write

College English, vol. 34 (February 1973), pp. 666–673.

plainly about whatever he knows. "Write in your own voice," we tell him. "Pick a topic familiar to you, a theme you can support." We urge him to expose his private feelings. Surely that is something he knows something about. We tell him to give evidence, to be specific, to use examples, to be concrete, and, in *telling* him, we are doing exactly what we are telling him not to do. It is not surprising that students should do as we do, not as we say. It is not surprising that they should learn more from *how* we teach than from what we teach.

The fact is that *no one,* in the decade of the seventies, is convinced by being told. Yet students and teachers go on telling with greater and greater embellishments as if extravagant rhetoric could obviate simple illustration. And we are all turned off, students and teachers alike.

The teacher, concerning himself primarily with the product rather than the process, grades in silence, grimly revising his transmogrifying comments. The student is expected to learn language by writing in silence, later by observing his "corrected" errors, often in contrast to an accomplished writer's "model essay." Alone in his study, suspecting somehow he is responsible, the teacher tries to devise means to help the student reorder his thoughts. Removed from the process, he is inclined to think in terms of form aside from content. Should he decide, in the name of Order or Expediency, to impose a pre-determined form upon his students' raw material, he runs the risk of alienating his students from language. Pleasure in language may be lost, and with it the opportunity to see writing as a process of discovery.

Much of the graceless language we are confronted with comes as a direct result of student attempts to put together too much too soon, using someone else's format. Much of this writing is simply a reflection of the degree to which the student has become alienated from language which should be as naturally his as love. Susanne Langer ("The Lord of Creation," *Fortune,* January, 1944) writes, "The process of transforming all direct experience into imagery or into that supreme mode of symbolic expression, language, has so completely taken possession of the human mind that it is not only a special talent but a dominant, organic need." If this be so, then why should writing be considered such an unpleasant task by so many students?

In the opinion of this writer, there can be no pleasure in language in the classroom so long as students write and teachers grade in painful isolation from one another. Yet teacher involvement in the process of writing has all too often meant interference, a dictating of form or content, a coming in with red pencil in hand, an approach which tends to separate teacher from student, form from content, and ultimately, student from language.

We need to get involved in the process together, all together, to mutually re-discover that language lives, that the word is alive, that writing is a process of discovery.

The sort of teacher involvement I am advocating brings teacher and students together in exploring the problems we all have in common when we try to write. It means sharing the pleasure we all can experience through writing. It means a shift in emphasis from teacher-student to student-peer evaluation, and an opening up of the classroom to let in real problems, as opposed to those artificially set up to "train" the student into logic or to "prepare" him for entrance into some other institution.

As a poet and as a teacher I have come to see the creative process as a process of scattering, then bringing together of various parts into a new whole. One does not know beforehand what form that whole will take, but that is how discoveries are made, and that is what makes writing, or any other creative act, exciting. It is the excitement of writing creatively which needs to be restored to the English classroom.

What follows is not a course description, but rather an attempt to illustrate some of the discoveries I and my students made while becoming involved together in the process of writing.

Attempting to illustrate a process is a little like trying to communicate a color in braille. I comfort myself with what I say to students: "All writing assignments are impossible. Though we can summon things to us with words (which is miracle enough), the word can never be the thing, and since writing is a process of selection, always we are compelled to leave things out, and to fear we have left the 'wrong' things out." With this a priori limitation in mind I shall try to illustrate the value of "spontaneous" writing in the classroom, and to show how certain techniques of fiction can be used to teach a multi-purpose writing skill to many who have become alienated from language, as well as to those who love language.

The class I refer to in the paragraphs which follow is a three unit freshman transfer composition class made up of students who placed themselves.

The class met three times a week. During the first week, after arranging our seats in a kind of circle, we began our discussion of writing. From the beginning we agreed that writing is a very complex and difficult task. I explained to the students that all of the writing assignments would be impossible; that I would not be looking for the perfectly executed assignment, but that I would be most concerned to see that each person had grappled in his or her way with the problem posed by the assignment. "What is it that makes writing so frustrating and so painful?" was the subject of the first of a series of five to ten minute write-ins designed to help students recover the excitement of using language expressively.

I suggested the students write on one side of the paper only, and with a smooth ball point pen. Much of the frustration connected with writing comes because the mind moves so much faster than the hand. Pencils move too slowly, and the process of erasing stops the forward movement. Often what has been erased turns out to be useful later on. It is less frustrating and more productive to scratch out and later revise.

I wrote along with the students. This helped me to discover more about my own processes, and it served the purpose of encouraging the students, and of keeping me in closer touch with what was happening to them. I tried to make the most of my own "mistakes" to *reinforce* the idea that we were not aiming for perfection. Spelling, sentence structure, punctuation were all matters to be considered on a final draft, but not for now. Since we were not aiming for perfection the students were soon freer in their writing, and at the same time, less hesitant in reading aloud what they had written. Sometimes it was fun, sometimes serious, often it was both at the same time.

One student's response to the question "What makes writing so painful?" provoked a very serious and stimulating discussion. She wrote, "Writing is difficult because everything you write down is there forever. When you *say* something you get feelings back right away, and it's easier to know how to respond. But writing is stating something—not being able to take anything back."

We discussed whether or not it is true that we can't take back what we say in writing. We decided that although it is not true, most people act as if it were true. And that is part of what makes writing painful. We tend to write every moment as if every one of our words were to be published and immortalized. And so long as we are wondering "Am I saying the right thing? Am I saying it the right way?" that is the object of our concentration, and not the subject we are writing about. Our powers of observation are cut off to the extent to which we internalize a voice of authority which constantly demands a perfect product, even on a first draft. Our motto became "Write first, think later. Don't try to be the writer and the critic at the same time."

I asked the students to write the next assignment on white, unlined paper. This assignment was to write for five minutes without stopping, on any subject. Those who "couldn't find" a subject were asked to write on just that. The aim was pure quantity. After five minutes we did a word count. The record was 193. The girl who won had written about being fired from her job. She had more than enough to say on that subject. The students "without subjects" began to realize that, in actuality, they had a great wealth of material. It was a question of tapping the source, the flow. Who hasn't failed at something? And, sadly, we always have much to say about our failures. We wrote for another five minutes to see if anyone could beat the record. No one did, but we discovered that no one had had time to be bored or intimidated by the prospect of writing.

I asked the students to hold up their papers. Facing each other, they made the not so surprising observation that nearly everyone had written as though his paper were lined, and as though the object were, not to expand thoughts, but to conserve paper. Thereafter, continuing to use unlined paper, and resolving to be more expansive and wasteful, we placed the waste paper basket in the center of the room, and used it freely as we wrote.

Released from the bondage of spelling, punctuation, erasers, and lined paper we were free wheeling. The students themselves began to provide the in-class writing assignments. We wrote on all sorts of objects, both strange and commonplace, and often grappled with unanswerable questions. If a hungry student began furtively to peel an orange so that the pervasive smell of rind reached us long before the sight of the orange, we wrote about that. Nothing was irrelevant, and thus much of the attention, the best concentration, which ordinarily goes out the window or toward some other "distraction," was caught and held.

The next planned assignment was to "put the classroom on paper" the way a novelist or short story writer puts a room into a sentence or a paragraph. After we had written for five minutes I asked the students what problems they were encountering. By this time they were aware of the great number of possibilities, angles of vision, open to the writer in describing any object or scene. The problem, they said, was where to begin. As we analyzed this problem it became clear the real problem was not where to begin, but *to begin.* The discovery that they could find so much to say had stopped them. We discussed writing as a process of selection. Selecting means making decisions, and the more importance we attach to each decision the more painful and difficult it becomes. The tendency to attach undue importance to each decision is minimized once the distinction between a first draft and a finished piece is clearly realized.

Gradually the students came to realize that it is more effective, more efficient, and less painful to write three drafts rapidly, each time adding and/or subtracting detail, rather than painstakingly attempting a polished, all inclusive piece the first time through. I suggested they concern themselves, not absolutely, but generally, with *what* they have to say on a first draft, with the *order* in which they say it on a second draft, and with *how* they say it on a third draft.

Constantly we *tell* students to revise, revise, but not until they have been through the process, not once, but a number of times, do they clearly see the value of what we are telling them. This is partly because students are all too inclined to treat a first draft like a final draft; to approach it at the last minute, and with great intensity, until they exhaust themselves half way through. Perhaps this is because teachers themselves have tended to ask for "first drafts" while looking for neatly structured outlines, perfect sentence structure, precise punctuation, and perfect spelling. For whatever reason, most students initially rebel at the thought of going through, what seems to them, the very tedious process of writing a second or third draft.

Too often, I think, teachers have acted under the fear or the assumption that students, left to their own devices, will write sloppy, disorganized papers. One has only to leave them to their own devices to discover that students are no more resistant to the mind's need for order than the rest of us, and that their desire for order is, in fact, very great. It then becomes the function of the teacher, not to leap in with a magic formula five paragraph theme to assure the student of what will please him, the teacher, but rather to help the student through the wilderness of his own thought, to encourage him to use language expansively until he discovers what it is he wishes to give order to. Free of any pressure to pre-order his thoughts, the student can then experience the excitement of seeing form evolve out of content as his scattered thoughts come together into a new whole.

By the time the students caught on to the advantage of writing freely and of doing several drafts, we were already into more sophisticated assignments related to their reading of literature. Thus far I have mentioned only in-class writing assignments and related discussion. The students were, at the same time, reading short stories and poems outside of class. The first few out-of-class writing assignments simply required the students to react in a personal way, positively or negatively, to the literature assigned. Gradually the in-class and out-of-class assignments came together. For example, having attempted to put a room on paper ourselves, we then examined the way writers of fiction accomplish this.

One in-class assignment was to write from memory a description of a character from one of the stories. We then went through the story line by line listing all concrete details in order to determine what had been left out, or perhaps of greater interest, what had been added, by each of us. The next out-of-class assignment was to describe a person so everyone in the class would either like or dislike him. As we reacted to each description it soon became clear that the most convincing pieces of writing were those in which the writer paid close attention to concrete detail, attempting to show rather than tell. Increasingly the students grew to trust one another to evaluate and criticize constructively. Their writing improved as they continued to write for an audience beyond themselves or their teacher.

At one point I read the students the first few pages of Kafka's *The Metamorphosis*, up to the point where Gregor's mother calls to him from the other side of the door. I then asked the students to finish the story as they saw fit. This led to some hilariously funny writing, but they were able to see the limitless possibilities which confront, and at the same time offer themselves to the writer of fiction. We discussed how and why Kafka might have made certain decisions as he wrote, and how writing decisions in general are made. We played with the idea of a metamorphosis, trying to decide how other characters we had encountered would have reacted had each, like Gregor, found himself transformed into an insect. Or what if Gregor had turned into an antelope instead of an insect? The students could readily envision many variations on a single theme. Perhaps the most important discovery they made while tackling this assignment was how much easier it is to write when one has hold of a plot or a theme interesting enough to be self-propelling.

The next step was to prepare for a longer, more formal, out-of-class paper. I suggested possible themes, but recommended that the students develop their own. They were free to write a formal essay or to try writing a short story. The only requirement was that the paper must relate to the literature assigned. A short story, for example, could be modeled on Kafka's *Metamorphosis.*

I asked the students on a Friday to bring in a statement of theme for Monday. Though they had been quite good about doing assignments, when Monday came, less than two thirds of the students had done the assignment. I asked how much time each of them had spent worrying about the assignment in the midst of week end activities. That was another matter. One girl estimated she had spent as many as twelve hours worrying about not doing the assignment. I suggested we take five minutes to write a statement of theme. In five minutes the student who had spent twelve hours worrying about the assignment had written a statement satisfactory to me. She had given herself a far more difficult assignment than I had because she unconsciously assumed, despite all indications to the contrary, that she would be held to her statement, tied to this one decision. Instead of writing a statement of theme she was attempting to write the entire paper in her head—a little like trying to put a puzzle together in one's head without looking at the pieces. I pointed out that an initial statement of theme should be simply a tool to explore with, and added, somewhat didactically, "He who postpones the assignment, does it a hundred times."

Next I asked those who had statements of theme to begin their first drafts. I reminded them that a first draft should simply amount to getting the pieces of the puzzle out on the table. I suggested they write only one set of ideas or images per page on one side of the page in order to achieve greater mobility when the time came to put their ideas back together in new form. Those who did not yet have a statement of theme I asked to write for five minutes at a time on several potential themes suggested by other students. When a student found something he wanted to continue writing on, I suggested he pursue that.

Though not every student found his theme that day, nearly everyone discarded a few dead ends. One by one the students were discovering that they had themes of their own, and could develop them. I wanted them to understand, also, that certain themes, unanswered questions, run through our entire lives, and that in writing a single paper, one only begins to tap a major theme.

Increasingly the students were coming to find they did not want to stop writing after five or ten minutes, that writing for "five" minutes was a good way to begin, a way to get past that time just prior to writing when the mind rebels. At one point I asked a student if the five minute write-ins were helping him. "No," he replied, "I want to keep writing."

Before the papers were due the students brought them into class for criticism. I suggested they divide into groups of three so that each student would have an audience of two. Each student read his paper aloud and was given general criticism. Then I asked them to exchange papers and to make specific comments in writing. I asked that the papers be typed, not just because a typed paper makes a better impression on the reader, but because I am convinced that typing a paper improves the quality of writing. The pen may be friendlier in the beginning, but typing a paper finishes it.

Despite student enthusiasm and the opportunity for much criticism beforehand, the papers were not all A's, and I would have been happier had I not had to put a grade on some of them. Some of the students had a problem with sentence structure until the very end, and I do not mean anywhere to imply that some of them would not have benefited from a grammatical approach. I will say that much of the rough sentence structure I encountered in the beginning had become smoother by the end of the course. I could particularly see a change in the writing of those who began with the sort of cramped style so evident in the piece of student writing first quoted in this paper. "Correcting" such writing is nearly impossible, and any attempt to do so is likely to produce more pain than anything else. It is not enough to *tell* such a student to be concrete, to give examples. She needs to discover the examples she needs by learning to explore ideas freely through writing.

I was generally pleased with the final papers the students turned in and also with the improvement I could see in their in-class writing. But more than that I was pleased to hear some of them say they were, for the first time, enjoying writing, that they were even beginning to write letters! I was pleased, not because I think learning must always be "fun," but because I know that one does more of what one enjoys and by doing more, one becomes better, and so enjoys doing more. A new and positive cycle is begun. Writing is, and always will be, one of the most difficult of human endeavors. This we understood and accepted from the beginning. The discovery, for some of the students, was that writing could be pleasurable and rewarding.

These, then, are some of the highlights, some of the high points we attained during the semester. There is much, of course, which I have not covered. Once involved in the process, I found the discoveries to be endless. Certainly participating in the write-ins brought back to me the difficulty of the task facing students when we ask them to sit down to write in a classroom situation. For better or for worse, I discovered I had this paper on my mind. And I doubt that I'd have written it had I not sat down to write "five" minutes at a time with ball point pen on unlined paper.

The greatest problem I encountered throughout the course was that of evaluation. I postponed grading by making comments rather than corrections on the short out-of-class papers. In making comments I tried to re-enforce the positive, rather than emphasize errors. In addition, I told the students that I would, at any time, accept a paper to be graded, should anyone wish to know where he stood grade-wise. This worked for the better students who were more readily able to move from expressive to communicative language. But one semester is hardly enough time for the weaker student to make such a transition. It would have been better had these students been allowed to continue writing expressively without having to "get it altogether" for a grade. The course would have been more effective for all concerned, and more readily adaptable to individual needs, had it been offered on a credit, no credit basis.

It could be asked at this point "Where and how will the student learn his basic grammar, his spelling and punctuation?" It is by no means my intent to discount this very real and valid concern. I can only say that if the student has not acquired his basic English in twelve years of schooling, it would be presumptuous to think that as college teachers we have the magic to teach him all this in one or two semesters. But we can, by *allowing* him to find pleasure in language, by encouraging him to expand his thoughts until they become interesting to him, help him to find the motivation to pursue the more mechanical aspects of language.

On the last day of class I asked the students to write for five minutes in response to the following question: "Has your attitude toward writing changed at all since the beginning of the semester?" I think the following anonymous response best illustrates how writing can be a process of discovery.

> Not really—If I have a good topic I get interested—If I don't, it's just another assignment—I've always enjoyed writing when I'm interested in the subject. I've become a lot more critical of my writing. I guess my attitude has changed—I now feel that what I write must be a total expression of me—rather than just writing to fulfill the assignment—True, I am writing to fulfill this assignment but I'm also saying things I mean rather than a lot of the bullshit I'm capable of producing.

To Be Read

KEN MACRORIE

We ask students never to judge ideas or events out of context, but fail to see our composition classes in any larger world. That is why they are such astonishing failures. For decades we have been smearing the bloody marks *(sp, awk, gr)* in the margins of what we call "themes." These papers are not meant to be *read,* but *corrected.*

Now we are living in a great series of revolutions, testing whether the present forms of school, church, state, family, and relationships between blacks and whites will endure. Already high school students are following the lead of college students—publishing underground newspapers, asking for a voice in making the rules of their schools. Tomorrow they will be suggesting or forcing changes in the classroom—in what they are asked to read, to write, and in how their work is to be evaluated.

A textbook named *Correct Writing, Forms A, B, C, and D* is likely to receive only a hoot of derision from students who are communicating with each other and with administrators and teachers in dozens of new ways. As the television generation, they are not any longer going to suffer learning in grade school that the White House is where the President lives, in junior high what the President's name is, and in senior high that the house is located on Pennsylvania Avenue. Many of them have been there, and to the Pentagon as well.

These are perilous moments for American establishments. They will be destroyed or they will reform. We have a small chance to keep our students from turning our schools into the shambles remaining after revolutions in Watts, Newark, and Detroit. But it is a chance.

Four years ago I stumbled into a way to induce students to write so they excited each other and me. Now that I have worked out a program and seen it elicit lively and valuable writing from all levels of students (from seventh grade through graduate school) and all ranges of students (from "remedial" to "honors"), I know trying to reform writing in the schools and colleges makes sense.

English Journal, vol. 57 (May 1968), pp. 686–692.

Here is the program:

1. Ask students to place themselves outside of class anywhere they can be alone and quiet. Then write for ten minutes as fast as they can, putting down whatever comes to mind. If they can't think of a word, they should start by reporting what they see in front of them. Let the mind and pencil go until they fill a large-sized notebook page. Twice, so they have two papers to bring to the next class.

2. Ask for honesty. Say you know school doesn't often nurture it, that at times you will be dishonest, as everyone is without realizing—but you will try to speak truth. Pass out an example of phony writing—pretentious, empty:

> But the area which caused Henry and I to become steadfast friends was outdoor sports.

Also pass out an example of honest writing, like this:

> He doesn't have legs. Not ones that feel or move. It's been that way almost four years now. Wheels. I was scared to talk at first, felt like a kid asking what it is that everyone's talking about. But we did. We used to goof around and tell dirty jokes. I always felt a little fake. Dan and I took him to the bathroom every day. Had to be done in a special way. We were there once, Dan asked a question—I don't remember what it was—something involving my ability to work.
>
> "What do you think I am, a cripple?" That's what I said. I didn't look at anyone, just the wall. For about half an hour. I felt very whole, but my stomach was tin foil. They were quiet, both of them. Quiet as being alone. I wished someone would cut off my arms.

3. Ask students to keep all papers in a folder. At the end of the semester you will choose the six to ten best papers and give a course grade on them. If the student needs a grade earlier—to convince his father he should buy him a car or so he can apply for college—you will grade his folder as of the moment. His classmates and you will be constantly commenting on his papers in this seminar-style class, and some papers will be reproduced as examples of fine writing; so he will know how he is doing.

If students' free writings turn out too personal or confessional, they should try others. Ask them not to submit writing that embarasses them because of its intimacy. If they write close to their heart, they may ask you to withhold their names when their papers are presented to the class.

4. Ask students to bring two free writings to the second meeting and to exchange papers with another student. They should underline (or indicate in the margin) any phrases or sentences they like for content or expression, or both.

5. Discuss the marked passages with students. Ask students to comment on some before you praise them. Look for truth and liveliness. Take

papers home, mark passages or phrases you like. Ditto these excerpts. Write nothing on the papers.

6. At the third meeting continue discussion of good passages. Tell students that for the first month or so they should make only positive comments on each other's writing. If the class numbers no more than twenty, begin the first few meetings with the group seated in a circle, or around a giant table made from a number of tables. If the class is more than twenty, for part of the period separate students into smaller groups. Seven is good because it puts pressure on writers so they cannot dismiss criticism—good or bad—as merely a gesture from friend or enemy. Do not visit the groups. In the first month ask no student to read his paper aloud to others unless you think it a smashing success. Otherwise, you read it to the class or ask students to exchange papers several times so they may be read aloud without the class knowing who wrote them.

7. Ask students to write two fifteen-minute free papers trying to focus on one subject, not letting the mind skip as freely as in the first writing. If they get off the subject and are going marvelously, they should continue on the detour.

8. As you and the students discuss the writing, allow them to react even when they can't say what they like about the writing. Twelve heads nodding up and down in appreciation will charge any writer's batteries. Begin now occasionally to point out why a writing is good: strong metaphor, rhythmic sentences, tension between two ideas or facts, fresh expression instead of clichés, insight, memorable sensuous details. Don't feel obliged to offer all the papers to class criticism, even if you have a two-hour period in which to work.

9. Show students how to tighten writing. Ask them to choose their best free writing and cut all wasted words—outside of class. Urge what professional editors suggest (not necessarily what English textbooks emphasize): for example, eliminating unnecessary uses of *which, that,* and *who.* Show students where they have repeated words powerfully.

10. Ask students to write a forty-five minute free paper focusing on one subject.

11. Encourage and encourage, but never falsely. When you get a fine piece of writing with a weak beginning and ending that need chopping, type it on a ditto master in the most powerfully cut version you can arrange without changing any words, and then—if the author approves—post it on the bulletin board in the hall. Correct all spelling errors and mechanical weaknesses before publishing it in any way. Publishers never knowingly embarrass their writers.

Try to place several writings in the student newspaper or magazine early in the semester. Don't expect students to take that initiative. For years they have been indoctrinated to believe they can't write. Their papers have been massacred—all that blood in the margins.

12. Ask students to write an informal case history of a day or hour (or several days, hours, or weeks condensed into one) on a job, or in a process or activity they've gone through many times. Or to tell what happens during a half-hour in the school library at a certain spot. They should put the reader there, not try for clinical detachment unless they need it. If they wish, they can write freely several times about the experience and then try to find a center (some tension, meaning, or lack of meaning) in the activity that helps tell them which details to discard and which they need more of. This paper may run two pages or ten.

13. Read aloud a few of these case histories the day they are due. Ask students to point out anything they like. Take them home, read them, try not to comment unless you have a major suggestion. Do not correct. Do not mark mistakes. Ditto two to four (one or three if your class lasts only fifty minutes) that you think compelling.

Occasionally during the semester you will find a paper that becomes excellent when cut massively. Ditto the cut version, then append the cut paragraphs or sentences. Remind students that this surgery is only one possibility and that the author has the *authority* to restore any of the material cut. After class discussion of case histories, ask all students to take their papers home and do their own revising and adding to. Let them know reworking of papers is expected in all major assignments, except when a paper seems strong all the way through upon first writing. Tell students that the wastebaskets of professional writers are full of discarded pages.

14. Ask students to record short fabulous realities in a notebook or journal. Examples:

a. Boy and girl talking, he standing in gutter, she on curb, for better eye-to-eye contact.
b. Sign downtown: "Four Barbers, No Waiting," and then below: "Television While You Wait."

Written skillfully these fabulous realities embody six essentials of most good writing: The writer (1) makes an event happen before the reader, (2) locates it significantly, (3) presents materials that create a tension or point, (4) uses only details that bear upon that tension or point, (5) does not waste words, and (6) saves the punch till the end, where it gains from suspense. The first fabulous reality above could be improved by reordering:

> Boy and girl talking—for better eye-to-eye contact she stands on the curb, he in the gutter.

The surprise is now at the end.

15. Ask students to think of expanding one fabulous reality into a little story. If they have nothing expandable, they needn't try. Conduct this class for writers, not hothouse scholars. When writers have worked hard and nothing goes right, they give up a project and start another. Good writing

usually is produced half by civil engineering and half by hidden springs that suddenly start flowing.

16. Ask students to write a longer paper remembering some childhood incident that shook them up. They should put the reader there, not generalize about feelings. Start with "One day—" and recreate that young world.

In this, and in all of their writing, do not allow clichés. If students can't think of another way of saying "It rained cats and dogs"—one that hits precisely the mood and intensity they want—let them say, "It rained hard." In casual conversation clichés are to be expected and endured; in writing—inexcusable. A writer asks his reader to look at his sentences. His first duty is not to bore him.

17. When childhood papers come in, introduce the elementary kinds of organization—Before-After, The Journey (we did this or went here and then did that and went there—whether this is a movement in ideas or action), and The Hook (at the end tying back to the beginning, perhaps with irony). Suggest that students may want to use one of these patterns in reshaping their childhood papers. (Call writing "writing" or "papers," never "themes." Whoever would voluntarily read something called a "theme"?) From now on in seminar sessions point out weaknesses in students' writings as well as strengths, but in front of the class don't be hard upon the paper of a student not yet praised by the group.

18. Ask students to keep a journal for three weeks or more, making entries only when they see or think of something striking. Present excerpts from strong journals, like Thoreau's, to show range and diversity of entries.

Ask students to try several short free writings in their journals, and not to worry if they don't hit a subject that goes beautifully. A journal is a place for many failures and a few successes. Ask that entries be communications to others, not Dear Diary private statements. In five or ten years the student looking at this journal should be able to put himself back in his experience. He can't do that with comments like these: "What a terrible week it has been. Tommy just isn't the sort of guy I thought he was going to be. I'm really miserable." He can with an entry like this:

> We went for a ride in the fog last night, out on Ravine Road. There are no lights and no houses. So in the fog we were isolated. All that existed in the universe was about ten yards of yellow ribbon and my eyes, and that curving conveyor belt which I had to steer my eyes along—very much like my life at times.

19. Ask students to try word play in journals. Read Lewis Carroll's *Through the Looking Glass,* the text for word play. Make words speak to each other, as Shakespeare or a good newspaper headline writer does. Puns, rhymes. Revive dead metaphors. Record good word play heard in TV commercials or seen in advertisements, or around school. Examples:

a. Love Is a Many Splintered Thing. [student word play]
b. Watch how Gossard [girdles] makes tummies disappear in ten seconds flat.

20. Ask students to write an article for the school magazine or newspaper. They must think of readers and give them news in fact or expression—something that hits the writer and will hit the reader. At the outset, the article should grab and hold and tell the reader enough to satisfy his need for completeness. What persons say should be exploited, but only the words that strike hard in what they say or how they say it.

21. In assigning the article suggest that students try and discard and try again. Let them know you expect some of the articles to be published. Ask them to study campus publications for length of story, style, and kinds of responsibility shown by the writer. Don't restrict students to a tight, "straight" news article. Allow feature stories or columns of personal opinion if the writing seems to move in that direction.

22. Let students know that at any time in the semester you will allow them to depart from an assignment if they have motive and materials boiling. This freedom must be balanced with discipline. About halfway through the course, when students are apt to slough off (feeling wearied and harried, like you) by using rewriting possibilities as an excuse for not turning in work, begin the practice of requiring two pieces of writing every week, even if only short free writings. You are developing writers. They are persons who write.

23. When you use professional models, whenever possible point out how students have employed the techniques you are pointing to. You have dittoed student work to refer to. For example, this paper—

> I had always wanted a BB gun, but I never had one until now. We were going out to a friend's farm near Paw Paw and my dad bought me one to take along. At first I took it home to practice. I thought it was a big thing to hit an empty Joy bottle from twenty feet.
>
> After I got to the farm, the owner asked me to shoot some blackbirds for him. For a long time no blackbirds came around. At last one landed in a walnut tree in the yard. I walked under it quietly so I wouldn't scare it. The stupid thing just sat there begging to be shot. I fired my first shot. I saw the little gold BB fly past his head. Dumb bird. It still didn't move. I shot again and the bird's face reacted with pain. It fell over, hanging upside down by one foot from its branch. I shot again. It still hung there. I could see blood on its feathers even from where I stood. With the fourth shot, it fell, its black feathers red.

The last phrase, "its black feathers red," exhibits poetic concentration and carries the weight of the boy's revelation. During the experience he changed his feelings from sadism to sympathy, but he lets the reader infer the change.

He does not tell him. He speaks no joy or condescension after "the bird's face reacted with pain." Like a professional writer, he allows some of the smallest details to rise to the surface, and they turn out aptly ironic and symbolic. Practicing to kill, he is shooting a Joy [name of a detergent] bottle. He uses gold BB's for blackbirds. He probably did not intend these extra meanings, but they are present, they work, and he did not excise them.

Because this paper on shooting blackbirds is a small piece of literature, it embraces many of the qualities of good explanatory or persuasive writing, while carrying a different intention and purpose. Show students how "personal" writing usually makes up part of all good critical essays and descriptions and explanations, like those written by Emerson, Bernard Shaw, or E. B. White. The sharply chosen details of the story about the blackbird constitute evidence for its large and unexpressed assertions. "Too subjective," says one teacher. Nonsense. The writer here looked hard at himself over a period of time that gave him distance, recreated the thoughtless killer he once was, took the reader inside his sadistic attitude, and then revealed the change through action rather than explanation. Subjectivity and objectivity are both present and never confused. A trainer of literary critics could ask for no more. (The stories about the boy in the wheelchair and the shooting of blackbirds were written in classes of John Bennett, teacher at Central High School in Kalamazoo, who has used this approach to teaching writing.)

24. After three weeks of journal keeping, ask students to turn in journals. Excerpt from them some of the best writing and ditto it for students. You need not look at journals again if you do not want to. You may suggest to students that journals make useful banks for ideas and beginning pieces of writing.

25. Ask students to write a paper about something they have read. They should tell how and why some part of the work delighted, enraged, or stamped itself onto their memories. At the beginning and end of the paper they may present experience from their lives that illuminates the work. They may discuss book, magazine, short story, poem, sign, instruction sheet, letter, whatever. For this assignment one boy wrote of how successful Truman Capote had been in making the murderers in *In Cold Blood* seem human. The boy showed that in many ways they lived and thought like his own acquaintances and friends, who were not violent, sadistic, or murderous. Students should make their experience touch the experience in what they read, but not distort the author's world. Sometimes only part of this paper will go well. That part may be so good it can be lifted out to stand by itself.

26. Call attention to sound effects in both professional and student writing. Ask for several free writings (in journals or elsewhere) that experiment with sounds.

27. Ask students to write an indirect paper, in which they say the opposite of what they mean, create a fantasy that parallels some life situation,

or speak in a pompous or otherwise false voice in order to satirize. Remind them frequently that they use these techniques in conversation with other students when they mimic, speak praise when they mean blame, or talk roughly to convey admiration or love. Don't use the word "satire." In this writing they must maintain one approach and tone. They cannot write "straight" part of the time and ironically the rest of the time.

Explain that some contemporary writers and artists using what has been called the "Put-On" mix tone and approach so the audience is never sure where the communicator stands. This ploy is sometimes appropriate and effective but more often irresponsible. In every activity of this course, except the assignments on word play and indirect writing, a few sophisticated students may feel they are being pushed into an old-fashioned, traditional mold. If you sense this reaction, say that most artists master the traditional techniques and forms of their art before significantly breaking them.

28. Throughout the course take up matters of usage and dialect when occasions present themselves. Language styles change. Today what we teachers once considered unpublishable vulgarity and obscenity is being printed, frequently by good writers and editors. Make students justify any use of material that shocks you. Does the material, the occasion, the audience, seem to the students to call for the language employed? You don't have to like it yourself, but don't inhibit the student's language to the point that he loses the rhythms inherent in his voices. Remember he has many voices. Frequently he should be able to find one that speaks clearly and excitingly to his classmates, to you, and to him.

By reading aloud passages from students' writing, constantly remind them of the differences between rhythmic sentences and stiff, flat, awkward sentences—the authentic and the badly borrowed. This emphasis on genuine voice does not mean you need to encourage only one style—informal, conversational, of the alley. Most good writers of ideas and experience—Shakespeare, Emerson, James Baldwin—employ a style which alternates between homely, kitchen language and elevated words. This alternation provides variety and tension and insures precision without artificiality.

29. Tell students that if they attend this seminar-style class regularly and write and criticize others' writing, they will write several, perhaps half a dozen, pieces that deserve to be published to the whole school community. That is a promise.

Expect student seminar criticism to improve slowly. Students need to test your assertion that you want truth. They need to discover ways of helping writers rather than injuring them. They need your more sophisticated and experienced judgment. Several times a week for periods of fifteen to twenty minutes, talk about writing clearly and authoritatively. If you do not know a great deal more about craft than most students, you should learn or quit teaching. In valuable seminars the teacher lets the students do most of the talking but comes forward strongly when he feels he can inform or lead. He is never the authoritarian but often authoritative.

In general, do away with individual conferences with students about their papers. Most teachers dominate those sessions. Few such conferences provide the long-term support a writer needs to improve on his own. The teacher-student dialogue in the office has bad connotations for the student. In this course you are doing something different for him: providing praise from both his fellow students (whom he must trust more than you at the outset) and the most convincing approval—publication of one kind or another.

When you find a student who is not improving, take him aside and ask for four or five free writings again. Look for what is good in them. If nothing, try again. Bring him out of his doldrums or fear by honest praise for what he has done well, if only a sentence or paragraph.

30. Finally, the students' writing will be as good as the amount of discovery and wonder it contains. Old ideas, if held dearly, are valuable when expressed in new ways. Otherwise, the materials students present to others and to you should be news. The surest way for a writer to find newness is to try almost unbearably for truth. Last year in *The Reporter* magazine, Gene Baro said of Edward R. Murrow: "He told the truth in order to see it."

Creative Expression in Great Britain

JOHN DIXON

Everything grows from a context. The requisite context for the sudden flourishing of creative expression over the last decade in Great Britain has been a narrow but academically tough exam at sixteen plus. A written exam based on the essay. So the first target of its critics was a new vision and critique of written English about the age of fourteen to sixteen. Call it "creative" writing if you will—though with a term so widely and blatantly extended today, we shall have to clarify it in the course of discussion.

I begin then with creative *writing*—and McLuhan would laugh—because this represents the strongest challenge to traditional views of our subject, English.

Some would say that all writing is creative. I wish it were. The Writing Research Unit at the London Institute of Education recently reported a simple observation of profound importance to us English teachers. We might all check it in our own schools. Given a sample of pupils' writing across the whole range of school subjects, we should ask the question: How much of this written work involves learning while in the act of writing? And how much of it, on the other hand, is offered to the teacher as evidence that somewhere back in the lesson *things were learnt*—or even that a certain kind of performance can now be gone through? On a first sample the London group found that roughly 90 per cent of a student's writing at the secondary stage does not show clear signs of learning in the act of composition. Now if we want—as I do—to use the word "creative" to suggest the process of making and fashioning things to stand for a world we experience, this is a telling observation. One can see a new value in the writing that goes on in English lessons, because here at least is the opportunity to stress the *fashioning,* the act of finding and choosing anew from the infinite system of words what will come closest to experience as we meet it day by day.

Originally delivered as a paper at the NCTE Convention in Honolulu, November 1967, and published in *English Journal*, vol. 57 (September 1968), pp. 795–802.

At the Dartmouth Seminar I learnt to ask not "What is English?" but "What—at our best—are we doing in English lessons?" And in general terms the answer was this: "We are using language to bring articulation and coherence to our living experience." I want to challenge right here those who think "this is only self-expression." Let us be quite concrete. This is my first experience of Honolulu—and back in college I know already the friends and students who will want to ask what it has meant to me. Now I could begin with waking at dawn to a tropic sky, with palm trees in sunlight, with children and doves under the tables at breakfast, or with the faint white of breakers gliding in to the beach as you sit at night under a banyan—I could begin with this and much more, but from this *matrix* of the felt world of Honolulu would come questions and revisions—the recollection of the morning cars and dustcarts throbbing against the dawn chorus, the nostalgia of friends who remembered fallen palm groves and who regretted skyscrapers, the issues of town planning and finance, the discussions of the meaning and purpose of life in a city like this, or in all cities. All this and much more are part of a week's experience. To get it exact, to find language adequate to this experience, I will have to draw not on some mythical "self" for *self*-expression, but on a range of impressions and recollections that only the most precise use of language will make real and immediate again.

Day-by-day experience, indeed, becomes the starting point for much of the writing in English lessons. And this draws the teacher into a new search —alongside his class—for those moments in their experience that raise a need to say exactly what was involved. Take as an example this extract from a piece by a fourteen-year-old on "My First Dance" (in the London Association for the Teaching of English booklet, *Assessing Composition*):

> It was a Sunday evening, and I was at a local dance hall. I arrived there with an elder friend who had been there many times before, and he was trying to impress me a little by saying "hello" to all the girls that he knew there. There were not many people there then, for it was early. I certainly did not want to dance until the hall was more crowded, if I danced at all. For the moment, however, I just walked around with my friend, trying to be as friendly as I could with everyone he spoke to. Eventually, the place was packed out, with hardly room to move. The mixture of intense heat and thick cigarette smoke stifled me. The group was playing its music tremendously loudly, and this helped to cure me of my nervousness. Then my friend announced that he was "going to have a dance." Not wanting to be left on my own, I followed him to the dance floor.
>
> I stood nearby, watching him dancing with what looked like a seventeen years old girl, but who was probably nearer thirteen, but wearing a great deal of make-up.

> I tapped one foot in time to the rhythm of the music, but could not find anything to do with my hands. I put one in my pocket, but it sweated so much I soon had to take it out. Eventually I decided to light a cigarette, although I had never previously smoked. I lit one, and immediately felt more like the majority of the people there. Immediately after I finished it, I lit another one, because I wanted something to help me pluck up courage to dance. At the beginning of the next song, I strode out on to the dance floor and asked a girl to dance. I did not really care who the girl was. I began to dance very self-consciously, trying to make every movement of the dance look how I would have liked it to look.

The desire to feel "like the majority of the people there" is in conflict with the continual effort "to make every movement of the dance look how I would have liked it to look." It's the perennial problem we face in entering new circles of people, and the writer, Jonathan, is just beginning to probe what went on. Other people besides him, he notices, were trying to make an impression—his friend who hailed the girls, and the girl who was made up like a seventeen-year-old. But equally candidly, when he invited a girl to dance, he notes "I did not really care who the girl was." At such moments a perceptiveness is beginning to develop and with a good class of fourteen-year-olds I would hope to see them take up and extend some of these perceptions as they talk over what Jonathan has written. The demand would probably be for precision, for exactness to experience as we know it. In discussion, and possibly in further writing that sprang from it, one or other of the class might try to penetrate behind such relatively stereotyped phrases as "trying to be friendly" or "helped to cure me of my nervousness."

In such *personal* writing, as it has come to be called, the teacher is looking for an effort to achieve insight—to brush aside the everpresent invitation to take the world as other people have found it, adopting ready-made their terms and phrases (their image of us). Writing is a way of building a personal world and giving an individual rather than a stereotyped shape to our day-by-day experience. Personal writing has to take feeling as well as thought into account, attitudes as well as observations. Characteristically it uses prose as an undifferentiating matrix that blends discussion of ideas with the sense of felt experience. In its way, then, this is a starting point to which we continually recur.

But what developments do we also foresee and encourage? Primarily, I believe, a growing awareness of the range of purposes that this matrix of personal prose gives rise to. Let us take a twelve- to thirteen-year-old looking at an experience not too distant from Jonathan's. Living in Southwark—a downtown district of London, I think you'd say—she looks across at life "over the water" in the West End.

THE CINEMA AND THE THEATRE

Unlike the Cinema
I find the Theatre more classy.
They have bars where posh old gents drink.
And usherettes full of charm who won't rest till they find your place.
The cinema has orange drinks with containers you can see through.
And you're guided to your seat by a torch-light which sometimes abruptly switches off and leaves you stranded.
Behind you someone's eating crisps or apples.
But in the theatre you hear ladies saying,
"How dreadful the costumes are,"
And referring to their programmes criticise and discuss the designer.
Parties of foreign people.
Germans, Americans, Indian people all go to the theatre,
How nice it must be to step out and go straight into a taxi.
Not to stand and wait for the "63"
That comes packed
Yet how lovely to eat chips smothered with vinegar while walking and talking.
Not to sip a cup of tea,
While eating dainty, small cakes.

Georgina has looked at experience, yes, but highly selectively, searching to find the things that will stand for and epitomise two opposed worlds. There is an element of play, of laughing at a world she can't know, but momentarily she does reach out towards it and from a wider perspective looks back to laugh at her own world too. One could discuss this at length: I must be satisfied to point out here the new range given to language when it speaks with the oblique vision of poetry and makes very simple things like "orange drinks with containers you can see through" stand in some elementary way for larger parts of our world. And poetry reminds us too that a prose account of human experience is never complete, because its direct vision, its urge to state just what is there, easily eliminates whatever is half-defined or less than clear. But how much of experience remains uncertain and yet calls for articulation is suggested by a poem such as this from a seventeen-year-old girl (in *Poems from Bristol Schools*, collected by the Bristol Association for the Teaching of English):

YOUTH

We stand together
Hand in hand,
He so earnest, so concerned
in my tears.
Why do I cry?
What questions he asks!
Why do I cry?
How can I tell?
I could have laughed,
I could have stood
and screamed
at the dull drips of rain,
his fond stupidity,
his wiry hair,
his youth.
But no,
I stand and cry.

The value of such poems, and indeed of all writing that tries to penetrate and search the elusive fluidity of experience, is that it enables the writer to take on the role of spectator. Difficult, subtle, complex experiences can be recalled and reenacted with a new sense of distance, of dispassionate understanding. And if I have stressed these aspects of personal experience rather than the more cognitive, it is because for many students the English lesson is their one opportunity to come to terms with bewildering feelings and uncertainties in their personal lives. Some objectors may call this therapy, implying a clinical role for the teacher and a gross mental disorder in the student. I do not want to usurp the role of the psychiatrist. I would merely ask whether for us mature adults an exposure to the modern world doesn't at times leave us uncertain or bewildered—glad to talk things out with our wives or with trusted friends.

I believe, then, that such writing, arising from personal experience, invites students to make more of language than they have done in the past—to explore the world of people and things at their most concrete, at their most general, and at their most indefinable. It is not such an easy invitation to accept, as those of us who have tried to write will know. For literature, as Lionel Trilling has said, is "the human activity that takes the fullest and most precise account of variousness, possibility, complexity, and difficulty." The writing of the English classroom, while it may never fully become literature, can work to give just such an account of experience. But to do so, the act of writing must become an act of learning.

As has already been hinted, work in creative expression cannot stop short at writing. The private findings of the writer depend on his inner sense of an audience. A decade ago I would have said that it is the teacher or the *class,* or both, who make up the public, appreciative audience, and thus confirm the writer in his inner sense of being attended to. In those days pieces like Jonathan's and Georgina's would generally have emerged after a class discussion or dramatic improvisation on going to strange places, feeling isolated and uncertain—or excited and fascinated. The talk and the improvised drama, it seemed, were there to lay a foundation for such writing. Today it is necessary not so much to deny as to qualify this position. I still believe that, divorced from rich classroom talk and drama—both of them drawing on and extending personal experience—"creative writing" very easily becomes an unreal exercise in "responding to stimuli." However, what was lacking in my earlier notion was a full sense of the expressive possibilities of natural and of dramatic speech—for their own sake.

Secondary teachers like me were brought up in a tradition of *classwork.* Before we could make the most of talk and drama we had to learn to use *group work.* Take natural speech first. In the silent classrooms of two decades ago the best we could offer was a formal debate, a lecturette, or a class discussion led by the teacher. I am concerned now not to condemn these things but to expose their limitations—linguistic and educational. BBC radio programmes showed us the way, though I for one took ten years to realise it. First, they showed the small panel, on equal terms, talking over matters of common interest, learning as they did so—and sharing a satisfaction in this process for its own sake. With a panel of four to six persons, language began to be used less as a medium of public pronouncement, more as an exploratory medium. As Alan Purves has pointed out to me, dialogue offers many students a special opportunity to use language in an exploratory way, because it does not leave us on our own, like writing—it offers the help and encouragement of other people's efforts alongside our own. In a *small* group, interchange served a different function from that in a large class: as if a group were using a different strategy—expecting to work together to produce a common statement. There were difficulties as soon as an audience was introduced. But, we noted, the presence of an adult—even if he was silent—could have important effects on level, heightening the group's awareness and their expectations of what their talk would achieve. It is worth bearing in mind Nancy Martin's comment that such talk may be an art, which like the novel "can inform and lead into new places the flow of our sympathetic consciousness."

About five years ago came a second new influence—again from BBC radio. It was based on a partnership between Charles Parker, an interviewer and artist with a passionate concern for what he takes to be a dying oral culture, and two folk singers—Peggy Seeger and Ewen McColl. Together they produced what came to be known as radio "ballads." Take a typical example, "Singing the Fishing"—a collage in sound that evokes the herring fishing, blending with the voices of old and young fishermen, telling the quality of their lives, the natural sounds of the sea and the men at work, and songs of the herring fleet (sometimes traditional ballads, sometimes original songs by McColl). Largely through Parker's enthusiasm, many teachers are beginning to look again at a mode of oral expression not based on books—in the speech of local miners, mill workers, steel men, etc., and of course in their pupils' speech, very often. Portable tape recorders are just becoming available in schools. We are just getting a generation of young teachers who *sing* traditional ballads rather than read them. So this work is in its infancy, like talk in small groups, but where it exists it is vigorous and thriving.

Back in the classroom, then, we are beginning to find more of a workshop atmosphere. A group may be out, for instance, interviewing local shopkeepers or policemen or a football team about a chosen aspect of their work and life experience. Or they may be listening together to the playback of similar interviews, noting and discussing the significant remark that can later be built into a taped ballad. Or they may be talking over the experience they have gathered and drawing on related things from their own lives—taping their discussion for future reference and maybe for use by the teacher. In a few schools there will be a group searching for and trying over ballads, perhaps writing their own songs too. Like improvised drama and film, this kind of work has often started outside the English classroom in evening or Saturday morning clubs, but it is gradually being drawn into the lessons themselves. It reminds us that, as Sapir said in another context, "the history of writing is in essence the long attempt to develop an independent symbolism on the basis of graphic representation, followed by the slow and begrudging realisation that *spoken language is a more powerful symbolism than any graphic one can possibly be.*"

I believe that we are only at the beginning of understanding, developing and controlling that power which Sapir recognised in the spoken language. Listening, as I did recently, to a collection of un-selfconscious utterances by children between the ages of three and eleven, one feels humbled by a sense of the resources we have not yet learnt to tap in secondary school. And I was reminded of this at the present convention by a splendid comment from Ruth Strickland that our work in language "must start with listening to children" and young people. I now foresee a decade's work in taping students' talk in small groups, varying the roles and situations so that we find the optimum conditions for learning through talk. In London an excellent foundation is already being laid in the work of Harold Rosen, Nancy Martin, and Margaret Tucker (chairman of the "Talk & Talkers" group of the London A.T.E.).

Fortunately, some of those resources are being tapped directly and successfully, in drama—especially improvised drama. Drama offers a dual basis for expression: expressive movement is as important as language here.

But then in all the natural talk and interaction of the classroom, language, gesture, stance, and "attitude" are interwoven. Thus, if we teachers are concerned with the need to explore the power of speech, improvised drama offers us an enormous widening of the classroom situations in which speech and movement can potentially work together.

Over the past decade, more and more secondary schools have come to see drama as an essential part of English lessons. Perhaps one should here acknowledge the early and widespread influence of Peter Slade, and less directly of the production methods used by Joan Littlewood. By now, classroom drama—much of it improvised—is probably as widespread as creative writing, and in a sense the same questions have to be asked: when is improvised drama a medium for learning in its fullest sense? When, on the other hand, is it largely an indication that sometime ago things have been absorbed?

My answer today owes a good deal to a recent discussion led by Joe Reed, an education officer with the Schools Broadcasting Council closely connected with a series of BBC TV films on drama in schools now being generally released. Much of improvised drama *illustrates* life without really penetrating its surface. Improvising speech from situations in daily life—on a bus, in a shop, at a coffee bar, among soldiers, among members of a gang, etc. —is an interesting and an important kind of play which all younger children seem to enjoy out of school, and which secondary pupils too can enjoy if their inhibitions are loosened by music or percussive sound or other means. But this is the foothills of drama. To find the peaks we must look for situations that involve pupils—and us—to the full and that set us to work to clarify and realise the complexities of life. Once seen, these situations are strikingly obvious. Thus, suppose we watch and listen to a group of younger pupils working on a situation like this:

> We're in a northern village in England 300 years ago. Joanna, whose son is sick, faces a group of neighbours including the Beadle. One of them is sure her son has the plague. Joanna won't be convinced. Is she a liar—or are they panicking? They know the plague has reached London. It's more like witchcraft, says Joanna, looking at Margaret. So they commence. The dialogue continues, engaged, rapid—overlapping into an outburst at times. He must be moved and isolated, the Beadle decides. Yes, in an old place, somewhere away. Why an old house? He's a human being, not an animal. He's not an ordinary human being. . . . The Beadle has to override both Joanna and the owner of the hut they put the boy in. Why take the Beadle's orders? Joanna has taken them, and they will take them. Then, Joanna must stay. She'll go in there—she'll catch the Plague off her own son. There's nothing we can do, except paint the cross on the door.

This sketch is drawn from a tape made by the pupils of Tom Stabler, a West Hartlepool teacher working in a disadvantaged neighborhood, I think you would say. He has talked over the outline of the story and the tape represents their first effort to realise it for themselves. Over a period of weeks the class went on to develop this improvisation, helped by the teacher to find out more fully both what the roles involved, and what were the circumstances of the period.

Such an improvisation, as Reed says, raises two different kinds of issue. The first becomes an argument about proof, about motives, and about authority. The second involves others beside the mother in a conflict between fears, compassion, a sense of duty—and ultimately between self-preservation for the group and for the individual. This issue had to be resolved in *action.* But in a situation of this kind there is a special demand to use language to render explicit our feelings, attitudes, and ideas.

In dramatic situations such as this we realise as deeply as we can the conflict of sympathies, attitudes, and ideas that real experience faces us with sooner or later. Learning to contain that conflict and to find what it really involves is part of growing up—a growing up that doesn't end at twenty-one. Improvisation enables a group of pupils to explore and penetrate more deeply into the roles and the issues that are to be faced. As in real life they do this through action and interaction, but as in real life language is inextricably bound up with their sense of the meaning and interpretation of every act. When such a group are fully engaged, occasionally there is a flash of imagination and for a moment the spoken word (with all its potential power unleashed) epitomises a whole attitude, a whole way of looking at what goes on in life.

I have chosen, not by accident, a dramatic story built on historical foundations. Well before Walter Scott and the prose authors, drama was *the* medium for entering into the experience of people distant from us in time or in place and culture. One thinks of its native English origins in the mystery plays. More obviously than any other form of expression, dramatic improvisation draws on more than the personal experience we daily acknowledge to ourselves, and yet it personalises a kind of knowledge that would otherwise remain detached and alien to us.

I am already making, you will notice, a general answer to those who ask: what justifies work in "creative expression"? My answer is that it leads to *knowledge,* a unique knowledge of one's self and the world. Only in an age dazzled by science would this fail to be obvious. For we have come to think of knowledge as concerned with alien *things,* which we detach ourselves from as the scientist does, not with fellow *men,* whom we know and understand only by involving ourselves in their purposes. As English teachers, the model we should recall is that of literature, the knowledge of which is always in part knowledge of what *we make* in the act of reading (our subjective world) as well as knowledge that we recognise in part as experience itself (the objective world).

And at this point we should ask: what conditions does work in "creative expression" demand? I would like to propose these four:

> First, a sharing of experiences, outside the classroom as well as inside.
>
> Second, a gradual introduction to individual choice by the student from the range of media and forms that might help him penetrate an experience.
>
> Third, something less fragmented than five or six sessions, each of thirty-five minutes or so, scattered through the school week.
>
> Fourth, a readiness to help the student draw on expertise and interests throughout the humanities—not merely those of the English specialist.

Over the past decade I have seen two phases in the growth of "creative English" and a third is just beginning. In the first phase, the purposes of writing were redefined, and we realised how writing could become a medium for learning. In the second phase, with group work in an open classroom, natural speech and dramatic speech have been and are being re-evaluated. In the third phase, which we are just entering in Great Britain, an effort will be made to apply these new-seen possibilities in language to a broader field of study, and to link them with similar discoveries in the visual arts and in music. Through the Schools Council of England and Wales, teachers are being invited to join a pilot project in the humanities. In each of fifty schools teams of teachers—including specialists in English, history, religious education, and geography—will work together for full days or half days on themes such as War or Sex or Cities or Law and Order.

With the help of a national team, coordinating and developing resources, material, and a pool of ideas, these teachers will try to find the optimal conditions for learning from human experience. In so doing, some of them, I feel sure, will find and develop new and more complex forms of creative expression.

On Clock Watching and Composing

STEPHEN JUDY

It takes nine months to make a Bulova watch. It's our baby and nothing, not even fancy new machines can rush us. We find the more time we put into a watch the less trouble you have afterwards. When you know what makes a watch tick, you'll buy a Bulova. (Bulova Watch Company, Inc., 1966)

In an age of overpopulation and underachievement, of instant credit and a growing knowledge industry, some processes still take time. By investing extra time in preparing parts and materials, the Bulova people suggest, they produce a superior product—clock watching has no place in watchmaking.

Nor, it seems to me, does it have any place in the teaching of composition. Too often we ask students to produce "instant" compositions, and it is thus not surprising that we have so much trouble afterward. By allowing more time for the production of a paper and by guiding the student through the stages of gathering and shaping material for his composition, we are less likely to have so much remedial work after a paper has been written.

Most current composition textbooks ostensibly supply some help in these pre-writing stages, at least in the sense that the content of most texts is to be learned before the student writes. The composition thus becomes a test of the student's mastery of his material. But most texts seem to think that writing can be learned by analyzing the parts of *completed* compositions—that watchmaking can be learned by taking watches apart. The texts teach writing by showing the abstract form of "prose"; they assume that if a student knows organizations and forms that he can organize and form a paper. Thus for most texts, pre-writing instruction becomes a study of language particles. Students master the correct form of the sentence (supposedly the smallest linguistic unit that contains a "complete thought") through study of grammar and usage. Next comes the paragraph, a longer version of the complete thought, characteristically having a topic or thesis sentence, some form of logical "development" or "body," and a summarizing or "clincher"

English Journal, vol. 57 (March 1968), pp. 360–366.

sentence. Paragraph development is said to follow particular patterns: examples, details, comparison and contrast, small to large, reasons, and analogy. (The list varies somewhat from text to text.)

Finally, the texts invite the student to move on to "the whole composition," which is itself a sort of complete thought, a detailed discussion of a single theme or "main idea." The student prepares a formal outline, breaking his thoughts into convenient, numbered categories, and writes his essay, paragraph by paragraph, one paragraph for each main heading of the outline, each paragraph developed by a logical pattern, and each paragraph linked to its fellows by "transitional devices." [1] When the student adds an introduction (a sort of extended topic sentence) and a conclusion (the "clincher"), his composition is ready for grading.

The mechanical nature of this attack, which programs students to think and write logically on any topic that happens their way, is no doubt already evident, but there are deeper problems with this traditional approach. One of these is rhetorical: the textbooks simply don't describe the properties of good contemporary writing accurately. In the early and mid-nineteenth century, when the "rhetoric" of current composition texts was developed, essayists wrote highly structured, rather formal pieces, but the outlinable, neatly paragraphed essay with topic and clincher sentences and clear-cut patterns of development has been rejected by twentieth-century writers; only newspaper editorials, and perhaps sermons, show much resemblance to the old nineteenth-century essay form.[2]

As most college freshmen discover during their first weeks of class, few lectures can be fit into a formal outline, chiefly because that is only one of many legitimate forms that material can take. The outline is best suited to topics that can be split into "aspects" or equally weighted parts: "There Are Six Amazing Things about the Dolphin," "Three Stages of Hawthorne's Literary Development," "Seventeen Ways To Lose Weight Gracefully." But most writing does not develop in chunks; it "flows," with statements developing from and modifying previous ones while simultaneously preparing the reader for more complex, more detailed generalizations. Topics are not parallel, but subordinate. Points developed early in an essay are dropped momentarily and are picked up later in the piece. Several strands of an argument are developed separately, to be woven together at the close. Attempts to fit most good modern prose into a formal outline are generally

[1] One text even includes a list of important transitional phrases: "nevertheless, moreover, however, on the other hand, to the contrary, . . ." Presumably the student can select the appropriate phrase for his particular problem and place it before the topic sentence of his new paragraph, neatly bridging the gap between one heading in his outline and another.

[2] One of the reasons for the decline of the highly structured nineteenth-century paragraph may have been the development of the split-column page. Created toward the end of the century, this convention of printing (not rhetoric) would have made such paragraphs seem excessively long when set in type.

unsuccessful; an accurate diagram looks more like a road map than a chessboard.

Similarly, terms like "comparison and contrast," "examples," "reasons," and "analogy," while describing legitimate ways of supporting assertions, do not describe paragraph structure itself very accurately. For one thing, paragraphs are often as much visual as logical; editors frequently adjust paragraph length to achieve an aesthetically satisfactory printed page, with neat blocks of type—not too long, not too short—lined up on the page. A little experimentation will show that almost any paragraph of several sentences can be broken into two or three shorter paragraphs without destroying the structure or the logical coherence of either the paragraph or the entire piece.

Yet even if the textbooks did describe the forms of modern prose accurately, it is questionable whether we should teach these forms to our students. The basic premise of the traditional approach is that students learn the process of writing by studying abstract structures, but this premise does not lead to good pedagogy because it tends to separate form and content and makes the structure of writing more important than its message. Note, for example, the following exercise, paraphrased from a current composition textbook:

> Write three paragraphs describing the life of a literary figure from a period you are studying. Use a different method of development for each paragraph.

The student is sent out, not to find information for a good biography, but to find material that will satisfy structural requirements. He selects an author, say Byron, and three modes of development, perhaps "example," "comparison and contrast," and "analogy"; he then heads off to the library where he sifts through Byroniana until he finds matter that will fit. The following day he turns in three neatly penned paragraphs:

> Development by Example: "Byron was very sensitive about his injured leg. For example, ..."
>
> Comparison and Contrast: "In many ways Byron was similar to his uncle, Mad Jack Byron, but there were many differences, too. . . ."
>
> Analogy: "Lady Byron was like an albatross hanging on her husband's neck. . . ."

He produces three hothouse paragraphs, sterile and pointless, but "correct" in every respect. More important, he has probably learned nothing about how to compose a successful essay, because he has not encountered any of the "real" problems of writing.

Students do not need practice filling out *a priori* forms or structures; their problem is finding material appropriate to their message and molding it into a successful shape. Content and structure cannot be neatly separated, because a good essay can be produced only if the author considers the material he has on hand, what he wants to do with it, and the audience for whom he is writing *before* he begins to write. The stages of gathering and shaping material cannot be dichotomized without distorting the writing process.

It is in this stage of gathering information and finding appropriate ways of presenting it, the "invention" stage of composition, that the textbooks are most deficient, generally stressing the trappings of invention—outlining, notetaking (invariably on 3 × 5 cards), using the library, and narrowing a topic. But students can become quite adept at using the card catalog and preparing bibliographies without really learning "where to look" or "what to look for" when planning a paper.

To illustrate what seem to be some of the major problems which students encounter when preparing to write, I want to examine a pair of impromptu themes written by two students from average ability, ninth-grade English classes in a Chicago high school. Each student was given a "thought provoking" essay and was asked to write a critique or a response to it, focusing his paper on a heterogeneous audience such as he might find reading the daily newspaper. One of the essays attacked the television viewing habits of American adolescents; the other recommended that some rather stringent restrictions be placed on teenage drivers. Here are the students' responses:[3]

ON TELEVISION

(1) When he starts out, his essay he states that he seldom turns on the "tube" as he calls it. (2) So in one night's time he just about condemns everything that ever was on the screen. (3) He is just one person! (4) Just because the shows he watched didn't agree with him he says a flat statement about what all like. (5) The shows he saw.

(6) The television networks I feel are putting out what they can and what the public is demanding. (7) For if they put out what only above average intelligence people can get a "vague" understanding what is the other half of the population going to do (8) When people come home from school or work they want to have and enjoyable evening at home with his family and friends. (9) Watching T. V. is a

[3] The Impromptu Theme is a genre seldom produced outside the examination room or the composition class, chiefly because it unrealistically provides little time for invention. Topics like these are "successful" only in that they elicit "the spontaneous overflow of powerful feelings"; students have a ready supply of opinions and can verbalize without much preparation. I am presenting these essays *not* as the products of a good writing assignment, but as illustrations of student writing in a sort of natural state, from which we can determine a plan of instruction.

The essays are reproduced without correction. I have numbered the sentences for reference.

relaxing evening and if they only put "serious" stuff, what is enjoyable about that!!

(10) Government Controll!! (11) I think that would be a bunch of hogwash. (12) That will be interfering with one of the basic principals, to live without (more or less) government interference. (13) In the middle of his essay he says, "that teen-agers should have something better to do." (14) No one tells us to put on the T. V. and watch it. (15) We have homework, study and books to read.

(16) Television certainly is not as bad as he says it is. (17) For mostly you can't say that all television is just great, but it is mostly all right. (18) and if one program doesn't agree with someone they can always turn to something else.

(19) It is stated that the good old American teen-ager spends more time watching T. V. than most anything else, what about the good old parent.

—Deborah M.

On Teen-age Drivers

(1) This story is as good as goop. (2) He never stopped to think about banding people of 65 years or more from the road, because they think they eldors and they have more right to the road. (3) Point number three is real dumb, about drivers under 21 years having there driver license suspended for three years for speeding. (4) That's like saying all people with blond hair walking out on the left hand side of the street wearing gym shoes is against the law. (5) Also if the age for licenses are raised, teenagers at sixteen can always say they are eighteen. (6) The younger the driver the more he can learn, after all you can't teach an old dog new tricks. (7) This Ramsay guy is really *off-the-wall about the age for owning a motor vehicle. (8) I mean you can be fourteen and own a car but who says you have to drive it. (9) He might be saving it for when he's 16, and also could you see a forty five year old person riding a Honda or a Yakahama. (10) The only point that I think is good is about taking the driving course from a pro driver. (11) The only thing I see wrong is why can't a driver over 21 take the course if a driver 16 does. (12) After all there both new at it.

*off-the-wall, means: could you picture some one bouncing himself off a wall.

—Richard S.

Obviously the writing assignment was not successful; neither paper even begins to come up to the standards of well-written prose, and neither is especially persuasive (if indeed persuasion of an audience is the mark of a successful paper). The essays are argumentative goulash, lists of opinions that could be rearranged in any order without destroying their non-existent development. Deborah and Richard simply started writing with the first argument that occurred to them and ended when they had exhausted the supply.

But before we throw up our hands and dismiss these two as members of the hopeless generation, we need to look a little more closely at the cases they present. If we "translate" their arguments and do a little reading between the lines, we can find a good deal of substance. Deborah's essay contains the elements of a thorough critical analysis, one of which the debate coach might be proud. She demonstrates the fallacies of her opponent's argument:

> The author generalizes about all television from a single night's viewing (sentences 1 and 2).
>
> He attempts to apply his own taste universally (3–5).
>
> He unfairly aims his arguments at teens, rather than at the entire television viewing audience (19).

She undercuts his arguments:

> The television networks supply what the people demand, and the people demand entertainment, not serious stuff (6–9).
>
> Government control violates one of the fundamental principles of democracy (10–12).

And finally, she introduces her own counter-arguments:

> Contrary to what he says, teen-agers do have plenty to do (13–15).
>
> No one is obligated to watch bad programs (18).
>
> Television, while not great, isn't all that bad (17).

Similarly, Richard shows that his opponent's argument is incomplete (sentences 2 and 11–12) and prejudicial (3–4). He presents a contrary argument (6) and discloses his opponent's fallacies (7–9). He *is* cavalier about suggesting teen-agers can obtain licenses fraudulently, but this seems to be more an error of ignorance than logic—one suspects that he doesn't fathom the difficulty of and the penalties for falsifying documents.

There would seem to be little question that Deborah and Richard know "how to think"; given the time limitations of the impromptu theme, they have marshalled an impressive set of arguments. But they have produced only the skeletons of successful papers; the logical arguments are "there," but are inarticulate and incomplete. The reader is forced to go beyond the page to deduce how the arguments function in relation to the whole essay and in several cases has to fill in details or evidence of his own. Deborah doesn't tell us what she means by "serious" or enjoyable programs; she doesn't expand her assertion that television is "not as bad as he says it is." She fails to elaborate her shrewd observation that freedom from government control is "(more or less)" the American way of life. Richard's interesting analogy between drivers under twenty-one and people with blond hair walking on the left side of the road wearing gym shoes is left incomplete, and he passes off the "old dog-new tricks" bromide as a truism.

The lack of overall form in these papers, as well as their incompleteness, would seem to result from a common weakness of student writers, the lack of audience consciousness or audience sensitivity. The essays are aimed in the general direction of a tyrannical adult world, but statements like "this story is as good as goop" and "this Ramsay guy is really off-the-wall" are cast in the language of a teen-ager among his peers. (Note Richard's careful footnote to a phrase that isn't in the old folks' lexicon.) Indignant questions like "what is enjoyable about that?" or "what about the good old parent?", while perhaps fair, repel rather than persuade an adult audience. The sketchiness of the various arguments suggests that Deborah and Richard failed to consider their audience and made no attempt to clarify things that were probably quite obvious to themselves but by no means apparent to the reader.

Nevertheless, there is much that the teacher could do to help these students develop their writing. If we regard these papers as notes, the products of a short brainstorming session, we have material for what could be some stimulating class discussion and valuable prewriting "instruction." The teacher might lead students in both Deborah's and Richard's classes in an examination of the issues raised by the original essayists. What were the writers proposing? Where are the weaknesses in their arguments? Do they have any points that we must acknowledge as good ones? The students, of course, have already done some thinking on these matters, but through tactful questioning and by asking for proof and clarification, the teacher can help the students see that their own cases are not particularly detailed and are not based on substantial evidence. Deborah and Richard may be right, but unless they beef up their cases, no one will pay attention to them.

The discussion can then shift to the question of information: What kinds of evidence do the students need to support their arguments? Equally important, where can they find it? On what basis has Deborah concluded that television is "mostly all right"? How can she prove it? Where can Richard find statistics on the driving records of adults and teenagers? Through class discussion, each student can develop a list of items he wants to investigate on his topic. Some of these may take him to the library, but others will probably carry him outside the school-and-books environment. Deborah may decide to analyze an issue of *TV Guide* or spend an evening of her own in front of the tube; she may want to visit the local television station or the advertising offices of a prime-time sponsor. Richard may choose to interview an automobile insurance salesman or an official from the Motor Vehicles Office, or to observe driver behavior at a busy intersection.

This process of exploration would obviously require several days or a week. In the meantime, the class periods might be spent helping the students focus on the audience for their papers. Who is likely to be concerned about these problems? Who reads the daily paper? Is the audience likely to be made up of adults or teen-agers? What sorts of preconceived beliefs will have to be changed if the essays are to be successful?

A collection of published letters to the editor might provide useful models for this discussion, not that we need be deeply concerned with the letter as a literary form, but because letters frequently provide an interesting study of audience sensitivity. In any daily paper students can find a variety of letters on local issues: one writer feels his neighborhood is not getting adequate police protection; a second urges parents to vote for the school bond issue; a third wants to know why someone doesn't do something about some deplorable situation.

Through discussion of such letters, the students can begin to relate the author's "tone" and "stance" and his method of presentation to his overall success as a writer. What attitude does the writer take toward his readers? Does he treat them like intellectual equals? like children? like subjects for a sermon? What image of the writer as a person does the letter conjure up? Is he a grey-templed, pipe-smoking man of common sense? a tub-thumping country fair orator? a *sotto voce* neighborhood scandal monger?

The students can also examine the ways in which the writer presents his case. To what extent is his plea built on reason or emotion? Which arguments are most successful? Can we find a "reasonable" blend of rational and non-rational appeals? Do writers tend to begin with positive or negative points? How do they conclude their essays? Which of these ways seem better?

It is not likely that the students will discover strict rules for writing argumentative pieces from such analysis; nor, it seems to me, is that particularly desirable. But they will, in all probability, return to their own papers with a sharper awareness of the audience they are writing for and some knowledge of attacks that will and will not prove successful.

At this point, each student in the class should have completed his "research" and found some "original" information that he is interested in communicating, not only to the general audience, but to his fellow students as well. Thus the process of organizing papers might be done in small groups where the students explain their discoveries to their classmates. Deborah can describe what she learned by studying *TV Guide*, how this relates to her case, and how she wants to present it in her paper. Simply "talking through" these ideas and plans will help Deborah clarify them for herself, but her classmates can give her considerable assistance, serving both as a test audience and as a group of experts on letters to the editor. If Deborah is not clear, her peers will ask her to explain things a second time; if they think she will offend her readers, they will tell her so. In a sense she pre-writes her essay with a "live" audience, and when she finally puts pen to paper, it will be with confidence that she knows what she is going to do and how she is going to do it.

After this kind of pre-writing work, the actual process of writing the paper should be relatively easy (perhaps even enjoyable) for the students, although the teacher would still need to allow plenty of time for writing and encourage the students to discuss the problems they encounter while writing.

After preparing so carefully for this assignment, the students (and teacher) would probably enjoy seeing the final essays collected and duplicated in a class magazine, or, if this is impossible, displayed on the board, read aloud to the class, or flashed on the overhead projector. There are also many possibilities for "follow-up" exercises based on the papers. The essays might be left anonymous and exchanged between students or entire classes for analysis of the writer's image and success. But we need to be careful about over-analyzing student papers; when the student puts down his pen and declares "That's it," he needs positive reader reaction more than commentary and criticism.

Deborah and Richard probably won't write essays that would make the editors of the *New Yorker* (or businessmen or college professors) jump for joy; it would be surprising if they were to write pieces that were good enough to be accepted by the daily paper. But if the teacher spends time on meaningful pre-writing instruction rather than the textbook formalities of paragraphs, outlines, and clincher sentences, the students will, I believe, produce as good a pair of essays as they are capable of writing. Time will take care of much of the rest.

Teach Writing as a Process not Product

DONALD M. MURRAY

Most of us are trained as English teachers by studying a product: writing. Our critical skills are honed by examining literature, which is finished writing; language as it has been used by authors. And then, fully trained in the autopsy, we go out and are assigned to teach our students to write, to make language live.

Naturally we try to use our training. It's an investment and so we teach writing as a product, focusing our critical attentions on what our students have done, as if they had passed literature in to us. It isn't literature, of course, and we use our skills, with which we can dissect and sometimes almost destroy Shakespeare or Robert Lowell to prove it.

Our students knew it wasn't literature when they passed it in, and our attack usually does little more than confirm their lack of self-respect for their work and for themselves; we are as frustrated as our students, for conscientious, doggedly responsible, repetitive autopsying doesn't give birth to live writing. The product doesn't improve, and so, blaming the student—who else?—we pass him along to the next teacher, who is trained, too often, the same way we were. Year after year the student shudders under a barrage of criticism, much of it brilliant, some of it stupid, and all of it irrelevant. No matter how careful our criticisms, they do not help the student since when we teach composition we are not teaching a product, we are teaching a process.

And once you can look at your composition program with the realization you are teaching a process, you may be able to design a curriculum which works. Not overnight, for writing is a demanding, intellectual process; but sooner than you think, for the process can be put to work to produce a product which may be worth your reading.

What is the process we should teach? It is the process of discovery through language. It is the process of exploration of what we know and what

The Leaflet, November 1972, pp. 11–14. Reprinted by permission of Frances L. Russell, Treasurer, The New England Association of Teachers of English.

we feel about what we know through language. It is the process of using language to learn about our world, to evaluate what we learn about our world, to communicate what we learn about our world.

Instead of teaching finished writing, we should teach unfinished writing, and glory in its unfinishedness. We work with language in action. We share with our students the continual excitement of choosing one word instead of another, of searching for the one true word.

This is not a question of correct or incorrect, of etiquette or custom. This is a matter of far higher importance. The writer, as he writes, is making ethical decisions. He doesn't test his words by a rule book, but by life. He uses language to reveal the truth to himself so that he can tell it to others. It is an exciting, eventful, evolving process.

This process of discovery through language we call writing can be introduced to your classroom as soon as you have a very simple understanding of that process, and as soon as you accept the full implications of teaching process, not product.

The writing process itself can be divided into three stages: *prewriting, writing,* and *rewriting.* The amount of time a writer spends in each stage depends on his personality, his work habits, his maturity as a craftsman, and the challenge of what he is trying to say. It is not a rigid lock-step process, but most writers most of the time pass through these three stages.

Prewriting is everything that takes place before the first draft. Prewriting usually takes about 85% of the writer's time. It includes the awareness of his world from which his subject is born. In prewriting, the writer focuses on that subject, spots an audience, chooses a form which may carry his subject to his audience. Prewriting may include research and daydreaming, note-making and outlining, title-writing and lead-writing.

Writing is the act of producing a first draft. It is the fastest part of the process, and the most frightening, for it is a commitment. When you complete a draft you know how much, and how little, you know. And the writing of this first draft—rough, searching, unfinished—may take as little as one percent of the writer's time.

Rewriting is reconsideration of subject, form, and audience. It is researching, rethinking, redesigning, rewriting—and finally, line-by-line editing, the demanding, satisfying process of making each word right. It may take many times the hours required for a first draft, perhaps the remaining fourteen percent of the time the writer spends on the project.

How do you motivate your student to pass through this process, perhaps even pass through it again and again on the same piece of writing?

First by shutting up. When you are talking he isn't writing. And you don't learn a process by talking about it, but by doing it. Next by placing the opportunity for discovery in your student's hands. When you give him an assignment you tell him what to say and how to say it, and thereby cheat your student of the opportunity to learn the process of discovery we call writing.

To be a teacher of a process such as this takes qualities too few of us have, but which most of us can develop. We have to be quiet, to listen, to respond. We are not the initiator or the motivator; we are the reader, the recipient.

We have to be patient and wait, and wait, and wait. The suspense in the beginning of a writing course is agonizing for the teacher, but if we break first, if we do the prewriting for our students they will not learn the largest part of the writing process.

We have to respect the student, not for his product, not for the paper we call literature by giving it a grade, but for the search for truth in which he is engaged. We must listen carefully for those words that may reveal a truth, that may reveal a voice. We must respect our student for his potential truth and for his potential voice. We are coaches, encouragers, developers, creators of environments in which our students can experience the writing process for themselves.

Let us see what some of the implications of teaching process, not product, are for the composition curriculum.

Implication No. 1. The text of the writing course is the student's own writing. Students examine their own evolving writing and that of their classmates, so that they study writing while it is still a matter of choice, word by word.

Implication No. 2. The student finds his own subject. It is not the job of the teacher to legislate the student's truth. It is the responsibility of the student to explore his own world with his own language, to discover his own meaning. The teacher supports but does not direct this expedition to the student's own truth.

Implication No. 3. The student uses his own language. Too often, as writer and teacher Thomas Williams points out, we teach English to our students as if it were a foreign language. Actually, most of our students have learned a great deal of language before they come to us, and they are quite willing to exploit that language if they are allowed to embark on a serious search for their own truth.

Implication No. 4. The student should have the opportunity to write all the drafts necessary for him to discover what he has to say on this particular subject. Each new draft, of course, is counted as equal to a new paper. You are not teaching a product, you are teaching a process.

Implication No. 5. The student is encouraged to attempt any form of writing which may help him discover and communicate what he has to say. The process which produces "creative" and "functional" writing is the same. You are not teaching products such as business letters and poetry, narrative and exposition. You are teaching a product your students can use—now and in the future—to produce whatever product his subject and his audience demand.

Implication No. 6. Mechanics come last. It is important to the writer, once he has discovered what he has to say, that nothing get between him and his reader. He must break only those traditions of written communication which would obscure his meaning.

Implication No. 7. There must be time for the writing process to take place and time for it to end. The writer must work within the stimulating tension of unpressured time to think and dream and stare out windows, and pressured time—the deadline—to which the writer must deliver.

Implication No. 8. Papers are examined to see what other choices the writer might make. The primary responsibility for seeing the choices is the student. He is learning a process. His papers are always unfinished, evolving, until the end of the marking period. A grade finishes a paper, the way publication usually does. The student writer is not graded on drafts any more than a concert pianist is judged on his practice sessions rather than on his performance. The student writer is graded on what he has produced at the end of the writing process.

Implication No. 9. The students are individuals who must explore the writing process in their own way, some fast, some slow, whatever it takes for them, within the limits of the course deadlines, to find their own way to their own truth.

Implication No. 10. There are no rules, no absolutes, just alternatives. What works one time may not another. All writing is experimental.

None of these implications require a special schedule, exotic training, extensive new materials or gadgetry, new classrooms, or an increase in federal, state, or local funds. They do not even require a reduced teaching load. What they do require is a teacher who will respect and respond to his students, not for what they have done, but for what they may do; not for what they have produced, but for what they may produce, if they are given an opportunity to see writing as a process, not a product.

Part Three

A Reluctant Medium: The Sentence

"*No class hour should pass without attention to sentences.*"

J. N. HOOK

As ironic as it may seem, the most neglected rhetorical unit in the teaching of composition is the sentence. Much current textbook treatment of the sentence takes a negative slant, consisting largely of "rules for salvaging misbegotten sentences." In the composition course itself, a disproportionate emphasis often falls on broad, global concerns and theme-length efforts, with little attention given to the sentence.

Yet the sentence *is* important. It may be, as Simeon Potter noted, "the most important unit of English speech." It is important, first of all, because many of the flaws which occur in writing occur at the sentence level. If the writer is insensitive to his audience, it shows up in his sentences. If he uses an awkward expression, it is the sentence which is awkward. Furthermore, many rhetorical principles which ostensibly apply to longer stretches of prose can first be seen in microcosm in the sentence. The principle of subordination, for example, can be seen in the arrangement of ideas in the fully developed essay, but it is also at work in the paragraph as well as the sentence. Above all, the sentence is important because—to borrow Richard Ohmann's term—it is "the primary unit of understanding." Or to put it rhetorically, it is the primary medium of written expression: *we write in sentences.*

The first essay in this section is an original effort of my own in which I have attempted to sketch out a sequential approach for teaching the structure of the English sentence. In trying to cover so much ground in so little space, it is inevitable that some aspects should remain undeveloped. The ensuing essays, however, focus on the particulars of the sentence and treat many significant details which I have neglected or only touched upon.

The variety of rhetorical effects which can be achieved through the modulation of "so simple a construction as the series" is the theme of Winston Weathers' "The Rhetoric of the Series." Weathers identifies three specific ways of influencing the impact of the series: (1) varying the number of elements, (2) inserting or deleting conjunctions, and (3) controlling the level of parallelism. An appeal for more attention to the study of parallelism appears in Robert L. Walker's essay, "The Common Writer: A Case for Parallel Structure." After examining samples of current writing, Walker concludes that parallel structure is "the most common and fundamental of the rhetorical schemes." In view of its pervasive and fundamental nature, he argues, we should make an all-out effort to teach this important form to our students.

Several recent research studies have deepened our understanding of the nature of syntactic growth. In a pioneer work that must be considered one of the major studies of the century, Kellogg W. Hunt found, after looking at scores of grammatical measures, that mean T-unit length is the most reliable indicator of syntactic growth. (The term T-unit refers to a main clause plus any appended clauses or phrases.) Hunt discusses the pattern of regular and progressive growth from grade four through adulthood in his article, "A Synopsis of Clause-to-Sentence Length Factors." Hypothesizing that long T-units result from embeddings within the main clause, other investigators found that young people show dramatic gains in T-unit length after studying a transformational grammar which clearly shows the process of embedding. Following this lead, still other investigators found that these same dramatic changes would occur, not after a study of grammar, but merely after students had practice in combining sentences. A concise guide to the process of sentence combining and embedding appears in Charles R. Cooper's "An Outline for Writing Sentence-Combining Problems."

In one of the most influential essays of our time, "A Generative Rhetoric of the Sentence," Francis Christensen champions the cause of the cumulative sentence—a sentence with a short main clause with a series of added modifiers, usually appositives, participles, adjective phrases, or absolutes. In the asymmetrical form of the cumulative sentence, with its myriad possibilities for coordinate and subordinate modification, Christensen sees the potential for teaching a range of rhetorical structures. "Thus the mere form of the sentence generates ideas," he writes, indicating something of its value to the role of Invention. Christensen's ideas have given classroom teachers some new insights into the teaching of composition, and in "On the Practical Uses of a Grammatical System: A Note on Christensen and Johnson," A. M. Tibbetts provides a thorough analysis of these ideas. Tibbetts's discussion of the relationship between form and idea is especially enlightening; it concludes with a felicitous metaphor:

> Like two crafty, powerful courtiers, Idea and Grammar whisper, cajole, and argue at the ear of the writer—more, sometimes they demand. Sometimes one of them gets his way almost by force.

Nevertheless, we still have just scratched the surface of an important subject. A definitive rhetoric of the English sentence has yet to be written, and until it is, much of our efforts in teaching the sentence must remain intuitive.

A Strategy for Teaching Sentence Sense

RICHARD L. GRAVES

In a recent journal article, Geneva Smitherman published an example of a student paper with an unusually large number of errors. It is the kind of writing that teachers at all levels have seen at one time or another, the kind that makes one question whether he has chosen the right profession. The paper is reproduced below:

> I think the war in Viet Nam bad. Because we don't have no business over there. My brother friend been in the war, and he say it's hard and mean. I do not like war because it's bad. And so I don't think we have no business there. The reason the war in China is bad is that American boys is dying over there.[1]

When I ask prospective teachers in my undergraduate classes what is wrong with the paper, they invariably come up with the same kinds of answers. The student needs work on punctuation and capitalization, they say. He needs to learn how to form the possessive. He needs to learn about subject-verb agreement. He needs to put in some obviously missing words. His vocabulary needs enlarging. He should eliminate the double negatives. He needs to improve his usage in general. And on and on their answers go, all very much the same.

My prospective teachers always seem puzzled by the paper and vaguely dissatisfied with their own response to it. They seem to recognize that while all their answers are right in a technical sense, in another more profound sense they are all wrong. Somehow the traditional categories of grammar and usage do not get at the real problem. Rather, they seem to be symptomatic of some deeper problem which is more difficult to identify, more difficult to define with any degree of precision. The teacher to whom the paper was submitted also seemed puzzled by it, for as Smitherman notes, the teacher's only response was, "Correct your grammar and resubmit."

[1] Geneva Smitherman, "English teacher, why you be doing the thangs you don't do?" *English Journal*, 61 (January 1972), p. 65. Excerpted from Geneva Smitherman, *The Black Idiom: Soul and Style.*

The most obvious problem is that there are so many problems one hardly knows where to begin. The teacher's first impulse might be to dismiss the paper as "horribly bad" and go on to give the student an "F" on it. On the other hand a conscientious teacher might laboriously correct every minute detail, spending far more time reading and correcting the paper than the student did writing it. But neither of these courses of action produces the desired result, which is to help the young person gain some measure of control of his written expression. Indeed, both courses are unsatisfactory, for both produce unnecessary frustration and anguish—in the first instance on the part of the learner and in the second on the part of the teacher. This brings us back again to the original question: "What is wrong, *really wrong*, with the paper? Is there some major underlying weakness that can be identified and remedied?"

I would like to suggest that the major problem in the paper is two-fold: first, the writer lacks understanding of (and therefore skill in using) English sentences, and second, he lacks understanding of how such sentences are put together to form paragraphs. Until these two matters are solved, he is not likely to show much improvement in written expression, no matter how much grammar he is taught (traditional, transformational, or whatever), or how much he is drilled in usage or cajoled to change his dialect. Some may object that this solution may seem too obvious, yet an examination of the paper reveals that most of its failures occur at the sentence level. Until the fragments are expanded and filled out, until the redundancies are eliminated or combined with something else, until the whole thing is taken apart and put back together in good English sentences, then all other corrections are just so much tinkering and so much window dressing.

My purpose here is to outline a strategy for solving the first of these problems, that is, to help the young person achieve a better understanding and command of the English sentence structure. In order to be successful our strategy must take into account the learner's present level of knowledge; it must "begin where he is," as we say. But even more important is that it must take him beyond his present level of understanding. We cannot be satisfied unless he gains command of the full range of rhetorical structures which govern sentence sense.

The Simple Sentence

It is sometimes assumed that slow learners are prone to use simple linguistic structures (such as simple sentences), and average and above average learners complex structures (such as complex sentences). A perusal of the Smitherman passage reveals that this is not true. All the sentences in the passage are either complex or compound-complex, which suggests that the writer does have some control of the subordination process. His major weakness, rather, lies in his insensitivity to the simple sentence. He needs to come to see that the sentence is much like a lump of clay in the hands of a potter. Just as the potter molds and shapes earthen vessels, so too the writer molds and shapes sentences, making their very form and meaning bend to his will. At the outset the young writer needs to learn this "feel" for the simple English sentence.

Of the several aspects of this goal, the ability to distinguish between sentences and nonsentences should receive early attention. In essence this entails an understanding of *the limits of the sentence.* The run-on violates sentence limits by exceeding them; the fragment violates them by falling short of them. The traditional definition of the sentence is not much help here, for as yet no one has been able to distinguish between a complete thought and an incomplete one. A more promising approach may lie in the use of examples.[2] Since most people appear to learn the distinction by observing examples of sentences and nonsentences, it is logical to assume that remedial students would learn in the same way. Remedial students, however, may need more examples, and they may need more explicit explanation about them. Regardless of how the skill is taught, it remains crucially important. It may well be that the most consistent rhetorical failure of poor writers is the failure to distinguish between sentences and nonsentences.

A second way of developing an awareness of the sentence is by studying the basic English sentence patterns, or *the syntax of the sentence.* It is important for the student to recognize that while the possibilities for expressing a given idea are limitless, the sentence patterns into which that idea will fit are finite. The reason for studying sentence patterns, it should be understood, is not to insure that every paragraph the student writes, or even every paper, include a variety of sentence patterns. Such a motive would lead inevitably to a strained and grotesque style, or what Francis Christensen called "pretzel prose." What such knowledge does accomplish, however, is to give the writer a repertoire of possible forms which always lurks in the background during the composing process. It is one example of how grammar can serve rhetoric.

Once the learner understands the concept of complete sentence and knows a variety of sentence patterns, it is then important for him to see that the same idea may be expressed in any number of ways. In short, he needs to comprehend something of *the plasticity of the English sentence.* A familiar example of this is the transformation of the active sentence into the passive, and vice versa, but transforming clauses, phrases, or even words is also good exercise. He should know how to transform a word from one form class to another *(beauty, beautify, beautiful, beautifully)*, a process which is roughly the

---

[2] Thirteen seventh-graders whose I.Q. scores ranged from 54 to 83 and who were identified as "deficient in language skills" studied sentences and nonsentences in magazine advertising. Though not conclusive, the results of the experiment can be termed "promising." See J. F. Watkins and R. L. Graves, "Using Advertising To Teach Sentence Sense: A Promising Technique for Slow Learners." *Elementary English*, 49 (May 1972), pp. 721–724.

grammatical equivalent of the rhetorical device *polyptoton.* Understanding this function of language is useful in revising and recasting sentences.

Throughout his education the young writer should be encouraged to make sure that every sentence has something to say. The purpose of such encouragement is to instill within the student a healthy regard for the sentence as a vehicle of communication. It is to remind him that the good sentence is something to be achieved, the inane sentence something to be avoided. The ultimate purpose perhaps is to teach him that one's writing is an extension of oneself, and honest writing represents the fact of being honest.

The Compound Sentence and Coordinate Structure

Once the learner understands the rudiments of the simple sentence, it is then possible to explain that any element in the sentence may be duplicated, or reduplicated—words may be, phrases may be, clauses may be, the sentence itself may be. Thus are introduced the ideas of coordination and simple parallel structure, which in turn lead to a consideration of the compound sentence.

The structure of coordination presents an opportunity for teaching two other rhetorical concepts which are important in the composing process, the concepts of *redundancy* and *ellipsis.* After the learner becomes familiar with the fundamentals of coordinate structure, it is a relatively simple next-step to teach him that the second element of a series should not repeat the first (except in special cases for emphasis), as in the "hard and mean" in the Smitherman passage. Coordinate structure also provides the basis for explaining that certain parts of the second or later elements in a series may be omitted, as in the sentence from Donne:

> Some are translated by age, some [are translated] by sickness, some [are translated] by justice . . .

Thus the process of coordination serves not only to introduce concepts of redundancy and ellipsis but also to prepare the way for teaching more complex rhetorical concepts, such as subordination and modification, and beyond that topics such as balance and rhythm and sentence symmetry.

The Complex Sentence and Subordinate Structure

Whereas the idea of equality permeates coordination, it is that of inequality which is basic to subordination. In coordination two relatively equal things are balanced on each side of a conjunction, but in subordination it is unequal things which are joined together.

A device for illustrating this difference is suggested in the work of the late Francis Christensen. As most English teachers are aware, Christensen's method of analyzing sentences and paragraphs makes use of a number sequence in which a base clause (or topic sentence) is labeled "1" and subsequent modifiers of that clause are labeled "2." In turn the modifiers of the level "2" modifiers are labeled "3," and so on. The point that I want to make here is that once the learner has grasped the difference between the 1–2–2 sequence and the 1–2–3 sequence, he has in reality gained insight into the difference between coordination and subordination, for the two sequences represent the two processes reduced to their simplest forms, *to their lowest common denominators*, so to speak. Once the learner sees this difference, he then has the background for understanding complex examples of the two processes.

Although the Smitherman passage reveals a very high subordination ratio (seven dependent to six independent clauses), it also includes a repetition of the same subordinating devices—five instances of *that* (including the deleted form) and two of *because.* The writer seems unaware of the range of subordinating conjunctions and relative pronouns available to him. It is not a question of whether he knows that such words exist—simple words such as *how, what, who, where, why, when*, and so on. Any native speaker knows these words. Apparently the problem is that during the composing process it did not occur to him to make use of the knowledge he already possesses. A strategy for teaching sentence sense should therefore include some activities designed to make the writer aware of the possible relationships between the independent and dependent clause.

One way of achieving this awareness is through practice in clause- or sentence-combining, the kind described by John Mellon in the NCTE research report *Transformational Sentence-Combining*. Although Mellon's research employed transformational techniques, the real value of his work—as Mellon himself states—lies not so much in the kind of grammar as it does in the kind of exercise:

> Here some readers of this study may wish to conclude that it has confirmed a belief about schoolroom grammar long posited as a simple article of faith, namely, that grammar study "improves" sentence structure. In fact, however, this experiment proves no such thing and should not be said to. Clearly, it was the sentence-combining practice associated with the grammar study, not the grammar study itself, that influenced the syntactic fluency growth rate.[3]

Mellon's conclusion about sentence-combining has been substantiated in a recent study at Florida State University.[4] Frank O'Hare found that seventh graders who had extensive practice in sentence-combining

[3] John C. Mellon, *Transformational Sentence-Combining: A Method for Enhancing the Development of Syntactic Fluency in English Composition* (Champaign, Illinois: National Council of Teachers of English, 1969), pp. 73–74.

[4] Frank O'Hare, *Sentence Combining: Improving Student Writing Without Formal Grammar Instruction* (Urbana, Illinois: National Council of Teachers of English, 1973).

without grammar showed remarkable improvement in both syntactic growth and overall quality of writing. O'Hare offers convincing evidence that practice in sentence-combining should be a regular part of the composition curriculum.

If such practice is as beneficial as these two studies suggest, then it can be reasonably argued that two other kinds of practice might also be helpful, practice in clause expansion and clause reduction. The process of expansion begins with a small unit which, through elaboration and embedment, becomes a longer one. A word may be expanded to a phrase, a phrase to a clause, a clause to a full sentence. The process of clause reduction is just the opposite. This time the sentence is reduced to a clause, or the clause to a phrase, or the phrase to a word. Activities in expansion stress the value of enrichment of detail; those in reduction stress economy of expression.

Of these two kinds of exercise, expansion is somewhat less difficult than reduction. My experience with the writing of college students confirms what James Moffett observed in children's writing: "But children's sentences must grow rank before they can be trimmed. . . . I feel certain from studying children's writing that they have to spin out long clauses before they can learn to reduce them." [5]

The Cumulative Sentence and Its Modifiers

With its concise base clause and its modifiers all following the base clause, the cumulative sentence offers a refreshing change from regular English sentence syntax. More than other sentence types, the cumulative sentence allows the reader to move in concert with the writer, to follow the eye of the writer from one detail to another. Moreover, the cumulative sentence serves as a hedge against the "lumpy" sentence, the kind "in which lumpy, vague subject clusters are connected to lumpy, vague complement clusters by a form of *to be*."

Since the modifiers in the cumulative sentence normally occur in the same place (after the base clause), it is possible to use the cumulative sentence as a vehicle for teaching certain kinds of modification, specifically the noun appositive, the participle, and the nominative absolute. The strategy would begin by showing how a noun modifier is added to the base clause:

> Melrose wrapped his ankle with the cloth bandage, an old *shirt* which he had found nearby.

The next step would employ the same base clause, but instead of a noun modifier it would add a participial construction, such as the following:

> Melrose wrapped the cloth bandage around his ankle, *knowing* full well the possibility of infection.

---

[5] *Teaching the Universe of Discourse* (Boston: Houghton Mifflin, 1968), p. 172.

Once these types of modification have been presented, the nominative absolute construction can then be shown as a combination of the two, that is, as a combination of *noun plus participle*, as in the following example:

> Melrose wrapped the cloth bandage around his ankle, his *fingers working* nimbly to tie the knot.

Unless students have a fairly thorough understanding of the noun appositive and the various types of participles, it would likely be difficult for them to comprehend the nominative absolute. On the other hand, going from noun to verb to noun-plus-verb provides a convenient and logical sequence for learning these constructions.

Sentence Style: The Uses of Rhythm and Balance

The last step in the strategy is concerned with those subtle yet important qualities which sometimes fall under the heading of "style"—sentence rhythm, balance and parallelism, antithesis, devices for achieving repetition, and so on. At first glance these qualities may seem merely decorative, but a closer examination reveals that they are indeed very practical, for in deciding what may be balanced with what, or what is the opposite of a certain thing, or what in the first clause may be effectively repeated in the second—in deciding all these things the writer is engaged in the process of coming to know even more about his subject.

The rhythm of prose is so uncertain and delicate that it is difficult to know how to teach it. We might make a start by pointing out that good prose does have a subtle, almost imperceptible rhythm. One way of developing an ear for prose rhythm is through practice in oral reading. Essentially this involves reading aloud one's own writing, but it might also include the writing of others, especially passages from well-known authors. A colleague has developed a technique in which he first reads aloud to a class a passage of prose which has a marked rhythm (say, from Thomas Wolfe) and then reads aloud the same passage but this time paraphrased so that the meaning is retained but the rhythm is lost. Students are usually quick to sense the difference between the two passages.

Balanced and antithetical expressions represent a fortunate blending of form and content, and they appeal to the mind's need for order and symmetry. Such expressions have a way of sticking in the mind. Who could forget John F. Kennedy's famous, "And so, my fellow Americans, ask not what your country can do for you; ask what you can do for your country"? The complete writer should be familiar with these and similar rhetorical structures, and he should be able to use them appropriately.

Since such structures often occur within the context of one or two sentences, it is relatively simple and very effective to project them on a screen for discussion.[6] The Kennedy sentence, for example, might be shown as follows:

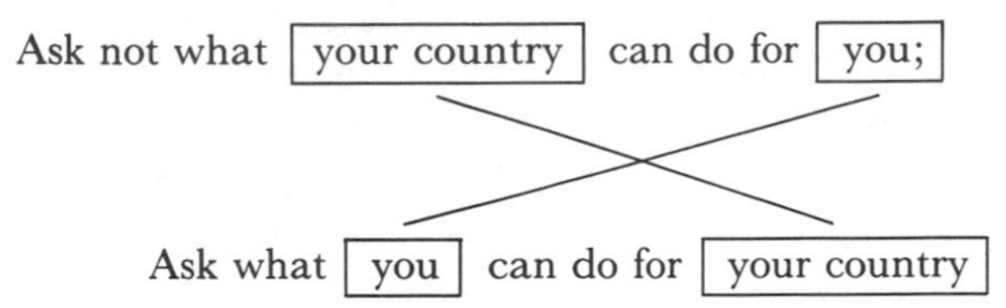

The "X" indicates the criss-crossed members, *you* and *your country*, each of which can be highlighted with a different color to show more vividly the structure of the sentence.

Various patterns of repetition can be illustrated with a series of boxes and lines, the boxes illustrating the element which is repeated, the lines those which are different. The repetition at the beginning of successive clauses *(anaphora)* might be shown as follows:

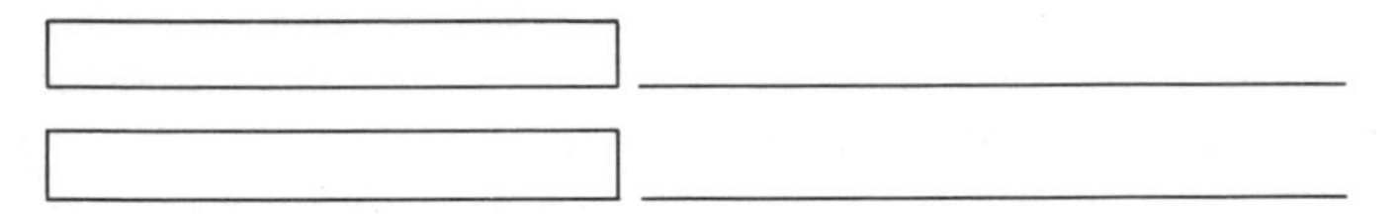

The example can then appear as an overlay, thus:

Ask *not what your country can do for you;*

ask *what you can do for your country*

The purpose in the visual presentation is to make the abstract concrete, and with the abundance of new materials and new techniques in electronic media, the potential here seems limitless. It should be recognized, however, that media does have certain limitations, especially where the teaching of composition is concerned. The primary function of media is showing, and there is no guarantee that showing young people what good prose is will lead them to produce it themselves. But it is not a far step from seeing-something-done to doing-it-yourself, especially if one has reliable feedback and ample opportunity for practice.

At this point the reader may wonder whether or not it is possible to achieve this final step, or indeed even some of the intermediate steps. He may recall all the flaws and imperfections in the Smitherman passage and grow fainthearted at the writer's prospects of ever mending them. Perhaps this is too much for the disadvantaged, he may reason; perhaps we should settle for something less. But it should be brought back to mind that our original purpose was that the learner gain command of *the full range of rhetorical structures which govern sentence sense.* "Settling for something less" might be easier

[6] A more detailed account of this technique appears in "A Primer for Teaching Style," *College Composition and Communication*, 25 (May 1974), pp. 186–190.

on the teacher, but for a vast portion of our population it can only mean a placebo education, or what Sunny Decker has called "an empty spoon." A compromised, second-rate education is a one-way street which dead ends in second-rate citizenship. "Settling for something less" does indeed say something, not about the student but about the limited vision of the teacher. It indicates that in teaching composition the student's lack of capacity to learn may not be as great a problem as the teacher's lack of knowledge and skill. Ego and pride prefer "They haven't learned," when "I haven't taught" is closer to the truth—and of course we can always bury our mistakes with red ink.

Compared to the full-length paper, the sentence looks small and insignificant. Many teachers assume that their students already know its structure, having learned it from someone "last year." That teacher who stresses the term paper and neglects basic rhetorical skill is like someone who sets out to build the Great Wall of China, only to find that nobody knows how to mix mortar. The overall plan is important, of course, but transforming the plan into a finished product requires technical competence, good craftsmanship, and careful attention to detail.

The achievement of widespread literacy in written expression is a noble and worthwhile goal, but it is one that will not come without effort. As our present age has shown little interest in discipline and hard work, the prospects for achieving it in the near future seem dim. Whether it is achieved in our generation—whether it is ever achieved—is still an open question.

The Rhetoric of the Series

WINSTON WEATHERS

Style is the art of choosing, and one of our tasks, as writers and teachers of writing, is to identify as many compositional choices as possible. Our comprehension—and practice—of style improves as we organize verbal locutions and construction into areas of choice and indicate how the choice within any given area is to be made. Any such exercise seems valid, even if our conclusions are not always definitive or absolute.

I would like to discuss in this article so simple a construction as the series. "I went to the store and bought bread, milk, butter, and eggs." Nothing could be more common than that. And yet the stylist must be concerned with it. For style actually begins with the simple constructions—and if we cannot organize and interpret the simple things, how can we hope to have anything like a serious rhetoric that embraces more complicated structures and devices?

I would begin by noting that the series—as the result of the number of items it contains, the presence or absence of conjunctions within it, and the degree of parallelism in its presentation—functions rhetorically in a number of different but simultaneous ways. By manipulating the series in three different areas at once, the writer can determine what sort of intellectual or emotional appeal he wishes to make to his audience, and can add to the actual meaning of the series—via implications about the duration of the series, the individuality of the items, the importance of the series as a whole. Creating the basic rhetorical effect by series length and then modulating that effect by the use of conjunctions and parallelism, the writer achieves an overall effect appropriate to the content and meaning of his essay.

First of all, the length of the series. Surely every writer has asked himself and every style-conscious reader has asked the writer: Why did you present a series of three illustrations rather than two, why four events rather than three, why two rather than five?

College Composition and Communication, vol. 17 (December 1966), pp. 217–222.

And the answer is that the writer can construct one of three kinds of series in terms of length, each kind having its own particular rhetorical quality. He can write the two-part series and create the aura of certainty, confidence, didacticism, and dogmatism. He can write the three-part series and create the effect of the normal, the reasonable, the believable, and the logical. He can write the four-or-more part series and suggest the human, emotional, diffuse, and inexplicable.

Let us look at these possibilities.

When Arnold Bennett, in *An Author's Craft*, describes a dog's encounter with a London fire engine, "He glances casually at a . . . vermilion construction . . . whizzing towards him on four wheels, preceded by a glint of brass and a wisp of steam," Bennett has chosen a two-part series ("glint of brass and wisp of steam") because the two-part series creates the effect of massive, abrupt, and final summary. The effect would have been different had he said, "whizzing towards him on four wheels, preceded by a glint of brass, a wisp of steam, and a thunder of engines." The sense of the abrupt and total would have been diminished. Likewise, Swift uses the two-part series when he says that the hides of young children "will make admirable gloves for ladies, and summer boots for fine gentlemen." Surely juvenile skins would make more things than that—say lampshades?—but Swift chose two, not three, not four items for his series, since the effect he desired, consciously or unconsciously, was that of the two-part series alone: the effect of "nothing more need be said."

This sense of finality and totality is closely related, of course, to the authoritarian tone. Consider the use of the two-part series by the didactic Mr. Fowler in *A Dictionary of Modern English Usage*: "A sentence or a passage [two-part series] is rhythmical if, when said aloud, it falls naturally into groups of words each well fitted by its length and intonation [two-part series] for its place in the whole and its relation to its neighbours [two-part series]. Rhythm is not a matter of counting syllables and measuring the distance between accents [two-part series]. . . ." In this authoritarian passage, Fowler has used four separate two-part series.

There is indeed something abrupt and unquestionable in the two-part that is the secret of its effect.

But when the writer chooses the three-part series, he is seeking the effect of something more reasonable, ordinary, and more truly representative. The three-part series, the most frequently used, is the norm, for it has the touch of the common and understandable about it. It has the aura of the true and believable sample. One hears this when Chesterton says, "I liked the quality of brownness in October woods, or in beer, or in the peat-streams of the North." The sense of abruptness and finality in the two-part series is gone; the sense of the reasonable and even logical has been added. If Chesterton had said, "I liked the quality of brownness in October woods or in beer" there would have been an either-or quality to the series, a greater sense of an unbending position. With the three-part series he softens the list, expands its dimensions just enough to make it reasonable.

This use of the normative three-part series is clearly seen in this passage from Thoreau: "That age will be rich indeed when . . . the Vaticans shall be filled with Vedas and Zendavestas and Bibles, with Homers and Dantes and Shakespeares." Thoreau's very breaking up of a longer series into two distinct three-part series is revealing. And the same predilection for the normative series is seen in this Thoreau passage: "It is time that villages were universities and their elder inhabitants the fellows of universities. . . . Shall the world be confined to one Paris or one Oxford forever? Cannot students be boarded here and get a liberal education under the skies of Concord? Can we not hire some Abelard to lecture to us? Alas . . . we are kept from school too long."

The effect of the three-part series is normality and reasonableness, and it is related distantly to the syllogism. But when the writer creates the third kind of series, of four-or-more parts, he achieves another effect: that of plethora, abundance, the unlimited, or what Professor Corbett calls in his *Classical Rhetoric for the Modern Student*, the "weighty and exhausting." At times the effect is extended to that of the diversity that is confusion. With this longer series, the writer moves from the certainty of the two-part, from the reasonableness of the three-part, to the more complicated emotional realism of the catalogue.

Dostoevsky, for instance, wrote in a letter to his brother Mihail: "There remains in me my heart and the same flesh and blood which can also love, and suffer, and desire, and remember, and this, after all, is life." Dostoevsky's four-part series does contribute to the effect of life, just as Bartolomeo Vanzetti's five-part series contributes to the effect of emotion in a letter to Dante Sacco: "You shall know, when you will be able to understand this tragedy . . . how good and brave your father has been with you . . . during these eight years of struggle, sorrow, passion, anguish, and agony." Being a series of life and emotion, the four-part becomes the series of plea and petition also, as for example in Shelley's attempt to persuade Keats to come to Italy: "I spare declamation about the statues, and the paintings, and the ruins, and in a greater piece of forebearance, about the mountain streams, fields, the colours of the sky, and the sky itself." All in all, the catalogue series suggests a world human, pluralistic, and emotional.

By using these three different kinds of series the writer can achieve different rhetorical effects—and he can adapt his writing to his subject and audience. In fact, each series may lend itself to a particular kind of writing, to certain broad areas of utterance.

Consider that a writer, recording and arranging the words of a divine figure, may tend to use the two-part series, as in this Biblical passage that J. Middleton Murry says "stirs your depths": "Come unto me, all ye that labour and are heavy laden [two-part series], and I will give you rest. Take my yoke upon you, and learn of me [two-part series]; for I am meek and lowly [two-part series] in heart; and ye shall find rest unto your souls. For my yoke is easy, and my burden is light [two-part series]." This use is appropriate, for, being a series of confidence, certainty, even dogmatism, it meets the very conditions of religious and apocalyptic statement.

But if the writer is a political leader, concerned with making his own position tenable, reasonable, and acceptable to followers, he may tend to use the three-part series. Julius Caesar's famous, "I came, I saw, I conquered," is a choice made, no doubt, out of many possibilities. Caesar could have written, "I came and I conquered," but that suggests dogmatism and tyranny. He could have written, "I came, I saw, I fought, I conquered, I claimed, and I kept," but that suggests something less than heroic, filled as it is with busyness, even confusion. Caesar obviously chose the three-part series because it avoids the extremes of more-than-human certainty on the one hand and a kind of emotional pleading on the other. Or consider Lincoln's "of the people, by the people, for the people." His choice of the three-part series suggests a desire to create the effect of the believable and judicious selection. Milton, in a passage Murry describes as "irresistible," uses the three-part series in discussing matters of state: "When complaints are freely heard, deeply considered, and speedily reformed, then is the utmost bound of civil liberty attained. . . ."

But yet, what if the leader of a people is not trying to make reasonable new ideas or events that have already taken place or his own actions? What if he is trying to persuade, convince, and speak to the emotions? He may move on to the four-or-more-part series, as Winston Churchill does in his famous "blood, sweat, toil, and tears." How different the effect if Churchill had said, "blood, sweat, and tears," how much more ordinary and common; how much different had he said, "blood and tears," how definite and complete, with no more possible sacrifices to be made.

Any one writer, of course, can make a demonstration of all three possibilities as his subject matter changes. Bacon does this when he uses the two-part series to achieve the didactic effect for which he is noted; to imply, "This is the way it is, you don't have to question it." "Truth may perhaps come to the price of a pearl, that showeth best by day; but it will not rise to the price of a diamond or carbuncle, that showeth best in varied lights." But Bacon can move on to the three-part series to make his statements less didactic, more reasonable, as he does when he writes on the subject of studies: "Studies serve for delight, for ornament, and for ability. . . . Crafty men condemn studies, simple men admire them, and wise men use them." Obviously Bacon knew that in talking about studies, a potentially unpopular subject, one might well take less a dogmatic tone, more a reasonable one. And when Bacon deals with subjects of emotional nature, or certain subjects and aspects of human behavior, somehow beyond the reasonable, he can move to the catalogue series: "Groans and convulsions, and a discolored face, and friends weeping, and blacks, and obsequies, and the like show death terrible." Or "Revenge triumphs over death; love slights it; honor aspireth to it; grief flieth to it; fear pre-occupieth it." The mystery of death seems to deserve the longer list of items.

I realize that these interpretations of rhetorical effect are open to discussion. Yet I think this is part of our task as writers and stylists—to venture forth with at least proposed interpretations; we can always refine and polish, or even change. To leave rhetorical devices blank and unevaluated is to avoid the whole matter and to leave style in as nebulous a condition as ever.

Writers do, of course, manipulate more than the length of the series. Whatever the basic rhetorical effect achieved through length, modulation can occur by manipulation of conjunctions and parallelism.

Looking at the use of conjunctions, we observe that the writer works from a norm—if he has no reason to do otherwise, he constructs his series with the normal single conjunction: "blood, sweat, toil, and tears." From this norm, he can go in either of two directions—he can add conjunctions or omit them.

When the writer omits conjunctions, he adds to the series an implicit statement: "in a hurry," or "all at once." When Priestly says, "If . . . in July 1914 . . . everybody, emperors, kings, archdukes, statesmen, generals, journalists had been suddenly smitten with an intense desire to do nothing . . . then we should all have been much better off than we are now," he is saying, via asyndeton, that everybody all at once, without debate, in a hurry, would have done so and so. Likewise, when H. Caudwell says of the artist, "His nature leads him constantly to explore, constantly to seek new aspects of truth," the omission of the conjunction suggests the idea of simultaneity, of two things occurring at once. But asyndeton suggests also integrity, not only that a number of things are happening at once, but that a number of things are really one thing: one act, quality, or person. That is why Caesar said, "I came, I saw, I conquered." If Caesar had said, "I came, I saw, and I conquered," he would have lost the effect of a single integrated act. If he had said, "I came, and I saw, and I conquered," he would have created the effect of separated, even isolated events. And, in addition, he would have created the effect of slow rather than rapid time.

Caesar's decision not to use polysyndeton suggests what the stylistic effect of the many conjunctions is. Polysyndeton adds to the series the statement "and in no hurry" or "these things definitely occurred one after the other." A good example is from Lewis Mumford: "Time-keeping passed into time-serving and time-accounting and time-rationing." With time as his subject, Mumford appropriately chose to add the effect of slow time by the use of polysyndeton. Or consider this example from Yeats' *Autobiography*: "My first memories are fragmentary and isolated and contemporaneous, as though one remembered some first moments of the Seven Days." Here again, the writer is dealing with the very subject of time's passing, of memory of the past, and to support that subject he adds the modulation of polysyndeton.

Polysyndeton also moves a series into separateness, making increasingly discrete and clear the various items. When Swift says, "They are every day dying and rotting, by cold, and famine, and filth, and vermine, as fast as can be reasonably expected," he has included in the series not only the idea that death is taking place over a long period of time, but he is making sure the reader is aware of each single way of dying. If Swift had said they are dying "by cold, famine, filth, and vermine," he would have reduced the discrete quality of each item; and if he had said "by cold, famine, filth, vermine" he would have suggested not multiplicity of the problems, but that the problems were all of one simple, contained category.

If a writer does not wish to suggest either simultaneity or great duration or does not wish to suggest either the singleness or multiplicity of his ideas, then he will use the normal single conjunction. But as he wishes to add any of these ideas to the basic rhetorical effect of his series, he can take advantage of conjunction modulation.

Likewise, the writer can manipulate parallel structure of the series in order to say something about the importance of the series as a whole. Parallelism is the propriety of the series, but the writer, without disturbing that propriety, can establish choices that will determine the degree of intensity, emphasis, and significance that he wishes the series to have. Perfect parallelism creates the greatest emphasis—it is the device a writer uses to say "this series is to be especially noticed" or "this series is to be read on a high level of consideration." Then, as the writer wishes to de-emphasize his series or to relieve it of its obviousness, he moves away from perfect parallelism.

Manipulation of parallelism is primarily a matter of interrupting the parallelism or of diversifying the length of the various elements put into parallel relationship. The writer can construct exact parallelism, as Lewis Mumford does when he says, "The modern industrial regime could do without coal and iron and steam." The series of "coal and iron and steam" is presented in exact word-for-word parallelism. But in another series in the same essay, Mumford chooses to reduce the impact of such parallelism: "In its relationship to determinable quantities of energy, to standardization, to automatic action, and finally to its own special product, accurate timing, the clock has been the foremost machine in modern techniques." This is a four-part series with each of the items of different length: "determinable quantities of energy" [four words: a syntax of adjective, noun, adjectival, prepositional phrase]; "standardization" [one word]; "automatic action" [two words: adjective, noun]; and "its own special product, accurate timing" [six words: three adjectives, a noun, a two-word appositive]. Note also that there is an interruption between the third and fourth items with the word "finally."

This process of interruption and diversification can be extended to the point that the parallelism is almost entirely muted or disguised, with the author, in effect, removing the series from the spotlight—though in his manipulations, the writer cannot move so surely from one category to another, as he can with length or conjunctions. With parallelism the writer is dealing with degrees rather than categories and is moving along a spectrum. Nevertheless we might suggest that the writer generally makes his choice from among perfect parallelism; moderately interrupted and diversified parallelism; and extremely interrupted and diversified parallelism. This at least helps suggest three basic possibilities.

This then is the outline of a proposed rhetoric of the series. With choices to be made concerning the number of items in a series, the use of conjunctions, and the degree of parallelism, the writer can construct for himself a paradigm of at least twenty-seven possible presentations. Establishing these twenty-seven choices, the writer is in a better position to make the particular selection he needs in order to say what he really wants to say. The paradigm has probably always existed in the unconscious of the successful stylist, but for the sake of pedagogy, if nothing else, we need to bring this paradigm (and all such paradigms) out into the open, present it to the writer and would-be writer, and help him make more than hit-and-miss stylistic decisions.

All we really say to the student of writing now about the series is that series do exist, that a series of equal ideas should be presented in compound, co-ordinate form, that parallelism is the proper structure for so doing, etc. I don't believe we say much about the choices that can be made and why they should be made.

I offer this paper as prolegomenon in that direction.

The Common Writer: A Case for Parallel Structure

ROBERT L. WALKER, O.P.

What we should teach the common writer—our students—depends upon the practice of the uncommon writer—the professional. With this principle in mind I propose to make a statistical study of the style of ten representative twentieth-century writers, five British and five American, analyzing one hundred consecutive sentences from each. My aim is to draw some conclusions about the sentence as found in contemporary nonfictional prose and about how to teach it. Professor Francis Christensen has said that the cumulative sentence is the "typical sentence of modern English."[1] I propose to test that assertion. He has also said that we should not emphasize the subordinate clause and complex sentence in teaching, but the cumulative sentence.[2] I hope to correct that statement.

The first question that arises is one of definition. When is a sentence cumulative and when is it not? According to Christensen, the cumulative sentence "has a base or a main clause . . . usually short, and one or more final modifiers." The noncumulative sentence usually has "long noun and verb phrases" and free modifiers, if any, "in the initial and medial positions."[3] "Free modifier," or "sentence modifier," is an essential term in this definition. I shall use it to mean unbound or nonrestrictive phrases (and occasionally clauses and adverbs); appositives and appositive adjectives; verbal, absolute, and sometimes prepositional phrases.[4]

College Composition and Communication, vol. 21 (December 1970), pp. 373–379.

[1] *Notes Toward a New Rhetoric* (New York: Harper and Row, 1967), p. 5. Hereinafter referred to as *Notes.*

[2] "Symposium on the Paragraph," *College Composition and Communication*, XVII (May 1966), pp. 61–62. Hereinafter referred to as "Symposium." Mrs. Sabina Thorne Johnson has questioned Christensen's definition of a mature style in "Some Tentative Strictures on Generative Rhetoric," *College English*, XXXI (November 1969), pp. 155–165. But my method differs from hers. She counted the relative number of words in T-units, base clauses, and free modifiers. I count grammatical types of sentences. My indebtedness to Christensen for my inductive, statistical method of sampling is obvious. See "Sentence Openers" in *Notes.*

[3] *Teacher's Manual: The Christensen Rhetoric Program* (New York: Harper and Row, 1968), p. 7.

[4] See *Notes*, p. 2, also Paul Roberts, *English Sentences* (New York: Harcourt Brace and World, 1962), Chapters 19–21.

Another question is the application of the definitions, something that depends on judgment, about which there can be disagreement. In order to give the cumulative sentence every possible statistical advantage, I have broadened my definition to include any sentence that has several free modifiers prominent in proportion to the rest of the sentence, regardless of their position—initial, medial, or terminal. Not just the simple sentence but any of the other types—compound, complex, and compound-complex—may be cumulative. Such a broader definition is justified by Christensen's own practice.[5]

I shall give some examples, all taken from sentences actually counted in Tables I and II below:

A. Free modifier (in italics) and bound modifier (in boldface): "Four doctors in their scarlet robes were observed **advancing** upon the royal party across the quadrangle, *carrying* a canopy." (Waugh)

b. Noncumulative sentence: "You must be capable not only of great finesse or perception, but of great boldness of imagination if you are going to make use of all that the novelist—the great artist—gives you." (Woolf)

C. Cumulative sentences (free modifiers in italics):

1. Simple—"The little theater movement has swept the whole country, *enormously augmenting the public interest in sound plays, giving new dramatists their chance, forcing reforms upon the commercial theater.*" (Mencken)
2. Compound—"I heard the siren scream but that was all there was to that—*an eighteen inch margin again.*" (White)
3. Complex—With free modifiers attached to a subordinate clause and/or a subordinate clause embedded in a phrase—"This is the very pattern which persists today—*a central sphere of molten iron, very nearly as hot* **as it was two billion years ago,** *an intermediate sphere of semi-plastic basalt, and a hard outer shell, relatively quite thin and composed of solid basalt and granite.*" (Carson)
4. Compound-complex—
   a. With terminal free modifiers—"The summer traveller swings in over Hell Gate Bridge and from the window of his sleeping car as it glides above the pigeon lofts and back yards of Queens looks southward to where the morning light first strikes the steel peaks of midtown, and he sees its upward thrust unmistakable: *the great walls and towers rising, the smoke rising, the heat not yet rising, the hopes*

[5] See *Notes*, pp. 5, 9, 20; also *The Student Workbook: The Christensen Rhetoric Program* (hereinafter referred to as *Workbook*), pp. 61, 62, 82, 100, 115, 116, 137, 177.

and ferments of so many awakening millions rising—this vigorous spear that presses heaven hard." (White)

b. With medial free modifiers—The man who went out with the cape in both hands after the bull had been run, and cited him from in front, *standing still as the bull charged, and with his arms moving the cape slowly just ahead of the bull's horns close by his body with a slow movement of the cape, seeming to keep him controlled, in the folds of the cape, bringing him past his body each time as he turned and recharged; doing this five times and then finishing off with a swirl of the cape that turned the man's back on the bull and, by cutting the bull's charge brusquely, fixed him to the spot;* that man was called the matador and the slow passes that he made were called veronicas and the half pass at the end a media-veronica. (Hemingway, Chapter 7)

In my two statistical tables I have counted and classified the four traditional, grammatical types of sentences in order to discover the percentage of sentences which have subordinate and coordinate main clauses as well as the percentages of simple sentences that contain any free modifiers, any parallelism, and notable parallelism. "Notable parallelism" is a relative term, depending on the length and construction of the sentence. It means that there is sufficient weight of parallel elements to make parallelism the principal rhetorical feature of the sentence: for example, three items in a series in a short sentence, or more and lengthier ones in a longer sentence; or balance as a means of contrasting or emphasizing the important parts of a sentence.

In Table I, I have counted the first one hundred consecutive sentences in each work listed, excluding all fragments, dialogue, and sentences containing substantial quotations from other authors. I have made the same exclusions in Table II, in which all sentences are otherwise consecutive. By "sentence" I mean the normal, complete sentence: S = NP + VP. There are two lines for each work listed in Table I. The first line gives the totals of the items named at the head of the columns; the second, with figures in parentheses, lists the number of cumulative sentences. The total of the figures on the first line in the first four columns, added horizontally, is always one hundred. The total of the figures in parentheses in the first four columns on the second line will be found in column five. Column six includes column five. All figures, except those on line eleven are percentages. In any vertical column, the figures in parentheses subtracted from those immediately above them give the number of noncumulative sentences. In column seven the figures in parentheses represent the number of cumulative sentences with parallel free modifiers.

In Table II, I have attempted to verify the figures in Table I. I chose other chapters from Hemingway in order to check the frequency of cumulative sentences at greater length in an author—a favorite of Christensen—who is supposedly a rich source of cumulative sentences. Also because chapter seven contains a fine description of a bull fight, and cumulative sentences supposedly abound in narrative-description.

On line fourteen I present figures on 222 sentences from thirty-four model paragraphs in Christensen's *Workbook*, pp. 191–239. These paragraphs are by seventeen named and five anonymous authors. They represent the kind of plain, clear, expository prose that Christensen recommends and aims to teach, prose taken from a wide variety of sources and types of writing, some of it from textbooks. Percentages are indicated immediately below the figures to which they pertain.

A word about column six in Table I—free modifiers. These are practically all phrases. I do not attempt to distinguish them from nonrestrictive clauses, which play a very minor role in the cumulative sentence.[6] In the thousand sentences in Table I, seventy-nine of which are cumulative, only three nonrestrictive clauses in three sentences (two by Baldwin, one by Snow) can be classified as free modifiers having the same function as phrases at the end of the sentence. All three of these are noun clauses used as appositives.

Finally, a concession. Certain long compound-complex sentences, if repunctuated with periods instead of semi-colons, would produce more cumulative sentences. In other words, parts of such sentences are rhetorically cumulative. By repunctuating such sentences, three more cumulative sentences could be added to the total for Waugh (making thirteen in place of ten) and one to the total for White (making nine instead of eight); and the total for all authors would be eighty-three instead of seventy-nine. I have not counted these possible sentences, however, since I prefer to classify all sentences strictly as their authors wrote them.

My figures show that the cumulative sentence is not the "typical sentence of modern English." It is a minority sentence, an unusual sentence. Only 7.9% of the thousand sentences classified in Table I are cumulative. The highest percentage for any author is twelve (Carson), the lowest, one (Snow).

Table II supports this conclusion. The percentages for Hemingway are slightly below his average in Table I and below the total average. The percentage of cumulative sentences in Christensen's *Workbook* (9%) is slightly above the average in Table I. The cumulative sentence comprises a small minority also in a description of the opening of a bull fight in chapter six of Hemingway's *Death in the Afternoon.* In this passage of three long paragraphs, the last three in the chapter, Hemingway wrote forty-two sentences, of which

[6] In the thousand sentences in Table I, bound clauses outnumber unbound more than two to one (55 to 24) in 31 sentences which contain both free modifying phrases and subordinate clauses. Most subordinate clauses used with such phrases are either embedded in phrases or have phrases attached to them. The same is true of the model paragraphs in section twelve of Christensen's *Workbook.* Out of 222 sentences, 131 contain 199 subordinate clauses, only 48 of which are unbound (less than 1 in 4). Of these 48 only 1 occurs in a cumulative sentence.

Table I

Author–Title	1 *Simple*	2 *Compound*	3 *Complex*	4 *Comp.-Complex*	5 *Totals**	6 *Free Modifiers*	7 *Notable Parallelism*	8 *Any Parallelism*
1. Mencken: "The Sahara of the Bozart," (*Prejudices: Second Series*, 1920). Polemical essay.	58 (7)	11	21 (1)	10 (1)	100 (9)	18	36 (5)	61
2. Hemingway, *Death in the Afternoon*, chapter I, 1932. Travel book.	7 (1)	6	37 (4)	50 (2)	100 (7)	28	16 (7)	80
3. Woolf: "How Should One Read a Book?" (*The Second Common Reader*, 1932). Literary criticism.	31 (4)	18	30 (1)	21 (1)	100 (6)	17	43 (5)	77
4. Waugh, *Edmund Campion*, chapter I, 1946. Biography.	25 (5)	20	25 (4)	30 (1)	100 (10)	29	21 (4)	52
5. White: "Here Is New York," 1949. Travel essay from *Holiday* magazine.	39 (4)	14 (1)	32 (2)	15 (1)	100 (8)	18	29 (4)	65
6. Carson: *The Sea Around Us*, chapter I, 1950. Nature book.	28 (5)	11	45 (7)	16	100 (12)	27	11 (4)	59
7. Orwell: "Such, Such Were the Joys," 1950. Autobiographical essay.	21 (4)	14 (1)	44 (6)	21	100 (11)	19	19 (3)	59
8. Baldwin: "Stranger in the Village," (*Notes of A Native Son*, 1955). Autobiographical essay.	11 (2)	12	41 (5)	36	100 (7)	25	25 (5)	76
9. A. Huxley, "Tomorrow, and Tomorrow, and Tomorrow," 1956. Essay.	42 (7)	10	39 (1)	9	100 (8)	17	28 (4)	65
10. Snow, "The Two Cultures," 1959. Essay.	38	7	40 (1)	15	100 (1)	15	11 (1)	51

11. Totals	(1,000)	300	123 (2)	354 (32)	223 (6)	1000 (79)	213	239 (42)	645

* Totals include the number of sentences on the first line of each item (based upon the first 100 consecutive sentences of each work) and the number of cumulative sentences in parentheses on the second line.

Table II

Author–Title	1 *Simple*	2 *Compound*	3 *Complex*	4 *Comp.-Complex*	5 *Totals*	6 *Free Modifiers*	7 *Notable Parallelism*	8 *Any Parallelism*
12. Hemingway, *Death in the Afternoon*, chapter II, 120 consecutive sentences.						8 6.6%		
	(1) .83%	(1) .83%	(4) 3.3%	(1) .83%	(7) 5.8%			
13. Hemingway, *Death in the Afternoon*, chapters VI, VII, VIII; 200 sentences.	51 26.5%	22 11%	72 36%	55 27.5%		54 27%	67 33.5%	110 55%
	(2) 1%	(1) .5%	(7) 3.5%	(1) .5%	(11) 5.5%			
14. 222 sentences from 34 model paragraphs in Christensen *Workbook*, pp. 191–239.	72 32.4%	19 8.5%	102 45.9%	29 13%		40 18%		
	(8) 3.6%		(11) 4.9%	(1) .45%	(20) 9%			

only three (9%) are cumulative; but seven are noncumulative with free modifiers, and thirty-three are without any free modifiers.

To get the totals of sentences with subordinate clauses, add columns three and four horizontally. The percentages of noncumulative sentences vary from twenty-nine in Mencken to eighty-one in Hemingway, with Waugh and Woolf in the middle at about fifty percent. The average for the whole thousand sentences is 54.9%. These figures suggest that "our faith in the subordinate clause and complex sentence" does not seem to be "misplaced," as Christensen says it is. (*Notes*, xiii)

The figures for sentences with coordinate main clauses are also revealing. To get totals, add columns two and four horizontally. The percentages for noncumulative sentences vary from 20 in Mencken to 54 in Hemingway, with Waugh at 49, Baldwin at 48, Woolf at 38, and Orwell at 34. The total for the entire thousand sentences is 33.8%.

My conclusion from these statistics is that we should teach subordinate and coordinate main clauses and all kinds of sentences, including the cumulative sentence. We should thank Professor Christensen for teaching it to us. It is beautiful and useful. It is a sign of mature style, but only one of many signs. We should teach free modifying phrases not just as parts of the cumulative sentence, not just in the terminal position, but in the other positions as well, especially in the medial position. They are useful schemes in any appropriate position.

We should teach sentences in sequence and the function of various types of sentences in context. For example, the short, simple, noncumulative sentence to vary pace, to pile up detail (as in White), to deal a series of sledge hammer blows (as in Mencken), to make transitions and to form topic sentences (as in Waugh).

Columns seven and eight suggest that in the short time we have with freshmen, we should drill parallel structure into them, parallelism in all parts of the sentence: in words, in phrases, and in clauses, including free modifiers. It is the most common and fundamental of the rhetorical schemes. Christensen's rhetoric, of course, is based on parallelism and presumes knowledge of it in the student. But Christensen makes no provision to teach it outside of the cumulative sentence. He grants its importance in good prose but implies that somehow it will teach itself. (*Notes*, pp. 1–2) Such has not been my experience. I find that I must drill students in it in order to prevent them from stumbling, as in the following sentence on the illusory effects of marijuana: "These include *colors* that seem brighter and richer to the user, *values* in works of art that previously seemed to have no meaning to him, *and music seems to be appreciated more.*"

Coordinate clauses, whether main or subordinate, are as much a sign of mature style as the longest, most elaborate, most purple cumulative sentence ever written. Christensen suggests that because children use subordinate clauses easily, a better criterion of the mature style is the free modifier. ("Symposium," pp. 61–62) The fact is that both children and professional writers use clauses, main and subordinate, because they are so fundamental. It all depends on how they are used. Professionals use them in a sophisticated way, frequently in parallel or balanced structure.

Christensen is also of the opinion that compound sentences are "a feature of paragraph rather than sentence structure." [7] This may be true of some very long sentences or of some that might be repunctuated to bring out their relation to other sentences more clearly, but not of most compound and compound-complex sentences. Authors use them for various purposes, for example, to relate similar, associated events: "And outside the donkey brays, the women gossip at the pump, the colts gallop across the field." (Woolf) Another purpose of such a sentence is to give variety; Woolf uses the donkey, women, and colts twice again in her essay as symbols of ordinary, random sensory experience, each time in a different syntax from the first.

A further example from Woolf illustrates balance in the compound-complex sentence: "The thirty-two chapters of a novel—if we consider how to read a novel first—are an attempt to make something as formed and controlled as a building; but words are more impalpable than bricks, reading is a longer and more complicated process than seeing." In this sentence the second and third clauses are balanced against the first in order to explicate it by contrast.

These two compound, noncumulative sentences, so exquisitely formed and polished, so perfectly adapted to their purpose, so imperceptibly uniting form and content, represent an important facet of a mature style, the deft use of coordination, a facet that is quantitatively more important than terminal free modifiers. An untutored schoolboy could no more have written them than he could have written Caesar's *veni, vidi, vici.*

Parallelism must be taught too. It is essential.

---

[7] See Francis Christensen, "The Problem of Defining a Mature Style," *The English Journal*, LVII (April 1968), p. 579.

A Synopsis of Clause-to-Sentence Length Factors

KELLOGG W. HUNT

If an experienced writing teacher looks for the first time at language development studies for the last half century, hoping to find there some clear and coherent picture of what changes occur in sentence structures as students mature, he will be sadly disappointed. He may even be shocked that so many studies could all add up to so little. We have a rich tradition of rhetorical intuition but no significant body of quantitative information.

But some pioneering work has been done. Thirty years ago Lou LaBrant studied the writings of students from Grades 4 to 12, plus the writings of eminent psychologists. She was skeptical about the significance of sentence length and did not study it. But she did study the length of clauses and the frequency of subordinate clauses and main clauses. Unfortunately, she did not count as one clause what most of us would call a clause.

In the thirty years since LaBrant's study we have added very little to our instruments for investigation. Investigators have continued to use these same measures: sentence length and subordination ratio.

In addition to them, certain novel concepts have been tried. Some people have used weighing scales. One of these scales assigns some arbitrary number of points for writing a main clause, some different number for a subordinate clause, some still different number for a subordinate clause related to another subordinate clause, etc. Though the number of points assigned in this fashion is quite arbitrary, depth of subordination is indeed a significant index of maturity.

In addition to such weighting scales, certain subjective units have been tried. They undertake to segment a discourse into "complete thoughts" or "complete communication units" or "complete expressions." But how many words there are in a thought is a subjective matter, so these units are like tape measures made out of elastic.

Thinking seems to have crystallized into what I will call "the standard view" about writing development. McCarthy expressed it ten years ago. "The standard view" holds three tenets: (1) sentence length is a

English Journal, vol. 54 (April 1965), pp. 300, 305–309.

significant index of language maturity; (2) sentences get longer because a larger proportion of subordinate clauses appears in them; (3) the length of clauses remains constant, or nearly constant. Apparently this view is in need of revision, as we will see.

Indexes of Maturity in Writing

The study I am reporting here reevaluated these widely-accepted tenets and searched for more significant objective indexes of maturity. I will not tell you about all the blind alleys we scurried into, nor all the false starts we made. First we studied the writings of average students at three grades: fourth, eighth, and twelfth. Since then we have studied expository articles in *Harper's* and *Atlantic*. I will refer to this fourth group as superior adults. From each of our writers, both schoolchildren and superior adults, we took a one-thousand word sample. We took an equal number of writers in each of the four groups. In each grade, equal numbers were boys and girls. Since the number of words written by every individual and by every group is the same, we can compare the frequency of any structure without needing to repeat continually "in equal bodies of writing." We analyzed thousand-word samples from 18 writers in each of the four groups: 72 writers with a total of 72,000 words.

First, we studied the average length of sentences as they were punctuated with capital letters and periods by the writers. Second, we studied the average length of clauses. We considered a clause to be any expression with a subject (or coordinated subjects) and a finite verb (or coordinated verbs). We did not try to count the length of each clause individually: for instance, a main clause containing a noun clause as object. But we did count the number of clauses, both subordinate and main; and then we divided the total number of words by the total number of clauses to get the average length of clauses. Third, we studied the proportion of subordinate clauses to main clauses. For each of these three measures we computed the score for each individual, each grade or group, and each sex within grade. The statisticians then checked our figures for statistical significance.

We became more and more interested in the unit which I will describe as one main clause plus whatever subordinate clauses happen to be attached to or embedded within it.

In the hands of older students that whole unit will get longer as more subordinate clauses are put into it. The unit will also grow longer as more non-clausal structures are packed into each clause. The length of this unit will not be affected by the tendency of certain young students to write abominably long sentences, using *and* after *and* after *and* where they should use periods.

A piece of writing can be sliced up into such units just as a pork loin roast can be sliced up into chops. The person slicing needs to watch where the joints come so he does not cut into solid bone.

A passage sliced up into such units would be sliced into its shortest possible grammatically allowable sentences. Two main clauses joined by *and* or any other coordinating conjunction would be cut into two units, that is, two simple sentences. The *and* would begin the second unit, just as mature writers begin so many sentences today. Each unit would be like a simple sentence or a complex sentence. All compound sentences or compound-complex sentences would be cut up into two or more shorter units.

Here is a sample. It is a single theme written by a fourth-grader who punctuated it as a single 68-word sentence.

> I like the movie we saw about Moby Dick the white whale the captain said if you can kill the white whale Moby Dick I will give this gold to the one that can do it and it is worth sixteen dollars they tried and tried but while they were trying they killed a whale and used the oil for the lamps they almost caught the white whale.

That theme, cut up into these unnamed units, appears below. A slant line now begins each clause. A period ends each unit, and a capital begins each one.

1. I like the movie / we saw about Moby Dick, the white whale.
2. The captain said / if you can kill the white whale, Moby Dick, / I will give this gold to the one / that can do it.
3. And it is worth sixteen dollars.
4. They tried and tried.
5. But / while they were trying / they killed a whale and used the oil for the lamps.
6. They almost caught the white whale.

Minimal Terminable Units

These units I am talking about need a name. I would like to call them "minimal sentences" except that the word *sentence* means too many things already. A fresh technical-sounding name would be better. We might christen these units "minimal terminable units," since they would be minimal in length, and each could be terminated grammatically between a capital letter and a period. For short, the "minimal terminable unit" might be called a "T-unit." I would hesitate to use both initials and call it an MT unit. "T-unit" is the name used in this investigation.

The unit has the advantage of preserving all the subordination achieved by a student, and all of his coordination between words and phrases and subordinate clauses.

The unit's length is not affected by coordination between main clauses, or, more accurately, between T-units, and that turns out to be a virtue of the index. Fourth graders use so very many *and*'s between T-units that in that position *and*'s prove to be a mark of immaturity statistically significant at the .01 level.

The T-unit turned out to be a useful tool. We applied it to our 54,000 words from fourth, eighth and twelfth grades, and also to our superior adults. According to the statisticians who analyzed our data using a chi-square and a contingency coefficient, the T-unit length is probably a better index of grade level than any of the other indexes evaluated. Sentence length is the poorest index. Subordination ratio is somewhat better. Mean clause length is still better, and mean T-unit length is at least as good as any, and apparently the best of all.

The T-unit is a useful grammatical concept for bridging the gap between the clause and the sentence. The clauses inside it are glued together by subordination devices. For example, look at the second T-unit in that fourth grade theme. That T-unit contains a main clause with a noun clause as direct object of the transitive verb *said,* but the noun clause has both an adverb clause and an adjective clause embedded in it. That one T-unit is made up of four clauses. Sentences can be the same size as T-units, or bigger if two or more are joined. For example, look at the fourth T-unit in the theme. A mature writer would probably join T-unit number 4 to T-unit number 5, punctuating them as one sentence. Actually, of course, this fourth-grader strung all these six T-units together as a sentence.

The concept of the T-unit now helps us to see at what points the growth occurs from grade to grade as these children mature. I will present what we might call a synopsis of clause-to-sentence factors. First, however, let me present an easy example to review the relation between these various factors. Suppose the clauses for some student averaged ten words apiece. Suppose too that his T-units averaged 1½ clauses apiece. The length of his average T-unit would be 1½ times ten words, or 15 words. Now suppose that on the average he joins two of these T-units into sentences. His average sentence length will be two times 15 words, or 30 words. Now, look at the actual figures for our groups in Table I. Synopsis of Clause-to-Sentence Factors. We will look at three grades first, and then afterward at the superior adults.

Reading down the left hand column you have the average number of words per clause written by the four groups: first, 6.6 words, for fourth-graders, then, 8.1 words for eighth-graders, then, 8.6 words for twelfth. Let us stop there momentarily. Underneath the number of words is the percentage of twelfth-grade achievement. Between fourth and eighth grades the percentage growth is from 77 percent to 94 percent, a difference of 17 percent. From eighth to twelfth grade the difference is only 6 percent. We can say then, that most of the growth in clause length occurred early in the school years. Students learned to pack more words, and consequently more grammatical constructions into their clauses in the earlier period of their growth.

Table I. A Synopsis of Clause-to-Sentence Factors

	Average length of clauses	Ratio of clauses per T-unit	Average length of T-units	Ratio of T-units per sentence	Average length of sentences
Grade 4	6.6 words ×	1.30 =	8.6 words ×	1.60 =	13.5 words
	77%	77%	60%	137%	80%
Grade 8	8.1 words ×	1.42 =	11.5 words ×	1.37 =	15.9 words
	94%	85%	80%	117%	94%
Grade 12	8.6 words ×	1.68 =	14.4 words ×	1.17 =	16.9 words
	100%	100%	100%	100%	100%
Statistical significance for 3 grades and both sexes by analysis of variance, 2 × 3 factorial	for grade at .01 level, and for sex at .01 level	for grade at .01 level, and for interaction of sex and grade at .05 level	for grade at .01 level	for grade at .01 level, for interaction of sex and grade at .05 level	for sex at .05 level and for grade at .05 level
X^2	33.10	17.66	50.35	3.07	17.03
Contingency coefficient	.616	.496	.694	.230	.489
Superior adults	11.5 words ×	1.74 =	20.3 words ×	1.24 =	24.7 words
	136%	104%	140%	105%	147%

Now let us look at the second column, the number of clauses per T-unit. Let me remind you that there will always be just one main clause to a T-unit. So the decimal to the right of the one indicates the average number of subordinate clauses added to that one main clause. We see that fourth-graders added a subordinate clause about a third of the time, whereas twelfth-graders added a subordinate clause twice as often, about two thirds of the time.

If we now look down the percentages in the second column, we find that they tell a story of late growth. Relating subordinate clauses to a main clause occurs more in the late period than the early one.

The third column, on average T-unit length, shows the effect of both these first two growth factors. You will recall that the number of words in a clause times the number of clauses in a T-unit gives the number of words in a T-unit. Since school children develop one of these facilities early, and the other late, T-unit length smooths out the two, showing strong and steady growth from fourth grade to twelfth.

The fourth column indicates the number of T-units per sentence. You will recall that our fourth-grader strung six T-units together to form one sentence. That was an extraordinary occurrence. Looking down the column we see that the percentages from fourth grade to twelfth decline instead of increasing as the others did. Coordinating a great many T-units together into a sentence is, in general, a mark of immaturity, not maturity. This negative factor counter-acts some of the increase which otherwise would occur in sentence length. It explains one of the reasons why sentence length is not so good an index of maturity as is T-unit length.

We can summarize the relative strength of the various growth factors from clause length to sentence length. T-unit length is a better index of maturity than sentence length because the excessive stringing together of T-units by young writers detracts from the growth which otherwise would be carried forward to manifest itself in sentence length. What growth there is in sentence length and T-unit length between Grades 4 and 12 is due about equally to an increase in clause length and in number of subordinate clauses.

Comparison with Superior Adults

Now let us see how these average twelfth-graders compare on these criteria with superior adults writing *Harper's* and *Atlantic* articles. The adult clauses are a big 36% longer. That difference is greater than the difference from Grade 4 to Grade 12. But these adults produce only a trifling 4 percent more clauses per T-unit. The much longer clauses plus the slightly larger number of subordinate clauses produces a T-unit length that is 40 percent greater than that for twelfth-graders. Adults write a trifling 5 percent more T-units per sentence, but that increase plus the big increase in T-unit length produces a sentence length that is 47 percent above that for twelfth-graders.

More than 70 percent of the gain in sentence length is caused by the increase in clause length alone.

Clause length more than any other single factor measured here distinguishes superior adults from average twelfth-graders. The superior adult packs a great many non-clause structures into his clauses. The average twelfth-grader has approached the ceiling on the number of subordinate clauses, and on the number of T-units per sentence, but he has not approached the limits of development in clause length.

If we look at the statistical test by analysis of variance for the three grades we see that sentence length is significant for grade at the .05 level, but the other four are significant for grade at the .01 level. Furthermore, according to the contingency coefficients, T-units length is the best indicator of grade level; clause length is second best; the frequency of subordinate clauses is third best; and sentence length is fourth best.

Re-appraisal of Criteria

On the basis of this synopsis of factors we can re-evaluate the opinions expressed in what has been called "the standard view." First, "sentence length is a significant index of maturity." It is, but three other indexes are more significant—at least for these average students from Grades 4 to 12. Second, "The chief factor contributing to the increase in sentence length is an increase in the frequency of subordinate clauses," and third, "the length of clauses remains constant or nearly constant." The length of clauses certainly does not remain constant while the number of subordinate clauses increases. Instead, from Grades 4 to 12, the percentage increase of the one is just the same as that for the other. But superior adults distinguish themselves by a notable increase in clause length but only a trifling increase in number of subordinate clauses per main clause. In view of all this, the "standard view" certainly needs to be overhauled.

There is a little more that needs be said about T-unit length. For instance, the number of short T-units declines markedly from one grade to the next. If we set eight words as the maximum for "short" T-units, then we find that 43 percent of all the words written by fourth-graders appear in "short" T-units; only 21 percent of all the words written by eighth-graders appear in "short" T-units; for twelfth-graders the percentage is 10 percent; for superior adults the percentage is 6 percent. Each of the older groups cuts the previous group's percentage in half. The frequency of short T-units is a most significant index of maturity. (The chi-square is 52.87; the contingency coefficient is .70.) When the layman says that younger children write short sentences, it must be the T-unit rather than the sentence that has caught his eye.

The T-unit, and the synopsis of sentence length factors which it makes possible, has broader applications. For instance, it is useful in describing what a conspicuous stylist does to achieve his special effects.

(Especially for fiction, sentences containing no dialogue need to be handled separately from those containing dialogue.) The non-dialogue sentences in Faulkner's "Barn-Burning" are greatly extended in clause length (150 percent of that for Grade 12). They are greatly extended in T-unit length (157 percent of that for Grade 12). So the average sentence length is 200 percent of that for Grade 12. But the ratio of clauses to T-units is only 105 percent of Grade 12 performance. Again the average twelfth-grader has approached the mature stylist in the number of subordinate clauses he uses.

What is in many ways an opposite extreme appears in Hemingway's "The Killers." Here the non-dialogue sentences are little more than stage directions. The clause length is 8.7 words, almost exactly that of the average twelfth-grader. The ratio of clauses to T-units is 1.17, even lower than that for fourth-graders. So the T-unit length is 9.4, between those for fourth and eighth graders. The ratio of T-units to sentences is 1.08, an extremely low figure. So the sentence length is only 10.2 words, shorter than the length of fourth-grade sentences. The only factor which Hemingway has not reduced drastically is clause length. The only factor which Faulkner has not greatly extended is the number of subordinate clauses per main clause or T-unit. Those two exceptions are notable contradictions to the tenets of "the standard view."

But "The Killers" is not typical Hemingway. The various factors for the non-dialogue sentences in his "Short Happy Life of Francis Macomber" fall about half-way between the scores for "The Killers" and for "Barn-Burning." The scores are fairly close to those for the non-fiction of the *Harper's* and *Atlantic* articles. However, at the climax of this story Hemingway twice puts six T-units into one sentence and twice puts nine.

The T-unit and the synopsis should have still other applications. They can tell us something about the prose of earlier centuries. Whether they will have significance in the study of speech development remains to be seen. No doubt readability formulas would have greater significance if sentence length were replaced by T-unit length.

This still does not tell the writing teacher what he needs to know. He needs to know what happens inside those clauses that they become so decisively longer in the hands of older and better writers. When he knows that he may be able to plan his program long range. The T-unit and the synopsis are only an entering wedge.

An Outline for Writing Sentence-Combining Problems

CHARLES R. COOPER

Every teacher would welcome a systematic classroom activity that would enable his students to write sentences of greater structural variety and complexity. Every child does eventually come to write more complex sentences—and several recent studies have traced that development[1]—but every teacher watching this glacially slow development feels compelled to intervene. He cannot avoid asking what Piaget calls the American question: "How can I speed it up?" Now that formal grammar study has been discredited as an instructional tool for enhancing syntactic dexterity,[2] the well-informed upper elementary or secondary teacher has been relying on naturalistic methods for strengthening his students' sentence dexterity, methods such as wide silent reading, reading aloud, dramatic activities, discussion, sentence games, much writing and the informal examination of the students' own sentences. Probably all language activities foster syntactic dexterity, and there is no reason why the teacher must consider it a separate, isolated problem.

However, beginning in Grade 4 there may be a distinct developmental gain in control of written syntax for most children if they are asked to direct their attention to syntax. Grade 4 is about the time when complexity of written syntax catches and surpasses complexity of spoken syntax (O'Donnell, p. 95). As teachers know, students seem to make a breakthrough here in willingness to write and in sheer quantity of writing. It seems an appropriate time to provide them direct help with sentences. Boys particularly appear to need this help, since they temporarily fall behind the girls in written sentence

English Journal, vol. 62 (January 1973), pp. 96–102, 108.

[1] Kellogg W. Hunt, *Grammatical Structures Written at Three Grade Levels*, 1965; Walter Loban, *The Language of Elementary School Children*, 1963; and Roy C. O'Donnell *et al.*, *Syntax of Kindergarten and Elementary School Children*, 1967. All published at Urbana, Illinois, as research reports of the National Council of Teachers of English.

[2] See the very thorough and readable review of research on grammar and writing in John C. Mellon, *Transformational Sentence-Combining* (Urbana, Illinois: National Council of Teachers of English, 1969).

dexterity (though never in spoken language dexterity) at about this point (O'Donnell, p. 96).

How can the teacher provide this direct assistance? A significant recent research report by John Mellon[3] provides evidence that sentence-combining problems of a special kind can enhance the syntactic dexterity of students' written sentences. The problems are presented apart from the writing program (which should be concerned with whole pieces of discourse); they confront the student with sentences more complex than ones he would be likely to write at that point in his development; they ask the student to write out fully-formed sentences and they provide him the content of the sentences so that his attention can remain focused on the *structural* aspects of the problem. The appended Outline offers examples. The first problem asks the student to write out a new, well-formed sentence by embedding the sentence, "The canary is yellow," in the sentence, "The canary flew out the window." Simple indentation indicates which sentence is the insert. Sentence ID shows a multiple embedding problem. Clues for making the insertion are included for adjective clauses and for noun substitutes.

The studies in language development referred to above show that the structures covered in Parts I and II of the Outline are highly significant in distinguishing mature from "immature" syntax. In other words, the teacher can accelerate growth toward written syntactic maturity if he can help students increase the amount of modification around their nouns and help them use noun substitutes (phrases and clauses) in place of single-word nouns.

Loban's study of oral language development implies that there is no point in having the student write sentence patterns he already controls (in the manner of most grammar texts); what the student needs—and what separates high-verbal from low-verbal students—is to expand the patterns themselves. This is Loban's often-quoted conclusion: "*Not pattern but what is done to achieve flexibility within the pattern* proves to be a measure of effectiveness and control of language at this level of language development" (Loban, p. 84; italics his).

Hunt's study of grammatical structures written at Grades 4, 8, and 12 leaves no doubt that critical factors in written language development are longer and more varied nominals (using noun phrases and clauses in place of simple-word nouns) and amount and depth of adjective modification of nouns. In discussing the implications of his study for instruction in the classroom, Hunt has this to say: "This study suggests a kind of sentence-building program that probably has never been produced, or at least not systematically and fully. The aim would be to widen the student's span of

[3] Mellon, *op. cit.* A replication of Mellon's study by Frank O'Hare of the University School of Florida State University supports Mellon's findings. Working with seventh-graders, Mellon got two years' growth in one in syntactic dexterity. Working with eighth-graders, O'Hare got four years' growth in one: his subjects were writing words per T-unit, words per clause, and a ratio of clauses to T-units, equal to that of twelfth-graders.

grammatical attention and concern. The method would be for him to reduce independent clauses to subordinate clauses and non-clauses, consolidating them with adjoining clauses and T-units. He could work up to structures of considerable depth and complexity comparable to those exhibited by twelfth-graders and superior adults" (Hunt, p. 157).

Mellon, the first researcher to examine the effects in the student's own writing of a sentence-building program like the one recommended by Hunt, concludes that sentence-combining problems "will increase the rate at which the sentence structure of the student's own writing becomes more highly elaborated (or differentiated) and thus more mature." Mellon thinks that ". . . this increase in growth rate is of sufficient magnitude to justify one's regarding the programs that produce it as valuable supplements to reading, writing, and discussing, which will obviously remain the staple activity content of elementary and junior high school English and language arts curriculums" (Mellon, p. 73).

In building a case for using sentence-combining problems in the classroom on a systematic basis, I do not want to ignore two important criticisms of this approach. One comes from James Moffett, who argues that any nonnaturalistic approach to language development should be avoided, that workbooks and exercises should be thrown out, the teacher working only with the student's own language production. And yet Moffett does recommend one sentence-writing activity that is very much like these sentence-combining problems. His activity has elementary children practice expanding and filling in the telegraphic speech of babies.[4] I am satisfied that these problems do not violate Moffett's curriculum if they are regarded as another language game in the teacher's repertory and if they are used in the spirit of a game, a set of puzzles to be solved.

The other criticism comes from Francis Christensen, who argues that the cumulative sentence, rather than the embedded sentence, is more characteristic of modern prose styles.[5] The cumulative sentence with its final free modifiers is very common in modern prose, but it has not replaced the embedded sentence, an impression one can get on reading Christensen. Embeddings and accumulations can occur in the same sentences, of course. The fact remains that mature syntax is characterized *in large part* by amount and depth of embedding, and this is a developmental task the child must master. To meet this criticism the teacher could also prepare some sentence-*additive* problems based on those in *The Student Workbook, The Christensen Rhetoric Program: The Sentence and the Paragraph* (Harper and Row, 1969). One exercise format very much like the format of Mellon's sentence-combining problems appears three times in Christensen's workbook (pp. 53,

[4] *A Student-Centered Language Arts Curriculum, Grades K–13: A Handbook for Teachers* (New York: Houghton Mifflin, 1968), pp. 150–152.

[5] *Notes Toward a New Rhetoric* (New York: Harper and Row, 1967).

65, 67), but in every other exercise format the student is writing to a pattern, making up the content of the sentence out of his own head.

My considered opinion is that teachers should be using these sentence-combining problems on a regular basis with their students. Used with an informal approach in correcting deviancy from standard English usage and punctuation (Mellon, pp. 5–7),[6] they permit the teacher to guiltlessly eliminate the teaching of a formal grammar, since both these activities—informal approach to deviancy and sentence-combining problems —fulfill the traditional goals of grammar study: standard usage and control of written syntax. Presented as another language game in a class where there is also an engaging writing program, they will increase the child's facility with the nominal and adjective structures of written English. Even so, the increased facility will still come very slowly. Learning to write sentences is like learning to read—a lifelong process. In "A Week on the Concord and Merrimack Rivers," Thoreau said it well: "A perfectly healthy sentence, it is true, is extremely rare."

Teachers can easily write all the sentence-combining problems they need. The Outline is a guide to constructing them systematically to cover all the kinds of embeddings and substitutions students need to practice. For children in the upper elementary grades the emphasis should be on the adjective problems (Part I). Beginning in Grade 7 the problems can be balanced between adjective embeddings and noun substitutions (Part II). Multiple embeddings and substitutions (ID and IIC) should be presented as soon as the students can handle them. Very capable high school students can move almost immediately to multiple embedding and substitution problems.

The sentence-combining problems can be presented a few at a time on a single worksheet. In doing further research on the value of these problems, I have been presenting them to large numbers of fourth- and seventh-graders of all abilities in schools in San Bernardino, California. Students do two worksheets in class each week (a total of ten or twelve problems) in connection with whatever other language activities the teacher has planned. Like Mellon, I have found that students seem to remain interested in "solving" the problems. Obviously, they can be given to the entire class at once, or they can be independent work for each student or for students who choose the activity. Pairs or small groups of students can work together on the problems. The teacher can put up a key somewhere in the room for students to check their new sentences against. The worksheets should never be presented as tests or as punishment or as time-fillers. Ideally the problems would be designed so that all the students write out perfect solutions, although some may puzzle over the problems longer than others.

---

[6] Mellon reviews the research on the utility of learning usage rules in correcting usage problems and concludes that the informal or incidental approach to correcting usage problems is more efficient and successful.

An Outline for Writing Sentence-Combining Problems: Noun Modifiers and Noun Substitutes

I. Noun Modifiers

A. Adjective word embeddings

1. Simple

a. before subject

The canary flew out the window.

The canary is *yellow.*

• The yellow canary flew out the window.

b. before object

I saw a canary.

The canary is *yellow.*

• I saw a yellow canary.

c. before predicate nominative

He was a student.

The student was *serious.*

• He was a serious student.

d. before object of a preposition

He was in the house when it caught fire.

The house was *old.*

• He was in the old house when it caught fire.

He fell from the roof.

The roof was *steep.*

• He fell from the steep roof.

2. Participle

a. *ing*

He saw the dog.

The dog *sleeps.*

• He saw the sleeping dog.

The plane crashed into the house.

The plane *burns.*

• The burning plane crashed into the house.

b. *ed*

The house had a pool.

The owners *abandoned* the house.

• The abandoned house had a pool.

The police captured the convict.

The convict *escaped* from prison.

• The police captured the escaped convict.

The students did their homework.

The homework was *assigned.*

• The students did their assigned homework.

Compound-adjectives

He dated the girl.
The girl *loves fun.*
• He dated the fun-loving girl.
He saw the dog.
Fleas bite the dog.
• He saw the flea-bitten dog.

4. From adverbs

The man is a fireman.
The man is *outside.*
• The man outside is a fireman.
The number is the answer.
The number is *below.*
• The number below is the answer.
The sky was full of stars.
The sky was *above.*
• The sky above was full of stars.
The people on the boat asked us to come aboard.
The boat was *alongside.*
• The people on the boat alongside asked us to come aboard.

B. Adjective phrase embeddings

1. Prepositional phrases

The man is my teacher.
The man is *in the room.*
• The man in the room is my teacher.
We sailed in the boat.
The boat was the one *with the blue sail.*
• We sailed in the boat with the blue sail.

2. Appositive phrases

My old friend is a plumber.
My old friend is *Bill Jones.*
• My old friend Bill Jones is a plumber.
My neighbor took me around the track.
My neighbor is *the race car driver.*
• My neighbor the race car driver took me around the track.

3. Participle phrases

a. *ing*

I stepped on the ant.
The ant was *carrying a crumb.*
• I stepped on the ant carrying a crumb.
The runner wins.
The runner was *making the best effort.*
• The runner making the best effort wins.

b. *ed*

We ate the food.

The food was *prepared by the chef.*

• We ate the food prepared by the chef.

The homework took too long.

The homework was *assigned by the math teacher.*

• The homework assigned by the math teacher took too long.

4. Infinitive phrases

We were given food.

The food was *to eat.*

• We were given food to eat.

The team was our next opponent.

The team was the one *to beat for the championship.*

• The team to beat for the championship was our next opponent.

C. Adjective clause embeddings (using who, when, which, that, when, or where)

People shouldn't throw stones.

People live in glass houses. (who)

• People who live in glass houses shouldn't throw stones.

The man is a congressman.

The man is the one I admire most. (whom)

• The man whom I admire most is a congressman.

He read a story.

The story had a surprise ending. (which)

• He read a story which had a surprise ending.

There are days.

I am discouraged. (when)

• There are days when I am discouraged.

That was the town.

We stopped for a hamburger. (where)

• That was the town where we stopped for a hamburger.

D. Multiple adjective embeddings (use of two or more embeddings from A–C)

The girl went to San Francisco.

The girl was *tall.*

The girl was *slender.*

The girl won the beauty contest. (who)

The contest was *local.*

The girl competed in the finals. (where)

The finals were *state-wide.*

• The tall, slender girl who won the local beauty contest went to San Francisco, where she competed in the state-wide finals.

II. Noun Substitutes

A. Noun clauses

1. Fact clauses

SOMETHING pleased him.

It snowed. (the fact that)

• The fact that it snowed pleased him.

SOMETHING alarmed his parents.

He might not have grades high enough to get him into Mugwamp College. (the fact that)

• The fact that he might not have grades high enough to get him into Mugwamp College alarmed his parents.

SOMETHING made the teacher feel very good.

Jimmy volunteered to give a report to the class. (that)

• That Jimmy volunteered to give a report to the class made the teacher feel very good.

The policeman was convinced (of) SOMETHING.

He had caught the guilty person. (that)

• The policeman was convinced that he had caught the guilty person.

Each of the candidates said SOMETHING.

He was the best man for the office of student body president. (that)

• Each of the candidates said that he was the best man for the office of student body president.

2. Question clauses

Johnny never did understand SOMETHING.

The teacher made him stay after school for some reason. (why)

• Johnny never did understand why the teacher made him stay after school.

SOMETHING made her angry.

She read something in the note. (what)

• What she read in the note made her angry.

Suzy tried to figure out SOMETHING.

The gift was for SOMETHING. (what)

• Suzy tried to figure out what the gift was for.

The fans wondered SOMETHING.

The coach would send in the second string sometime. (when)

• The fans wondered when the coach would send in the second string.

We didn't know SOMETHING.

Those other guys came from somewhere. (where)

• We didn't know where those other guys came from.

The pilot tried to explain SOMETHING.
He had drifted so far off course somehow. (how)
• The pilot tried to explain how he had drifted so far off course.
His scoutmaster could best tell him SOMETHING.
His money will go so far on the trip. (how far)
• His scoutmaster could best tell him how far his money would go on the trip.
The engineer knew exactly SOMETHING.
The cables should be so long. (how long)
• The engineer knew exactly how long the cables should be.
The coach knew just SOMETHING.
A fullback had to be so tough. (how tough)
• The coach knew just how tough a fullback had to be.
Janet was afraid to find out SOMETHING.
She had so much make-up work to do in algebra. (how much)
• Janet was afraid to find out how much make-up work she had to do in algebra.
(others: how often, how little, how few, how many, etc.)
My guitar teacher did not say SOMETHING.
Someone practices the chords so often. (how often to)
• My guitar teacher did not say how often to practice the chords.
My father is not sure of SOMETHING.
Someone calls someone if the car breaks down. (who + to)
• My father is not sure who to call if the car breaks down.
The fisherman didn't know SOMETHING.
Someone finds worms someplace (where + to)
• The fisherman didn't know where to find the worms.
Leinegen wondered about SOMETHING.
Someone stops the ants somehow. (how + to)
• Leinegen wondered about how to stop the ants.
Suzy could not decide SOMETHING.
Someone does SOMETHING next. (what + to)
• Suzy could not decide what to do next.

B. Noun phrases
1. Gerund phrases
SOMETHING was his favorite way of exercising.
He ran on the beach. (running)
• Running on the beach was his favorite way of exercising.
He enjoyed SOMETHING.
He wrote his name on fences. (writing)

• He enjoyed writing his name on fences.

The teacher could not understand SOMETHING.

Jim did not finish the homework. (Jim's + *ing*)

• The teacher could not understand Jim's not finishing the homework.

SOMETHING causes night and day.

The earth rotates on its axis. (the earth's + *ing*)

• The earth's rotating on its axis causes night and day.

2. Infinitive phrases

SOMETHING was his dream.

He wanted to win an Olympic medal in swimming. (to win)

• To win an Olympic medal in swimming was his dream.

He tried SOMETHING.

He avoided hitting the tree. (to avoid)

• He tried to avoid hitting the tree.

My recommendation would be SOMETHING.

The councilmen build more parks. (for + to)

• My recommendation would be for the councilmen to build more parks.

SOMETHING is very hard.

A smoker gives up the habit. (for + to)

• For a smoker to give up the habit is very hard.

C. Multiple embeddings (use of two or more embeddings from I A–C and II A, B above)

SOMETHING upset my father.

The smog persisted for ninety days above the danger level. (the fact that)

The smog was deadly.

My father sat down and wrote a letter to the governor. (who)

The letter was long.

The letter was angry.

• The fact that the deadly smog persisted for ninety days above the danger level upset my father, who sat down and wrote a long, angry letter to the governor.

My friends and I enjoy SOMETHING.

We race our bicycles around the paths in the park. (racing)

Our bicycles are lightweight.

Our bicycles are ten-speed.

The paths are narrow.

The paths are winding.

• My friends and I enjoy racing our lightweight, ten-speed bicycles around the narrow, winding paths in the park.

SOMETHING is highly frustrating to a(n) student.

Some teachers only exhort students to write sentences. (the fact that)

The teachers are naive.

The sentences are mature.

The sentences are deeply-embedded.

The student is eager.

The student recognizes his lack of fluency but cannot see SOMETHING. (who)

The fluency is syntactic.

He can correct this deficiency somehow. (how to)

• The fact that some naive teachers only exhort students to write mature, deeply-embedded sentences is highly frustrating to an eager student who recognizes his lack of syntactic fluency but cannot see how to correct this deficiency.

A Generative Rhetoric of the Sentence

FRANCIS CHRISTENSEN

If the new grammar is to be brought to bear on composition, it must be brought to bear on the rhetoric of the sentence. We have a workable and teachable, if not a definitive, modern grammar; but we do not have, despite several titles, a modern rhetoric.

In composition courses we do not really teach our captive charges to write better—we merely *expect* them to. And we do not teach them how to write better because we do not know how to teach them to write better. And so we merely go through the motions. Our courses with their tear-out work books and four-pound anthologies are elaborate evasions of the real problem. They permit us to put in our time and do almost anything else we'd rather be doing instead of buckling down to the hard work of making a difference in the student's understanding and manipulation of language.

With hundreds of handbooks and rhetorics to draw from, I have never been able to work out a program for teaching the sentence as I find it in the work of contemporary writers. The chapters on the sentence all adduce the traditional rhetorical classification of sentences as loose, balanced, and periodic. But the term *loose* seems to be taken as a pejorative (it sounds immoral); our students, no Bacons or Johnsons, have little occasion for balanced sentences; and some of our worst perversions of style come from the attempt to teach them to write periodic sentences. The traditional grammatical classification of sentences is equally barren. Its use in teaching composition rests on a semantic confusion, equating complexity of structure with complexity of thought and vice versa. But very simple thoughts may call for very complex grammatical constructions. Any moron can say "I don't know who done it." And some of us might be puzzled to work out the grammar of "All I want is all there is," although any chit can think it and say it and act on it.

The chapters on the sentence all appear to assume that we think naturally in primer sentences, progress naturally to compound sentences, and must be taught to combine the primer sentences into complex sentences—and that complex sentences are the mark of maturity. We need a rhetoric of the sentence that will do more than combine the ideas of primer sentences. We need one that will *generate* ideas.

For the foundation of such a generative or productive rhetoric I take the statement from John Erskine, the originator of the Great Books courses, himself a novelist. In an essay "The Craft of Writing" (*Twentieth Century English*, Philosophical Library, 1946) he discusses a principle of the writer's craft which, though known he says to all practitioners, he has never seen discussed in print. The principle is this: "When you write, you make a point, not by subtracting as though you sharpened a pencil, but by adding." We have all been told that the formula for good writing is the concrete noun and the active verb. Yet Erskine says, "What you say is found not in the noun but in what you add to qualify the noun. . . . The noun, the verb, and the main clause serve merely as the base on which meaning will rise. . . . The modifier is the essential part of any sentence." The foundation, then, for a generative or productive rhetoric of the sentence is that composition is essentially a process of *addition.*

But speech is linear, moving in time, and writing moves in linear space, which is analogous to time. When you add a modifier, whether to the noun, the verb, or the main clause, you must add it either before the head or after it. If you add it before the head, the direction of modification can be indicated by an arrow pointing forward; if you add it after, by an arrow pointing backward. Thus we have the second principle of a generative rhetoric—the principle of *direction of modification* or *direction of movement.*

Within the clause there is not much scope for operating with this principle. The positions of the various sorts of close, or restrictive, modifiers are generally fixed and the modifiers are often obligatory— "The man who came to dinner remained till midnight." Often the only choice is whether to add modifiers. What I have seen of attempts to bring structural grammar to bear on composition usually boils down to the injunction to "load the patterns." Thus "pattern practice" sets students to accreting sentences like this: "The small boy on the red bicycle who lives with his happy parents on our shady street often coasts down the steep street until he comes to the city park." This will never do. It has no rhythm and hence no life; it is tone-deaf. It is the seed that will burgeon into gobbledegook. One of the hardest things in writing is to keep the noun clusters and verb clusters short.

It is with modifiers added to the clause—that is, with sentence modifiers—that the principle comes into full play. The typical sentence of modern English, the kind we can best spend our efforts trying to teach, is what we may call the *cumulative sentence.* The main clause, which may or may not have a sentence modifier before it, advances the discussion; but the additions move backward, as in this clause, to modify the statement of the main clause or more often to explicate or exemplify it, so that the sentence has a flowing and ebbing movement, advancing to a new position and then pausing to consolidate it, leaping and lingering as the popular ballad does. The first part of the preceding compound sentence has one addition, placed within it; the second part has 4 words in the main clause and 49 in the five additions placed after it.

The cumulative sentence is the opposite of the periodic sentence. It does not represent the idea as conceived, pondered over, reshaped, packaged, and delivered cold. It is dynamic rather than static, representing the mind thinking. The main clause ("the additions move backward" above) exhausts the mere fact of the idea; logically, there is nothing more to say. The additions stay with the same idea, probing its bearings and implications, exemplifying it or seeking an analogy or metaphor for it, or reducing it to details. Thus the mere form of the sentence generates ideas. It serves the needs of both the writer and the reader, the writer by compelling him to examine his thought, the reader by letting him into the writer's thought.

Addition and direction of movement are structural principles. They involve the grammatical character of the sentence. Before going on to other principles, I must say a word about the best grammar as the foundation for rhetoric. I cannot conceive any useful transactions between teacher and students unless they have in common a language for talking about sentences. The best grammar for the present purpose is the grammar that best displays the layers of structure of the English sentence. The best I have found in a textbook is the combination of immediate constituent and transformation grammar in Paul Roberts' *English Sentences.* Traditional grammar, whether over-simple as in the school tradition or over-complex as in the scholarly tradition, does not reveal the language as it operates; it leaves everything, to borrow a phrase from Wordsworth, "in disconnection dead and spiritless." *English Sentences* is oversimplified and it has gaps, but it displays admirably the structures that rhetoric must work with—primarily sentence modifiers, including nonrestrictive relative and subordinate clauses, but, far more important, the array of noun, verb, and adjective clusters. It is paradoxical that Professor Roberts, who has done so much to make the teaching of composition possible, should himself be one of those who think that it cannot be taught. Unlike Ulysses, he does not see any work for Telemachus to work.

Layers of structure, as I have said, is a grammatical concept. To bring in the dimension of meaning, we need a third principle—that of *levels of generality* or *levels of abstraction.* The main or base clause is likely to be stated in general or abstract or plural terms. With the main clause stated, the forward movement of the sentence stops, the writer shifts down to a lower level of generality or abstraction or to singular terms, and goes back over the same ground at this lower level.[1] There is no theoretical limit to the number of structural layers or levels, each[2] at a lower level of generality, any or all of them compounded, that a speaker or writer may use. For a speaker, listen to Lowell Thomas; for a writer, study William Faulkner. To a single independent clause he may append a page of additions, but usually all clear, all grammatical, once we have learned how to read him. Or, if you prefer, study Hemingway, the master of the simple sentence: "George was coming down in the telemark position, kneeling, one leg forward and bent, the other trailing, his sticks hanging like some insect's thin legs, kicking up puffs of snow, and finally the whole kneeling, trailing figure coming around in a beautiful right curve, crouching, the legs shot forward and back, the body leaning out against the swing, the sticks accenting the curve like points of light, all in a wild cloud of snow." Only from the standpoint of school grammar is this a simple sentence.

This brings me to the fourth, and last, principle, that of texture. *Texture* provides a descriptive or evaluative term. If a writer adds to few of his nouns or verbs or main clauses and adds little, the texture may be said to be thin. The style will be plain or bare. The writing of most of our students is thin—even threadbare. But if he adds frequently or much or both, then the texture may be said to be dense or rich. One of the marks of an effective style, especially in narrative, is variety in the texture, the texture varying with the change in pace, the variation in texture producing the change in pace. It is not true, as I have seen it asserted, that fast action calls for short sentences; the action is fast in the sentence by Hemingway above. In our classes, we have to work for greater density and variety in texture and greater concreteness and particularity in what is added.

I have been operating at a fairly high level of generality. Now I must downshift and go over the same points with examples. The most graphic way to exhibit the layers of structure is to indent the word groups of a sentence and to number the levels. The first three sentences illustrate the various positions of the added sentence modifiers—initial, medial, and final. The symbols mark the grammatical character of the additions: SC, subordinate clause; RC, relative clause; NC, noun cluster; VC, verb cluster; AC, adjective cluster; A + A, adjective series; Abs, absolute (i.e., a VC with a subject of its own); PP, prepositional phrase. The elements set off as on a

---

[1] Cf. Leo Rockas "Abstract and Concrete Sentences," *CCC*, May 1963. Rockas describes sentences as abstract or concrete, the abstract implying the concrete and vice versa. Readers and writers, he says, must have the knack of apprehending the concrete in the abstract and the abstract in the concrete. This is true and valuable. I am saying that within a single sentence the writer may present more than one level of generality, translating the abstract into the more concrete in added levels.

[2] This statement is not quite tenable. Each helps to make the idea of the base clause more concrete or specific, but each is not more concrete or specific than the one immediately above it.

lower level are marked as sentence modifiers by junctures or punctuation. The examples have been chosen to illustrate the range of constructions used in the lower levels; after the first few they are arranged by the number of levels. The examples could have been drawn from poetry as well as from prose. Those not attributed are by students.

1

1 He dipped his hands in the bichloride solution and shook them,
  2 a quick shake, (NC)
    3 fingers down, (Abs)
      4 like the fingers of a pianist above the keys. (PP)

Sinclair Lewis

2

  2 Calico-coated, (AC)
  2 small-bodied, (AC)
    3 with delicate legs and pink faces in which their mismatched eyes rolled wild and subdued, (PP)
1 they huddled,
  2 gaudy motionless and alert, (A + A)
  2 wild as deer, (AC)
  2 deadly as rattlesnakes, (AC)
  2 quiet as doves. (AC)

William Faulkner

3

1 The bird's eye, / , remained fixed upon him;
  2 / bright and silly as a sequin (AC)
1 its little bones, / , seemed swooning in his hand,
  2 wrapped . . . in a warm padding of feathers. (VC)

Stella Benson

4

1 The jockeys sat bowed and relaxed,
  2 moving a little at the waist with the movement of their horses. (VC)

Katherine Anne Porter

5

1 The flame sidled up the match,
  2 driving a film of moisture and a thin strip of darker grey before it. (VC)

6

1 She came among them behind the man,
  2 gaunt in the gray shapeless garment and the sunbonnet, (AC)
  2 wearing stained canvas gymnasium shoes. (VC)

Faulkner

7

1 The Texan turned to the nearest gatepost and climbed to the top of it,
  2 his alternate thighs thick and bulging in the tight-trousers, (Abs)
  2 the butt of the pistol catching and losing the sun in pearly gleams. (Abs)

Faulkner

8

1 He could sail for hours,
  2 searching the blanched grasses below him with his telescopic eyes, (VC)
  2 gaining height against the wind, (VC)
  2 descending in mile-long, gently declining swoops when he curved and rode back, (VC)
  2 never beating a wing. (VC)

Walter Van Tilburg Clark

9

1 They regarded me silently,
  2 Brother Jack with a smile that went no deeper than his lips, (Abs)
    3 his head cocked to one side, (Abs)
    3 studying me with his penetrating eyes; (VC)
  2 the other blank-faced, (Abs)
    3 looking out of eyes that were meant to reveal nothing and to stir profound uncertainty. (VC)

Ralph Ellison

10

1 He stood at the top of the stairs and watched me,
  2 I waiting for him to call me up, (Abs)
  2 he hesitating to come down, (Abs)
    3 his lips nervous with the suggestion of a smile, (Abs)
    3 mine asking whether the smile meant come, or go away. (Abs)

11

1 Joad's lips stretched tight over his long teeth for a moment, and
1 he licked his lips,
  2 like a dog, (PP)
    3 two licks, (NC)
      4 one in each direction from the middle. (NC)

Steinbeck

12

1 We all live in two realities:
  2 one of seeming fixity, (NC)

3 with institutions, dogmas, rules of punctuation, and routines, (PP)
4 the calendared and clockwise world of all but futile round on round; (NC) and
2 one of whirling and flying electrons, dreams, and possibilities, (NC)
3 behind the clock. (PP)

Sidney Cox

13

1 It was as though someone, somewhere, had touched a lever and shifted gears, and
1 the hospital was set for night running,
2 smooth and silent, (A + A)
2 its normal chatter and hum muffled, (Abs)
2 the only sounds heard in the whitewalled room distant and unreal: (Abs)
3 a low hum of voices from the nurses' desk, (NC)
4 quickly stifled, (VC)
3 the soft squish of rubber-soled shoes on the tiled corridor, (NC)
3 starched white cloth rustling against itself, (Abs) and, outside,
3 the lonesome whine of wind in the country night (NC) and
3 the Kansas dust beating against the windows. (NC)

14

1 The beach sounds are jazzy,
2 percussion fixing the mode—(Abs)
3 the surf cracking and booming in the distance, (Abs)
3 a little nearer dropped bar-bells clanking, (Abs)
3 steel gym rings, / , ringing, (Abs)
/4 flung together, (VC)
3 palm fronds rustling above me, (Abs)
4 like steel brushes washing over a snare drum, (PP)
3 troupes of sandals splatting and shuffling on the sandy cement, (Abs)
4 their beat varying, (Abs)
5 syncopation emerging and disappearing with changing paces. (Abs)

15

1 A small Negro girl develops from the sheet of glare-frosted walk,
2 walking barefooted, (VC)
3 her bare legs striking and coiling from the hot cement, (Abs)

4 her feet curling in, (Abs)
5 only the outer edges touching. (Abs)

16

1 The swells moved rhythmically toward us,
2 irregularly faceted, (VC)
2 sparkling, (VC)
2 growing taller and more powerful until the shining crest bursts, (VC)
3 a transparent sheet of pale green water spilling over the top, (Abs)
4 breaking into blue-white foam as it cascades down the front of the wave, (VC)
4 piling up in a frothy mound that the diminishing wave pushes up against the pilings, (VC)
5 with a swishsmash, (PP)
4 the foam drifting back, (Abs)
5 like a lace fan opened over the shimmering water as the spent wave returns whispering to the sea. (PP)

The best starting point for a composition unit based on these four principles is with two-level narrative sentences, first with one second-level addition (sentences 4, 5), then with two or more parallel ones (6, 7, 8). Anyone sitting in his room with his eyes closed could write the main clause of most of the examples; the discipline comes with the additions, provided they are based at first on immediate observation, requiring the student to phrase an exact observation in exact language. This can hardly fail to be exciting to a class: it is life, with the variety and complexity of life; the workbook exercise is death. The situation is ideal also for teaching diction—abstract-concrete, general-specific, literal-metaphorical, denotative-connotative. When the sentences begin to come out right, it is time to examine the additions for their grammatical character. From then on the grammar comes to the aid of the writing and the writing reinforces the grammar. One can soon go on to multi-level narrative sentences (1, 9–11, 15, 16) and then to brief narratives of three to six or seven sentences on actions with a beginning, a middle, and an end that can be observed over and over again—beating eggs, making a cut with a power saw, or following a record changer's cycle or a wave's flow and ebb. (Bring the record changer to class.) Description, by contrast, is static, picturing appearance rather than behavior. The constructions to master are the noun and adjective clusters and the absolute (13, 14). Then the descriptive noun cluster must be taught to ride piggy-back on the narrative sentence, so that description and narration are interleaved: "In the morning we went out into a new world, a glistening crystal and white world, each skeleton tree, each leafless bush, even the heavy, drooping power lines sheathed in icy crystal." The next step is to develop the sense for variety in texture and change in pace that all good narrative demands.

. . . The same four principles can be applied to the expository paragraph. But this is a subject for another paper.

I want to anticipate two possible objections. One is that the sentences are long. By freshman English standards they are long, but I could have produced far longer ones from works freshmen are expected to read. Of the sentences by students, most were written as finger exercises in the first few weeks of the course. I try in narrative sentences to push to level after level, not just two or three, but four, five, or six, even more, as far as the students' powers of observation will take them. I want them to become sentence acrobats, to dazzle by their syntactic dexterity. I'd rather have to deal with hyperemia than anemia. I want to add my voice to that of James Coleman (*CCC*, December 1962) deploring our concentration on the plain style.

The other objection is that my examples are mainly descriptive and narrative—and today in freshman English we teach only exposition. I deplore this limitation as much as I deplore our limitation to the plain style. Both are a sign that we have sold our proper heritage for a pot of message. In permitting them, the English department undercuts its own discipline. Even if our goal is only utilitarian prose, we can teach diction and sentence structure far more effectively through a few controlled exercises in description and narration than we can by starting right off with exposition (Theme One, 500 words, precipitates *all* the problems of writing). There is no problem of invention; the student has something to communicate—his immediate sense impressions, which can stand a bit of exercising. The material is not already verbalized—he has to match language to sense impressions. His acuteness in observation and in choice of words can be judged by fairly objective standards—is the sound of a bottle of milk being set down on a concrete step suggested better by *clink* or *clank* or *clunk*? In the examples, study the diction for its accuracy, rising at times to the truly imaginative. Study the use of metaphor, of comparison. This verbal virtuosity and syntactical ingenuity can be made to carry over into expository writing.

But this is still utilitarian. What I am proposing carries over of itself into the study of literature. It makes the student a better reader of literature. It helps him thread the syntactical mazes of much mature writing, and it gives him insight into that elusive thing we call style. Last year a student told of rereading a book by her favorite author, Willa Cather, and of realizing for the first time *why* she liked reading her: she could understand and appreciate the style. For some students, moreover, such writing makes life more interesting as well as giving them a way to share their interest with others. When they learn how to put concrete details into a sentence, they begin to look at life with more alertness. If it is liberal education we are concerned with, it is just possible that these things are more important than anything we can achieve when we set our sights on the plain style in expository prose.

I want to conclude with a historical note. My thesis in this paragraph is that modern prose like modern poetry has more in common with the seventeenth than with the eighteenth century and that we fail largely because we are operating from an eighteenth century base. The shift from the complex to the cumulative sentence is more profound than it seems. It goes deep in grammar, requiring a shift from the subordinate clause (the staple of our trade) to the cluster and the absolute (so little understood as to go almost unnoticed in our textbooks). And I have only lately come to see that this shift has historical implications. The cumulative sentence is the modern form of the loose sentence that characterized the anti-Ciceronian movement in the seventeenth century. This movement, according to Morris W. Croll,[3] began with Montaigne and Bacon and continued with such men as Donne, Browne, Taylor, Pascal. To Montaigne, its art was the art of being natural; to Pascal, its eloquence was the eloquence that mocks formal eloquence; to Bacon, it presented knowledge so that it could be examined, not so that it must be accepted.

But the Senecan amble was banished from England when "the direct sensuous apprehension of thought" (T. S. Eliot's words) gave way to Cartesian reason or intellect. The consequences of this shift in sensibility are well summarized by Croll:

> To this mode of thought we are to trace almost all the features of modern literary education and criticism, or at least of what we should have called modern a generation ago: the study of the precise meaning of words; the reference to dictionaries as literary authorities; the study of the sentence as a logical unit alone; the careful circumscription of its limits and the gradual reduction of its length; . . .[4] the attempt to reduce grammar to an exact science; the idea that forms of speech are always either correct or incorrect; the complete subjection of the laws of motion and expression in style to the laws of logic and standardization—in short, the triumph, during two centuries, of grammatical over rhetorical ideas.

Here is a seven-point scale any teacher of composition can use to take stock. He can find whether he is based in the eighteenth century or in the twentieth and whether he is consistent—completely either an ancient or a modern—or is just a crazy mixed-up kid.

[3] "The Baroque Style in Prose," *Studies in English Philology; A Miscellany in Honor of Frederick Klaeber* (1929), reprinted in *Style, Rhetoric, and Rhythm: Essays by Morris W. Croll* (1966) and A. M. Witherspoon and F. J. Warnke, *Seventeenth-Century Prose and Poetry,* 2nd ed. (1963). I have borrowed from Croll in my description of the cumulative sentence.

[4] The omitted item concerns punctuation and is not relevant here. In using this scale, note the phrase "what we should have called modern a generation ago" and remember that Croll was writing in 1929.

On the Practical Uses of a Grammatical System: A Note on Christensen and Johnson

A. M. TIBBETTS

The work of Francis Christensen on grammar and rhetoric is important and interesting. Sabina Johnson's recent article on Christensen in *College English* is also important and interesting, particularly so because she raises some issues that are not sufficiently discussed in these times. Also, she shows in some detail that a few of Christensen's premises are not quite as solid as he (and many of us) thought they were.

But good as it is, Mrs. Johnson's article does not go into detail concerning several merits in the Christensen grammar, nor does she discuss certain implications of the grammar. I do not mention these as being flaws in her article. I am not out to attack her (or for that matter Christensen, much of whose work I find valuable in certain specific ways). Let my essay be considered as a gloss upon his work and hers, and also as a brief commentary upon certain practical issues in the teaching and use of grammar.

First, unlike either structural or transformational, Christensen's grammar can be taught in the schools. Modern grammars—and this includes much of modern traditional grammar—tend to be so complex and sophisticated that they can't be understood or used by most teachers, students, or members of the educated public. A really useful grammar is, after all, a part of public property. And, over a period of years, it is the educated public which will determine whether a grammar will have more than just a brief, vivid life in the scholarly journals. A merit of his school grammar, which is outlined in his *Rhetoric Program*, is that Christensen provides an understand-

Editor's Note: In this article Professor Tibbetts evaluates the work of Francis Christensen and comments on an earlier analysis of Christensen written by Sabina Thorne Johnson. The Christensen materials to which Tibbetts refers are as follows: "The Problem of Defining a Mature Style," *English Journal*, vol. 57 (April 1968), pp. 572–579; *Notes Toward a New Rhetoric* (New York, 1967); *The Christensen Rhetoric Program* (New York, 1968). Mrs. Johnson's article, "Some Tentative Strictures on Generative Rhetoric," appeared in *College English*, vol. 31 (November 1969), pp. 155–165.

College English, vol. 31 (May 1970), pp. 870–878.

able set of directions and a group of exercises which go far to improve student writing. He has, for instance, some of the best exercises on subordination in modern school texts.

Essentially, most of Christensen's exercises consist of "pattern practice," in which the student learns to arrange base clauses, bound modifiers, and free modifiers effectively. The student is expected to respond to a visual pattern of slots and levels of generality that is given to him as a problem. He solves the problem using his own words. For example, in *The Rhetoric Program* the student may be given three levels of generality:

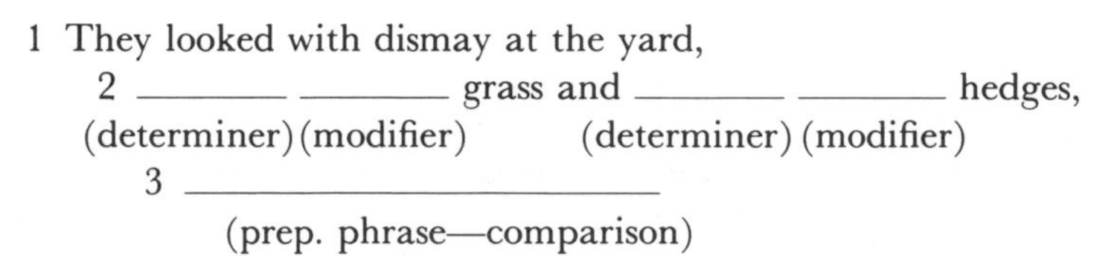

1 They looked with dismay at the yard,
2 _______ _______ grass and _______ _______ hedges,
(determiner)(modifier) (determiner) (modifier)
3 ____________________
(prep. phrase—comparison)

A possible solution, as suggested in the teacher's version of the *Program* (p. 31), is:

1 They looked with dismay at the yard,
2 that overgrown grass and those towering hedges,
3 like the lean ghosts of a deserted home.

Such exercises require the student not only to know his grammar rather well but also to practice his rhetoric. It is as important in the example above for the student to give a vivid figurative description of the hedges as it is for him to know that *like the lean ghosts of a deserted home* is prepositional. Knowing, and using, both his grammar and rhetoric should give his prose more accuracy and precision—and also make it easier to read.

A second merit in Christensen is that he shows students how to avoid what he calls "pretzel prose," one characteristic of which is a sort of unreadable jargon. This jargon is often created, says Christensen, by the writer's use of "the long noun phrase as subject and the long noun phrase as complement, the two coupled by a minimal verb" ("Defining a Mature Style," p. 575). Christensen continues:

> One of the hardest things to learn in learning to write well is how to keep the noun phrases short. The skillful writer is the writer who has learned how to keep them short. On nearly every page of this paper I have had to resort to syntactic devices to keep them within bounds—devices, such as this appositive, that are practically unknown to our textbook writers. Northrop Frye might have written this sentence: *The curriculum is at best, however, a design to be interpreted by teachers with varying degrees of ability and insight for children with different equipment in intelligence and language background.* Instead, he wrote this one: *The curriculum is at best, however, a design to be interpreted by teachers,*

> *for students—by teachers with varying degrees of ability and insight, for children with differing equipment in intelligence and language background.* As a skillful writer he has found a device to avoid a long noun phrase of twenty-four words. Although his sentence is longer by four words, it is immeasureably clearer and more emphatic. (p. 575)

Essentially, much pretzel prose consists of badly made SVC patterns in which lumpy, vague subject clusters are connected to lumpy, vague complement clusters by a form of *to be.* I have been collecting such SVC sentences for several years, and I conclude from examining them in their contexts (and from talking to the people who wrote them, when they were available), that Christensen is right. A high percentage of bad prose is pretzelized, and he has given us an excellent method of teaching students how to avoid it. The ordinary methods used—changing terms in the clusters, or changing *to be* to "a more active verb"—ordinarily don't work very well. Nor do most exercises in predication. What does work fairly well is to have the student rewrite his own pretzel prose using more specific words in short base clauses and precisely stated free modifiers. Unlike Christensen, I would also prescribe practice with a few balanced phrases or clauses, antitheses, and periodic sentences—these involve an issue to which I'll return in a moment.

A third merit in Christensen is that he understands, mainly, what the proper relationship between grammar and rhetoric should be. I quote the opening paragraph of "Defining a Mature Style":

> The topic assigned me for this paper was "Grammar and Rhetoric—Putting the Two Together," and I proposed to deal with two questions—*whether* they can be brought together and *how* they can be brought together. But reflection on these questions, together with some recent reading, made me face up again to another question. *Grammar and rhetoric are complementary, but their procedures and goals are quite different. Grammar maps out the possible; rhetoric narrows down the possible to the desirable or effective.* [Italics added.] In the area of style or, more narrowly, of syntax as style, our province in this paper, the key problem for rhetoric is to know what is desirable or effective. In matters of style, how do we as teachers know what to say *yes* to and what to say *no* to? Unless, as some appear to contend, we are merely to turn on the spigot and watch the water flow without attempting to direct the flow, where do we direct it? How do we avoid mere subjective impressionism or, worse, mere caprice and whim? (p. 572)

Implicit everywhere in his grammar is Christensen's belief that the study of literature, rhetoric, and grammar should be genuinely integrated, not just placed side by side in the curriculum. The student should learn something grammatical from his reading of literature and something literary from his study of grammar. And in his writing he should draw on both. One of the major strengths in *The Rhetoric Program* is that it often succeeds in integrating the different "procedures and goals" of grammar and rhetoric. In fact, it is mainly this integration which makes possible the first two merits of the Christensen grammar that I mentioned.

Yet with all its merits, the Christensen grammar has some weaknesses, several of which Mrs. Johnson discusses in her admirable article. One of these weaknesses may be summed up in her comment: "I suspect that Christensen, in seeking to remedy the errors inherent in the more traditional approaches to composition teaching, has presented his theories and his method in far more absolute terms than they warrant" (p. 165). Her observation is accurate. Christensen is fond of saying things like: "Anyone who learns to use the full range of free modifiers will be a skillful writer" (*The Rhetoric Program*, Teacher's Manual, p. vi). And: "The principle that underlies the entire program is that of 'addition'—a writer makes his point clearer by adding" (p. vii).

The trouble with both of these remarks, and they are typical of a part of Christensen's approach, is that they are simply not empirically true as they are stated. A person will be a "skillful writer" only if he has good control over many more things than just free modifiers, which are but one element in good writing. And a writer does not necessarily make "his point clearer by adding," although in practice this is quite possible. He may make a point clearer by using fewer words, by using more specific or concrete words, or by recasting his sentence.

A second weakness in the Christensen grammar is created by what I call the *fiction fallacy*. In a general way, this is the fallacy of believing that fiction, especially as represented in the modern short story or novel, is of great value to the student in teaching him to be a good writer. Without doubt, fiction is of some value. But I am inclined to think that the fictional mode of writing no longer overlaps the rhetorical mode as much as it once did. This is especially true in the matter of style, which in the hands of modern writers of fiction has tended toward the personal and the poetic, neither of which is ordinarily of much use to the rhetorician. Of course I am limiting *rhetoric* here to the arts of argument and persuasion, a limitation which is amply justified by the history of rhetoric.

The fiction fallacy occurs in Christensen's grammar because he apparently believes that students should learn to write like writers such as Eudora Welty, William Faulkner, and Irwin Shaw. These and other writers of modern fiction appear in the important section on "Levels of Generality" in *The Rhetoric Program*, a section which seems to be typical of the *Program*. In the "visuals," which form the basis of instruction for the section, the only writer of non-fiction who appears is E. B. White, and his sample sentence is a piece of narrative prose.

Much of the narrative or fictional prose in *The Rhetoric Program* is highly "creative" and self-conscious. Take, for instance, the following sentence by Wallace Stegner, which appears in the section on "Levels of Generality":

> The hunter moved his shoulder under the weight of the ducks, his mind full for the moment with the image of his father's face, darkly pale, fallen in on its bones, and the pouched, restless, suspicious eyes that seemed always looking for someone. (p. 31)

The use of such a prose model for high school students—and remember that *The Rhetoric Program* was designed for them—seems misguided. For one thing, it requires no accurate observation or logical analysis on their part. Indeed it may well encourage them to manufacture the arty, false descriptions of adolescent mental states that are the rage among college undergraduates these days. It is difficult to break bad habits in writing, and a few years of being trained to write sentences like the one just quoted will probably do some damage to impressionable minds. If you teach young writers that it is good, as Christensen believes, "to become sentence acrobats, to dazzle by their syntactic dexterity" (*Notes Toward a New Rhetoric*, p. 14), then you are likely to get what you deserve—dextrous rhetorical acrobats who dextrously tell untruths. In disagreeing with Christensen on this issue, Mrs. Johnson appropriately comments: "I want students to dazzle me with their ideas and to astonish me with their powers of persuasion" (p. 160).

In his *Notes Toward a New Rhetoric*, Christensen anticipated the objection "that my examples are mainly descriptive and narrative—and today in freshman English we teach only exposition." He continued:

> I deplore this limitation as much as I deplore our limitation to the plain style. Both are a sign that we have sold our proper heritage for a pot of message. In permitting them, the English department undercuts its own discipline. Even if our goal is only utilitarian prose, we can teach diction and sentence structure far more effectively through a few controlled exercises in description and narration than we can by starting right off with exposition. . . . This verbal virtuosity and syntactical ingenuity [used in description and narration] can be made to carry over into expository writing. (p. 15)

I doubt the validity of two premises here. For one thing, English departments have traditionally believed (and rightly so) that their "discipline" includes the rhetoric of the literary periods as well as their fiction and poetry. Most of us who teach literature would no more leave out Mill or Carlyle from a survey of Victorian literature than we would omit Tennyson or Browning. Would Christensen, or anyone else, seriously suggest that we teach a course in the last half of the eighteenth century and omit Boswell, Johnson, and Burke simply because they did not generally write poetry and fiction? For another thing, I doubt that as a rule "verbal virtuosity and syntactical ingenuity" *should* be "made to carry over into expository writing."

For what we are generally after in expository writing is accuracy rather than cleverness.

Christensen's excessive use of modern literary models begs the question concerning what he calls "the idiom of our own day" ("Defining a Mature Style," p. 572). Certainly, much of the modern fictional idiom is self-indulgent and somewhat decadent. And one gets the impression from the work of many who imitate the fictionists, but who are themselves writers of reportage, that the idiom of our day has become less a way of expressing truth than a stylistic mannerism. In using the idiom of a modern cumulative rhetoric, such non-fiction writers often seem unable to develop an idea clearly. They bumble about in a paragraph, tacking on one notion after another, hoping—perhaps like a latter-day Henry James—that if they put in enough bits and pieces the material will add up to something profound.

In "Defining a Mature Style," Christensen uses as a model of the modern idiom a paragraph from an article by David Halberstam called "Love, Life, and Selling Out in Poland" (*Harper's*, July 1967). This is the paragraph (Christensen puts in roman type the base clauses and the coordinators that join base clauses; in italics he puts the free modifiers):

> These countries were once the center of the storm, and *as the Curtain was coming down* their hotels were filled with *correspondents, pushing and crowding each other, playing what is known in the trade as journalistic boomerang (you take a rumor, throw it out, and by the end of the day it has touched so many other people that it comes back to you fresh and vital, passed on by people you haven't even spoken to).* The storm is now in Saigon, *where several hundred* correspondents *cover the story of whether that country will or won't go Communist.* Their editors are in a sense right; for there is little news from Eastern Europe—*some change, some restlessness, but little hint of revolution.* These are small countries: you can take all the political developments in the Polish Communist party in one year, and *perhaps* it will be one story. Yet *for me* it was an extraordinary time. My colleague David Binder, *who shared the lower half of the tier, the Balkans, with me,* agreed emphatically. *When the Times wanted to transfer him to Bonn, a bigger story and a bigger bureau,* he went reluctantly, *leaving what he had come to call "my people."* We shared, *I think,* the same feeling for being a reporter there, *of watching and in a way being involved in the simple yet moving business of the daily struggle of these people with the state. Cast in the most unnatural circumstances,* they go on in the struggle relentlessly, *living lives with an infinite degree of moral complexity, daily courage, daily honor, daily dishonor* (p. 578).

What's wrong with this as an example of "good" writing? First, it is weakly organized; it lacks logical order, jumping erratically from point to point in almost a stream-of-consciousness fashion. Also, although Halberstam uses a lot of fancy stylistic footwork, he doesn't really say much. He gives the impression of great knowingness and intellectual superiority: "Their editors are in a sense right, for there is little news from Eastern Europe—some change, some restlessness, but little hint of revolution." Such is the modern reporter's typically stylish way of seeming to be on top of a story while not having in his possession any hard facts. Finally, one senses that Halberstam's cumulative sentence rhetoric itself may be a mistake, that it may be a mannerism which prevents him from putting his ideas as precisely as he might. Unless the writer uses it carefully and with discretion, the cumulative sentence can tempt him to deviate from his logical course, causing him to pitch and yaw about in his paragraphs. What the fictional fallacy may ultimately prove is that the modern fictional idiom is a questionable model to use in non-fictional rhetoric, whose main strategy is to find and express truth.

Christensen's lack of interest in the truths of the objective world is a third weakness in his grammar (and it is one which is present in all grammars to some extent). This weakness, which grows out of the first two I mentioned, is the most important. I do not, of course, mean to imply that his work is dishonest. It is honest; and, given his premises, logical. But his grammar, which is also a rhetoric, is not designed to teach young people how to do the most valuable things any grammar-rhetoric should be designed to teach—how to think; how to separate and define issues; how to isolate fallacies; how to make generalizations and value judgments. In brief, how to express the truths and realities of our time, and how to argue for improvements. Next to these matters of moment, the stylistic dexterities of a Fitzgerald or a Hemingway are as insubstantial airy nothings.

It may be objected that my list of items which a grammar-rhetoric should teach deals with rhetorical matters other than the sentence. To some degree, this is true. But the basic unit of both grammar and rhetoric *is* the sentence. And whether we approve of the process or not, we are forced by the very nature of the human mind to express our sense of reality and value in linguistic segments that we choose to call "sentences." So it follows that the better we can teach students to write "truthful" sentences—omitting for the moment other issues in rhetoric—the better writers they are likely to become.

I remarked at the beginning that Christensen's premises were occasionally weak. It is useful to discuss the implications of one of these premises: That the grammatical form of a sentence can "generate" ideas. As Christensen puts it, "Thus the mere form of the sentence generates ideas" (*Notes Toward a New Rhetoric*, p. 6).

The generalization does not seem very accurate. In fact, something like the reverse can be true. Often the writer's *idea* will "suggest" *form.* If he sees Jim kiss Sally, and he knows both of them by name, he will likely write: *Jim kissed Sally.* If Sally reports to the writer that she was kissed in the midst of a crowd and that she doesn't know who kissed her, a different form may be suggested: *Sally was kissed,* or *Sally was kissed by somebody, we don't know who.* If *Sally was kissed, hugged, and (after a minute) indecently proposed to,* the form of the grammatical parallelism, including the parenthesis, is suggested by the reality and sequence of events. I do not balk, by the way, at using narrative for grammatical illustration of this limited nature. I am not writing a grammar. If I were, Sally's osculatory propensities would be exercised in a full range of logical as well as narrative relationships.

Mrs. Johnson comments as follows on the issue of form generating content: "This is perhaps the heart of my hesitancy about the Rhetoric Program. Christensen seems to believe that form can generate content (*Program*, p. vi). I don't believe it can, especially if the content is of an analytical or critical nature" (p. 159).

Her generalization isn't entirely accurate either. For, in expressing the inchoate idea, the writer has in most contexts a surprisingly small number of choices in sentencing, and these choices are dictated in some part by the idioms and grammatical structures he has available to him. In other words, form can have an important influence on content. Consider how few ways, for instance, there are to express explicitly most logical causations in the English sentence. In keeping track of the possible corrections of "bad cause" sentences that students write, I have found that, given the context of their sentences, about four out of five have to be constructed using one of the familiar multi-clause patterns with *since* or *because* as a signal. When Jim tries to make both sense and grammar out of his kissing Sally, out of the welter of reasons which cross his mind he may well decide upon something like: *I kissed her because she was beautiful,* or *Since I loved her, I kissed her,* or *I kissed her, since she was standing there and I couldn't think of anything else to do.* The fact that such grammatical structures are familiar, easily available to the literate mind, and usable in most contexts should have some influence, however little, on the idea expressed.

Or consider how few ways English provides for expressing *is*-ness involving subjects and complements. The writer is ordinarily stuck with a Subject-Linking Verb-Complement structure; and this structure, along with its semantic content, not only influences what he has to say but also limits his choices of bound and free modifiers and their placement in the sentence. As an example of the problem, here is a sentence written by a student:

> *One of the most striking features of plays in this genre* [modern realistic drama] *is the compromise between the events of everyday life and traditional forms of art.*

This is a typical example of Christensen's *pretzel prose,* which he has diagnosed so clearly. But the choices available to the student for producing a better sentence are to a surprising degree limited by (1) the context, which we will here ignore; (2) the ideas implied in words like *striking features, compromise,* and so on; (3) the grammatical constructions available to express the idea; (4) the reality or truth of the idea. I consulted an expert writer who is also a scholar in the drama, and asked him: Can you rewrite the sentence to make it readable, grammatical and truthful? [1] He quickly jotted down four versions, with his comments:

> (A) *One of the most striking features of modern realistic drama is the compromise which playwrights always make between the demands of traditional art and the events of everyday life.*
>
> But this sentence is still a joylessly long buzz of words. I'll try again:
>
> (B) *one very striking feature of modern realistic drama is its compromise between reality and art. However earnestly the playwright wants to depict everyday life, he alters it to fit it into dramatic form.*
>
> Once more:
>
> (C) *The trouble with modern realistic drama is that form compromises fact.* [*Plus second sentence to explain.*]
>
> You will object that in my second and third tries I've spoiled the game by using more than one sentence. This, however, is the best way out of the difficulty—the real difficulty being that the original "bad" sentence attempts to include too much. So, to put it effectively, one expresses the nugget idea in a sentence of the fewest possible words; then, in one or more sentences following, one expands and explains. The opening sentence may be simply factual, or enigmatic, or even sensational: its communicative intention is to catch attention, even perhaps to startle and challenge attention, so that the reader wants to read on.[2]
>
> I'll try a razzle-dazzle version:
>
> (D) *Realistic drama is a lie. The playwright pretends to show the truth of everyday life, to tell it like it is. But he is so trapped by the demands of dramatic technique that he compromises the truth, or even forgets it, long before his play is written.*
>
> Maybe I'd better not try any more! Thanks for the game: better than solitaire, which I never play anyway.

I have gone a long way round to make a point about whether form does, or does not, generate content. Where both Christensen and Mrs. Johnson may err in their premises is in taking too seriously the idea of

---

[1] When I tried a revision of the sentence, I wrote this: *In modern realistic drama, the most striking feature is that the author is forced to compromise between the demands of traditional art and the events, as he experiences them, of everyday life.* The revision is bad, perhaps as bad as the original; I didn't know the subject and was afraid to say anything specific about it. My consultant's first comment: "Change *the most striking* to *one of the most striking* because *the most* here is simply not true. I would also change *author* to *playwright*—for exactness."

[2] Note how my consultant's own sentences, scribbled down in haste, exemplify nicely Christensen's excellent theoretical statement on the good cumulative sentence. The base clauses are short and clear. The free modifiers add to, explain, and qualify the ideas presented in the base clauses.

"generating." Unfortunately, the term implies an act of creation. Looking at my newest desk dictionary (*The American Heritage*), I find that it defines *generate* as meaning (1) "to bring into existence; cause to be; produce"; (2) "to engender (offspring); beget." As Christensen uses it, the term is probably misleading, since it seems unlikely that a grammatical form, in any precise sense of the expression, "brings into existence" any ideas.

The relationship between grammar and idea needs to be stated with greater accuracy than either Mrs. Johnson or Christensen has been able to state it. For such a statement, I suggest that we return to Richard Weaver:

> Rhetoric in its practice is a matter of selection and arrangement, but conventional grammar imposes restraints upon both of these. All this amounts to saying what every sensitive user of language has sometimes felt; namely, that language is not a purely passive instrument, but that, owing to this public acceptance, while you are doing something with it, it is doing something with you, or with your intention. It does not exactly fight back; rather it has a set of postures and balances which somehow modify your thrusts and holds. The sentence form is certainly one of these. You pour into it your meaning, and it deflects, and molds into certain shapes. (*The Ethics of Rhetoric* [Chicago, 1965], p. 116)

The central metaphor here is one of wrestling, and it expresses very well the reality of the conflict between what the writer wants to say and what the grammatical choices available to him keep "persuading" him to say. Earlier, I used the words *suggest* and *influence.* Like two crafty, powerful courtiers, Idea and Grammar whisper, cajole, and argue at the ear of the writer—more, sometimes they demand. Sometimes one of them gets his way almost by force.

Now for a conclusion about grammar, a conclusion which is implied in certain words in my title: "the practical uses of a grammatical system."

First, all grammatical systems are at bottom surprisingly unsystematic. This is particularly true of school grammars, which are likely to leave a lot of philosophical loose ends hanging out. Edward Sapir put it best: "Unfortunately, or luckily, no language is tyrannically consistent. All grammars leak" (*Language* [New York, 1949], p. 38). We should accept Sapir's judgment gracefully and be prepared to spend the rest of our lives bailing furiously.

Second, any school grammar which is designed to be taught, learned, and used should employ as many strategies of writing the good sentence as it can. Since (for example) balance, antithesis, and the periodic sentence are excellent devices, we should teach them right along with Christensen's ideas about the base clause and the free modifier. We should avoid telling students that they are learning a tight system, instead that they are learning practical ways to write more truthfully and clearly.

Third, the good sentence is a product of art and craft. It depends on:

(a) precision of word choice
(b) truth of statement
(c) context of statement
(d) shape of statement
—grammatical shape
—rhetorical shape

Items (a) and (d) represent important issues in "coding" the writer's message. On the level of sentencing, both grammar and rhetoric force the writer to ask a single question: *How can I make a true statement which my reader will understand and find convincing?* Unless he uses precise wording, and the appropriate grammatical/rhetorical "shapes," the writer's code will not be understood and his statement will not be persuasive.

I left one thing out of this formula, which should be ingested by the reader with as much salt as he needs to make it palatable. It is that no grammar will be successfully taught or learned without intelligence, luck, and God's grace.

Part Four

The Paragraph and Beyond

> *The paragraph, indeed, is the microcosm of the discourse and admits and demands a very extended study in any scheme of instruction in English.*
>
> ALEXANDER BAIN

Present-day efforts to discover new insights into the composing process are sometimes called "new rhetorics." Among the most promising of the new rhetorics is that area of study concerned with patterns of organization in units of prose "beyond the sentence." Research in this area has opened up intriguing new vistas for understanding the paragraph and longer passages. Edward P. J. Corbett has said that the May 1966 issue of *College Composition and Communication*, which included a symposium on the paragraph, "has more sensible things to say about the rhetoric of the paragraph than have ever been gathered together between the covers of a single publication."

One approach has grown out of the study of tagmemics, a study pioneered by Kenneth L. Pike, Richard Young, and Alton Becker at the University of Michigan. Borrowing from the field of physics, tagmemic theorists argue that language can be fully comprehended only when viewed from three perspectives: as *particle*, as *wave*, and as *field*. In "A Tagmemic Approach to Paragraph Analysis," Becker explains what it means to view a paragraph in these three ways. Although tagmemic theory may seem unnecessarily abstruse, it has many practical uses for the public school classroom: I have personally seen Becker's concept of paragraph structure successfully taught at the ninth-grade level. Those teachers who are willing to read Becker with care and to develop appropriate activities based on his work will be amply rewarded for their efforts.

In "A Generative Rhetoric of the Paragraph," Christensen demonstrates that the paragraph is an expanded cumulative sentence, the base clause and added elements of the sentence corresponding to the topic sentence and added sentences of the paragraph. Both Becker and Christensen provide some important new approaches which previously have been unavailable to the teacher of composition. In many ways the two systems are alike, one of the main differences being that Becker employs semantic description ("Topic, Restriction, Illustration"), whereas Christensen relies on a numerical classification to indicate the level of generality.

Another way of looking at the structure of prose appears in Paul Rodgers' essay "The Stadium of Discourse." According to Rodgers, the key to structural relationships lies "in the psychology of literary intention." An author may complete what he has to say in one simple statement, but if he needs to expand a given statement, he may do so in one of two ways: by either *adjunction* or *accretion*. Rodgers explains *adjunction* as the process of adding explanatory material, and *accretion* as that of adding new material which provides an even deeper insight into the subject. When several such units are combined into one coherent whole, they form a new unit which Rodgers calls the "stadium of discourse." A stadium may include several sentences, but it is not necessarily a paragraph.

Yet another method is revealed in Josephine Miles' "What We Compose." After looking at many pages of printed text, hoping to find a simple pattern of organization, Miles hit upon a solution which includes the following features: (1) assertion (the subject-predicate relationship), (2) development (modifying elements), and (3) connection (conjunctions and prepositions). In her article Miles examines selected passages from literature to illustrate how these features distinguish "the grain of the living wood . . . , the character of the language by which we live and compose."

Do textbook admonitions accurately reflect current practice in paragraph structure? Richard A. Meade and W. Geiger Ellis ("Paragraph Development in a Modern Age of Rhetoric") give a resounding "No." After analyzing three hundred paragraphs from professional journals and from letters to newspaper editors, these investigators found that more than half the paragraphs analyzed would not fit into categories described in textbooks, and that the most popular kinds of development are development by examples and by a combination of methods. Meade and Ellis not only give some sound advice about teaching composition but also provide some provocative leads about further research.

Frequently a rhetorical principle that can be extended from the sentence to the paragraph can also be extended to the fully developed essay. In "A Generative Rhetoric of the Essay," Frank J. D'Angelo shows how coordinate and subordinate relationships which Christensen explored in the sentence and the paragraph also function in the essay. The value of this approach should not be overlooked. It means that once mastered, a small feature may have many uses far beyond its original purpose. Like the pebble dropped into a pool, the small feature often sends its ripples far out into unexpected places.

A Tagmemic Approach to Paragraph Analysis

A. L. BECKER

In order to be of more than peripheral interest to rhetoricians and literary scholars, linguistic research must move beyond the sentence, even though passing over this threshold vastly complicates linguistic theory. However, the initial steps toward a theory of language which explains both grammatical and rhetorical patterns can probably be made by extending grammatical theories now used in analyzing and describing sentence structure. The purpose of this paper is to illustrate how one such theory, tagmemics, can be extended to the description of paragraphs.[1]

Tagmemic theory can be characterized in many different ways depending upon one's primary assumptions about language. Among the various linguistic theories currently respectable—signals grammar, slot and substitution grammar, finite-state grammar, phrase structure grammar, and transformational grammar—tagmemics is probably closest to slot and substitution grammar, the sort of grammar exemplified in Charles C. Fries' *The Structure of English* and A. S. Hornby's *A Guide to Patterns and Usage in English* (to mention two works known to most English teachers), although it would be false to describe tagmemics as merely a slot and substitution grammar, for it includes features of all these grammars and is probably the broadest and most flexible of them—and it is the only one of them which contains theoretical motivation for carrying language description beyond the sentence.

In tagmemic theory, the central concept in the process of parti-

College Composition and Communication, vol. 16 (December 1965), pp. 237–242.

[1] This work is the result of my collaboration with Kenneth L. Pike and Richard Young in research on rhetoric, sponsored in part by the Center for Research on Language and Language Behavior, University of Michigan, under a grant from the Language Development Branch, U. S. Office of Education. Tagmemic theory is developed in Kenneth L. Pike, *Language in Relation to a Unified Theory of the Structure of Human Behavior* (Glendale: Summer Institute of Linguistics, Part I, 1954; Part II, 1955; Part III, 1960). See also Robert E. Longacre, *Grammar Discovery Procedure: A Field Manual* (The Hague: Mouton and Co., 1964); for a brief description using English examples, Robert E. Longacre, "String Constituent Analysis," *Language*, XXXVI (1960), pp. 63–68.

tioning patterns is the tagmeme, which can be defined as the class of grammatical forms that function in a particular grammatical relationship. For instance, the grammatical relationship (or function) *subject* can be manifested by a limited number of grammatical forms or constructions, including noun phrases, pronouns, nominalized verb phrases, clauses, etc. Another way of defining tagmemes might be to say that they are spots or slots in a system where substitution is possible, and they include both the functional spot or slot and the set of substitutable forms. As composites of both form and function, tagmemes reflect an important axiom in tagmemic theory: that meaning cannot be separated from form or form from meaning without serious distortion. Put in terms of partitioning, this means that a whole is not the sum of its parts (if by "parts" we mean only the isolated segments), but only of its parts plus their relationships.

The concept of the tagmeme is useful in the rhetorical analysis of structures beyond the sentence. It gives us criteria for partitioning discourse in a significant way, though it is by no means a completely new idea to divide a sequence of discourse into functional slots and filler classes. The traditional syllogism can be viewed as a system of slots and filler classes; there are rigid restrictions on how each slot (or term in a premise) can be filled, and only a limited number of patterns (or moods) are correct. Also the strategies of argumentation and the forms of definition have traditionally been conceived of as something like functional slots and classes in a larger pattern in which expectations are aroused and fulfilled.

Before I illustrate the use of the tagmeme in describing paragraph structure, let me first emphasize that partitioning a paragraph into functional parts reveals only one aspect of its structure. Like sentences, paragraphs are multisystemic. In addition to its systems of functional parts, a paragraph has two other structural features in the tagmemic approach: there is continuity or concord between the parts, and there is a system of semantic relationships in which the reader's expectations are aroused and fulfilled.[2] Each of these three perspectives on the paragraph is necessary for a complete description, and the isolation of only one perspective tends to distort the description somewhat by suppressing other features of paragraph structure.

To further limit my focus, I will discuss only the structure of expository paragraphs. Narrative, descriptive, and argumentative paragraphs have quite different structures from those I will present, though the methods

---

[2] This three-part definition of the paragraph reflects the assumption in tagmemic theory that three perspectives are necessary to a complete description of behavior: a *particle* perspective, which views behavior as made up of discrete contrasting parts; a *wave* perspective, which emphasizes the unsegmentable continuum of behavior; and a *field* view, in which units are seen in context (sequence, class, or ordered set). This article focuses on paragraph tagmemes as particles in sequence. For a fuller explanation of tagmemic trimodalism, see Kenneth L. Pike, "Language as Particle, Wave, and Field," *The Texas Quarterly*, II (Summer, 1959), pp. 37–54; and Pike, "Beyond the Sentence," *CCC*, XV (October 1964), pp. 129–135.

of analysis I use are the same, and the grammatical markers of paragraph slots are nearly identical for all types of paragraphs.

There seem to be two major patterns of paragraphing in expository writing. These two patterns can be derived experimentally by giving students samples of expository paragraphs and asking them to partition them in ways that seem significant. There are disagreements about how particular paragraphs ought to be partitioned, but also a striking percentage of agreement, especially after students have partitioned enough paragraphs to recognize recurring patterns.

The first expository pattern has three functional slots, which can be labelled **T** (topic), **R** (restriction), and **I** (illustration). In the **T** slot the topic is stated, in the **R** slot the topic is narrowed down or defined, and in the **I** slot the topic, as restricted in **R**, is illustrated or described at lower level of generality. These slots seem to reflect what Kenneth Burke calls "an internal form," a natural way of talking or writing about something.[3]

These three slots usually correspond to three levels of generality in the paragraphs, and one of the signals of a new slot is a noticeable shift in level of generality. The recent work of Francis Christensen emphasizes this aspect of paragraph structure;[4] indeed, he makes layers of generality central to his theory. It is, however, extremely difficult to be very precise about one's ability to recognize, say, *Hereford* as a particular instance of *cow*—difficult, that is, without a lexical theory which makes levels of generality explicit.

Each of the slots in a **TRI** paragraph can be filled in various ways; that is, certain rhetorical types of sentences typically occur in certain slots. For instance, the **T** slot can be filled by a simple proposition, or a proposition implying a contrast, comparison, partition, etc. The **R** slot is frequently a restatement of **T** at a lower level of generality, a definition of **T** or a term in **T**, a metaphoric restatement of **T**, etc. The **I** slot can be filled by one or more examples (often in a narrative or descriptive pattern), an extended analogy, a series of specific comparisons, etc. For each slot there is a general function and a set of potential fillers. Each slot and its fillers constitute, therefore, a paragraph-level tagmeme.

The following paragraph is an example of the **TRI** pattern:

> (**T**) The English Constitution—that indescribable entity—is a living thing, growing with the growth of men, and assuming ever-varying forms in accordance with the subtle and complex laws of human character. (**R**) It is the child of wisdom and chance. (**I**) The wise men of 1688 moulded it into the shape we know, but the chance that George I could not speak English gave it one of its essential

[3] Kenneth Burke, *Counter-Statement* (Chicago: University of Chicago Press, 1957), pp. 45–46.

[4] Francis Christensen, "A Generative Rhetoric of the Paragraph," *CCC*, XVI (October 1965), pp. 114–156. See also Christensen, "A Generative Rhetoric of the Sentence," *CCC*, XIV (October 1963), pp. 155–161.

> peculiarities—the system of a Cabinet independent of the Crown and subordinate to the Prime Minister. The wisdom of Lord Grey saved it from petrification and set it upon the path of democracy. Then chance intervened once more. A female sovereign happened to marry an able and pertinacious man, and it seemed likely that an element which had been quiescent within it for years—the element of irresponsible administrative power—was about to become its predominant characteristic and change completely the direction of its growth. But what chance gave, chance took away. The Consort perished in his prime, and the English Constitution, dropping the dead limb with hardly a tremor, continued its mysterious life as if he had never been.
>
> Lytton Strachey, *Queen Victoria*

In this paragraph we note that the **T** slot is filled by a metaphoric proposition *(The English Constitution . . . is a living thing . . .)*; the **R** slot by a mere specific instance of that metaphor *(living thing* → child); and the **I** slot by a set of examples ordered historically in one dimension and categorically according to the "parentage" *(wisdom and chance)* of the "child" (the Constitution) in the other.

The second major pattern of expository paragraphs has two slots, which can be labelled **P** (problem) and **S** (solution). The **P** slot, often in question form, is the statement of a problem or an effect which is to be explained, and the **S** slot states the solution or cause of **P.** If it is extended, the **S** slot very often has an internal structure of **TRI** (an example of embedding at the paragraph level). This second pattern is shown in the following paragraph, which also illustrates two other features of paragraph structure (which will be considered later)—that is, the combining of what could be two paragraphs into a single paragraph (i.e., the slot **S** occurs twice, giving two contrasting answers to the question in **P**), and the appending of transitional sentences to formally unified paragraphs. These transitional sentences make paragraphs indeterminate units, for, as transitions, they are shared by two paragraphs and usually could occur as well at the end of one paragraph as at the beginning of the next. The majority of the disagreements in experimental student partitioning of paragraphs involved transitional sentences.

> (**P**) How obsolete is Hearn's judgment? (**S_1**) (**T**) On the surface the five gentlemen of Japan do not themselves seem to be throttled by this rigid society of their ancestors. (**R**) Their world is in fact far looser in its demands upon them than it once was. (**I**) Industrialization and the influence of the West have progressively softened the texture of the web. Defeat in war badly strained it. A military occupation, committed to producing a democratic Japan, pulled and tore at it. (**S_2**) (**T**) But it has not disappeared. (**R**) It is still the invisible adhesive that seals the nationhood of the Japanese. (**I**)

Shimizu, Sanada, Yamazaki, Kisfi and Hirohito were all born within its bonds. Despite their individual work, surroundings and opinions, they have lived most of their lives as cogs geared into a group society. Literally as well as figuratively speaking, none of them has a lock on his house door. [transition] In 1948, long after Hearn had gone to his grave, a Japanese sociologist, Takegi Kawashima, could write with much justice about the behavior of his contemporaries: [A long quotation follows, beginning a new paragraph.]

Frank Gibney, *Five Gentlemen of Japan*

Although there are more kinds of expository paragraphs than these two, I would say that the majority of them fall into one of these two major types. Many expository paragraphs which at first appear to be neither **TRI** or **PS** can be interpreted as variations of these patterns. In this sense these two patterns can be called kernel paragraph patterns. Furthermore, narrative, descriptive, and argumentative paragraphs frequently occur in expository works and sometimes combine with expository paragraphs to produce mixed patterns. There are also minor paragraph forms (usually transitional paragraphs or simple lists)—and, finally, there are "bad" paragraphs, like poorly constructed, confusing sentences.

The variations of these two patterns (**TRI** and **PS**) can be seen as the results of four kinds of operations: deletion, reordering, addition, and combination. Slots may be deleted, especially the **R** slot—though this slot appears to be deleted more often in poor student paragraphs than in high quality expository writing. Frequently, especially at the beginnings and endings of essays, the pattern is reordered by inversion, e.g. **TRI** → **IRT.** Inversion gives the paragraph a completeness or closure that is lacking in the more open-ended **TRI** order. Students, asked to evaluate paragraphs *out of context,* prefer **IRT** paragraphs almost exclusively when the choice is between **TRI** and **IRT**. Another way of making a **TRI** paragraph less open-ended is by addition—for example, repeating the **T** slot at the end (e.g. $\mathbf{T_1RI} \rightarrow \mathbf{T_1RIT_1}$ in which the fillers of the two **T** slots are semantically equivalent). This expanded form of the **TRI** pattern seems to occur most frequently when the discourse is complex or long and the reader is not likely to retain the controlling idea of the paragraph. And, finally, two paragraphs may be combined, especially when they are either contrastive or parallel semantically. The paragraph by Gibney above contains an illustration of paragraph combination.

So far in this article the procedures for partitioning paragraphs have been pretty much intuitive; that is, I have not talked about formal markers of paragraph structure. I have generalized about the patterns my students and I find, and I have sketched out the basis for a taxonomy of expository paragraph patterns. Now I would like to describe the formal markers of paragraph tagmemes.

The formal signals of the internal tagmenic structure of paragraphs are both rather indeterminant and redundant. For instance, there are almost no simple markers of paragraph slots similar to the relatively simple plural or tense markers in English grammar. The markers of paragraph tagmemes are complex—usually redundant combinations of graphic, lexical, grammatical, and phonological signals.

The simplest of these is the graphic marker, indentation, which, like other punctuation marks, is related to all three linguistic hierarchies (i.e. lexical, grammatical, and phonological). Indentation sets off a unit which has a certain kind of internal structure allowable by the rules of the language, just as an independent clause is punctuated by a period or a period substitute. At the paragraph level, however, the grammatical constraints are much looser than, say, at the phrase level. This greater grammatical freedom allows the writer to create interesting tensions in paragraphing by skewing the lexical, grammatical, and graphic markers of the paragraph—similar to enjambment in poetry where the poet uses the end of a line (a graphic marker) as a device to achieve emphasis in counterpoint with regular grammatical and lexical emphasis.

The lexical markers of paragraphs are of two sorts, equivalence classes[5] and lexical transitions. In the Strachey paragraph above, the lexical *head* of the paragraph is the term *English Constitution,* which designates an equivalence class that occurs throughout the paragraph *(English Constitution, indescribable entity, It, it, . . . , English Constitution).* The domain of this equivalence class is the entire paragraph. Other lexical equivalence classes in the paragraph are dependent on this head class, and their domains extend over only parts of the paragraph. For instance, the domain of the class which includes the human forces which shaped the constitution *(wise men of 1688, George I, . . . , The Consort)* covers only the **I** slot and is a lexical marker of the **I** slot—that is, a feature of the structure of the paragraph which allows readers to partition it in predictable ways. A further study of the lexical equivalence classes in the paragraph reveals that the domains of these classes clearly distinguish the three slots (**TRI**) of the paragraph.

Lexical transitions are words and phrases which mark the semantic concord of the paragraph, words like *but* and *then* in slot **I** of the Strachey paragraph. Certain of these words are closely associated with particular slots: slot **I** is often marked by *for example,* slot **R** by *in other words,* etc. Lexical transitions may also signal continuation of a slot, e.g. such words as *furthermore, likewise,* or (as in the Strachey paragraph) *then.*

Although the paragraph seems most clearly marked as a lexical unit, chiefly by the equivalence classes, paragraph tagmemes are also marked by

[5] The theory of equivalence classes or equivalence chains is from Zellig S. Harris, *Discourse Analysis Reprints* (The Hague: Mouton and Co., 1963), pp. 7–10. Tagmemic discourse analysis is developed in Kenneth L. Pike, "Discourse Analysis and Tagmeme Matrices," *Oceanic Linguistics,* III (Summer, 1964), pp. 5–25.

numerous grammatical constraints with domains beyond the sentence. There are clear, though not yet adequately defined, relationships between the domains of the lexical equivalence classes and the grammar of the sentences in the paragraph. Though these relationships are many and complex, a few of the more interesting and subtle relationships can be mentioned here. I will concentrate on grammatical parallelism and the sequence of verbs.

A sequence of lexical units in an equivalence class, including substitutes like pronouns and demonstratives, establishes what might be called lexical parallelism. These lexical units have certain grammatical roles (e.g. subject, object, agent, locative, etc.) in the sentences of a paragraph, and, to a great extent, these grammatical roles are maintained throughout the paragraph. Consequently, major changes in the grammatical roles of equivalence classes, especially the head classes, signal either new slots or new paragraphs. In the Strachey paragraph, for instance, the head class (the *English Constitution* class) fills the subject slot in the first two sentences, which are grammatically and lexically parallel. Then, in the **I** slot, this lexical class shifts to the object slot *(The wise men of 1688 moulded it. . . .)* and remains there in the following sentence *(The wisdom of Lord Grey saved it. . . .)*, while a new lexical class (human agents of change) fills the subject slot in these sentences. This shift is another marker of the **I** slot in the paragraph, and it illustrates the clear relationship of grammatical patterns in a sequence. One particular pattern which seems to have as its chief function the continuance of lexical and grammatical parallelism (though it does not appear in the illustrations I have given) is the passive transformation; the passive allows the writer to retain grammatical focus on a particular lexical class in a discourse.

Verb sequences are also important markers of paragraph structure. A shift in verb form frequently marks a slot in a paragraph. Expanded verb forms (e.g. the "progressive" and "perfect" forms) seem especially important in marking major shifts in focus in a discourse, particularly in paragraphs, and shifts in tense likewise usually mark new paragraph slots. The **I** slot in the Strachey paragraph is marked by a shift to past tense, and the changes in verb form in the Gibney paragraph also correspond to the slot structure. These constraints on verb form, however, need to be specified more precisely; we appear to have but scratched the surface of a very subtle area of inquiry, the sequence of verb forms in English.

Finally, there are the phonological markers of paragraph structure. Paragraph tagmemes seem to be marked by shifts in pitch register, tempo, and volume when paragraphs are read aloud.[6] While these signals can be perceived by a trained phonetician, they have not been adequately described in the laboratory, and their written counterparts have not been identified.

---

[6] These phonological signals are discussed in Kenneth L. Pike, *Language*, Part I (Glendale: Summer Institute of Linguistics, 1954), pp. 66–72.

This paper rests on the evidence that readers can partition paragraphs in a consistent and predictable way, that there are shared conventions of grouping sentences into higher-level units, and that there are structural cues which signal these patterns beyond the sentence. In outlining the tagmemic approach to paragraph analysis, however, I have made at least two major omissions. I have not, first of all, acknowledged our debts to traditional rhetoric, though the reader has undoubtedly recognized them. The similarities are many; it would be surprising if one were to find something entirely new in a field as old and as diligently studied as rhetoric. What is new, I think, is the attempt to relate rhetorical and grammatical patterns and to use a few general concepts to describe language patterns from phonemes to paragraphs and, hopefully, beyond paragraphs.

The second major omission is that I have not discussed rhetorical field structure—the network of semantic categories that, for instance, allows us to add to Strachey's paragraph: we carry his illustrations into the twentieth century without any difficulty, continuing to specify the alternating forces of wisdom and chance that have shaped the historical development of the English Constitution. It is through field analysis that we begin to understand the organic nature of the paragraph, its ability, like a poem's, to shape itself once its dimensions have been specified.[7]

---

[7] Field theory is described broadly in Edward R. Fagan, *Field: A Process for Teaching Literature* (University Park, Penn.: The Penn. State University Press, 1965), and it is applied to problems of rhetoric in Kenneth L. Pike, "Beyond the Sentence," *CCC*, XV (Oct., 1964), pp. 129–135.

A Generative Rhetoric of the Paragraph

FRANCIS CHRISTENSEN

In my article "A Generative Rhetoric of the Sentence," I said that the principles used there in analyzing the sentence were no less applicable to the paragraph. My purpose here is to make good that claim, to show that the paragraph has, or may have, a structure as definable and traceable as that of the sentence and that it can be analyzed in the same way. In fact, since writing that paper, I have come to see that the parallel between sentence and paragraph is much closer than I suspected, so close, indeed, that as Josephine Miles put it (in a letter) the paragraph seems to be only a macro-sentence or meta-sentence.

The chapters on the paragraph in our textbooks are so nearly alike in conception that one could almost say that, apart from the examples, the only striking difference is in the choice of *indention* or *indentation.* The prescription is always the same: the writer should work out a topic sentence and then choose one of the so-called methods of paragraph development to substantiate it. The topic sentence may appear at the beginning or at the end of the paragraph or anywhere in between, or it may be merely "implied," a sort of ectoplasmic ghost hovering over the paragraph. Besides this, some books speak of "paragraph movement"—chronological (as in narrative), spatial (as in description), logical (as in discursive writing). If the movement is logical, it may be inductive or deductive or a combination of the two, and some books offer diagrams, as systems analysts use flow charts, to picture the thought funneling down from the topic sentence or down to it.

This prescription for writers and the analysis it is based on are even more unworkable than the conventional treatment of the sentence as simple-compound-complex, with emphasis on the complex, or as loose-balanced-periodic, with emphasis on the periodic. I doubt that many of us write many paragraphs the way we require our charges to write them or that we could find many paragraphs that exemplify the methods of development or the patterns of movement.[1]

From *Notes Toward a New Rhetoric* by Francis Chistensen, pp. 52–81, Copyright © 1967 by Francis Christensen. Reprinted by permission of Harper & Row, Publishers, Inc. Originally appeared in *College Composition and Communication*, vol. 16 (October 1965).

[1] In this article I propose to deal only with the paragraphs of discursive writing and to exclude from these the short introductory and transitional and concluding paragraphs.

First, the methods of paragraph development. These methods are real, but they are simply methods of development—period. They are no more relevant to the paragraph than, on the short side, to the sentence or, on the long side, to a run of several paragraphs or to a paper as long as this or a chapter. They are the topics of classical rhetoric. They are the channels our minds naturally run in whether we are writing a sentence or a paragraph or planning a paper. There is no point in restricting a class (as for a whole semester in a freshman course I once taught) to a single method of development until the last week, when we reached what the textbook called a "combination of methods." It is almost impossible to write a paragraph without employing a combination of methods or to find paragraphs that do not.

In "A Lesson from Hemingway," I maintained that in representational (or narrative-descriptive) writing, where the aim is to *picture* actions and objects, there are only three methods of development, or description, as I called them, only three things one can do to present an image. These methods are to point to (1) a quality or attribute or to (2) a detail or (3) to make a comparison. A single sentence may exemplify all three: "The gypsy was walking out toward the bull again, walking heel-and-toe, insultingly, like a ballroom dancer, the red shafts of the banderillos twitching with his walk"—Hemingway. These methods are exactly parallel to the methods of development or support in discursive writing. The great difference is that in representational writing the methods are so few and in discursive writing so many. In either kind of writing the methods of description or development are hard to discern except in the light of what may be called a "structural analysis."

In the light of such a structural analysis, most paragraphs are like the sentences I called "cumulative." They exemplify the four principles proposed for the rhetoric of the sentence. Let us think of the topic sentence as parallel to the base clause of a sentence and the supporting sentences as parallel to the added sentence modifiers: clusters, absolutes, and nonrestrictive subordinate and relative clauses. (1) Then it is obvious that there could be no paragraphs without *addition.* (2) When a supporting sentence is added, both writer and reader must see the *direction of modification* or *direction of movement.* Discerning the direction is easier in the sentence because the sentence is self-contained and the elements added differ in form from the base clause. The direction of movement in the paragraph is explained below. The failure to see the relation of each upcoming sentence to what has gone before is probably one source of the difficulty many people have in reading. (3) When sentences are added to develop a topic or subtopic, they are usually at a lower *level of generality*—usually, but not always, because sometimes an added sentence is more general than the one it is added to. (4) Finally, the more sentences the writer adds, the denser the *texture.* The paragraphs our students write are likely to be as thin-textured as their sentences, and teachers can use this structural analysis of the paragraph to *generate* paragraphs of greater depth.

I have arranged the details of this approach to the paragraph under nine headings.

1. The Paragraph May Be Defined as a Sequence of Structurally Related Sentences.

By a sequence of structurally related sentences I mean a group of sentences related to one another by coordination and subordination. If the first sentence of a paragraph is the topic sentence, the second is quite likely to be a comment on it, a development of it, and therefore subordinate to it. The third sentence may be coordinate with the second sentence (as in this paragraph) or subordinate to it. The fourth sentence may be coordinate with either the second or third (or with both if they themselves are coordinate, as in this paragraph) or subordinate to the third. And so on. A sentence that is not coordinate with any sentence above it or subordinate to the next above it, breaks the sequence. The paragraph has begun to drift from its moorings, or the writer has unwittingly begun a new paragraph.

2. The Top Sentence of the Sequence Is the Topic Sentence.

The topic sentence is comparable to the base clause of a cumulative sentence. It is the sentence on which the others depend. It is the sentence whose assertion is supported or whose meaning is explicated or whose parts are detailed by the sentences added to it. In the examples that follow, it will always be marked 1, for the top level.

3. The Topic Sentence Is Nearly Always the First Sentence of the Sequence.

The contrast between deductive and inductive, or between analytic and synthetic as it is sometimes put, seems to have led us to assume that the one kind of movement is as common as the other and that the topic sentence therefore is as likely to appear at the end as at the beginning. The many scores of paragraphs I have analyzed for this study do not bear out this assumption. Except as noted in point 7 below, the topic sentence occurs almost invariably at the beginning. In fact, I do not have clear-cut examples of topic sentences in the other theoretically possible positions. Readers may check their own actual practice and mine in this piece.

In connected writing, the topic sentence varies greatly in how explicit it is in designating the thesis of the paragraph. Sometimes it is quite explicit; sometimes it is a mere sign pointing to the turn the new paragraph is going to take. Sometimes it is the shortest sentence of the paragraph; sometimes it is not even a grammatically complete sentence. Sometimes it is a question. It seems to me that these differences are irrelevant, provided only that the reader gets the signal and the writer remembers the signal he has called.

4. Simple Sequences Are of Two Sorts—Coordinate and Subordinate.

Here the parallel between sentence and paragraph becomes fully evident. In analyzing the rhetoric of the sentence, I described what I called the two-level and the multilevel sentence. Here is an example of each and a paragraph exactly parallel in structure with each. The two sets of terms seem to me necessary to put the emphasis where it is needed in teaching and to avoid conflict with the use in grammar of *coordination* and *subordination.*

A. Two-Level Sentence

1 [Lincoln's] words still linger on the lips—
  2 eloquent and cunning, yes,
  2 vindictive and sarcastic in political debate,
  2 rippling and ribald in jokes,
  2 reverent in the half-formed utterance of prayer.

Alistair Cooke

A. Coordinate Sequence Paragraph

1 This is the essence of the religious spirit—the sense of power, beauty, greatness, truth infinitely beyond one's own reach, but infinitely to be aspired to.
  2 It invests men with pride in a purpose and with humility in accomplishment.
  2 It is the source of all true tolerance, for in its light all men see other men as they see themselves, as being capable of being more than they are, and yet falling short, inevitably, of what they can imagine human opportunities to be.
  2 It is the supporter of human dignity and pride and the dissolver of vanity.
  2 And it is the very creator of the scientific spirit; for without the aspiration to understand and control the miracle of life, no man would have sweated in a laboratory or tortured his brain in the exquisite search after truth.

Dorothy Thompson

B. Multilevel Sentence

1 A small Negro girl develops from the sheet of glare-frosted walk,
  2 walking barefooted,
    3 her brown legs striking and recoiling from the hot cement,
      4 her feet curling in,
        5 only the outer edges touching.

B. Subordinate Sequence Paragraph

1 The process of learning is essential to our lives.
  2 All higher animals seek it deliberately.

3 They are inquisitive and they experiment.

4 An experiment is a sort of harmless trial run of some action which we shall have to make in the real world; and this, whether it is made in the laboratory by scientists or by fox-cubs outside their earth.

5 The scientist experiments and the cub plays; both are learning to correct their errors of judgment in a setting in which errors are not fatal.

6 Perhaps this is what gives them both their air of happiness and freedom in these activities.

J. Bronowski, *The Common Sense of Science* (Vintage), p. 111.

The analytical procedure for discovering the structure is really quite simple. There is no problem in locating the base clause of a sentence, and one can assume—provisionally (see 6 and 7 below)—that the first sentence of a paragraph is the topic sentence. Then, going sentence by sentence through the paragraph, one searches in the sentences above for likenesses—that is, for evidences of coordination. In both sets of two examples, the second element is *unlike* the first one; it is different and so it is set down as subordinate—that is, it is indented and numbered level 2. With the third element the two sets part company. In the examples marked A, the third element is *like* the second, it is parallel to the second, and so it is set down as coordinate. The clearest mark of coordination is identity of structure at the beginning of the sentence. The fourth element is like both the second and third; and the fifth is like the second, third, and fourth. All the elements marked 2 have the same relation to one another; they are siblings. And because of this, they all have the same immediate relation to level 1, the base clause or topic sentence; they are all children of the same mother. In the examples marked B, on the other hand, the third element is *unlike* the second, and of course unlike the first; the fourth is unlike the third or any other above it, and so on. Search as you may, you will find no signs of parallelism. So, instead of two generations, there are five in the sentence and six in the paragraph. No element after the second is related immediately to level 1; it is related to it only through all of the intermediate generations.[2]

The fact that there are two kinds of sequences makes all the difference in what we can say about the paragraph.

It should be evident how we must treat the methods of development or support. In the coordinate sequence, all the coordinate sentences employ the *same* method—in paragraph A they enumerate the *results* or *effects*. In the subordinate sequence, every added sentence may, and likely will, employ a *different* method. There is no theoretic limit to the number of levels, and the

[2] I use *generation* here metaphorically, in the biological sense, not in the sense of "levels generated."

lists of methods in our textbooks are far from exhausting the whole range of what we may say in discursive writing to develop or support a topic.

It should be evident, also, that we need two separate sets of yardsticks for measuring such things as unity, coherence, and emphasis. Take coherence, for example. The repetition of structure in A is all that is necessary to join sentence to sentence at the same level. Any connectives other than the simple *and* for the last member would be an impertinence—*again, moreover, in the same vein, in addition* would be a hindrance rather than a help. But repetition of structure *is* necessary; like things in like ways is one of the imperatives of discursive writing. Any attempt to introduce variety in the sentence beginnings, by varying the pattern or by putting something before the subject, would be like trying to vary the columns of the Parthenon. In a subordinate sequence, just as clearly, repetition of structure must be avoided. Each added sentence, being different in the method of development, must be different in form. In a subordinate sequence, the problems of unity, coherence, and emphasis are altogether different—and more difficult.

Another paragraph will illustrate two other points. First, a writer sometimes intends a coordinate sequence but, like the dog that turns around once or twice before he settles down, takes, and sometimes wastes, a sentence or two before he begins his enumeration. (For other examples see paragraphs E and J.) Second, the coordinate sentences need not be identical in structure; they need only be like enough for the reader to place them. In this paragraph it is evident that all three sentences at level 3 present *examples.*

C. Coordinate Sequence

1 He [the native speaker] may, of course, speak a form of English that marks him as coming from a rural or an unread group.
  2 But if he doesn't mind being so marked, there's no reason why he should change.
    3 Samuel Johnson kept a Staffordshire burr in his speech all his life.
    3 In Burns's mouth the despised lowland Scots dialect served just as well as the "correct" English spoken by ten million of his southern contemporaries.
    3 Lincoln's vocabulary and his way of pronouncing certain words were sneered at by many better educated people at the time, but he seemed to be able to use the English language as effectively as his critics.

Bergen Evans, *Comfortable Words*, p. 6

5. The Two Sorts of Sequence Combine to Produce the Commonest Sort—the Mixed Sequence.

Simple sequences, especially coordinate ones, are not common. More often than not, subordinate sentences are added to add depth to coordinate sequences, and coordinate sentences are added to emphasize points made in subordinate sequences. The resulting mixed sequences reveal their origin as derived from either coordinate or subordinate sequences.

My justification for the term *generative* lies here. The teacher can, with perfect naturalness, suggest the addition of subordinate sentences to clarify and of coordinate sentences to emphasize or to enumerate. With these additions the writer is not padding; he is putting himself imaginatively in the reader's place and anticipating his questions and resistances. He is learning to treat his subject home.

D. Mixed Sequence—Based on Coordinate Sequence

1 The other [mode of thought] is the scientific method.
  2 It subjects the conclusions of reason to the arbitrament of hard fact to build an increasing body of tested knowledge.
  2 It refuses to ask questions that cannot be answered, and rejects such answers as cannot be provided except by Revelation.
  2 It discovers the relatedness of all things in the universe—of the motion of the moon to the influence of the earth and sun, of the nature of the organism to its environment, of human civilization to the conditions under which it is made.
  2 It introduces history into everything.
    3 Stars and scenery have their history, alike with plant species or human institutions, and
    nothing is intelligible without some knowledge of its past.
      4 As Whitehead has said, each event is the reflection or effect of every other event, past as well as present.
  2 It rejects dualism.
    3 The supernatural is in part the region of the natural that has not yet been understood, in part an invention of human fantasy, in part the unknowable.
    3 Body and soul are not separate entities, but two aspects of one organization, and
    Man is that portion of the universal world-stuff that has evolved until it is capable of rational and purposeful values.
      4 His place in the universe is to continue that evolution and to realize those values.

Julian Huxley, *Man in the Modern World*
(Mentor), pp. 146–147.

This paragraph suggests careful calculation of what could be left to the reader and what must be made more explicit. Huxley took a chance on the first two items. What he added to the third made it a two-level sentence. The sentences he added to the last two made the paragraph a mixed one. He was under no obligation to expand all five items equally. The writer's guide is his own sense of what the reader must be told. In our classes we must work to develop this sense. The difference is often the difference between self-expression and communication.

E. Mixed Sequence—Based on Coordinate Sequence

1 An obvious classification of meaning is that based on scope.

1 This is to say, meaning may be generalized (extended, widened) or it may be specialized (restricted, narrowed).

2 When we increase the scope of a word, we reduce the elements of its contents.

3 For instance *tail* (from OE *taegl*) in earlier times seems to have meant 'hairy caudal appendage, as of a horse.'

4 When we eliminated the hairiness (or the horsiness) from the meaning, we increased its scope, so that in Modern English the word means simply 'caudal appendage.'

4 The same thing has happened to Danish *hale,* earlier 'tail of a cow.'

5 In course of time the cow was eliminated, and in present-day Danish the word means simply 'tail,' having undergone a semantic generalization precisely like that of the English word cited;

the closely related Icelandic *hali* still keeps the cow in the picture.

3 Similarly, a *mill* was earlier a place for making things by the process of grinding, that is, for making meal.

4 The words *meal* and *mill* are themselves related, as one might guess from their similarity.

5 A mill is now simply a place for making things: the grinding has been eliminated, so that we may speak of a woolen mill, a steel mill, or even a gin mill.

3 The word *corn* earlier meant 'grain' and is in fact related to the word *grain.*

4 It is still used in this general sense in England, as in the "Corn Laws," but specifically it may mean either oats (for animals) or wheat (for human beings).

4 In American usage *corn* denotes maize, which is of course not at all what Keats meant in his "Ode to a Nightingale" when he described Ruth as standing "in tears amid the alien corn."

3 The building in which corn, regardless of its meaning, is stored is called a barn.

4 *Barn* earlier denoted a storehouse for barley; the word is in fact a compound of two Old English words, *bere* 'barley' and *aern* 'house.'

5 By elimination of a part of its earlier content, the scope of this word has been extended to mean a storehouse for any kind of grain.

5 American English has still further generalized by eliminating the grain, so that *barn* may mean also a place for housing livestock.

Thomas Pyles, *The Origins and Development of the English Language,* pp. 306–307.

Here the development has proceeded so far that the four coordinate sentences (level 3) have become in effect subtopic sentences. The paragraph could be subdivided, making them the topic sentences of a series of paragraphs. The long paragraph looks well on a book page; the shorter paragraphs would look more palatable in narrow newspaper columns. Either way, the effect would not be essentially different.

The problem of a reader tackling a long paragraph like this is to identify the coordinate sentences. He reads one 3rd-level sentence and then some sentences explaining it as an example of semantic generalization. He must be aware when he has come to the end of that explanation and must then shift his attention back to level 3. He must recognize the direction of movement. The first three 3rd-level sentences are easy to spot because like things have been put in like ways: the italicized words chosen as examples have been made the grammatical subject or apposed to the subject. But the opportunity to make a deft transition led the author to vary the pattern for the fourth. I have seen readers stumble at this point, and I have seen some make Danish *hale* parallel to the four English words.

F. Mixed Sequence—Based on Coordinate Sequence

1 This is a point so frequently not understood that it needs some dwelling on.

2 Consider how difficult it is to find a tenable argument that *thrown,* say, is intrinsically better than *throwed.*

3 We can hardly say that the simple sound is better.

4 For if it were, we would presumably also prefer *rown* to *rowed, hown* to *hoed, stown* to *strode,* and we don't.

3 Nor can we argue convincingly that *throwed* should be avoided because it did not occur in earlier English.

4 Many forms which occurred in earlier English cannot now be used.

5 As we mentioned earlier, *holp* used to be the past

tense form of *help; helped* was incorrect.
5 But we could not now say "He holp me a good deal."
2 As for "me and Jim," the statement that *I* should be used in the subject position begs the question.
3 One can ask why *I* should be the subject form, and to this there is no answer.
4 As a matter of fact, *you* was at one time the object form of the second person plural, *ye* being the subject form.
4 But no one objects now to a sentence like "You were there."

Paul Roberts

I have included this paragraph to illustrate further the kind of clues that mark coordination: at the first level 3, *we can hardly say: nor can we argue;* at level 5, *used to be: now;* at the second level 4, *was at one time: now.* At level 2 there are no verbal clues; the reader just has to recognize that "me and Jim" is another example like "throwed" to illustrate the point that needs dwelling on.

G. Mixed Sequence—Based on Subordinate Sequence

1 The purpose of science is to describe the world in an orderly scheme or language which will help us to look ahead.
2 We want to forecast what we can of the future behaviour of the world;
particularly we want to forecast how it would behave under several alternative actions of our own between which we are usually trying to choose.
3 This is a very limited purpose.
4 It has nothing whatever to do with bold generalizations about the universal workings of cause and effect.
4 It has nothing to do with cause and effect at all, or with any other special mechanism.
4 Nothing in this purpose, which is to order the world as an aid to decision and action, implies that the order must be of one kind rather than another.
5 The order is what we find to work, conveniently and instructively.
5 It is not something we stipulate;
it is not something we can dogmatise about.
5 It is what we find;
it is what we find useful.

J. Bronowski, *The Common Sense of Science*, pp. 70–71.

This would be a simple five-level sequence but for the repetition at levels 4 and 5. It is a fair guess that the desire for rhetorical emphasis generated these additions. With five statements there could be five 5th-level sentences, but the author has chosen to put them in three groups. This is a matter of paragraph punctuation (see 9 below).

H. Mixed Sequence—Based on Subordinate Sequence

1 Science as we know it indeed is a creation of the last three hundred years.

2 It has been made in and by the world that took its settled shape about 1660, when Europe at last shook off the long nightmare of religious wars and settled into a life of inquisitive trade and industry.

3 Science is embodied in those new societies;
it has been made by them and has helped to make them.

4 The medieval world was passive and symbolic;
it saw in the forms of nature the signatures of the Creator.

4 From the first stirrings of science among the Italian merchant adventurers of the Renaissance, the modern world has been an active machine.

5 That world became the everyday world of trade in the seventeenth century, and
the interests were appropriately astronomy and the instruments of voyage, among them the magnet.

5 A hundred years later, at the Industrial Revolution, the interest shifted to the creation and use of power.

6 This drive to extend the strength of man and what he can do in a day's work has remained our interest since.

7 In the last century it moved from steam to electricity.

7 Then in 1905, in that wonderful year when . . . he published papers which made outstanding advances in three different branches of physics, Einstein first wrote down the equations which suggested that matter and energy are interchangeable states.

7 Fifty years later, we command a reservoir of power in matter almost as large as the sun, which we now realize

manufactures its heat for us in just this
way, by the annihilation of its matter.
J. Bronowski, *The Common Sense of Science*, pp. 97–98.

Conventionally, the "movement" of this paragraph might be called chronological; but it is only roughly so—it leaps, and at levels 4, 5, and 7 it lingers. Note the marks of coordination: level 4, *the medieval . . . passive: the modern . . . active;* level 5, *the seventeenth century: a hundred years later;* level 7, depending on *since* at level 6, *in the last century: then in 1905: fifty years later.*

The first sentence at level 4 ("The medieval world . . .") is interesting because the topic sentence limits the time to "the last three hundred years." One could easily read through levels 1–5 skipping "The medieval world . . ." The sentence has been inserted—extralogically and extra-chronologically—in order to set up a contrast. Such inserted sentences are fairly common and were at first very puzzling to me. Occasionally, also, one encounters and is puzzled by a parenthetic sentence. Such sentences should be set off by parentheses, but all sentences so set off are not extrasequential.

6. Some Paragraphs Have No Top, No Topic, Sentence.

I. Paragraph without Topic Sentence

2 In Spain, where I saw him last, he looked profoundly Spanish.
3 He might have passed for one of those confidential street dealers who earn their living selling spurious Parker pens in the cafés of Málaga or Valencia.
4 Like them, he wore a faded chalk-striped shirt, a coat slung over his shoulders, a trim, dark moustache, and a sleazy, fat-cat smile.
4 His walk, like theirs, was a raffish saunter, and everything about him seemed slept in, especially his hair, a nest of small, wet serpents.
3 Had he been in Seville and his clothes been more formal, he could have been mistaken for a pampered elder son idling away a legacy in dribs and on drabs, the sort you see in windows along the Sierpes, apparently stuffed.
2 In Italy he looks Italian; in Greece, Greek:
wherever he travels on the Mediterranean coast, Tennessee Williams takes on a protective colouring which melts him into his background, like a lizard on a rock.
2 In New York or London he seems out of place, and is best explained away as a retired bandit.
3 Or a beach comber: shave the beard off any of the self-portraits Gauguin painted in Tahiti, soften the

features a little, and you have a sleepy outcast face that might well be Tennessee's.

Kenneth Tynan, *Curtains*, p. 266.

The three sentences marked level 2 are clearly coordinate. But there is no superordinate sentence to umbrella them; that is, there is no level 1, no topic sentence. With paragraphs such as this the topic can usually be inferred from the preceding paragraph. But sometimes the topic sentence is actually part of the preceding paragraph, arbitrarily and illogically separated. Or, as in J, the preceding paragraph *is* the topic sentence; the two paragraphs of J constitute a single sequence. The basic pattern here is like that of C; but with the series of three examples disjoined, they stand alone in a paragraph that has no topic sentence. Paragraphs without topic sentences are always coordinate sequences, either simple or mixed.

J. Topic Sentence in Preceding Paragraph

1 The mystical artist always sees patterns.
  2 The symbol, never quite real, tends to be expressed less and less realistically, and as the reality becomes abstracted the pattern comes forward.
    ¶3 The wings on Blake's angels do not look like real wings, nor are they there because wings belong to angels.
      4 They have been flattened, stylized, to provide a curving pointed frame, the setting required by the pattern of the composition.
    3 In Hindoo art and its branches, stylization reaches its height.
      4 Human figures are stylized far beyond the point of becoming a type;
      they too are made into patterns, schematic designs of the human body, an abstraction of humanity.
    3 In the case of an Eastern rug all desire to express any semblance of reality has gone.
      4 Such a work of art is pure decoration.
        5 It is the expression of the artist's final withdrawal from the visible world, essentially his denial of the intellect.

Edith Hamilton, *The Greek Way* (Mentor), p. 33.

7. Some Paragraphs Have Sentences at the Beginning or at the End That Do Not Belong to the Sequence.

Occasionally a paragraph has one or more introductory (I) or transitional (T) sentences before the sequence begins. And occasionally one has a sentence or more added after the sequence has run its course; that is, the first of such sentences is not coordinate with any sentence above it or subordinate to the one next above it. They are related to the sequence, but are not a part of it; they form a conclusion or coda (C) or provide a transition (T) to what follows. To save space, I have quoted only enough to establish that the sentences so marked are extrasequential.

K. Paragraph with Introduction

I1 If you are at the beach, and you take an old, dull, brown penny and rub it hard for a minute or two with handfuls of wet sand (dry sand is no good), the penny will come out a bright gold color, looking as clean and new as the day it was minted.

1 Now poetry has the same effect on words as wet sand on pennies.

  2 In what seems an almost miraculous way, it brightens up words that looked dull and ordinary.

    3 Thus, poetry is perpetually 're-creating languages.'

      4 It does this in several ways.

        5. . . .

C. Day Lewis, *Poetry for You*, pp. 8–9.

Most of the examples of what I would call introductory sentences are like this in offering a comparison. The comparison is not carried through the paragraph, but is used only as a starter.

L. Paragraph with Transition

T1 So far I've been talking about some of the world-shapes out of which poetry is built.

  T2 But images, metaphors, and similes are not the only things which may go to make the pattern of a poem.

1 There are meter and rhyme.

  2 You may be surprised that I have not put meter first, after talking so much about rhythm in the last chapter.

    3 Well, the fact is that poetry can be made without meter or rhyme. . . .

C. Day Lewis, *Poetry for You*, p. 33.

Transitions from paragraph to paragraph are ordinarily embedded in the topic sentence, as a single word or a phrase, a subordinate clause, or the first part of a compound sentence. But sometimes, as here, they take a full sentence or more.

The first sentence of a paragraph may even be a major transition. It may be the topic sentence of a series of paragraphs or even the thesis sentence of an article.

M. Paragraph with Conclusion

1 When we follow the growth of science, we come to understand how that movement has been probing for these unifying concepts.

2 Look at the movement of biology since the days of Ray and Linnaeus: . . . .
2 Look at chemistry, from Dalton's law. . . .
2 Look at the march of physics to unity: . . .
3 We have seen this lead to the creation of energy from matter; to a picture of space as closed but possibly expanding; and now . . . .
C1 Science is a process of creating new concepts which unify our understanding of the world, and
the process is today bolder and more far-reaching, more triumphant even than at the great threshold of the Scientific Revolution.

J. Bronowski, *The Common Sense of Science,* pp. 132–133.

Concluding sentences are rather rare, and some of them, like this one, round off a sequence of paragraphs rather than the one they are joined to. Such concluding sentences are ordinarily at a higher level of generalization than the sentences they follow, and those who take the most general sentence to be the topic sentence may take them for topic sentences. They may say that the paragraph has two topic sentences, fore and aft. The practice of professional writers gives no support to the classroom notion that the paragraph should end with a "clincher."

8. Some Paragraphing Is Illogical.

N.

1 Rhymes, as you know, generally come at the end of lines.
2 They are put there because it helps to create and make clear the musical pattern of the stanza:
the ear learns to expect a rhyme, just as it expects a beat, at certain definite intervals, and
it's pleased when it finds one there.
1 But you may get a rhyme in the middle of a line, too: and some poets are extremely skilful in making assonances and other sound-echoes all over a poem.
2 This is often done by the use of alliteration.
3 For example,

I hear lake water lapping with low sounds by the shore.

¶4 Those three 'l's' make a pleasant liquid sound:
the sound here, in fact, corresponds with the sense.
4 So it does in

Dry clashed his armour in the icy caves,

where the hard 'c' of 'clashed' and 'caves' seems to dry one's mouth up when one speaks the line aloud.

C. Day Lewis, *Poetry for You,* pp. 35–36.

The two sentences marked 1 are clearly coordinate. One has to say, then, that the paragraph is compound (a reasonable solution; there are such paragraphs), or that the first two sentences are introductory or transitional, or that the paragraphing is simply illogical, breaking up a short sequence.

Paragraphing at level 4 is even more illogical. It breaks up a sequence at the most unexpected point. Perhaps the tired teacher will sigh "If gold rusts . . ."

On the other hand, many a run of four or five paragraphs totaling 500–600 words can be analyzed as a single sequence, with the paragraph divisions coming logically at the subtopic sentences. This is the consummation we should work for.

9. Punctuation Should Be by the Paragraph, Not by the Sentence.

O.

1 This brings me to the third failing of eighteenth century science, which I find most interesting.
  2 A science which orders its thought too early is stifled.
    3 For example, the ideas of the Epicureans about atoms two thousand years ago were quite reasonable; but
    they did only harm to a physics which could not measure temperature and pressure and learn the simpler laws which relate them.
    3 Or again, the hope of the medieval alchemists that the elements might be changed was not as fanciful as we once thought.
      4 But it was merely damaging to a chemistry which did not yet understand the composition of water and common salt.

J. Bronowski, *The Common Sense of Science*, p. 47.

This is a minor example of punctuating without an eye to the paragraph as a whole. The two sets at level 3 are the same in intent and, except for the punctuation, the same in form. Likes have been put in unlike ways.

Paragraph punctuation usually involves the choice of whether to make compound sentences or not. In paragraph G the same author wisely grouped five coordinate statements into three sentences, sorting them out on the basis of content. Paragraph E does not really have two topic sentences, and a semicolon would avoid that appearance. I have taken it as a rule that a sentence that merely restates another is on the same level with it. If this is a bad rule, then all the numbers for level should be raised one. In paragraph P the effects of repetition and balance would be obscured if the sentences were not punctuated as compound.

P.

1 Nowhere, at no time, have there been five and a half years so alternately wondrous, compelling, swift and cruel.

2 As the Sixties began, our aspirant astronauts had yet to enter space;
now, they practice giant steps to the moon.

2 Then, jet travel was a conversation piece;
now, we change the flight if we've seen the movie.

2 Then, we were about to be swamped by a recessionary wave;
now, riding history's highest flood of prosperity, we are revising our assumptions about the inevitability of ebbs in our economic life.

2 Then, our Negroes were still marshaling their forces;
now, they have marshaled the conscience of mankind.

2 Then, we were arguing over the fitness of a Roman Catholic to be President;
now, we subdue the nightmare of his murder.

2 Then, a Southerner in the White House seemed politically unthinkable;
now, a Southerner builds with the most emphatic mandate we have ever bestowed.

2 Then, John Birch was an unknown soldier, actresses still wore clothes at work, and dancing was something a man and woman did together.

Leonard Gross, *Look*, 6/29/65

The Stadium of Discourse

PAUL RODGERS

In his "Further Comments on the Paragraph," Mr. Leo Rockas reports on his recent all-out effort to grasp the nature of paragraph structure, remarking that he had trouble differentiating fact from fancy, reality from unreality. "There is no doubt," he writes, "that discourse is broken into sentences and that there are certain finite (but perhaps as yet unspecified) ways of adding them to one another." But does anything we can call "the paragraph" really exist? The claim that it does is a "whopping deductive assumption" which he's not about to make: "What nobody has ever proven is that groups of sentences always fall into neat units which existed long before there was any such mark of punctuation as a para-graph (¶). . . ."[1]

Rockas is quite right on this last point. No one has ever proved that all groups of sentences fall into neat units, nor will anyone ever do so—for prose isn't invariably unified and coherent. But whenever a passage of expository prose *is* unified and coherent, that passage possesses structure. And structure invariably implies the presence of distinct rhetorical units, which I call "stadia of discourse." And in the work of any competent prose writer, I think these units can be said to be rather neat.

In the present paper I shall try to relieve Mr. Rockas's ontological anxiety by demonstrating that prose structure does in fact exist, and that the paragraph—any effective paragraph—is a segment of structure emphasized by indentations, much as a channel among reefs is marked out by buoys. By "structure" I mean the web of argument, the pattern of thought-flow, the system of alliances and tensions among associated statements. Rockas mentions the problem of explaining how sentences "get connected." Here, I judge, he refers to what I think of as the problem of structure. When a discourse is structured—as it always is, to the degree that it is unified and coherent—it can be viewed as a configuration of connected predications.

Most of us, most of the time, perceive the connections quite spontaneously and automatically, as if by instinct or intuition. We may not know precisely *what* structure is, but we know *where* it is. And this knowledge

College Composition and Communication, vol. 18 (October 1967), pp. 178–185.

[1] Leo Rockas, "Further Comments on the Paragraph," *College Composition and Communication*, XVII (October 1966), p. 148.

suffices, because for most of us, as writers or as readers or as correctors of student compositions, it is enough to grasp prose structure in the same loose way that Aristotle, in Book VII of the *Poetics*, described plot structure:

> . . . a thing can be whole without being of any particular size. "Whole" means having a beginning, a middle, and an end. The beginning, while not necessarily following something else, is, by definition followed by something else. The end, on the contrary, follows something else by definition, either always or in most cases, but nothing else comes after it. The middle both itself follows something else and is followed by something else.[2]

This analysis opens few doors for anyone who does not already apprehend the reality of literary form. Had Aristotle found it necessary to analyze and explain formal integrity to an audience that did not already recognize it, then the *Poetics* would have been longer, needless to say. This is the situation I find myself in when I confront Mr. Rockas. I hope to be forgiven if I fall short of Aristotelian brevity and simplicity.

The key to structural relationships, to the "logical" aspect of thought-flow, seems to me to lie in the psychology of literary intention. To determine a statement's function, we must ask why it was written. Not why the writer chanced to think his thought, but why he phrased it as he did and why he recorded it at this precise point. When we do so, we discover two distinct categories of statements, reflecting two different motives. One group of statements conveys thoughts that are offered for their own sake, for their intrinsic value. These are the so-called topic statements. Statements in the second group serve a secondary purpose. They are set forth in order to justify or clarify or emphasize or in some way to heighten the probability that the reader will fully understand and accept and remember *other* statements, notably the topic statements.

Of course, this is not to claim we are conscious of purpose every time we touch pen to paper. Quite the contrary. We make assertions, and then sustain them with other assertions, simply because this seems the natural, sensible, normal thing to do. We do it constantly, routinely, in all our speaking and writing. But purpose (i.e., function) is served, whether or not we fully realize what we are doing. Some of our statements can stand alone, and we allow them to. Others need support, and this need, however obscurely felt or recognized, prompts us to make statements of the secondary type.

A second broad distinction is between simple and complex statements. A simple statement, as I am defining it, is a statement limited to a single independent clause, together with whatever modifying material may be necessary or appropriate. Having recorded it, the writer is satisfied that he has expressed his whole thought. Most statements are of this type: one

---

[2] Aristotle, *On Poetry and Style*, trans. G. M. A. Grube (Indianapolis, 1958), p. 16.

independent clause does the job. Sometimes, however, a second clause[3] may have to be added, and even a third, the resulting group entering into an intimate association in the reader's mind, making a sort of mental amalgam which serves (as Josephine Miles puts it) "to share ideas that need blending." [4]

"There are nine and sixty ways," wrote Kipling, "of constructing tribal lays." But his idea was not yet fully realized, so he added: "And every single one of them is right!" Here we have two independent clauses which together convey what Kipling obviously wants us to recognize as a single idea. The clauses "blend" in the mind by a process which, for the moment, I shall label *accretion.* This is no mere *adjunction* of clauses, the sort of thing we find in the following:

> *There are nine and sixty ways of constructing tribal lays;*
> *Twelve are found in Pakistan, the others in Bombay.*

Here the clauses of the second line merely support the claim made in the first. They convey information about it, occasioned by it, associated with it, but they do not *extend* it in the same way that Kipling's second clause extends the first. They can be glanced at and forgotten, and could be removed without disrupting the argument. But both of Kipling's clauses have to stand. His idea requires both. The components of his statement are not rhetorically distinct and separable in analysis, as are the components of my revision, wherein one clause receives support from a pair of "adjuncts."

Accretion occurs because we do not always manage to state a thought fully the first time we try. We blurt out something and then discover we've done little more than establish the subject of a sentence that still remains unwritten. So we follow up the first clause with a second, and sometimes the second with a third. Or again, we may encounter an idea that demands two clauses. At such times, the need for accretion may come upon us without our recognizing what we are doing, just as the need for adjunction does. But sophisticates like Kipling find subtle reasons for indulging in complex statement deliberately.

A third and final distinction arises from the fact that adjunctive support may either precede or follow the element it supports. When adjuncts follow, as they normally do, we have what is commonly called "analytic" movement; when they precede, the result is "synthetic" movement. When a writer works by analysis, he says something and then supports it with other statements (adjuncts) that make it clearer and more acceptable and more

---

[3] By "clause" (or "independent clause"), I mean not only the clause proper but also all its modifiers, including subordinate clauses. Lacking a name for such a unit, I shall simply call it a "clause" in this paper, abbreviating it as "C."

[4] Josephine Miles, "Symposium on the Paragraph," *College Composition and Communication*, XVII (May 1966), p. 81. Miss Miles refers to blends of paragraphs and sentences, but the general situation here would seem identical and her phrasing most appropriate.

memorable. Adjunctive statements typically turn out to be repetitions or obverse restatements of the base clause; or definitions of its key terms; or examples, instances, illustrations, or component details; or supporting quotations, or logical proofs; or statements of cause; or clarifying contrasts or comparisons. In synthesis, the same sort of material turns up, but it comes first, preparing the way for the base clause. Synthesis is what occurs when the writer foresees his conclusion and decides—for variety's sake, or for clarity, or for whatever reason—to state the evidence or the cause or the particulars first; or when he discovers his conclusion as he goes along, perhaps quite suddenly and unexpectedly, after laying out the supporting material in preliminary statements. In an analytic passage, the reader advances facing backward, so to speak, holding one main idea in mind as he considers the evidence advanced in support of it. In a synthetic passage, he faces forward; often he does not anticipate the conclusion that follows.

To summarize, *all* our statements are either simple or complex. (I shall call the latter type "accretion.") *All* our statements are either unsupported or supported. (I shall call the latter situation "adjunction.") And *all* supporting material either precedes or follows the material it supports, creating either "synthetic" or "analytic" movement throughout the passage. Any two structurally associated clauses will *always* be related either by accretion or adjunction; that is, the writer formulates his second clause either to complete an idea broached in the first, or to support the first. And any two clauses related by adjunction will *always* set up either a synthetic or an analytic movement of thought. . . .

Such units—each one containing a single topic, together with any accrete extensions or adjunctive support that may be present—are what I call, for want of a better name, "stadia of discourse." They are the basic rhetorical constituents of prose. But they are not paragraphs, necessarily.

Any stadium *may* become a paragraph, and many do. But a portion of a stadium may also become a good paragraph, providing that structural relationships remain clear; and a group of stadia may become a paragraph, providing the resulting bundle of material constitutes an acceptable blend. Discourse can be partitioned at so many points that Mr. Rockas concludes "you can justify an indentation before almost any sentence of sophisticated prose," and in this pronouncement he strikes close to the truth. . . .

The paragraph indentation is a multipurpose tool of punctuation with which we can identify and call attention to many of the varied simultaneous phenomena of prose discourse, but it must not be forgotten that the paragraph itself—the stretch of language silhouetted between indentations—must always reveal the boundaries of a unit of structure. If an indentation obscures structural relationships, it obstructs comprehension; if it points up structure, it clarifies. In the last analysis, perhaps the schoolboy's definition of the paragraph comes closer to the mark than the dictum of the learned professor. Let us modify it slightly (with a learned archaism) and say: "A paragraph is where you *invent.*"

What We Compose

JOSEPHINE MILES

The word *composition,* with its relation to *compose, component, composure,* is the word of the active composing artist and of the poised, the composed philosopher. When we try to teach composition, we are trying to teach art, and philosophy, and I cannot think of a better task. But it is a difficult task, and we often go wrong with it.

One reason we go wrong is that no one of us is a good enough philosopher or a clear enough thinker to be sure what we want to say. Our thoughts are not well enough composed because they are not even yet fully developed. Another reason we go wrong is that we are not good enough artists: that is, we do not seriously understand the powers of the medium in which we work to shape our thoughts. A sculptor would not leave to chance his choice of marble, clay, or wood to work in, a musician would not accidentally shift from key to key, yet the writer, because he has been using language all his life, forgets to treat with consideration the language which he must use formally to shape his thought. Further, not only artists but even scientists have had difficulty in standing away from their own language far enough to see it clear. So we have tended to understand our own mostly through other languages, and have developed a number of Latin, French, and German analogies for it, rather than a direct view of it. Now, by increasing the number of analogies to the most distant horizons, of Malay, Bantu, and Athabascan, we are able, often by the very absurdity of the distant relation, to see our own more clear.

But the question has naturally risen, how can such objectivizing, such particularizing of the traits of all languages, into phonemes, morphemes, sememes, serve the needs of art, which rather synthesizes and subjectivizes, which aims not to take apart but to put together, not to analyze but to compose? I think the simplicity of the answer lies in the question itself; to make a whole out of many parts requires some knowledge of the parts.

College Composition and Communication, vol. 14 (October 1963), pp. 146–154.

Composition needs components. The worker in wood needs to know the grain of the wood.

Over the years in which I have been teaching essay-writing and trying to write my own, I have looked many times at a page of printed text, hoping to see a simple pattern of thought on the page. Accustomed to poetry, where the visible and audible pattern is dominant, I have been steadily puzzled by the straight forward *pro* quality of prose, and have shared the sense of students that in writing prose they commit themselves to some sort of rushing tide of words. Where has been the design, where the pattern, of what I was reading and what I was writing? How amorphous were the materials of language with which I dealt? Memories of study of multiplicity of grammatical categories, and more recent acquaintance with form classes and immediate constituents, served to stress the unredeemable complexities of prose.

It was clear that for practical, describable purposes some sort of drastic simplification, a moving to a level beyond the molecular structure, to the grain of the wood, was necessary, but I did not know if it was attainable. Then three sorts of clues came together to aid my puzzling: first, reading the work of Zellig Harris, and discussing linguistic theory with Sheldon Sacks and Ann Stanford; second, debates with Bertrand Evans, Benbow Ritchie, Richard Worthen, and Leo Ruth, in problems of teaching; and finally, in relation to poetry, the reading of classic English prose, beginning in the Renaissance with Sir Thomas More and ending with Shaw and Russell. Suddenly one day when I looked at a passage of prose, I recognized a structural pattern in it, and when I tested my sense of this pattern, in a number of different writers, I found three or four major variations which served to suggest its relevance and pervasiveness. My specific method was to combine analysis of the frequencies of the main parts of speech in an eight thousand word prose text with a structural analysis of representative passages from the text.

The basic fact for observation is the tripartite articulation of utterance in formal prose: that is, first, the nucleus of predicated subject; second, the specification of context by adjectival, phrasal, and clausal modification; and third, the arrangement or composition by order and explicit connection. Thus the three main function-classes, each with its substitutable forms, are assertion (subject-predicate), development (modifying words, phrases, clauses), and connection (prepositional, conjunctival terms). Like a word, with its root and specifying affixes and connecting affixes, a sentence specifies and relates its nucleus of assertion; and like a sentence, an essay or formal prose passage also asserts, develops, and relates. The sentence then may well provide, over a span of recurrences, a microcosm for the choices of distribution and emphasis in the statement as a whole; and thus a style, a regularity of distribution of sentence-elements, an habitual set of choices and emphases from sentence to sentence, may be discriminable in certain main types in English prose. (Z. Harris, *Structural Linguistics*, pp. 352, 365).

The main difference between such a discriminating of types of articulation and those of some theorists today is that it is not binary or dichotomizing on the one hand, nor highly multiple on the other. Multiplicity leads to confusion of practical action, and binarism seems to me to cut across the central nucleus. Proposals ranging from immediate-constituent analysis, to noun and verb phrases, to Rulon Wells' suggestions for a basic division of styles into nominal and verbal (*Style in Language*, 1960), all seem to me therefore more theoretically usable. Nearly half the seventy or so main connectives in English may be used either phrasally or clausally, and all the prepositional phrases may modify either nouns or verbs, so when *the bird sings in the tree* or *the bird in the tree sings,* a binary division seems to me ruthlessly abstract. *The bird sings* is the important point; it may then be modified by *in the tree, in the morning, when he wishes, loud, loudly,* or what you will. A persistence in one or another of these choices will make for a characteristic of a whole style. The complex grammar of the subject-predicate, of pronouns, auxiliaries, and other substitutions and transferals I will assume here, in order to go on with the choices in the larger units of modification.

Take a number of units of assertion: "The bird sings. The bird is loud. The bird is on the branch. It is morning." One sort of style keeps such units as separate as possible, without subordination, with no more logic of order perhaps than a simple chronology. Other choices make various subordinations by assumption. "The loud bird sings on the morning branch" is adjectival and phrasal. Or, "The bird in its loudness on its branch in the morning sings" is highly phrasal. Or, "The bird which is loud when it is morning sings where it sits on its branch" is highly clausal. Subject, verb, object, each can be modified by word, phrase, or clause, and often by the same ones. Even connectives can take these alternative forms—"then," "in the morning," or "when it is morning."

One of the great insights into grammar is, I think, that not content alone, but also context, defines the working units; that both character and location are part of their definition. Thus we may see that the basic parts of speech, substantive, predicate, modifier, and connective, are not just items but are also functions, and perhaps any of the items may serve any of the functions interchangeably, and word-order may be as vital to meaning as word-form. So too with sentences. The root of the sentence has its affixes, that is, time—place—manner—modifiers, as does the root of the word; and the sentence like the word is not an independent unit, a free form, because its meaning is dependent upon order as well as on content. The order of "He did not sing. He wanted to sing," makes a meaning different from "He wanted to sing. He did not sing." Even more, the use of connectives rests upon order. "He did not sing. But he wanted to sing" is normally more meaningful than "But he wanted to sing. He did not sing." Content and context thus are accentable by the connective signals. In composition, the selection of material is supported and conditioned by the ordering of the material, its *position,* and by the devices of signaling order, the connectives, which make up a large part of the *com*—in *composition*—the signs which put the idea together, and put us together with it.

One of the simplest ways to observe and follow significant order, then, is to pay close attention to the connectives in a passage—to note not only whether the idea moves by words, phrases, or clauses, but also by which sort it moves—by additives like *and, then, also,* by comparatives like *as, so, how,* by disjunctives like *but,* by alternatives like *on the one hand . . . on the other,* by causal subordinates like *if, because, for,* by descriptive subordinates like *who* and *which,* by temporal and spatial locatives like *where* and *there, when* and *then.* Behind these guiding signs lie three or four basic logical patterns of which we profoundly need to be aware.

The major word-connectives we use today had their sources in other forms, in other parts of speech. *And* was *ante* or *anti*—two parties face to face across a border, one and the other. *But,* on the other hand, excluded, made an exception of the other party. *Because* was the phrase *by cause.* Most conjunctions, adverbs, and prepositions are signs of spatial, temporal, and conceptual relations, of separating and joining, preceding and following.

Let us look at their procedures in some vigorous and distinguished prose styles: for example, that of Emerson near the beginning of *Self-Reliance.* The subject-predicate units are italicized, in contrast to the modifiers.

> *Travelling* is a fool's *paradise.* Our first *journeys discover* to us the *indifference* of places. At home *I dream that* at Naples, at Rome, *I can be intoxicated* with beauty *and lose my sadness. I pack my trunk, embrace my friends, embark* on the sea, *and* at last *wake up* in Naples, *and there* beside me *is the* stern *fact, the* sad *self,* unrelenting, identical, that I fled from. *I seek the Vatican and palaces. I affect to be intoxicated* with sights and suggestions, *but I am not intoxicated. My giant goes* with me wherever I go.
>
> But *the rage* of travelling is a *symptom* of a deeper unsoundness affecting the whole intellectual action. *The intellect is vagabond,* and our *system* of education *fosters restlessness.*

Note the simple subject-predicates without connectives: *Travelling is a fool's paradise . . . I pack my trunk, embrace my friends . . . I seek the Vatican . . .* To these, what are the simplest additions? The modifying noun *fool's,* the adjectival *our first,* the phrases *to us* and *of places.* Then the patterned parallel additives, *at home, at Naples, at Rome;* and *on the sea, at Naples, beside me,* culminating in a pile-up of adjectives—*the stern fact, the sad self, unrelenting, identical.* Also then, the subordinate clauses, *the self that I fled from, but I am not, wherever I go,* are not very complicated, and, along with the phrases, less structurally important than the simple temporal sequence of verbs: *is, discover, dream, pack, embrace, wake up, seek, affect, go, fosters, travel, are forced.*

Notice that simple subject, predicate, and modification need no connectives: that connectives come in by adding place, time, manner, cause; that is, the phrasal and clausal specifications of simple modifiers. The proportioning of parts of speech is characteristic of Emerson's style—one adjective to three nouns, to two verbs, to two connectives—and this proportion is characteristic also of what we may call the predicative or active verbal style, typified by such a sentence perhaps as: *The bright boy came to the beach and built a boat.* Alternative emphases would increase either the adjectival or phrasal modification, on the one hand, or clauses and clausal connectives on the other—both thus with richer modification, with assumption, rather than statement, of qualifying data.

Emerson's style puts a maximum premium, for English prose, on the separate items of predication, the free functioning of active verbs. Whitman differs; he substantiates with phrasal connectives: *in, into, of, with,* and the comparative or alternative *or* and *than;* with the barest minimum of causal and relative terms. His adjectives and nouns and connectives are more than Emerson's, his verbs less; he is one of the few for whom many verbs are given the form of adjective participles, three times as many as Emerson's. In the third paragraph of *Democratic Vistas,* Whitman in effect introduces his style as well as his subject:

> But preluding no longer, *let me strike the key-note* of the following strain. First premising that, though the passages of it have been written different times, (*it is,* in fact, *a collection* of memoranda, perhaps for future designers, comprehenders,) and though it may be open to the charge of one part contradicting another—for there are opposite sides to the great question of democracy, as to every great question—*I feel the parts* harmoniously blended in my own realization and convictions, *and present them* to be read only in such oneness, each page and each claim and assertion modified and temper'd by the others. *Bear in mind,* too, *that they are not the result* of studying up in political economy, but of the ordinary sense, observing, wandering among men, these States, these stirring years of war and peace.

Here no more than a fifth of the material is direct predicate of subject, in contrast to Emerson's half. Whitman admits the possible charge of self-contradiction, but dismisses conscious contradiction, so strong for Emerson, from his style—"each claim and assertion modified and tempered by the others." Modification is the key-note, and sensory modification, not from argument, but from observing, wandering. *In, into, of, with, or, than:* "Our fundamental want today in the United States, with closest, amplest reference to present conditions, and to the future, is of a class, and the clear idea of a class, of native authors . . . accomplishing . . . a religious and moral character beneath the political and productive and intellectual bases of the States. . . . Never was anything more wanted than, today, and here in the States, the poet of the modern is wanted, or the great literatus of the modern."

Between these extremes of Whitman and Emerson, there is a middle ground—not a mere compromise, but a mode of its own, as its vocabulary exemplifies. Note Twain's chapters 15, 16, 17, in *Life on the Mississippi*, for example. The chief connectives are prepositional like Whitman's, but of a more directional adverbial sort; *about, at, between, on, through, to, under, upon;* with, like Emerson, a minimum of locative and possessive terms. While Whitman's prepositions of place show presence or possession, Twain's show action, befitting his stronger use of verbs:

> At the first glance, *one would suppose that* when it came to forbidding information about the river *these two parties could play equally* at that game; *but this was not so.* At every good-sized town from one end of the river to the other, *there was a "wharf-boat"* to land at, instead of a wharf or a pier. *Freight was stored* in it for transportation; waiting *passengers slept* in its cabins.

Here about a third of the material is direct predication of subject, between Emerson's half and Whitman's fifth, just as Twain's style in general balances adjectives and verbs.

One may well suggest that these distinctions I have been making are not a matter of style or choice, but are simply based on subject-matter. Emerson argues an idea, Whitman describes observations, Twain sets forth events; therefore the difference in verbs and connectives. But it is not so simple; while subject is a matter of style, so is attitude, and the habit of speech. So we may find in the Renaissance, in a trio of essays on morality, that the same stylistic contrasts occur. Sir Thomas More in his Utopian debate is like Emerson, spare in adjectives, strong in verbs and the logic of *by, how, that.* Ascham in a similar moralizing on education takes Whitman's role of blending alternatives and degrees in *amongst* and *in;* he ignores relative and *how* clauses. Bacon has Twain's vigor and crispness, his *to* directions, his moderately strong use of clauses.

Comparing Jonson, Milton, and Browne in the seventeenth century, we see that Jonson, the actively predicative writer, uses relatively few *and, of;* many *about, against, with, because, but, for, if, so, than, that.* Like More then, he combines simple verbs with clausal structures. His prepositions show especially a relation of opposition. Browne, on the other hand, uses little opposition, but much *above, from, in, of, into, upon,* the vocabulary of location. And Milton, in the middle, is characterized by the most *and, as before, now, into, out of,* prepositions of active direction like Twain's, as well as a high proportion of relative connectives *that, what, which, who.* In other words, we may see that certain styles vary but persist. In the twentieth century, the decline of subordinative clausal terms lessens the distinction of their whole style, but still retains in Lawrence's *because, if, what* a great contrast to Huxley's locational *between, from,* Russell's *about, since.*

On the other hand, to note the power of temporality, consider the prose of the sixteenth century as a whole, in such works as Tyndale's translation of St. Paul, Thomas More's *Apology*, Hugh Latimer's *Fifth* Sermon, Roger Ascham's *Schoolmaster*, Raphael Holinshed's *Chronicles*, Richard Hooker's *Laws of Ecclesiastical Polity*, John Lyly's *Euphues*, Philip Sidney's *Defense of Poesy*, Francis Bacon's *Advancement of Learning*, and Thomas Dekker's *Gull's Hornbook.* The fact that all of these but the *Schoolmaster* are strongly predicative, that is, use verbs twice the adjectives and two-thirds the nouns, suggests that more than individual choice was involved; and the variety of topics and genres suggests that time rather than type provided the common bond. Even certain specifications were agreed on in emphasis by a number of the writers: especially *to come, to find, to give, to know, to make, to see, to take.* These were related to adjectives *good, great, true, whole,* and nouns of human and social value like *mind, reason, word, work,* and to a multiplicity of major connectives, especially conjunctions.

So not only type of choice, but time, may provide meaningful generalizations. Time, with its general lessening of connectives, limits in its way the choices of a writer today, making probable the shortening of his sentences to forty, rather than an older seventy, words, cutting down the probabilities of strong logical connective use, and raising the chances for the adverbials. Within time and type then, the individual writer makes his own unique combinations of choice.

What it seems to me important for the young writer to know is what these choices are, how they have been made in the past, and how he may make them in the present. They are not infinitely various, for example, but limited and significant for certain tones and attitudes: the phrasal, for a receptive objectivity of observation, as in many scientific writers; the balanced, for a reasoned subordination; the active verbal for a commitment to natural temporal sequence, events as they happen. What the writer chooses to say about his subject, and how he develops and composes it is a matter of his awareness of, his power over, his thought and language. To think of him as only individual robs him of his participation in values, makes him a mere atom among the rest. But he is not. As an artist he is most solidly a worker in the values of his medium. So the student is the young artist too. Once he is able to see how others have worked before him, how others work around him, and once he is able to estimate the powers of his own language, he can consider deliberately, weigh and reject consciously, plan and proceed effectively, with a sense that his fate is at least partially, in composition, in his own hands; that he can decide where he wants to go, and then go there.

From choices, let us turn to necessities: the writer's commitments to predication. Suppose a student is considering the question, What does the first scene of *Hamlet* do for the play as a whole? And suppose he decides a good answer is: "The first scene establishes Hamlet in the view of his contemporaries, a view emphasized first by Horatio, then by Laertes, Rosencranz and Guildenstern, and Fortinbras." Then he knows first of all that his predicate is *establishes Hamlet* and that the steps of unfolding this predicate will be the steps of his paragraphs. The *first scene* is the subject; from it the material relevant to the predicate will be drawn. The predicate then is further modified by two phrases—*in the view,* and *of his contemporaries.* And finally, the last phrase of the question, *for the play as a whole,* is prepared to be dealt with in the apposition, *a view emphasized by Horatio, Laertes, and others.* In other words, both question and answer consider what possible predications can be made for Scene I, and then proceed to select and develop one of them. It is not the substance of Scene I which will guide the essay; rather, it is the pertinence which the predication will attribute to Scene I. In such a way, the writer is master of his material. He is not conditioned by his material, rather he is faithful to it in terms of the responsibility he takes toward it, and the evidence he finds and provides for the predication—in our instance, for the statement *establishes Hamlet*—and then for the views of Hamlet's companions throughout the play, even to the final speech of Fortinbras.

If I have a hero, the predication or idea, I have also a villain, the "preliminary outline." Lest you accept what I suggest too easily, and agree that of course we teach the following-out of a *thought,* not of a mere *subject,* remember the usually accepted form of outline, the outline of the "topic." Topic: Scene I of *Hamlet.* Outline: main steps of Scene I: A. The Guards, B. Horatio. And so on. Even in the writing of theses in graduate study, the student carries the confusion of such inertia with him, and provides outlines and bibliographies of such a field as "the early sixteenth century" or "the industrial novel," without yet knowing what he wants to say of it. For such a student, the beginning is not in the word, but in the hell of no intentions. So then he says, I have taken too big a subject; I must narrow this topic or this location; and looks puzzled when one asks: Will one industrial novel be easier to outline than *the* industrial novel? Will California be easier to outline than the United States? Will Berkeley be easier to outline than California?

Further, the standard outline conceals rather than reveals the crucial articulations of connectives. A, B, and C subordinations stress a sort of parallelism usually inherent in the subject according to certain taxonomic presuppositions, but not related to the main line of predication and the supplementary modifications which the writer must work along. To answer about the *who* and *what* of an event the main questions of time, location, cause, and manner, in *when, where, why,* and *how,* is to work through the words, phrases, or clauses of this information, with emphasis and alternatives most probably related to the main point the author is making about the event, and thus, transition for transition, marking the main stages in the development of that point.

You may notice that my example of a subject has been Scene I of *Hamlet.* I have a serious reason for this choice, namely, that fidelity to the relevant evidence in the subject-matter is best studied when the studying group shares the subject, has the text before it. No doubt all of us have done interesting experiments with the providing of common materials. My colleague, Jackson Burgess, for example, reports the effective use of the view from his classroom window. Charles Muscatine works with vast shared concerns like death. Benbow Ritchie works best with two or three translations of *The Odyssey* in hand at one time. For composers of all kinds I think the important point is that they compose responsibly in fields they are studying—literary students in literature, botany students in botany. As all of us think through the medium of our language, English, so all of us need to learn, and to teach, composition in whatever field we are working in and knowledgeable in, and to treat the material of that field with fidelity. "This is a young camel, though gray." How can we know whether such a statement is grammatical or ungrammatical, unless we know in the nature of camels whether indeed they are not gray when young? The connectives signal not only our argument but our knowledge. Every field of knowledge, every center of inquiry, carries its own responsibilities in its own language, English—if indeed it claims English as its language.

Almost twenty years ago, the Berkeley Plan for prose composition was begun under the direction of Professor Benjamin Lehman and later was worked out by Professor Benbow Ritchie and others. As it is now being worked out at the Davis Campus, it may well widen its name as well as its function. Central to the plan is the belief I have just expressed about subject-matter, that every department should teach composition in its own subject. Central too is the belief that well-constructed questions, in tests and assignments, will with a little care, get well-constructed answers in which a predication will carry the burden of argument, rather than a mere list of cue-items under the term "discuss." Central too is the belief that individual power over problems comes from practice in conscious choice of alternative relevant materials and structures, alternative modifications. Therefore the University of California Prose Committee, made up of members from a variety of academic departments, undertakes to give a course for readers and assistants in all interested departments, teaching them how to make assignments and how to guide and evaluate the resultant writing, even for large numbers of students at a time. This aid is not fully made use of because many departments feel that they more economically use their assistants in the guiding of laboratory experiments and reading of true-false questions. Nevertheless, in a range of subjects from music to economics, from classics to psychology and sociology, the advanced students may learn to teach the beginners the rudiments of thoughtful writing in their field.

Recently, colleges in this country have been confronted with a sad and true report by Professor Kitzhaber on the progressive deterioration of writing by students at Dartmouth. All the gloom, unease, queasy mediocrity, slipshod inadequacy of which teachers of composition are aware, and which are so tellingly set forth in this report, were felt too at Berkeley in interdepartmental studies of student-writing in 1950–53. But one further important fact should be noted: that deterioration is less in the supply of good writing than in the demand for it. That is, the student is apt to adapt himself to the demands of the course of study, and to supply only minimal cues rather than complex structures of thought, if these are all that the questions, or the readers of the answers, require.

So the upperclassmen in a wide range of departments at Berkeley also write badly, and write badly whether or not they wrote well previously in first year composition. But after only two widely-spaced half-hours of explanatory lecture, by instructor and assistant, on the sort of reasoning stressed in this essay, that is, the need for responsible predication of a subject adequately evidenced, over half of the students improve by a whole grade. In contrasting groups, without this compositional guidance, a fifth of the students improve by simply increasing their understanding of the subject-matter. Knowledge can be strengthened therefore by conscious awareness of responsibility. Every writer, in every sentence he writes, needs to relearn his method in relation to each new complexity of his medium. Composition does not work in a vacuum; it cannot be learned "once and for all." It works rather in a medium which grows increasingly complex as we learn more about it and requires further and further adaptation of the powers to compose.

In the word *grammar,* as admirable as *composition,* lies a fairly simple, or simplifiable, answer to our questions. Grammar gives us the articulations of language with which we can compose. And they are not infinitely multiple and confusing; rather they are fairly basic and elemental: the individual and powerful purpose of the predicate; the relevant substance of the subject; the specifiable details of manner and location in modifying clause, phrase, and word, and the explicit formal guidance of connectives: thus we compose our purpose in substance, quality, order and linkage. To know our purpose is not easy; it takes a philosophy. To know the malleability of our medium is not easy; it takes an art. But difficulty need not mean confusion. The composer in language, young or old, can look at his language and see its potentialities for his purposes and for purposes beyond him. Grammar for him can be as clear, strong, and potentially expressive as for the most accomplished artist. Our own best principles of coherence, would we apply them to our language, would tell us that we need not lose sight of the forest for the innumerable small branches of the trees.

It is the grain of the living wood we are after, the character of the language by which we live and compose.

Paragraph Development in the Modern Age of Rhetoric

RICHARD A. MEADE and W. GEIGER ELLIS

The decade of the 1960s has brought the teacher of composition to the modern age of rhetoric. Centuries ago Greek rhetoricians expounded principles that have been reemphasized today. Yet it is doubtful that English teachers have ever let go of all rhetorical matters. Much attention has been given to that phase of organization usually referred to as paragraph development. Because of the dearth of research investigations on rhetorical concerns, the teacher has been left to rely largely on the recommendations of textbooks.

Texts have over the years contained direction for practice in so-called "methods of paragraph development." In 1897 Scott and Denney advocated such methods as repetition, particulars and details, specific instances, comparisons and analysis, telling what a thing is not, contrast, cause and effect, and proofs.[1] In this early text the title of each chapter began with the words "How paragraphs grow—" followed by a colon and the name of one of these methods. Early in the 1960s a widely-used text told the reader that "in order to write well, you should know about several ways of developing a paragraph. . . ."[2] This statement preceded samples of paragraph development by facts, examples, incidents, comparison, contrast, arguments, and definition. A review of virtually all high school textbooks published in the 1960s produced the following list of most often cited methods of development: description, comparison, contrast, reasons, examples, definition, and chronology. Others presented under slightly different names seemed to be aspects of these or essentially the same.

Teachers have generally interpreted the presentation of paragraph development by these methods to mean that students should practice them, often in complete isolation from any broader context. This instruction seemed to be based on the assumption that a student should approach each

English Journal, vol. 59 (February 1970), pp. 219–226.

[1] Fred Newton Scott and Joseph Villiers Denney, *Composition-Rhetoric* (Boston: Allyn and Bacon, 1897), p. 72.

[2] John E. Warriner, Joseph Mersand, and Francis Griffith, *English Grammar and Composition: Grade 11* (New York: Harcourt, Brace and World, Inc., 1963), p. 363.

paragraph with this question in mind: "Now what method of development shall I use for my next paragraph?" There was the implication that the student would first choose a method of development, selected for some undisclosed reason, and next formulate a topic sentence to suit that method. Such a procedure when baldly described seems at once inane and futile. This certainly is not acceptable rhetoric, new or old.

What is the rhetoric at work as the student writes a paragraph? Recent pronouncements have served at least to show that a preponderance of thought about composing denies the value of traditional methods of paragraph development. Such teaching as a major strategy of rhetoric has been severely questioned. For example, in 1958 participants in a workshop during a meeting of the Conference on College Composition and Communication raised these questions: "How effectively do the textbooks describe the methods of paragraph development? Do the terms *comparison, contrast, space, time,* and so forth really oversimplify the actual process?" [3] In 1963 Albert Kitzhaber, speaking of composition instruction, wrote this paragraph:

> If a principal aim of the required freshman English courses is to teach students to improve their ability to write expository prose, some provision should be made in these courses for explicit instruction in those principles of rhetoric that are especially pertinent to exposition. Instruction in the principles of rhetoric should not mean studying . . . the nine—or nineteen—ways to develop expository paragraphs. This kind of rhetorical instruction is both sterile and stupefying.[4]

He reinforced this statement with the following words: ". . . the majority of handbooks present a dessicated rhetorical doctrine that has probably done a good deal more over the years to hinder good writing than to foster it—the position of the topic sentence and mechanical rules for developing expository paragraphs. . . ." No research to support these opinions was reported in *Research and Written Composition* by Braddock and others (NCTE, 1963). There was no review of any appraisal of the value of teaching these traditional types of paragraph development.

A dual attack on the problem appears to be in order. Do writers use these methods of paragraph development which have for so long claimed textbook space and classroom time? How do writers operate to incorporate in their writing whatever methods they do use? The first of these questions was the subject of a recent investigation by the writers of this article. They

[3] "The Rhetoric of the Paragraph: Principles and Practices," *College Composition and Communication*, 9 (October 1958), p. 196 (Workshop Report at the Conference on College Composition and Communication, Philadelphia, March 27–29, 1958).

[4] Albert R. Kitzhaber, *Themes, Theories, and Therapy: The Teaching of Writing in College*, The Report of the Dartmouth Study of Student Writing (New York: McGraw-Hill Book Company, 1963), pp. 135–137.

Table I. Occurrence of Paragraphs Developed by Textbook Methods

Method of development	*Saturday Review*	*Richmond Times-Dispatch*	*English Journal*	Totals	Total percentage
No textbook method	53	62	53	168	56.0
Examples	27	13	30	70	23.3
Reasons	7	15	6	28	9.3
Chronology	5	6	8	19	6.3
Contrast	4	0	1	5	1.7
Repetition	0	3	1	4	1.3
Cause-effect	2	1	0	3	1.0
Definition	1	0	1	2	.7
Description	1	0	0	1	.3
Comparison	0	0	0	0	0
Totals	100	100	100	300	99.9

examined three hundred paragraphs randomly selected from contemporary written material: one hundred from a magazine of recognized quality read by the general public, *Saturday Review*; one hundred from a professional journal, the *English Journal*; and one hundred from letters to the editor of the *Richmond Times-Dispatch*, a morning daily newspaper. Paragraphs from the first two sources were examined just as they appeared in print, for both editors reported that they change an author's paragraph formation only in rare instances. The paragraphs from the letters to the editor were taken from original copies provided by the newspaper, for journalistic style may require that letters on the editorial page be changed in paragraphing. Comparison of these letters with the printed versions produced examples of this practice. Indentations were often different and did not always adhere to the thought development of the letter writer.

For all three sources the traditional methods of paragraph development described in textbooks were present less than half the time. As shown in Table I, 56 percent (168) of the three hundred paragraphs were not developed by any textbook method. The remaining 44 percent followed only two of the textbook methods to any appreciable extent: reasons and examples.

Development by reasons involves one or more statements answering the question *why* about the theme. Two short paragraphs to the editor of the *Richmond Times-Dispatch* illustrate this procedure.

> (1) A Salvador Dali designed statue would certainly benefit Richmond (2) because it would be an esthetic change from the stereotype "Man on Horse" statue now dominant. (3) It would also attract and hold a person's attention much longer.

The theme stated in (1) is supported by reasons given in (2) and (3).

> (1) I can very well sympathize with Mr. Grimsley in his dilemma with regard to his article appearing in this paper Friday, May 6, concerning the payment of overdue parking tickets—(2) I have undergone the same awesome suspense, except for a longer period.

Statement (2) gives a reason for the idea expressed in (1).

Development by example involves one or more specific instances or cases to explain a general statement. All the sentences of the following paragraph from the *English Journal* (September 1966) except the first one describe a single example of the generalization made in the first sentence.

> (1) After analyzing these simpler examples, the role of affective and informative connotations should become more meaningful in structures such as similes, metaphors, and other devices of imagery. (2) For example, in the simple metaphor "My love is a red, red rose" analysis of the informative connotation of "love" and "rose" reveals some of what the poet is saying but leaves much meaning out. (3) Understanding the affective connotations of "love" and "rose" reveals much more and comes closer to the poet's meaning. (4) The positive and tender feelings associated with the love are transferred to the rose. (5) The beauty, frailty, completeness, and the sentimentality connected with roses are in turn transferred to the love. (6) In other words, simply understanding what a rose is will not reveal what the poet is saying about his love. (7) Only when we associate the feelings toward the rose with the love and allow these feelings to shift freely from one object to the other do we arrive at the poet's expression of feeling and his meaning.

The last three sentences of the following paragraph, also from the *English Journal* (September 1966), gave three specific examples of the fact that English teachers have "a great advantage that teachers of foreign languages lack."

> (1) But that our students already know the structure of spoken English when they come to us gives us English teachers a great advantage that teachers of foreign languages lack. (2) We do not

Table II. Occurrence of Paragraphs Not Developed by Textbook Methods

Method of Development	*Saturday Review*	*Richmond Times-Dispatch*	*English Journal*	Total for all sounds	Percent of the 168 paragraphs not developed by textbook methods	Percent of all paragraphs
A Combination of methods	18	25	19	62	36.9	20.7
Additional comment	19	14	25	58	34.5	19.3
Two themes	11	3	4	18	10.7	6.0
One sentence paragraphs	1	14	3	18	10.7	6.0
Opposition	4	2	1	7	4.2	2.3
Question	0	4	1	5	3.0	1.7
Totals	53	62	53	168	100.0	56.0

Table III. Occurrence of Four Most Frequently Used Methods of Paragraph Development

Method of Development	*Saturday Review*	*Richmond Times-Dispatch*	*English Journal*	All sources	Percent for all sources
Examples	27	13	30	70	23.3
A combination of methods	18	25	19	62	20.7
Additional comment	19	14	25	58	19.3
Reasons	7	15	6	28	9.3

> have to start our teaching of the structure of written English from scratch. (3) We can start with those features of English which are identical in both the written system and the spoken system and can build our teaching around them. (4) We can make use of the fact that our students already know—even if not consciously—those grammatical devices of English which are the same in both written English and spoken English.

The leading kind of paragraph development for all three sources taken together was examples. *Reasons* was first for letters to the editor, but *examples* was second. A kind of development not mentioned by any textbook—designated as additional comment—ranked in second place among the specific types for *Saturday Review* and the *English Journal*. Fifty-eight paragraphs in all were developed by this method, which ranked third actually, but was next to examples for paragraphs developed by a single method. In between came paragraphs developed by a combination of methods (see Tables I and II).

A paragraph from *Saturday Review* (November 12, 1966) is an example of additional comment:

> (1) There are 32,000 current words in *The Concise Oxford Dictionary*. (2) We don't know who invented them. (3) What an enormous inheritance! (4) Shakespeare used 10,000 of them. (5) It would take many more volumes than Shakespeare's to employ the 32,000 logically and cogently. (6) In a 5,000 word article I may use only 1,000. (7) Are 31,000 of these words superficial and extraneous to the reporting of what I have learned? (8) I have learned that you would think so if you ever saw a magazine editor at work on my work!

The first statement introduces the idea of the large number of words in the English language. The next five provide additional comment related to the initial statement. Sometimes, as in sentence (4), statement of additional comment provides information. Sentence (7) asks a question, and statement (8) furnishes additional comment related to the initial statement as well as to the question of sentence (7). This paragraph is obviously not developed by any of the traditional methods. There are no examples, no reasons, no definitions, no repetition, no causes or effects, nothing in chronological order, no description, no comparisons, and no contrasts. The method used supplies only additional comment in the sentences after the first one.

The second most frequent kind of development was by a combination of methods. Here is an example from *Saturday Review* (December 17, 1966):

> (1) From the tense days in Little Rock through the school boycotts in Northern cities a decade later, the whole thrust of the civil rights movement in education has been centered on the goal of integration.

> (2) Bussing, rezoning, pairing plans, educational parks, metropolitan planning have been the bywords of the civil rights movement. (3) Although there were demands for better schools in slums, too, the name of the game was integration. (4) But there have been few winners so far.

As stated in the first sentence, the theme of this paragraph is that all the efforts of the civil rights movement have been oriented toward integration. Statement (2) follows one textbook method and gives examples of these efforts. Statement (3) does not continue this method; it is largely a repetition of (1) but provides additional comment. According to the criterion used for classification, this paragraph could not be assigned to any particular method because no one method of development was used in over half of the supporting statements. This paragraph is typical of those with no single method but with a "variety of methods" instead.

The methods combined by authors most were the same as the specific methods most frequently used separately: example, reasons, and additional comments. The supporting statements for all paragraphs developed by a variety of methods were classified and counted. Most of these supporting statements consisted of the non-textbook additional comment, with examples second, and reasons third. Only two of the sixty-two paragraphs involved did not use one of these three kinds of supporting statements within them, and over half, thirty-eight, included at least two of these three kinds of statements.

If a conclusion may be based on the frequency of occurrence of methods of paragraph development discovered in the three hundred randomly selected paragraphs used for this investigation, it is that writers generally use paragraphs which reflect development by additional *comment, reasons,* or *examples,* either separately or in combination. A teacher may therefore question the validity of teaching all the methods textbooks include, whether or not they occur in a broader context. Certainly on the basis of the kinds of paragraphs appearing in the sources mentioned above, teachers would emphasize examples and reasons from traditional textbook methods, and they would give equal consideration to the new additional comment method as well as to the combination of these three methods.

Even so, the second question mentioned at the beginning of this article deserves consideration: "How do writers operate to incorporate in their writing whatever methods of paragraph development they use?" It was pointed out that traditional procedures have seemed to assume that choosing a method of development preceded paragraph composition. The question may be raised, however, as to whether a writer consciously selects a method of paragraph development. Perhaps what he does is only to act in accord with his purpose in writing. It would seem that a paragraph writer usually intends (1) to explain (often with examples), (2) to state his opinion (i.e., to comment), (3) to argue or to persuade (often supported with reasons), or (4) to fulfill two or more of these purposes. Could it be that the writer accepts whichever of these four purposes he feels within him? If so, he is likely to use examples when he explains, additional comment to state opinions, reasons to argue or to persuade, and a combination of two or more of these methods of paragraph development to fulfill a combination of purposes.

This procedure would seem to be in agreement with Robert Gorrell's theory that a writer makes a commitment with each sentence.[5] The response in one or more sentences to follow depends on the nature of this commitment. In one instance the first sentence or two of a paragraph may commit the writer to an immediate delivery of one or more examples. The nature of his topic sentence has dictated that first he must develop his paragraph in this way: i.e., by examples. In another instance, he may begin a paragraph, "The team should receive the support of the entire student body." Thus, he has committed himself to argue for this proposition and, therefore, to present reasons. Of course, if he then uses examples to defend these reasons, the resulting paragraph will show that methods of development sometimes overlap. A paragraph may demand a certain method because it fits the broader context directed in turn by the writer's overall purpose. A method of development may thus enter naturally and without conscious decision. Minor methods found only occasionally in writing—chronology, repetition, cause-effect, definition, contrast, description—may also occur naturally when required by an author's purpose.

Is there any necessity for direct instruction in particular methods of paragraph development as provided by the majority of textbook series? Should there be formal practice in methods that may be used without conscious decision? Much teaching in the English class in the past—attention to formal grammar, for example—was irrelevant to the real use of language. A similar danger exists in the modern age of rhetoric if the English teacher, in the name of rhetoric, turns to formalities of paragraph development irrelevant to the output of contemporary writers, both those who dash off a letter to the editor and those who compose considered paragraphs for *Saturday Review*, the *English Journal*, or some other periodical of recognized general or professional quality.

[5] Robert Gorrell, "Not by Nature: Approaches to Rhetoric," *English Journal*, 55 (April 1966) 409–416, 449.

A Generative Rhetoric of the Essay

FRANK J. D'ANGELO

Order in composition presents itself to observation as a set of necessary relations capable of exact description. The work of the rhetorician is to uncover these relations. Yet despite the countless number of composition and rhetoric texts dealing with arrangement, we know very little about order in composition. In many texts, arrangement is either neglected, or its treatment is woefully inadequate.

Although we have a number of useful studies describing patterns of arrangement beyond the sentence, very little has been done in describing units of discourse beyond the paragraph. Most notable of the approaches to form and structure beyond the sentence are the following: Zellig Harris's discourse analysis, Samuel Levin's analysis of linguistic structures in poetry, Francis Christensen's generative rhetoric of the paragraph, Alton Becker's tagmemic approach to paragraph analysis, and Paul Rodgers' discourse-centered rhetoric of the paragraph.[1]

Michael Grady, a former colleague of Christensen at Northern Illinois University, has attempted to apply the principles set forth by Christensen to the analysis of the whole composition.[2] Grady extends these principles in the following way: Every expository essay, states Grady, has an introductory sequence which is roughly comparable to the topic sentence of a paragraph. This introductory sequence is often included in the introductory paragraph (the topic paragraph), but if the essay is long, then the introductory sequence may be expressed in rather general terms. The

College Composition and Communication, vol. 25 (December 1974), pp. 388–396.

[1] A. L. Becker, "A Tagmemic Approach to Paragraph 16 Analysis." *College Composition and Communication* (December 1965), pp. 237–242; Francis Christensen, "A Generative Rhetoric of the Paragraph," *College Composition and Communication*, 16 (October 1965), pp. 144–156; Zellig S. Harris, "Discourse Analysis," in *The Structure of Language*, eds. Jerry A. Fodor and Jerrold J. Katz (Englewood Cliffs, N.J.: Prentice-Hall, Inc. 1964), pp. 355–383; Samuel R. Levin, *Linguistic Structures in Poetry* (The Hague: Mouton and Co., 1962); Paul C. Rodgers, Jr., "A Discourse-Centered Rhetoric of the Paragraph," *College Composition and Communication*, 17 (February 1966), pp. 2–11.

[2] Michael Grady, "A Conceptual Rhetoric of the Composition," *College Composition and Communication*, 22 (December 1971), pp. 348–354; "On Teaching Christensen Rhetoric," *English Journal*, 61 (September 1972), pp. 859–873, 877.

supporting paragraphs narrow down and add specific details and examples to the base sequence. "Thus the relation between sections of the body of the paper, and the Introductory Sequence is conceptually the same relationship that holds between the subsequent sentences in a paragraph, and the topic sentence of that paragraph." [3]

Grady's view that the supporting paragraphs in an essay are structurally related to the introductory sequence of the essay in the same way that the subsequent sentences of a paragraph are related to the topic sentence of that paragraph has some value. My own approach to discourse analysis, however, is one that conceives of units larger than the paragraph as primarily a sequence of structurally related sentences (i.e. a group of sentences which are related to each other by coordination and subordination) and secondarily as a sequence of structurally related paragraphs.

In this view, the essay is a kind of macroparagraph. The first sentence of the essay (or extended discourse) is the organizing sentence. (I shall call it the *lead sentence* to distinguish it from the traditional concept of the thesis sentence.) The lead sentence is the top sentence of the sequence; it is the sentence that gets the discourse going. Subsequent sentences in the discourse are related to it by coordination or subordination.

The method for analyzing the structure of an extended discourse is very similar to that proposed by Francis Christensen for analyzing the structure of a paragraph. But it also is related to the kind of analysis of the paragraph proposed by Paul Rodgers. To Rodgers:

> Paragraph structure is part and parcel of the structure of the discourse as a whole; a given stadium becomes a paragraph not by virtue of its structure but because the writer elects to indent, his indentation functioning, as does all punctuation, as a gloss upon the overall literary process under way at that point. Paragraphs are not composed; they are discovered. To compose is to create; to indent is to interpret.[4]

Rodgers contends that there are many reasons for indenting a new paragraph. The paragraph may in fact shift to a new idea. But oftentimes the writer decides to indent because of a change in tone, because of a shift in the rhythm, because of emphasis, or purely because of formal considerations. Christensen claims that he is always conscious of paragraphing when he writes. Rodgers asserts that he usually goes back after he has completed his writing and then makes his paragraph indentions. Surely the truth lies somewhere between. We invent paragraphs, and we discover paragraphs. At times we are highly conscious of the reasons for indenting a particular group of words as a paragraph; at times we are not.

---

[3] "On Teaching Christensen Rhetoric," p. 864.

[4] Rodgers, p. 43.

The procedure for analyzing the structure of an extended discourse along the lines indicated above is relatively simple. The reader assumes provisionally that the opening sentence of the essay is the lead sentence. Then he proceeds, sentence by sentence, through the whole discourse, searching for similarities and differences. If the second sentence is like the first, then it is set down as coordinate and given the same number as the first sentence. If the second sentence differs from the first, then it is indented as being subordinate to the first, and it is given the number 2. If the third sentence differs from the second, it too is indented and given the next number, but if it is coordinate to the previous sentence, then it is given the same number. A sentence may be either subordinate or coordinate to the sentence immediately above it.

The method of determining coordination and subordination between sentences is not always clear in Christensen's analyses of paragraph structure, which often seem to be based on an intuitive sense of semantic relationships between sentences. However, there are a number of ways of determining these relationships, many of which are well known to teachers and students. There are two main kinds of subordination between sentences: grammatical subordination and semantic subordination. Some typical examples of grammatical subordination include: the use of a pronoun in one sentence to refer to a noun in the previous sentence; the use of transitional markers such as *therefore, nevertheless, thus*, and the like, to tie sentences together; the repetition of a word or a part of a word (based on the same root) in a subsequent sentence to link it to a similar word in the previous sentence; and the use of a synonym to refer to an equivalent word in a previous sentence. Semantic relationships are much more difficult to discern, but in general these relationships are determined by noting the deductive or inductive movement of the meaning relationships in a discourse. Thus a sentence which gives an example, a reason, a statistic, a fact, or a detail is considered to be subordinate to a more general statement which precedes it.

Like subordination, coordination between sentences may be grammatical or semantic. One of the clearest signs of grammatical coordination is parallel structure as, for example, in anaphoric repetition. More often than not, grammatical parallelism will contain semantic parallelism, as in antithetical sentences, but if grammatical clues (for example, the repetition of similar syntactic structures such as nominals, prepositional phrases, or various kinds of clauses) are not present, then another way of determining semantic coordination is by looking for semantic groupings of examples, reasons, details and considering sentences which contain these groupings as coordinate. Clearly, much more work has to be done in delineating ways of determining relationships between sentences, but these examples do illustrate some of the more important methods.

As the reader considers each sentence in turn, indenting it as subordinate or setting it down as coordinate, when he reaches the end of the first paragraph, he then leaves enough space between the last sentence of this paragraph and the first sentence of the following paragraph so that the paragraph division becomes apparent. Then he continues his analysis, proceeding in the same manner as before. When he reaches the end of each subsequent paragraph, he leaves space between the paragraphs just as he did before.

Discourse Analysis

As an example of the kind of descriptive approach that I mean, I would like to analyze the following news article by Carl P. Leubsdorf, entitled "Contrasts Divide Goldwater Race and McGovern's," which appeared in *The Arizona Republic* on Friday, July 4, 1972:

Contrasts Divide Goldwater Race and McGovern's
Carl P. Leubsdorf, Associated Press*

1

1 Republicans hope, and many Democrats fear, that Democratic presidential nominee George McGovern is a Barry Goldwater of the left, an extremist doomed to defeat so overwhelming he will carry much of his party down with him.

2

2 Parallels do exist with Goldwater, the conservative GOP nominee routed in 1964 by Lyndon B. Johnson, but the contrasts appear to be far more striking as McGovern sets out to unify the Democrats to challenge President Nixon in November.

3

3 Like Goldwater, the liberal McGovern started with the narrow support of what was considered an extreme fringe of his party.

3 Like Goldwater, he is a pleasant man, with support from devoted followers.

4

3 As they did for Goldwater, supporters of McGovern packed the caucuses and state conventions to squeeze delegate representation often far beyond their real support among voters.

5

3 And like Goldwater, McGovern became leader of a deeply divided party with many key figures saying he not only couldn't win but meant party disaster.

* Reprinted by permission of the Associated Press, 50 Rockefeller Plaza, New York, N.Y. 10020.

6

2 Beyond the superficial, however, the differences between Goldwater and McGovern are broad and basic.

7

3 Goldwater was carried by his followers to a presidential nomination he never really wanted.

4 He regarded politics as an unpleasant chore.

8

3 McGovern, behind that blend of professor and preacher, is a politician who got his start by building a South Dakota Democratic Party that was basically a vehicle for electing George McGovern to Congress.

9

3 McGovern wants to be president, is determined to achieve his goal and confident he can.

10

4 He represents the nation's majority party that, even while divided, gives him a far stronger starting point than the divided and minority GOP gave Goldwater eight years ago.

11

3 Goldwater's nomination was fashioned in the confines of caucuses and conventions.

4 His primary record was weak until he squeaked through against Nelson A. Rockefeller in California.

12

3 McGovern's nomination is the product of political reforms that have made primary elections the dominant feature of the process.

4 Starting with a close run against Edmund S. Muskie in New Hampshire and a break-through in Wisconsin, McGovern swept victoriously through the last seven Democratic primaries and amassed two-thirds of his delegates at the polls.

13

3 Goldwater was an idealogue, a man willing, even eager to articulate and emphasize controversial positions even if it meant antagonizing large segments of his party.

14

3 McGovern envisions himself as a unifier.

4 Over the past month, he has sought to tone down his more controversial positions to increase their acceptability to potential rivals.

15

3 Goldwater sought the presidency when one president, John F. Kennedy, had just been assassinated, and his successor, Lyndon B. Johnson, was riding a wave of sympathy and support as he achieved success with a friendly Congress.

16

3 McGovern runs when the president is Richard M. Nixon.

4 While riding high after highly publicized trips to Peking and Moscow, he is still a disliked figure to a generation of Democrats who have fought him in five of the past six national campaigns.

17

2 Then, there are the issues.

18

3 Goldwater was cast, partly through his own statements, as the hawk in a nation of doves, the man who would escalate U.S. involvement in Vietnam against whom Johnson could campaign as the candidate of peace.

19

3 McGovern claims to have been "right from the start" on the central national political issue of the decade, the Vietnam War.

4 His opposition to the war has been at the heart of his public positions.

20

2 Is McGovern a Goldwater?

21

3 When the Arizona senator ran, he became the major issue of that campaign.

4 Political oratory revolved around his views, whether they were dangerous for the country.

22

3 In the last six weeks, political oratory has increasingly revolved around McGovern's proposals.

4 In California, this played a crucial part as Hubert H. Humphrey closed with a rush after polls had showed him a sure loser.

23

3 Similarly, in the fall campaign, President Nixon and his campaigners will seek to make McGovern the issue.

24

3 The South Dakota senator, in turn, will seek to make Nixon's credibility the issue.

25

4 Whether he succeeds or is forced to spend the next four months defending his record may determine whether McGovern meets Goldwater's fate.

This kind of analysis reveals a number of interesting things: the overall structure of the discourse, the organization of the paragraphs in relation to the larger structure of the discourse, the structural relationship of the sentences, and the logical presentation of the comparison.

As a macroparagraph, this essay is organized in much the same way as the "cumulative" paragraph, and it exemplifies the same structural principles. It is a sequence of sentences related to one another by coordination and subordination. The first sentence is the *lead sentence*; it acts as the organizing sentence of the entire discourse. The second sentence, which constitutes a new paragraph, is subordinate to the first. Sentences 3 and 4, which together comprise the third paragraph, are parallel structures which are coordinate to each other, but subordinate to the previous sentence. Sentences 5 and 6, each of which is a separate paragraph (paragraphs 4 and 5) are coordinate to each other and to the previous two sentences, but they are subordinate to sentence 2. Sentence 7 (paragraph 6), since it repeats a parallel idea, is coordinate to sentence 2. The remaining sentences are organized in much the same way as the previous sentences, i.e., they are related to each other by subordination or coordination.

If we next consider the discourse not merely as a group of structurally related sentences, but also as a sequence of structurally related paragraphs, we discover the following information. This essay consists of twenty-five paragraphs. The paragraphs vary in length from one sentence to two sentences (no paragraph is longer than two sentences) and from four words to fifty-four words. As a way of illustrating paragraph length, I have numbered the paragraphs consecutively from one to twenty-five, and I have included the total number of words contained in each paragraph in parentheses: 1 (36); 2 (39); 3 (32); 4 (26); 5 (25); 6 (14); 7 (21); 8 (33); 9 (15); 10 (28); 11 (26); 12 (54); 13 (25); 14 (28); 15 (38); 16 (43); 17 (5); 18 (35); 19 (35); 20 (4); 21 (26); 22 (36); 23 (17); 24 (14); 25 (22). The average number of words in each paragraph is 26.9. The average number of words in each sentence is 19.9. There is a total of 34 sentences in the discourse.

When we consider the relative length of the sentences and the paragraphs in relationship to the length of the sentences and paragraphs in other discourses, we cannot help but notice the paragraph divisions. What is the basis of the paragraph divisions? Is it logical, psychological, formal, or merely arbitrary? The logical basis seems to be the weakest, in my opinion. In terms of the conceptual structure of the comparison, I would consider paragraph 1 as a single unit, but I would group paragraphs 2, 3, 4, and 5 as a single paragraph; paragraphs 6, 7, 8, 9, 10, 11, 12, 13, 14, 15, and 16 as a unit; 17, 18, and 19 as another unit; and 20, 21, 22, 23, 24, and 25 as a final unit.

The opening paragraph sets up the basic antithesis ("Republicans hope/many Democrats fear") and thus logically could stand alone as a complete unit. Paragraphs 2, 3, 4, and 5 constitute another logical unit, dealing with the similarities that exist between Goldwater and McGovern, and these paragraphs could be structured as a single paragraph. In addition to the controlling idea, unity and coherence is further achieved by the repetition of parallel structures ("like Goldwater," "like Goldwater," "as they did for Goldwater," "and like Goldwater") at the beginning of the successive sentences, all referring back to the base clause, "parallels do exist with Goldwater." In fact it appears that all of the sentences marked level 2 could begin new paragraphs. The logical basis of the subsequent units would be the differences that exist between Goldwater and McGovern. In turn, each paragraph dealing with differences has a separate semantic basis. Paragraphs 6 through 16 (now considered as one unit) are based on "broad and basic" differences. Paragraphs 17, 18, and 19 revolve around "the issues." And paragraphs 20 through 25 deal with the personalities of the two candidates. So there could be a logical regrouping of the existing paragraphs into larger paragraph units. But the writer has decided, ostensibly for other reasons, to group his sentences into different units. This suggests that, at least in this discourse, Rodgers' view is valid, that is, that the paragraphs may have been discovered rather than invented.

The fact that this article appeared in a newspaper suggests some reasons why. In many newspaper articles, the sentences and the paragraphs do tend to be short. There are both psychological as well as formal reasons for this kind of structuring. Among these are the following: the educational level of the mass audience; the neat, orderly appearance that such a format presents; the readability of the paragraphs; the balance achieved by making the paragraphs the same average length.

If we regroup the sentences into new paragraph units as suggested above, the resultant structure would appear as follows:

1

1 Republicans hope, and many Democrats fear, that Democratic presidential nominee George McGovern is a Barry Goldwater of the left, an extremist doomed to defeat so overwhelming he will carry much of his party down with him.

2

2 Parallels do exist with Goldwater, the conservative GOP nominee routed in 1964 by Lyndon B. Johnson, but the contrasts appear to be far more striking as McGovern sets out to unify the Democrats to challenge President Nixon in November.

3 Like Goldwater, the liberal McGovern started with the narrow support of what was considered an extreme fringe of his party.

3 Like Goldwater, he is a pleasant man, with support from devoted followers.

3 As they did for Goldwater, supporters of McGovern packed the caucuses and state conventions to squeeze delegate representation often far beyond their real support among voters.

3 And like Goldwater, McGovern became leader of a deeply divided party with many key figures saying he not only couldn't win but meant party disaster.

3

2 Beyond the superficial, however, the differences between Goldwater and McGovern are broad and basic.

3 Goldwater was carried by his followers to a presidential nomination he never really wanted.

4 He regarded politics as an unpleasant chore.

3 McGovern, behind that blend of professor and preacher, is a politician who got his start by building a South Dakota Democratic Party that was basically a vehicle for electing George McGovern to Congress.

3 McGovern wants to be president, is determined to achieve his goal and confident he can win.

4 He represents the nation's majority party that, even while divided, gives him a far stronger starting point than the divided and minority GOP gave Goldwater eight years ago.

3 Goldwater's nomination was fashioned in the confines of caucuses and conventions.

4 His primary record was weak until he squeaked through against Nelson A. Rockefeller in California.

3 McGovern's nomination is the product of political reforms that have made primary elections the dominant feature of the process.

4 Starting with a close run against Edmund S. Muskie in New Hampshire and a break-through in Wisconsin, McGovern swept victoriously through the last seven Democratic primaries and amassed two-thirds of his delegates at the polls.

3 Goldwater was an idealogue, a man willing, even eager, to articulate and emphasize controversial positions even if it meant antagonizing large segments of his party.

3 McGovern envisions himself as a unifier.

4 Over the past month, he has sought to tone down his more controversial positions to increase their acceptability to potential rivals.

3 Goldwater sought the presidency when one president, John F. Kennedy, had just been assassinated, and his successor, Lyndon B. Johnson, was riding a wave of sympathy and support as he achieved success after success with a friendly Congress.

3 McGovern runs when the president is Richard M. Nixon.

4 While riding high after highly publicized trips to Peking and Moscow, he is still a disliked figure to a generation of Democrats who have fought him in five of the past six national campaigns.

4

2 Then, there are the issues.

3 Goldwater was cast, partly through his own statements, as the hawk in a nation of doves, the man who would escalate U.S. involvement in Vietnam against whom Johnson could campaign as the candidate of peace.

3 McGovern claims to have been "right from the start" on the central national political issue of the decade, the Vietnam War.

4 His opposition to the war has been at the heart of his public positions.

5

2 Is McGovern a Goldwater?

3 When the Arizona senator ran, he became the major issue of that campaign.

4 Political oratory revolved around his views, whether they were dangerous for the country.

3 In the last six weeks, political oratory has increasingly revolved around McGovern's proposals.

4 In California, this played a crucial part as Hubert H. Humphrey closed with a rush after polls had showed him a sure loser.

3 Similarly, in the fall campaign, President Nixon and his campaigners will seek to make McGovern the issue.

3 The South Dakota senator, in turn, will seek to make Nixon's credibility the issue.

4 Whether he succeeds or is forced to spend the next four months defending his record may determine whether McGovern meets Goldwater's fate.

This new alignment of the sentences and paragraphs clearly indicates that there is more to paragraphing than many conventional texts would have us believe. Surely the rhetorical effect of this new structure differs from that of the old. More importantly, this kind of analysis suggests that there may be a closer relationship between arrangement and delivery than previously supposed. Arrangement *(dispositio)* is that part of rhetoric concerned with the organization of a discourse. Delivery *(pronuntiatio)* is the division of rhetoric concerned with the manner in which a discourse is presented. Naturally, with the invention of printing and with the appearance of written discourse, delivery was neglected. But if we conceive of delivery in written discourse as the way in which a writer attempts to present his text in the most effective manner, clearly the relationship between delivery and arrangement takes on a new meaning. The orator could use modulations and inflections of the voice, gestures, and other mannerisms to present his text. The writer must use spelling, punctuation, indentations, and all of those devices that we usually associate with format to present his ideas. If this approach to delivery in writing seems too artificial, we should recall how effectively poets such as e. e. cummings have used these techniques in their own writing to please, to instruct, to move, or to persuade their readers.

If the study of form and structure in composition is to advance beyond the merely impressionistic (just allow the student somehow to discover his own form), the vaguely general (all that can be said about the structure of discourse is that an essay has roughly a beginning, a middle, and an end), and the prescriptive (be sure to have students outline their ideas before they begin to write), then much more attention must be paid to the rhetoric of the essay. If the ability to perceive form is so basic to our understanding of sentences and paragraphs, how much greater must it be for our understanding of extended units of discourse? Unfortunately the traditional concepts of unity and coherence have not been too helpful in this regard. Yet organization is of the utmost importance in all good writing. Usually the best writers are those who can perceive form in their own writing. Clearly then more work is needed in the analysis of the structure of extended units of discourse. This essay is merely a necessary first step in that direction.

Part Five

The Pedagogy of Composition

> *By and large, we who preside over the composition courses have refused to solve the problem of teaching, or have failed to solve it and some even to see that there is a problem.*
>
> FRANCIS CHRISTENSEN

There was a time not so long ago that the word "pedagogy" would almost automatically elicit a negative response from the academic community. The study of pedagogy, some seemed to believe, is the least profitable of all studies, and the office of pedagogue is reserved for the dullest scholar. But the word appears to be making a comeback. It is surprising how often it crops up at professional meetings, not in a negative way but in a positive and constructive light. Perhaps more segments of the academic community are coming to realize that the one thing above all else which is capable of making the finest aspects of research and scholarship available to the masses is pedagogy. After a half century of misteaching and non-teaching, the area of rhetoric and composition especially needs a sound pedagogy.

In "The Blockhead Writer: A Confessional," James E. Davis describes some of the effects of misteaching. Putting corrections on a paper may seem innocent enough to the teacher, Davis reminds us, but to the students those marks may go beyond the paper and sear the personality. One begins to wonder how many people today have deep, negative feelings about their ability to write, all because of some negative comments put on their papers long ago. The specifics have long since passed into oblivion, but the negative self-image which emerges from the experience lasts for a lifetime. We can be blockhead teachers as well as blockhead writers.

The next three essays all treat specific teaching techniques. Edmund J. Farrell ("The Beginning Begets: Making Composition Assignments") offers composition teachers some sound advice—both positive and negative—about making assignments. In "A Cumulative Sequence in Composition," James M. McCrimmon identifies three major rhetorical structures in the composing process: specification, comparison and contrast, and classification. "From specification to comparison to classification there is a straight line of sequence, and each segment of the line recapitulates the one before it," writes McCrimmon, thus indicating the relationships among the three. Classroom teachers will especially value the activities which the author suggests for teaching each of the structures. In the next article I describe a five-step teaching strategy. In all fairness I must give credit to a prospective teacher (whose name is now forgotten) who botched up a lesson in the methods class. "No, that's not the way to do it," I told her. "First, start with the Concept, *then* go to the Example," etc. By rearranging the first three steps, the approach may follow either an inductive or a deductive sequence.

The next group of articles in this section views the teaching and learning of composition at three different grade levels: elementary, secondary, and college freshman. In "Teaching Composition in the Elementary School," Mary Tingle explores the child's early attempts to bring order to his multifarious experiences. These early attempts to make order out of chaos provide "the foundations for growth in the composing process" in the elementary years. By the time young people reach high school, according to Richard L. Larson, they are ready to learn composition as "an art by which the writer tries to assure that his readers understand what he has to say, respect his opinions, and if they reasonably can, come to agree with them." Larson's proposals for achieving a rhetorical perspective include the following: (1) identifying a specific audience, (2) using questions as a heuristic procedure, (3) making rhetorical analyses of contemporary literature, (4) imitating the techniques of authors under study, and (5) using the "topics" to support argumentation.

In freshman comp classes, emphasis on a "kind of non-writing popularly known as Themewriting" often takes the place of real instruction in writing, writes William E. Coles, Jr., in "Freshman Composition: The Circle of Unbelief." Coles traces the source of the problem to the misuse of the broadly conceived, impersonal textbook. What happens when practicing writers teach freshman comp is described in Elizabeth Christman's vivid and refreshing essay "What Means? Who Says? Teaching College Freshmen to

Write Clearly." English teachers at all levels would do well to look closely at the composition curriculum at Saint Peter's College, a curriculum which features small classes, meticulous attention to concreteness and specificity, and a deliberate avoidance of verbosity and pretentiousness.

The reform of the English curriculum, writes Ann E. Berthoff in the concluding essay in this section, "is a matter immediately pedagogical, but it is nonetheless political and it is ultimately a philosophical matter." Berthoff offers a thoughtful and penetrating analysis of some of the current movements in English education, and concludes that an adequate theory of imagination can be found in the principles of rhetoric. Her account of the pervasiveness of rhetoric is eloquent.

> It is not a matter of introducing rhetoric as a separate discipline; rhetoric is already "there" since we cannot consider structure, function, shape, sound, voice, weight, pace, image, argument, allusion, meaning, intention, interpretation, context without thinking rhetoric. Rhetoric reminds us that the function of language is not only to name but also to *formulate* and to *transform*—to give form to feeling, cogency to argument, shape to memory. Rhetoric leads us again and again to the discovery of that natural capacity for *symbolic transformation*, a capacity which is itself untaught, God-given, universal.

It is in the language of rhetoric, in a *lexicon rhetoricae*, the author believes, that English teachers will find "the terms and the central notions for the philosophy of knowledge that we need, for a theory of imagination." The significance of this statement should not be overlooked. It implies that the principles of rhetoric are valuable not only as knowledge for its own sake but also as a means for discovering further knowledge. It signifies that rhetoric is not so much an artifact as it is a tool—a tool for understanding language, but even beyond that, for comprehending many aspects of one's environment. Although such an idea may be misinterpreted by some as claiming too much, to most of us, I believe, it provides a valid and worthy rationale to undergird the pedagogy of our subject.

The Blockhead Writer: A Confessional

JAMES E. DAVIS

Boswell tells us that Dr. Johnson, because of his indolent disposition, uniformly adhered to the following strange opinion: "No man but a blockhead ever wrote except for money." Boswell also admits that there are numerous instances in history to refute this, but I, for one, tend generally to believe Johnson's statement. But the world is full of blockheads and money grubbers. I, like many others I assume, find myself playing both roles from time to time, and occasionally at the same time. I would like to give a brief history of one human being's writing experiences which I have entitled "The Blockhead Writer: A Confessional." At the end of the confessional I hope to draw a few conclusions which may be worth considering in teaching composition, or perhaps I should more appropriately use James Moffett's term—the universe of discourse.

As far back as I can remember, certainly from age three or four, I liked to tell stories. Stories which through the encouragement of parents, older brother, and sisters grew ever more lengthy and complicated. I also liked to make up verses on practically any subject, and this for sheer fun. It must have been in the first grade, along about the time that I became a guest story teller for the second grade, that I knew I was destined to write. Remember that I had not written yet. But I had composed!

This story telling continued to be a very important part of my home and school life until it reached a kind of peak in the fifth grade when I had a teacher who much preferred to let the students in her class entertain than to teach dull subjects like mathematics and history. She was on a relevancy trip twenty-five years ahead of her time, and in Appalachia too! We not only told stories, but we even serialized them so that each new day offered cliff-hanging installments of our own, undoubtedly based on such models as "Nyoka, the Jungle Girl," "Zorro and His Fighting Legions," and "The Purple Monster Strikes." We made speeches that year too, and we discussed the war—the Second World War. Yes, we talked, talked, talked.

Elementary English, vol. 48 (March 1971), pp. 328–331.

But in the sixth grade, we were asked to do new things—study history, geography, fractions, and we were told at the beginning of the year that we would do a lot of writing. How thrilled I was! At last I would get a chance to begin my writing career. At last I would be able to write down some of the things I had been thinking and talking about for several years now. But when the teacher told us what we had to write about, I became less excited. No, it would not be stories or poems. The first topic on which we were asked to write was "How I Spent My Summer Vacation." How familiar I was to grow with that subject over the years! I had spent my summer vacation at home pretty much in the same way all the other kids had spent their summer vacations, and the few really interesting things I had done that I considered exciting and memorable were personal things that I did not particularly want to share with the teacher or anybody else. The teacher said it was a very bad paper. The spelling was bad. The punctuation was bad. The grammar was bad. It was not well-paragraphed. I needed topic sentences and on and on. . . . To prove how bad it really was, she had put red marks all over it and graded it F. A few more papers like this and I wasn't so sure about being a professional writer after all.

Through junior and senior high school I did not write a great deal in connection with classes. But when I did, here are some samples of criticisms I received from the teachers:

1. Your writing sounds too much like speaking. Speaking and writing are not the same.
2. You should make your writing more formal.
3. Always have topic sentences for your paragraphs.
4. Never use contractions.
5. Write on the topic assigned.
6. Don't make things up.
7. Don't use emotional words.

Occasionally there was an encouraging comment such as:

1. That sentence is grammatically correct.
2. Although the mechanics are terrible, you have some good ideas.
3. You have an occasional flair but need discipline.
4. Your spelling is improving, but you still have a long way to go.
5. This paper is better than your first one, but your first one was pretty bad.
6. Keep working!

You might reasonably conclude that by this time I had given up any possibility of becoming a writer. No, I had simply learned that there was a monstrous gap between what the teachers expected in writing and the topics they required us to write on and having something to say and saying it because you wanted to say it. So I did some bootleg writing on the sly.

By the time I arrived in college I found that I had a great deal of fear about the writing process and that I was learning more and more to avoid it. The general tendency that I had all through college, and still have, is to avoid writing as much as possible and to approach each new writing task as a life-death struggle in which I hold off writing to the last possible moment, convinced that it can't be done, and then compose in a kind of feverish desperation. This, according to my writing instructors in college, is not the way it should be done. One should choose a subject, or have one chosen for him. Next one should narrow the subject and collect all of the available material on it. Then he should decide what he wants to say about the subject and organize it in an outline, preferably in a sentence outline! Finally, the paper should be written being sure that it is clear, concise, coherent, orderly, and neat. Be sure that the paper has a good introduction, an adequate body, and a conclusive conclusion.

Realizing that my writing process did not follow what the teacher or the handbooks told me, I proceeded to grind out papers on through graduate school, with some guilt feelings because I did not always know what was happening. I played the blockhead role right on to the dissertation, which I think deserves more detail. I worked for months, full-time, gathering data for that dissertation. And then I worked for more months gathering additional data which I knew I did not need and could not use, gradually realizing that I was doing additional research simply to keep from writing. Finally, I had to face my stacks and stacks of notes. I tried formulating an outline, in fact tried doing all of the things I had been told for years would help a writer to get started. Nothing helped. I put away the notes and began a two month period of movie going, book reading, including a long stint with Agatha Christie, playing with my kids, and other devices to escape. Of course, I also worried about the dissertation. Finally, as the deadline drew nearer and nearer and realizing the work had to be done, I managed to complete the first draft in a few weeks of almost uninterrupted flow. I got the degree.

My indolent nature remained constant but money and professional interests continued to spur me on, in addition to the fact that I occasionally had something to say which I wanted very much to say to some audience. In those few instances, the writing came relatively easy. I frankly thought the dissertation would end my writing career, but I have since written some articles (I have 69 rejection slips to prove it) and have just this week completed the 19th (and I hope last) chapter in a high school text series on, ironically, composition.

I speak here today as a writer who, if he has learned anything at all about writing, has probably learned it all the wrong way. Possibly the main thing that has made me a blockhead writer is that I began writing too late. Dr. Johnson made a very insightful statement on that subject, "A man should begin to write soon: for if he waits till his judgment is matured, his inability through want of practice to express his conceptions will make the disposition so great between what he sees and what he can attain, that he will probably be discouraged from writing at all."

But while I do believe that during those early years in elementary school, I should have been writing as well as talking, I believe just as strongly that the opportunities I had to deal there with the whole universe of oral discourse was invaluable preparation for later writing. At the beginning of whatever this is that I have been doing—a kind of therapy (I composed it from the couch)—I promised that I would draw a few conclusions which might be worth considering in teaching writing. Here goes:

1. Talking, indeed the whole universe of discourse, is important. It is important in and of itself, but it is also important preparation for writing. In the talking, ideas are generated for composition. The talker may work himself toward a stance or a commitment on a subject.
2. Writing is commitment, and honest commitment is always difficult, for it is lonely. To force a writer to write at a more rapid rate than he is ready to write may force him to be dishonest and to pretend to be committed to what he is in fact not committed to.
3. Writing is highly individualized. There is no bag of tricks. Prescriptions do not work. Some writers say writing is easy; for me it is hard. Some writers do all of their planning on paper; others do most of it in their heads.
4. The subjects that a writer is going to write on should come from within, not from without.
5. Writings should have audiences. If a writer has something to say, and some reason for saying it, he will have come a long way toward discovering how to say it. Constructive criticism of writing can be helpful. Negative criticism tends to be frustrating and is generally self-defeating in that the flow is simply stopped.
6. In the teaching of writing, the process is more important than the product. Writing is a way of coming to know as well as a way of knowing.
7. Finally, writing cannot be done on a timetable. Theme a week and sentence a day approaches do not work. I believe that there are "happy moments" for composition. And since I began with Dr. Johnson, I think I shall end with him too.

Boswell says that "Somebody talked of happy moments for composition; and how a man can write at one time, and not at another—'Nay' said Dr. Johnson, 'A man may write at any time, if he will set himself *doggedly* to it.' " This may be true, but you ought to know that in his *Dictionary* Dr. Johnson defines *doggedly* as *sullenly, gloomily.* All too often writing and even more often the teaching of writing are engaged in sullenly and gloomily. This should not be the case.

The Beginning Begets: Making Composition Assignments

EDMUND J. FARRELL

Why teachers give so little time and thought to creating composition assignments has often perplexed me. Justifiably they protest the inordinate demands made upon them in the evaluation of students' themes, the laborious hours given to the written work of the too many students in the too many classes they daily meet. Yet, rather than mitigating this load by furnishing assignments that would stimulate students to write clearly and imaginatively, they seem to compound it eagerly with slap-dash assignments composed in the spur of the half-hour before school begins or, worse, in the five minutes between classes. I have even observed a few intrepid souls risk instantaneous creation during the few precious seconds they were able to turn their backs on classes, chalk in hand, to scribble furiously before chaos triumphed.

All teachers deserve respite from the daily sound of their own voices. It is a comfort indeed to wander aisles observing students quietly writing, to surfeit on silence, and not feel the pangs of guilt that showing a movie or spinning a record provoke. One can justify his existence: rather than mulcting the citizenry of tax revenues, he is having students write, an activity endorsed by the most conservative parental group in favor of bettering the education of the nation's youth.

But after the tranquility of the day comes the gnashing of the night, when the teacher who has lugged home the illiterate and puerile products he inadvertently has encouraged, suffers to find grace and sense where none exist. Their summer vacations were vacuous, their families a bore, their hobbies morally questionable, their syntax tortured, and their styles atrocious. And so, bleary-eyed to bed, red pencil blunted, morale dissipated, give-em-hell lecture contemplated, and source of problem ignored.

For some time now in the methods course I conduct on the teaching of English in secondary schools, I have had student teachers write lesson plans for a few short stories—Shirley Jackson's "The Lottery," J. D. Salinger's "The Laughing Man," and Hawthorne's "The Minister's Black Veil."

English Journal, vol. 58 (March 1969), pp. 428–431.

Included with each plan have been two composition assignments which the student teacher believed might suitably follow the teaching of the selection. From these hypothetical assignments I have culled and ordered those which exemplify a failure on the part of student teachers to anticipate what they are asking of students, to imagine themselves adolescents trying with as little cerebral friction as possible to fulfill the demands being made upon them. Based upon the work of the student teachers, the admonitions which follow are offered humbly, for I believe that each of us can find examples of his own pedagogical aberrations in the list and can recall the profitless hours of evaluating papers which resulted therefrom:

1. *Avoid assignments that can be answered yes-no, true-false:*

    Does man's need for self-preservation ever justify sacrificing others in order that he may live?

    People are the creation of their environment.

2. *Avoid assignments that lead to short, often fragmentary, responses:*

    How did you feel when you finished "The Lottery"? Why?

3. *Avoid assignments that lead to idle speculation or that may be treated frivolously:*

    Factors which might have caused Shirley Jackson to write such a story.

    The day I (my friends, our country, etc.) threw rocks at Tessie Hutchinson.

4. *Avoid assignments which are vague or which assume knowledge students may not possess:*

    Elaborate on the symbolism in "The Lottery."

    Trace the development of imagery in "The Lottery."

    Emphasize the recurring themes.

5. *Avoid assignments which, by posing numerous questions, provoke incoherency:*

    Compare the hero image of the Laughing Man with the movie hero image of James Bond. In your discussion, you may want to consider some of the following questions: What ingredients does the Laughing Man have or not have in comparison? Would the young boy in the story find James Bond a satisfying hero? Why or why not? Which image do you find more satisfying?

6. *Avoid assignments which a student may regard as too personal:*

    Relate the feelings of guilt experienced and expressed by Mr. Hooper and the townspeople to a personal experience in which you felt the pangs of guilt (e.g., cheating on an exam, lying to teacher or parent, defaming the character of a fellow student, receiving unearned praise for work which is not your own). Be specific. Use examples from the story to make comparisons.

Relate an instance in your own experience where you have inflicted injury (not necessarily physical) on another person as a member of a group. How did you feel at the time? How did you feel afterwards when you were alone?

7. *Avoid assignments which pit a novice writer against a professional:*

Decide what is the central idea, or cluster of ideas, carried by the story and then sketch out in several paragraphs a short story form, differing from that of "The Lottery," which might also be appropriate to carry these ideas. You may want to consider whether the story might be developed as a mood piece, as a strongly didactic piece, as a characterization, or whatever. To get started, you might consider how the short story authors we have studied so far might have presented such an idea—Saroyan, Steele, or Poe, for instance.

Write a story of your own, patterned after "The Lottery," but with the situation, events, and people that exist today in the South.

Select one part of the story, e.g., congregating of the people to distribute the lottery papers, the selection of Tessie Hutchinson as the victim and the consequent action. Write the selection as Hitchcock might write for presentation on TV.

Common to these assignments is the absence of a stipulated audience and/or purpose which would help the student to define himself in context, which would lead him to adopt an appropriate persona or "speaking voice" in his composition. Without prior knowledge as to why and/or to whom he is writing, even the professional author would be incapable of maintaining consistent tone, tone depending upon the individual's decision about who he is, a decision which can be made only in relationship to an occasion and audience. To belabor the obvious, an adolescent's discourse or the "self" he presents, is different on a date from what it is at home, different at home from what it is in the classroom.

Speaking at the CEE luncheon at the Honolulu convention of NCTE, Professor Walker Gibson observed:

> . . . When we can recognize that choices of language are dictated not alone by subject matter, and not alone by audience, but involve as well a self-creating act, the taking on of a role with a personality, an attitude, an identity—for some of us, at any rate, that perception offers a part way out of the woods. Thus a central activity of the

> composition course becomes the encouraging of students to take on various roles in their writing through exercises that may simply force upon them, however crudely, various rhetorical characters.

If Walker is correct, and I believe he is, then it behooves us to create composition assignments which stimulate students to role play, to indulge themselves in a gamut of personalities during their adolescent years. Only thus will they discover the range of rhetorical voices available to them in writing.

Let me now offer some composition assignments with built-in "selves" and indicate some of the available options as to audience and purpose. Again, the assignments were written by student teachers, some for classes they were teaching, but only after their initial efforts at composing assignments had been critically discussed in class:

1. *The "self" of an assignment may be internal to the selection, the purpose unspecified, and the audience private:*

   Assume that you are Lady Macbeth and that you keep a diary. Write the five entries which precede your suicide.

   Assume that you are the narrator in "The Laughing Man." You are in the bathtub on the evening after John Geduski has recounted the last episode of the Laughing Man story. What passes through your mind?

2. *The "self" and the audience may be internal to the selection and the purpose specified:*

   Word has reached the church fathers that Parson Hooper is dead. The Reverend Mr. Clark, who tended him at the end, was so impressed that he has petitioned the synod for permission to don a black veil and follow in Parson Hooper's footsteps. You have been asked to submit a report to a committee of church leaders stating why Mr. Clark should or should not be allowed to don a black veil.

   You are Tom and have been away from home now for three months. Write to Laura trying to explain to her why you left.

3. *The "self," audience, and purpose may be external to the selection:*

   A friend of yours comes to you with a copy of *Macbeth* and says, "I understand you've read this play in class. What should I look for in it so I can most fully understand it?" What advice would you offer?

   You have a pen pal in a foreign country. He asks you to recommend a book which captures the spirit of this country. From your reading in English III this semester, select the novel which you believe best satisfies your friend's request. Write to him, explaining why you are recommending the novel you have chosen.

4. *The "self" may be internal to the selection and the audience and purpose external:*

You are Sanger Rainsford and have undergone the experiences narrated in "The Most Dangerous Game." A group of high-school students, interested in starting a Rifle Club, have written to you, requesting that you speak to them. You accept the invitation. What have you to say?

You are one of the inhabitants of Spoon River who have died. You have an opportunity to speak out from the grave, summarizing your life in a paragraph or two. What comments have you to make?

In short, if assignments are composed carefully so as to assist students to produce appropriate voices or "selves" in their writing, if students are not asked to do what the teacher would not want to do, if they are given a choice of assignments as well as the opportunity to create their own, then their writing should be more pleasurable to read and much easier to evaluate.

But lest the reader be left believing that he has been furnished a panacea for all students' prose, he should be reminded of the anecdote about the teacher who asked that each of her students assume he was a famous personage in history writing to a beloved one in a time of crisis. From one boy came this memorable epistle: "Dear Josephine, I just wanted to let you know things didn't go so hot at Waterloo."

Humility, saith the preacher, in all things.

A Cumulative Sequence in Composition

JAMES M. McCRIMMON

"How can principles of rhetoric, logic, and grammar be arranged cumulatively according to the pupil's maturity level?" To avoid duplication with Professor Gorrell, who deals with the interrelation of grammar, and composition, and with Professor Hook, who deals with the interrelation of grammar, logic, and rhetoric, I will place my emphasis on what I shall call *rhetorical structure.* Let me explain that term.

The rhetorical structure is the organization of symbols to which we respond in any unit of communication. For example, Keats's sonnet, "On First Looking into Chapman's Homer," has at least three major structures—a grammatical structure, a metaphorical structure, and the generic structure of the Italian sonnet. All these together make up the rhetorical structure of the sonnet. I use the phrase *rhetorical structure* to get away from the divisiveness of the trivium—grammar, logic, and rhetoric. As Professor Hook has pointed out, rhetoric includes grammar and logic; it also includes semantics. Whatever elements in a communication affect our response are parts of the rhetorical structure of that communication.

What I want to do here is to illustrate how rhetorical structures may be arranged in a sequence which is cumulative in the sense that each new structure tends to include those preceding it, so that when a student learns how to handle one kind of structure, he can use that experience to master the next kind. The particular sequence I will illustrate for Grades 7, 8, and 9 has been influenced by the writings of Jerome Bruner, Albert Upton, and others, but it is chiefly the result of experiments and experience in the classrooms of the laboratory school of the University of Illinois. For the most part, the illustrations which I will use are lessons taken from the curriculum being developed at that school.

Specification

The first stage in the sequence I am concerned with is specification. If we ignore errors in spelling, punctuation, conventional sentence structure,

* *English Journal*, vol. 55 (April 1966), pp. 425–434.

and grammatical agreements of various kinds as matters of usage rather than of composition, I think we will all agree that the greatest weakness of inexperienced writers—and this holds true for college seniors as well as for seventh-graders—is their addiction to undeveloped, unsupported, and unexplained statements. For example, I ask a seventh-grader to write an essay about why he liked a particular short story, and he answers in a single sentence that he liked it because it was "interesting." He does not understand that his answer gives me no additional information, that he has merely substituted the abstraction "interesting" for the abstraction "likeable." I must now ask him what events in the story he found interesting. Only when his words point to specific events in the story does he begin to communicate to me.

Some of you will have noticed that part of the blame for this failure to communicate was mine. By asking a general question, I invited a general answer. Had I asked a more specific question, I might have guided the student into a more specific response, and such a response might have helped him to bring himself into a relation with the story and so evaluate its effect on him. As those of you who have read *how the french boy learns to write* must know, some of the bad writing we get from our students is a result of our failure to specify the assignment. Young students have to be guided into good writing. They can best be led into being specific by putting them into situations which require specific responses. This is especially true when they are being asked to revise inefficient work. It is not enough to ask them to be more specific; they must be shown what kind of specificity is wanted, and where. One way to direct such a revision is shown in the following assignment.

The purpose of this exercise is to revise a student essay so as to make it a more specific communication. At successive points in the essay, numbers have been introduced, and for each number a question is asked at the end of the essay. You are to answer these questions on a separate sheet of paper. When you have answered all the questions, you will be asked to revise the essay.

> *The Secret Life of Walter Mitty* tells about a man's daydreams.[1] His wife nags him[2] and he begins to dream. In his dreams he is a hero who has many adventures, such as a pilot and a doctor.[3] In real life he is a very ordinary person,[4] but he becomes a great man in his dreams.[5] He does a lot of exciting things.[6] His wife is not very nice.[7] She bosses him terribly.[8] The story tells how he escapes from her bossing in his daydreams.

1. Is the purpose of the story simply to tell about his daydreams, or are the dreams chosen for a special reason? State the purpose of the story.
2. Give examples of her nagging.

3. If a reader of this essay does not know the story, will he know what "such as a pilot and a doctor" means? What adventures is the author of this essay thinking of? State the adventures so that a reader will understand them.
4. What kind of ordinary person is he? Describe the "real" Walter briefly but specifically.
5. What kind of "great man"? Give an example.
6. If examples are given in 5, this statement will not be necessary, since the examples will show the exciting things he does.
7. In what ways is his wife not nice? If she is something more than bossy, give an example here. If she is only bossy, ignore this sentence.
8. Give examples of her bossiness.
9. Study your answers to these questions and group them under three headings: (1) the purpose of the story, (2) Mrs. Mitty's treatment of Walter and the way he accepts that treatment, and (3) his daydreams.
10. Starting with the purpose, rewrite the essay in the light of your answers.

This exercise was put on a transparency and projected on a screen for class discussion. I find it useful to do a good deal of this kind of work in the classroom. I have little confidence in the kind of help I can give a student by my written comments on his paper. That procedure is more useful for proofreading than for teaching composition. But I find that if selected essays are projected and discussed in detail by the whole class, not only is the revision more efficient, but the whole attitude toward revision is changed. It is no longer a question of a particular student's trying to appease a fault-finding teacher; it is an experience in communal authorship, which can be discussed at every stage of the composition. Teachers often complain—and rightly so—of the burden of grading compositions, but it seems to me that they often confuse evaluation with teaching. It is usually necessary at the end of each term to assign a grade which is a fair estimate of the quality of the student's work, but it is not necessary that every paper written during the term be graded. A graded assignment once a month would meet the evaluation requirements; the rest of the writing can be designed as learning experiences in which the class discovers by writing and criticism some of the differences between good and bad writing.

But I must return from this digression on grading. The best approach to specificity, I think, is through semantics. The minimum prerequisite is at least a rudimentary knowledge of the abstract nature of language and of the difference between words that point to things which we can see, hear, feel, taste, and smell and words which refer to classes of things. And the best pedagogical device for teaching this lesson is the abstraction ladder, which shows a range between very concrete and very abstract terms. The old distinction among proper nouns, common nouns, and abstract nouns is a less efficient method of teaching the same lesson. All nouns are abstract. It is only when they are restricted by modifiers and descriptive details that they point to individual and specific things. The following lesson illustrates this point:

The Meaning of Class Names
(X_1 is not X_2)

Here are pictures of two objects. A rectangle has been placed around them to indicate that they are to be understood as "real" objects, not pictures. You can cut them with a fork and eat them.

1. Are these objects the same? Alike? If you were hungry and were offered one, which would you choose, and why?
2. What do the names under the objects tell you about them? If the objects are different, why do they have the same name?
3. The apples in the pie at the left (No. 1) were first quality Jonathans grown in New York State. The flour was milled in Minneapolis from wheat grown in Kansas. The butter came from a Wisconsin dairy famous for its dairy herd. The pie was baked by the chef of the Waldorf Astoria from his own private recipe.

   I made the other pie (No. 2). I got the apples off our driveway where they had fallen from the old apple tree that I have been meaning for years to cut down. I cut out all the worms and most of the bruised spots and I rejected any apples that had been run over by the car. I got the flour from an open package at the back of the top shelf of the kitchen cabinet. I don't know how long it had been there, but it had no weevils in it, at least none that I could see. We were out of butter, so I used the contents of the can into which my wife drains the used cooking grease. I was very careful in preparing the crust, because I had never baked a pie before, but the recipe was so smudged that I had to guess at some of the measurements and ingredients. To make sure it was well cooked, I baked it in a hot oven for two hours. The crust got a little scorched but, except for that, it looked pretty good to me.

4. If you were hungry and were offered one of these objects, which would you choose, and why?
5. What does the name "apple pie" tell you about these objects? What does it not tell you? What do the numbers above the objects tell you about them?
6. What do we mean by the statement, "Apple pie_1 is not apple pie_2"?
7. If apple pie_1 is not apple pie_2, do you think a similar distinction can be made between $seventh\text{-}grader_1$ and $seventh\text{-}grader_2$? $Teacher_1$ and $teacher_2$? $Democrat_1$ and $Democrat_2$? X_1 and X_2, where X is any noun?
8. Using the example in 3 as a model, write a two-paragraph composition to illustrate *one* of the following statements: Woman $driver_1$ is not woman $driver_2$; $Redhead_1$ is not $redhead_2$; X_1 is not X_2, where X can be any class name you choose.

The lesson that class names, or common nouns, do not point to things but to characteristics that classes of things have in common is basic to specification. All description depends on it. The describer must use words that point through the class to the individual member with which he is concerned. This leads to what Matthew Arnold called writing with one's eye on the object, and one of the things that an emphasis on specification leads to is a concern with what the object actually looks like. It is not an exaggeration to say that at this stage in the teaching of composition we teach students to write by teaching them to see what they are writing about. Some of you, no doubt, remember the accounts of how Agassiz taught his students to understand the anatomical structure of fish by forcing them to look and look and look again at the structure of particular specimens. We composition teachers would be wise to follow his example, and to drill into our students that observation is a prerequisite for thinking, and thinking a prerequisite for writing. The structure of the writing must reflect in all significant details the structure of the subject as the writer perceives it. At least in the best of all possible worlds, rhetoric recapitulates experience.

This emphasis on the structure of the subject can be extended to the structure of a piece of writing. American children are supposed to have a genius for taking things apart to see how they work. They should be invited to take rhetorical structures apart and to see the interrelation of the parts. The following lessons invite them to take paragraphs apart to see how the general idea of the topic sentence is specified through examples.

Paragraph Structure

Study each of the following paragraphs and answer the questions that follow it.

(1)

(1) The greater the speed, the less control the driver has over the car. (2) For example, a man driving at 30 miles an hour needs only 73 feet to bring the car to a complete stop, but a man driving at 60 miles an hour needs 222 feet.

a. Which sentence expresses the main idea of the paragraph? Call that the *topic sentence.*

b. What is the relation of sentence 2 to sentence 1? Which sentence is lower on the abstraction ladder?

c. In the light of these answers, describe the structure of the paragraph.

(2)

(1) Beauty is a quality which tends to endure. (2) In a house that I know, I have noticed a block of spermaceti lying about closets and mantelpieces for twenty years, simply because the tallow-man gives it the form of a rabbit; and I suppose it may continue to be lugged about unchanged for a century. (3) Let an artist scrawl a few lines or figures on the back of a letter, and that scrap of paper is rescued from danger, is put in a portfolio, is framed and glazed, and, in proportion to the beauty of the lines drawn, will be kept for centuries. (4) Burns writes a copy of verses and sends them to a newspaper, and the human race takes charge of them that they shall not perish.

a. What is the topic sentence of the paragraph?

b. What is the relation of sentence 2 to sentence 1? Is sentence 2 higher or lower on the abstraction ladder?

c. What is the relation of sentence 3 to sentence 1? Which sentence is lower on the abstraction ladder?

d. What is the relation of sentence 4 to sentence 1? Which sentence is lower on the abstraction ladder?

e. In the light of these answers describe the structure of the paragraph.

f. Now suppose we added a final sentence to the paragraph:

(5) People treasure beautiful things and usually try to preserve them.

What is the relation of this sentence to sentence 1? Describe the structure of the expanded paragraph.

g. To save time and space we can use symbols to represent the parts of the structure of these paragraphs. We can use TS for "topic sentence," E for "example," and R for "restatement of the topic sentence." With these symbols we can describe the structure of the paragraphs as follows:

Paragraph 1: TS + E
Paragraph 2 (original): TS + E_1 + E_2 + E_3
Paragraph 2 (expanded): TS + E_1 + E_2 + E_3 + R

Once students have a good grasp of the structure of this kind of paragraph, they can extend it to multi-paragraph essays by using two or more sustained examples and allowing a paragraph for each example. The structure is generative in the sense that, once a student learns it, he can generate more examples for himself. Think what any normal 12-year-old could do by applying this structure to the theme, "Why don't grown-ups practice what they preach?"

I have spent so much time on specification because I think it is a prerequisite for almost everything else that the student will do in composition. If we divide composition into two major concerns—organization and development—we are here dealing chiefly with the problem of development. The student will always be dealing with that problem. But if, during the seventh and eighth grades, he acquires the habit of spelling out, through specific reference and illustration, the implications of general statements, he will have already reached a level of rhetorical maturity that many college freshmen never achieve. Yet that level is not beyond his capacity. It is not difficult to have him give an example of what he means or to have him point to specific things and events. He does this all the time with his peer group. The difficult thing is to persuade him that the standards of communication inside the classroom are not fundamentally different from those outside of it.

Before I move on to the next stage, I should like to add that this approach to specific communication has useful by-products. As we deal with the relation of topic sentence and paragraph development, of theme and examples, we are already beginning to lay a foundation of purpose and unity in a piece of writing. We are also, through our concern with these relations, creating an awareness of rhetorical structure.

Comparison and Contrast

In specifying we are concerned chiefly with reporting, with using words to point to things, and with explaining general statements by means of examples and illustrative details. In the next stage, comparison and contrast, we are getting into judgment. We are interpreting experience by selecting material and organizing it into some shape imposed by our interest in it, or by our purpose. Students who have already had some work in semantics will recognize this activity as part of the process of classifying. Indeed, observation, comparison, and classification are successive stages in a continuum. Each new stage subsumes the one preceding it, but in simple classifications the stages are so closely related that they seem to occur simultaneously. Since what experiences are selected in a comparison depends on the purpose for making the selection, work on comparison-contrast provides a natural introduction to the concept of purpose.

Exercises in comparison may be made as simple or as complex as the teacher thinks appropriate to the student's ability and previous experience. These exercises may be used for a wide variety of purposes—to compare two characters, actions, or themes in a novel or play; to explain different points of view, customs, or values; to explore alternative solutions to a problem or to weigh the advantages and disadvantages of a proposal. Since comparison-contrast is a common starting point for inference making, exercises in comparison lend themselves conveniently to inductive teaching in many subjects.

In developing a contrast of two subjects, A and B, we have a choice of two basic patterns, which I shall call A + B and A/B + A/B. In the A + B pattern we say all that we wish about A before saying anything about B, so that the paragraph or essay is structured as two balanced halves. In the A/B + A/B pattern the contrast is established cumulatively, sentence by sentence, and the balance lies within the sentence. As the Kennedy inaugural address illustrates, the second pattern is chiefly a ceremonial form today. For most purposes, and certainly in junior high school classes, the A + B structure is the more useful.

The following lesson requires students to analyze the structure of a paragraph which develops a contrast by first stating it generally in the first four sentences, then developing A and B in turn by illustrative details, and finally restating the theme in a concluding sentence. If this paragraph were expanded into a multi-paragraph essay, as it might be, its structure would be expanded but not changed. The first paragraph would be an introductory statement announcing the theme of the essay and explaining the contrast at a general and introductory level. The second paragraph would apply the theme to the ant society, the third to the goose society. The fourth paragraph would be a concluding restatement of the theme. In other words, the structure shows the same logical relation among the parts whether the comment is presented in one paragraph or several.

When a comparison or contrast follows an A + B structure, the essay or paragraph naturally tends to break into two parts. From your earlier work on paragraph structure, do you remember a structure in which the topic sentence was followed by two or more subtopic statements? Study the structure of the following contrast and answer the questions that follow.

> (1) The Wart's adventures as an ant and a goose were contrasted lessons in government. (2) Both adventures were designed by Merlin to prepare the Wart for kingship. (3) Each illustrated a society in operation and the values held by that society. (4) The Wart was expected to learn a lesson from the contrast. (5) As an ant he saw the tyranny of a dictatorship which reduced individuals to automatons. (6) The ants had no freedom. (7) They were brainwashed by

propaganda both in peace and in war. (8) They could make no personal choices. (9) All that was not forbidden to them by the state was compulsory. (10) Their lives were governed by "Done" and "Not done," and what was done or not was decided by their leader. (11) By contrast, as a goose, the Wart saw how individuals lived in a free society. (12) The geese chose their leaders freely for their skill in guiding the migrations. (13) They followed these leaders willingly but were not subject to them. (14) They accepted the mutual responsibility of taking turns as guards to warn of the approach of danger; but the thought of war with their own kind was so abhorrent to them that Lyo could not accept the Wart's question about war as serious. (15) When she realized that he was serious she was so shocked that she would not speak to him. (16) In the contrasted lessons of the ants and the geese Merlin showed the Wart society at its worst and best.

a. Which is the topic sentence of the paragraph? Mark it TS. Which two sentences serve as subtopic statements to introduce the ant and the goose adventures? Mark them st-1 and st-2 respectively. These divisions mark out the general outline of the paragraph. Is that structure A/B + A/B or A + B?

b. What is the function of sentences 2, 3, and 4? Do you remember what we called sentences like these? What is the function of sentences 6, 7, 8, 9, and 10? Of sentences 12, 13, 14, and 15? Of sentence 16?

c. If this paragraph were to be divided into two, where would the division occur?

d. If the paragraph were to be expanded into a four-paragraph essay, what would be the content of each paragraph?

I suggested earlier that comparison-contrast tends to include specification. The comparison establishes the main structural divisions—in this example, the topic sentence and the subtopic statements. But within these divisions the development is by specification. This specification is just as essential here as in our earlier examples. Without the illustrative details provided by sentences 6, 7, 8, 9, 10 and 12, 13, 14, 15, the contrast required by the purpose does not get adequately established. It is not surprising, therefore, that nine of the 16 sentences in this paragraph develop the theme by specification.

From comparisons of the kind we have been considering, it is a short step into analogy and metaphor, the structures of which can usually be described as a proportion: *a* is to *b* as *c* is to *d* in some identifiable sense. Thus Keats's first reading of Chapman's Homer was like an astronomer's first sight of a new planet in the sense of the thrill of discovery. The following assignment provides at least a rudimentary model from which a student may generate his own analogy.

Using the following short analogy as a model, develop an analogy for the following topic sentence: The relationship between a ______ and a ______ may be illustrated by an analogy with ______. Fill in the blanks with the terms of your choice.

> The relationship between a writer and a reader may be illustrated by an analogy with dancing. Anybody who has danced knows that both partners move in accordance with patterns which both understand and take for granted. The man, by his leading, indicates which pattern he wishes to set; the girl follows. If the man leads his partner to expect one kind of movement and then switches to another, the girl will have difficulty following.
>
> The relationship between a writer and a reader is similar. Each assumes that the other is familiar with the basic patterns of sentence structure. The reader, like the girl in the dance, must follow the writer's lead, and as long as the writer keeps to an accepted pattern the reader has no trouble. But if the writer sets one pattern in the first half of a sentence and then shifts to another, the reader is likely to be confused.

Every student can do something with a model like this, and some students will do surprisingly imaginative work. I had an eighth-grade student who filled in the blanks in this model to make the statement that the relationship between a teacher and a student may be illustrated by an analogy with photosynthesis. Then she went on to develop the figure that the teacher, like the sun, provided the light, and the student, like the plant, absorbed it and converted it into nourishment. But, she continued, photosynthesis is a function of the plant, not of the sun, and it occurs only when the plant is actively converting sunlight into food. When it stops converting, no chemical reaction takes place. The sunlight still falls on the plant, but nothing happens.

It is not difficult to give students—even quite young students—a sense of the structure of comparison, but, of course, the quality of what is said in that structure will depend on the talent that the student brings to the comparison. The perception of the similarities and differences between things is an intellectual activity, and the greater a student's mental powers are, the more sensitive, imaginative, and significant his comparisons will be. Nevertheless, I think that experience with the structure of comparison, especially if it is carried on through analogy and metaphor, will help students to think more efficiently. Professor Upton of Whittier College is said to have raised the IQ of a group of college freshmen by ten points by exercises in critical comparisons and analyses. Certainly if the new rhetoric is going to be worth cultivating, it must go beyond clarity and grace of expression and provide a procedure for helping students to improve the substance as well as the style of their comments.

CLASSIFICATION

The next stage after comparison is classification. As I suggested earlier, this is an extension of comparison. To be able to classify things, a student must first observe that they have something in common. But classification goes beyond this recognition and, by organizing and shaping perceptions, it creates new knowledge.

Classification may be approached inductively and deductively. Inductive classification is the heart of the discovery method. It is the means by which we organize and record experience. It is primarily a form of self-communication. Deductive classification is a method of communicating with others. When we have interpreted experience inductively, we explain the results to others deductively. The following assignment will illustrate both processes.

The following words illustrate the chief types of semantic change (changes in meaning) in English. For each word, the first meaning given in parentheses is the old or original meaning; the second meaning is the modern one. Look over the words, then follow the directions given below them.

1. *acorn* (various kinds of nuts—the seed or nut of oak trees)
2. *bonfire* (a fire for burning bones or corpses—any large outdoor fire)
3. *boor* (a farmer—an ill-mannered person)
4. *boycott* (an Irish captain who was ostracized by his neighbors—refusal to associate with any person or group)
5. *cad* (a younger son of an aristocratic family—an ill-mannered fellow)
6. *cattle* (property or wealth—cows, bulls, and steers)
7. *champagne* (wine from a French district—any wine resembling French champagne)
8. *corn* (a hard particle—the seed of a particular cereal crop)
9. *cunning* (knowing or skillful—tricky or meanly clever)
10. *dean* (an officer in charge of ten people—a major college administrator)
11. *deer* (any small animal—a particular animal with antlers)
12. *discard* (reject a card—throw something away)
13. *ferry* (travel—travel by boat)
14. *gossip* (a godparent—a spreader of rumors)
15. *hussy* (a housewife—a woman of low morals)
16. *knave* (a boy—a villainous man)
17. *knight* (a young male servant—a titled person)
18. *lady* (a breadmaker—a woman of quality)
19. *martinet* (a French general who was a stickler for discipline—any rigid disciplinarian)

20. *minister* (a servant—a clergyman or statesman)
21. *pedagogue* (a slave—an educator)
22. *shibboleth* (a password used in the Bible—any word or phrase that identifies a particular group)
23. *shirt* (a loose outer garment worn by either sex—a garment worn by a man)
24. *skirt* (a loose outer garment worn by either sex—a garment worn by a woman)

1. Examine the words to see if you can detect any patterns of change. That is, do you find certain words showing the same kind of change —for instance, *bonfire—boycott—discard* show one kind of change, and *boor—cad* another.
2. Group all the words that illustrate one type of change in a list and over the list write a heading which describes that change. This procedure will give you Class I and the name or description of that class. Repeat the procedure until you have established the four major classes of semantic change.
3. Convert your findings into an outline of the following form:

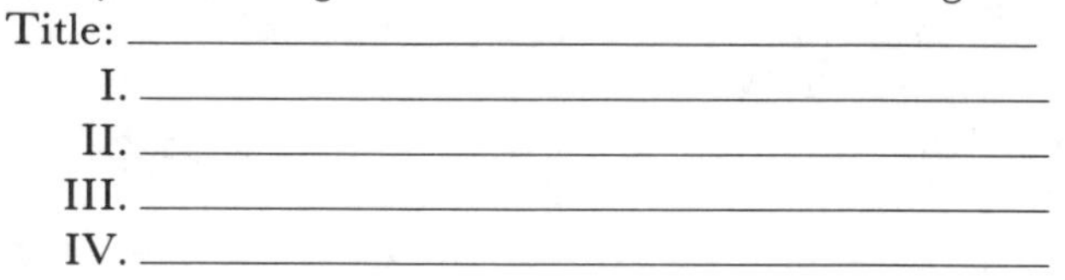

4. Fit the following words into the classes which you have already established:

   brat—child; *butcher*—a killer of goats; *campus*—a field; *citizen*—a city dweller; *clerk*—a cleric or clergyman; *count*—a companion; *cupboard*—a shelf for holding cups; *daft*—neat; *dismantle*—take off a cape; *eaves*—edges of any kind; *ferry*—to travel in any way; *fowl*—any bird; *frock*—a loose garment worn by a monk; *front*—forehead; *idiot*—a private person as contrasted with a public official; *liquor*—a liquid or fluid of any sort; *nice*—foolish; *a prude*—a modest person; *sergeant*—a servant; *silly*—happy or blessed; *starve*—to die in any manner; *steward*—the keeper of a pig sty.
5. For each of the four Roman numerals in the outline, write a paragraph consisting of a topic sentence developed by all the examples that are pertinent in that paragraph.
6. Now write an introductory paragraph which converts the title into a sentence which states the general conclusion of the study and explains that statement by one or more clarifying statements.
7. Finally write a concluding paragraph that sums up the content of the essay.

There are four things I'd like to point out about this assignment. First, difficult as the task may seem, it is really only a more challenging application of techniques which the student has already learned—the techniques of comparison and specification. Through comparison the student selects and organizes his material; through specification he illustrates the conclusions he has reached. What I am saying now is merely a restatement of what I said earlier. From specification to comparison to classification there is a straight line of sequence, and each segment of the line recapitulates the one before it.

Second, whether the assignment is difficult or easy depends more on the teaching procedure than on the subject matter. If students are required to work independently on this assignment, many of them will have difficulty and some of them will be frustrated. But if they are allowed to work as a group, sharing each other's insights and doubts, they will tend as a group to profit from individual contributions and to correct false leads. Indeed, it is at least theoretically possible that a brilliant student could lead the class to a quick break-through. He might see that *bonfire, boycott,* and *discard* were alike in that their meanings had become extended from narrow to wide. He might see that *boor* and *cad* had changed in the direction of taking on unpleasant meanings. He might then reason that for every class there is likely to be an opposite class, and so he might set up the hypothesis that the four changes were from narrow to wide, from wide to narrow, from good to bad, and from bad to good. If he tested that hypothesis, he would find that it worked, and he would have solved the problem without plodding through every word. I must admit that I have not actually had such a student, but I have had groups of students who, working together, achieved similar results.

Third, the teacher's contributions to the discovery is the structuring of the assignment. Once he has organized the specific steps in the total process, he withdraws from the solution, or at most limits himself to asking questions designed to challenge and invite reconsideration of a wrong turn in the thinking. If he obtrudes into the solution he will deprive the class of the thrill of discovery. He will then be like some critic telling Keats how wonderful Chapman's translation of Homer is. I doubt that any sonnet would ever have been written.

Finally, the method of doing this assignment can be generalized into a strategy for attacking other problems. The student has learned more than the common patterns of semantic change. He has learned an operational procedure which he can use in situations in which it is applicable, and these situations exist in all subject areas. As a result, the student is likely to have increased confidence in his ability to solve other such problems, perhaps even increased confidence in English as a subject.

One more point before I finish. I am not proposing this sequence as a universal composition curriculum for junior high schools. I am too clearly aware of individual differences among students and teachers alike to suggest that one sequence will satisfy everyone. I think it is important that there be a sequence in the composition work in successive grades, and I think that sequence should have some kind of explicit rationale—that is, it should be a true sequence, not just a succession of unrelated units. But I have no conviction that all students should follow the same sequence or that they should follow any sequence at the same rate. I am not, therefore, giving you a ready-made composition curriculum to apply in your own classes, but rather working out the implications of a point of view. There are other points of view, and many of them yield useful sequences. What is important, I think, is for the teacher to commit himself to some sequence, not necessarily to this one.

CEHAE: Five Steps for Teaching Writing

RICHARD L. GRAVES

English teachers are coming to realize more and more that the main problem in composition is not that we are teaching it *poorly*, but rather that we are not teaching it *at all*. We are discovering that in the typical assign-write-evaluate process there is really little or no actual teaching. Squire and Applebee found, for example, that English teachers on the average devote only fifteen percent of class time to composition, and most of this occurs *after* the papers are returned.[1] Dwight L. Burton has identified the ability to teach composition as one of the major gaps in the preparation of prospective teachers:

> Prospective teachers need to learn as much as possible about how to *teach* composition. This may seem an overobvious suggestion. Most prospective teachers have work in methods of teaching English in which there supposedly is concern with how to teach writing, but often there really isn't treatment of how to *teach* writing, but only talk of how to make writing assignments, how to evaluate student papers, etc. Even many experienced teachers don't know what to do about the matter except to motivate students as best they can, then criticize the works the students produce, and hope for the best the next time.[2]

The late Francis Christensen well understood this need when he shrewdly observed nearly a decade ago, "In composition courses we do not really teach our captive charges to write better—we merely *expect* them to."

We are discovering that *admonishing* students is not the same as *teaching* them. When we say that a paragraph should have unity, coherence, and emphasis, we are really being more the advice-giver than the teacher. We might as well say that a paragraph should be good, beautiful, and true, or that it should be well-written, or even that it should be groovy. The problem

English Journal, vol. 61 (May 1972), pp. 696–701.

[1] James R. Squire and Roger K. Applebee, *High School English Instruction Today* (New York: Appleton-Century-Crofts, 1968), pp. 121–122.

[2] Dwight L. Burton, "English in No-Man's Land: Some Suggestions for the Middle Years," *English Journal*, 60 (January 1971), p. 29.

is that an adjective such as *coherent* has such a vast range of meaning, it is unlikely that the students' understanding of the term will coincide with the teacher's. We might attempt to define the term, but in order to be successful such a definition must be comprehensive enough to include the best examples from the written language and yet succinct enough to be intelligible and useful. That alone would be a task in itself. Or we might walk into our classroom "cold-turkey, with no preparation" and demonstrate coherence by writing a coherent paragraph, but like Robert Zoellner I have never seen this done—nor have I done it myself. As Zoellner says, "We are very good at talking *about* writing—*but we never write.*" [3]

If forging a definition is too tedious and showing by demonstration too uncertain (if not nerve-shattering), then a third alternative may be in order. It may be possible to teach young people about coherence and other rhetorical and linguistic principles by showing them examples of it. In searching for and presenting the best available examples, we not only give our students a clearer approximation of the concept but bring our own understanding into sharper focus as well. This technique, it seems to me, is superior to working from a definition, because examples are more concrete and more specific. Too, prepared examples have the advantage of being more efficient than cold-turkey examples, although some of the cold-turkey variety would likely add spice to any composition course. This use of examples is a central part of a teaching technique which I have called CEHAE, a five-step sequence designed to promote the understanding and use of certain kinds of knowledge.

CEHAE, an acronym for *concept, example, highlighting, activity, evaluation,* is designed primarily for teaching certain rhetorical principles, but it may be used for teaching any principle which seems buried or obscured in extraneous material. The steps are sequential and closely related, each step being based on the one before it. There are two teaching goals inherent in the technique. The first is that students will understand the principle, *i.e.,* recognize it when they see it, distinguish it from other principles, etc., and second, they will be able to produce examples of it and use it as it is needed.

It should be emphasized that I view these five steps as *a* technique for teaching writing, not *the* technique. The situation in composition today is similar to that in linguistics a decade ago: there are several distinctly different approaches available to the classroom teacher, each with its own potential worth, its own techniques, its own peculiar assumptions about the nature of writing. Many of these, it seems to me, may be classified as either *structured* or *unstructured* approaches. The structured approaches usually begin with some form of teaching which leads to writing the paper. By contrast, unstructured approaches begin with motivational activities, especially those which capital-

---

[3] Robert Zoellner, "Talk-Write: A Behavioral Pedagogy for Composition," *College English*, 30 (January 1969), pp. 310–311.

ize on student interest, and include direct teaching only as the need arises. The first type may be characterized as *systematic,* the second as *functional,* or perhaps as *opportunistic.* To date, neither has been conclusively shown to be superior over the other. It may very well turn out that a decade from now (or even sooner) the best composition curriculums will be eclectic, utilizing the best of both approaches.

Following is a detailed description of the technique.

The first step is the identification of the *concept* or principle to be taught. At first glance this may seem obvious, but in reality it is fraught with hazard. The main problem is that we do not fully understand just what goes into good writing, much less great writing. We cannot say with much accuracy just what the components of good writing are, nor do we know how many there are. If we knew these things, the teaching of composition would be much simpler.

There is a danger then that this first step might easily turn into a Slough of Despond. Therefore, in order to avoid becoming bogged down, we might say this: Identify the concept *if possible;* if a specific concept cannot be identified, then proceed with caution. The technique can still be effective even though this first step is not completely satisfied. The concept may become clear *after* some of the other steps have been attempted, for the very process of working out the other steps may in itself shed light on the first step. It is always good to begin at the beginning, but if it is not possible we must then begin where we can.

For the purpose of illustrating the technique, let us assume the following as a concept or a teaching goal: *To achieve coherence in a paragraph structure through the use of definitions and counter-definitions.*

The second step, the presentation of an *example,* is an important one. Since this step embodies the basic technique of teaching by example rather than definition, the ultimate success of the whole program hangs on this point. A good example will often compensate for a vague concept, but there is no remedy for a bad example. Although the teacher may not be aware of it at the time, a large amount of learning will likely occur here. Many students who were confused at Step One will gain some understanding of the concept when they see it illustrated.

Sometimes a passage of literature may be useful not because it illustrates a particular concept, that is, not for any utilitarian purpose, but simply because it is valuable for its own sake. There are passages which we "feel" are very moving or very beautiful, and yet they do not seem to serve any immediate, practical purpose. Passages such as these can be effectively used as examples and should not be discarded just because they do not seem to fit the system. The instructor might show such a passage to his students and ask their opinion of it. If their opinion is favorable, he might then ask what rhetorical or linguistic principles led to its effectiveness. The first question is designed to encourage the expression of literary appreciation; the second attempts to provide some objective basis for it. The kind of discussion that follows would, ideally, involve both teacher and student in the process described in Step One, in a mutual search for discovering or clarifying or refining some underlying principle. Once this is accomplished, it may then serve as an integral part of the procedure.

There are a number of ways of presenting examples—anthologies, ditto sheets, Xerox sheets, etc.—but overhead projection is one of the most effective. The main limitation to overhead projection is the amount that can be shown—usually no more than one paragraph or five to eight sentences at a time. The advantages, however, far outweigh this drawback. In most instances the projector will be sufficient, but in those few cases where more space is legitimately needed, ditto sheets may be used. By presenting a passage on the screen in front of the room, the instructor can focus the attention of all his students at one place. Instead of saying, "Page 913, third paragraph from the top, right in the middle of that paragraph," he may point directly to the word or sentence in question. Furthermore, he may use all the accessories available with overhead projection—overlays, diagrams, charts, drawings, as well as the technique which is comprised in Step Three, Highlighting.

The following passage is an example of the concept identified in Step One, the achievement of coherence through the use of definitions and counter-definitions:

> It is not of supreme importance that a human being should be a good scientist, a good scholar, a good administrator, a good expert; it is not of supreme importance that he should be right, rational, knowledgeable, or even creatively productive of brilliantly finished objects as often as possible. Life is not what we are in our various professional capacities or in the practice of some special skill. What *is* of supreme importance is that each of us should become a person, a whole and integrated person in whom there is manifested a sense of human variety genuinely experienced, a sense of having come to terms with a reality that is awesomely vast.[4]

Highlighting the concept is the third step. This involves pointing out the specific principle under consideration and differentiating it from the other material at hand. This has the effect of creating a background and forefront, of setting up a sharp contrast between what is extraneous and what is to be taught. In the example the highlighting would look like this:

> [It is not of supreme importance that] a human being should be a good scientist, a good scholar, a good administrator, a good

[4] Theodore Roszak, *The Making of a Counter Culture* (New York: Doubleday Anchor, 1968), p. 235. Quoted by permission of the publisher.

> expert; it is not of supreme importance that he should be right, rational, knowledgeable or even creatively productive of brilliantly finished objects as often as possible. Life is not what we are in our various professional capacities or in the practice of some special skill. What *is* of supreme importance is that each of us should become a person, a whole and integrated person in whom there is manifested a sense of human variety genuinely experienced, a sense of having come to terms with a reality that is awesomely vast.

The advantage of the overhead projector at this point is obvious. The highlighting may be done with a suitable pen, or even better, with colored adhesive transparent tape placed on an overlay. If necessary, up to four overlays may be used with each base transparency, each overlay having a different color and representing some different principle to be taught. The result is that students can see one or several concepts clearly demarcated from the mass.

Until now the learner has been chiefly cast in role of observer, but in Step Four he becomes actively involved in process. This step represents the point at which the quintessence of teaching occurs, the point at which the teacher can see the tangible results of his work.

In Step Four the students are provided with an activity, but most important, an activity *based on the highlighting.* In effect, they are given a skeletal example of the concept and then asked to develop it fully. An activity based on the Roszak passage would look like this:

> It is not of supreme importance that ______________________.
> ____
> It is not of supreme importance that ______________________
> ____
> ______________ is not ______________________________.
> What *is* of supreme importance is that ____________________.

Like the example, the activity may either be dittoed or projected on a screen in front of the class. If individual work on the activity is preferred, the ditto would be suitable. If a group effort, or what James McCrimmon has called "communal authorship," is preferred, then overhead projection is superior. McCrimmon goes on to say that projecting work on the screen has the further advantage of efficiency and of establishing a good attitude toward revision:

> But I find that if selected essays are projected and discussed in detail by the whole class, not only is the revision more efficient, but the whole attitude toward revision is changed. It is no longer a question of a particular student's trying to appease a fault-finding teacher; it

> is an experience in communal authorship, which can be discussed at every stage of the composition.[5]

Ideally, the teacher would use both techniques—individual and communal authorship—so that his students might have the advantages of both.

For some reason all educational techniques seem to conclude with "evaluation," and this one is no different. The final step is to determine how well the students have learned the principle under consideration. "Learning" here means two things: the ability to recognize the principle in their reading and the ability to use it in their writing. To test the first situation, the teacher might present a new passage and then ask how it is organized. This kind of question requires the learner to *apply* what he knows to a new situation. The teacher might present his class with a passage such as the following from Kenneth Burke and ask how it is similar to the Roszak passage:

> Eloquence itself, as I hope to have established in the instance from *Hamlet* which I have analyzed, is no mere plaster added to a framework of more stable qualities. Eloquence is simply the end of art, and is thus its essence. Even the poorest art is eloquent, but in a poor way, with less intensity, until this aspect is obscured by others fattening upon its leanness. Eloquence is not showiness; it is, rather, the result of that desire in the artist to make a work perfect by adapting it in every minute detail to the racial appetites.[6]

It is to be hoped that the students will recognize in both passages that coherence is achieved through the use of definitions and counter-definitions, by telling what something *is* and what it *is not.*

The second kind of learning, using the principle in one's own writing, is much more difficult to evaluate—and much more important, I believe. The teacher might make a frontal attack on the problem simply by making a test based on the format of Step Four. With some slight alterations an activity can easily be transformed into an evaluative instrument. This kind of testing, however, does not completely satisfy the situation, for what the teacher really wants to know is whether the principle will be successfully used beyond the classroom. Will it be used in the office, in the home, in short, whenever and wherever it is needed? The answer to this question, unfortunately, can never be fully known. Our limited means of evaluation cannot penetrate far beyond the classroom walls. But we can hope, and our hopes will have a better chance of success if they are based on effective teaching.

[5] James M. McCrimmon, "A Cumulative Sequence in Composition," *English Journal*, 55 (April 1966), p. 427.

[6] Kenneth Burke, *Counter-Statement*, 2nd ed. (1931; reprinted Berkeley, California: Univ. of California Press, 1968), p. 41.

The reader may have observed that the technique described here is in some ways similar to those which employ models for writing. Step Two, the presentation of an example, is very similar, indeed identical, to some of those techniques. At least one difference, however, should be noted. Most "model" approaches simply announce that students should emulate Hemingway or Ben Franklin or someone else, but they do not give much advice about *how* it is to be done. By contrast CEHAE, in its emphasis on highlighting and in the subsequent activity, identifies precisely what the distinguishing feature is. Consequently, it might be said that CEHAE offers a much greater degree of specificity than is employed in most approaches that use models.

Implicit in the approach is the belief that form has the potential for generating ideas. It was Francis Christensen who said of the cumulative sentence, "Thus the mere form of the sentence generates ideas." What Christensen meant, I believe, is that if the young writer has conscious control of form, he then has within his grasp the means—a framework, if you will—for expressing his ideas. Seen in this manner, form is not intended to be used as a straitjacket for limiting or confining one's movement, though in the hands of a tyrannical teacher it might very well be. Rather, it should be viewed in just the opposite way; that is, as the means for *freeing* the writer, as an aid to assist him in developing his subject. Knowledge of form gives the writer a repertoire from which he might make appropriate choices during the writing process. But even more, the logic inherent in such knowledge of form may actually assist him in understanding his subject: it may cause him to see various possibilities for sequence and arrangement, for example. This view of creativity sees the need for both freedom *and* discipline.

To achieve the greatest success, the approach should be used in conjunction with other approaches and in programs which provide ample time for students to write. Any composition program which consists of all instruction and does not offer time for writing has lost sight of its original purpose. And of course, it will help if these five steps are employed by someone who is interested in teaching young people how to live better as well as how to write better, someone who is not only sensitive to human needs, but who is responsive as well. Someone who not only cares, but cares enough to teach.

Teaching Composition in the Elementary School

MARY J. TINGLE

When the kindergarten child announces to the teacher, "I have a new baby brother," he has engaged in the whole complex process of composing: he has abstracted from his whole repertory of experiences something that is significant to him, he has identified the audience with whom he wishes to communicate; he has been motivated by a purpose—to inform, to establish rapport; he has chosen the language and syntax to convey his communication; he has received some kind of response to his communication and has, through it, made a judgment about its effectiveness in relation to his purpose and audience. If he is encouraged by questions or comments, he will expand his composition to include related details which, in his mind, belong to this experience. He has somehow categorized the elements of the experience and brought them together to serve his purpose.

The tendency to categorize, to bring order to his personal world, seems to be intuitive to a child. The process of categorizing begins as soon as the individual becomes aware of any two elements of his environment that seem to belong together—a soft voice and presence of another person, gentle handling and food, loud voices and discomfort. How the individual does this is a matter of theory, but at a very early age—how early we do not know—he can sort out aspects of his total environment, bring certain ones together as a focus for a response, and eliminate others. The infant, through nervous responses and sensory perceptions, begins the process of grouping his experiences and responding to sets of circumstances by behaving one way in one set of conditions and another way in another.

As he grows, he learns that adults organize things differently from the way he would do it. He learns that you put a cap on the head, but not a bowl of Pablum; you wash hands in water but not in milk; you eat a cracker, but not soap; you kiss your mother but not the puppy. All around him are models of behavior, situations in which certain kinds of behaviors go together. Most of the models are called to his attention on his initial contact with them, but gradually he begins to observe and imitate. He comes to realize that

Elementary English, vol. 47 (January 1970), pp. 70–73.

certain things go together and make a unit of experience. He learns to make associations and differentiations; he learns that his experiences center about events—mealtime, bathtime, bedtime, storytime, the groupings of the routine day, and those of special occasions such as a visit to the grocery store or to grandmother's. He learns that events have beginnings, a main part, and a conclusion. A three-year-old girl watched her mother begin to clean up after her birthday party and said, "The happy birthday is all gone." For her this statement covered the beginning, the middle, and the end of an incident. The excitement of anticipation was gone, the surprise of opening packages was gone, the ice cream was gone. The significance of her simple statement is that she had identified a unit of experience. She could not retell the whole incident, but she was sensitive to the wholeness of it. A more mature person might have given an accurate report of it or drawn upon it for material for a personal essay, a satire, a bitterly realistic drama, or a poem. She could not do this, but someday in retrospect she may, for she had recognized the unitary nature of the experience.

By the age of two the child has learned the names of many items in his environment. He can see similarities among items to which a common term applies. He experiments, explores, talks, and questions, and as his range of experiences broadens, he develops confidence in making comparisons and in proposing cause and effect relationships through relating the unknown to the known. A young friend of mine explained that he put lightning bugs in the refrigerator because their tails were too hot. Chukovsky in his book, *From Two to Five*, cites many illustrations of children's attempts to express their perceptions:

> The ostrich is a giraffe bird.
> A turkey is a duck with a bow around its neck.
> Make a fire, Daddy, so that it can fly up to the sky and make the sun and stars.

These childish mistakes, delightful as they are to adults, are the child's serious and determined effort to bring order into his limited and fragmentary knowledge of the world. That the child attempts to classify objects of the material world and to compare them with other objects is evidence of his potential for flexible but orderly thought.

All that a speaker or writer has to draw upon for content of his composition is his own experiences, and all that he can do is present them as he sees them. They may be direct, vicarious, or imaginative, but in some way they become a part of him and he interprets their meaning to him whenever he chooses what he will tell about them. The teacher's responsibility in helping the learner broaden his base of choice lies in two directions: (1) to lead him to see in his experiences meanings that he has not previously seen and consequently to reevaluate their significance and (2) to open the way to new experiences.

The child may have to learn that he does have something to think, talk, or write about. He is a member of the human race and has participated in the affairs of a particular culture; he has only to recognize the significance of everyday experiences to have a limitless source of ideas to think and talk about. In addition to sharing the common experiences of mankind, he has had experiences that are peculiarly his own; he has perceptions that give particular meaning to his experiences; he is unique: he is a very special person with very special things to say.

However exhausting to adults may be the endless why, how, and what-does-it-do questions of three and four year olds, it is probable that the nature of the adult responses at this time determines the extent to which the child believes that the world is worth exploring, thinking about, and talking about. Without these beliefs he is not likely to learn either to talk or to write very well—certainly not as early as he might and perhaps never.

As the child grows through the experiences of infancy, he also develops a command of language. At first he is in a world of undifferentiated sounds, but from this mass of sound, some emerge as significant: footsteps, closing of a door, speech sounds associated with activities related directly to him. He makes sounds and finds that some of them are more important than others because they evoke responses that are consistent and meaningful. As conceptualization of experiences progresses, he develops a vocabulary and a grammar through which he can express his understandings. By the age of thirty-six months some children can produce most of the major varieties of English simple sentences up to a length of ten or twelve words. They have control of the common kernel sentences of the English language and are rapidly learning the transformations that can be derived from them.

The language the child uses is the language that he can use—whatever it is, it is all he has. It is a part of him. He learns it from the people who make his childhood world; through it he is able to establish himself as a member of the group that affords him all of the security that he knows, and if it enables him to live comfortably within his group, he has every reason to believe that it is the language valued by everyone.

When the child comes to school where everyone is not like him and where his language is not the only language spoken, he may become sensitive to the difference or he may be subjected to criticism by his peers and possibly by his teacher. Since he has no alternative language and therefore no way to meet the demands of his critics, he is reduced to silence, to active resentment, or to recurring frustrations, none of which is likely to lead to fluency in the use of language. If, however, he can be respected as a person who has something to say, just as everyone does, and as a person who uses the dialect of the community, just as everyone does, his interest and pleasure in communicating his ideas will make it reasonable to him to learn standard dialect so that his range of communication can encompass people other than those with whom he lives; he will be willing to risk experimenting with composition.

So when the child comes to school he brings with him the foundations for growth in the composing process: a background of experiences, the ability to make associations and discriminations, a vocabulary through which either literally or metaphorically he can express a wide range of meanings, a knowledge of the syntax of the language, and the ability to use all of these in simple oral compositions. We as teachers must take him from there.

Basic to the child's growth in composing is the development of sensitivity to a unit of experience—the beginning, the development, and the conclusion. There are several procedures that seem useful in developing this process.

(1) *Retelling well-structured stories.*

The child that has had contact with good literature all of his life has had a model of how man shapes his thoughts. He becomes sensitive to order, to sequence, to climax and to ending.

When he reads stories like "The Three Little Bears" he is able to retell the story by recognizing the parts of the story, the sequence of actions, and the repetition that ties one incident to another. The structure is obvious enough to become a pattern in the child's thinking, and he can relate the story. He is composing and producing an oral composition but under conditions of minimal demand because the entire story is already a part of his consciousness, the structure is ready-made, much of the language is already available to him, and he knows when he has completed the story.

As students grow older and the literature that they read becomes more complex, the teacher can help improve the skills of composition—oral and written—by teaching students the conventional structures of literature and helping them to recognize the ways in which an author composes a story, shows relationships, and chooses language to express his ideas.

(2) *Developing compositions in structured situations.*

Giving some cues to the structure of a story and yet permitting freedom in response to the cues enables a child to use his own judgment in shaping a sequence and selecting details but he does not have to determine the structure. A teacher can provide such situations through using pictures about which stories can be told, stopping at a crucial point in a story that the teacher is reading and asking children to tell what they think will happen, asking children to watch a pet and tell what he did, asking children to tell the story about a picture they have painted.

(3) *Developing compositions in unstructured situations.*

The child has the freedom to choose his subject, develop his own plan for telling the story, and tell it in his own way. The sharing periods are such situations. The teacher has the opportunity to ask questions and make comments that can help the child recognize relevant information that may be added, supply kinds of details that will help the audience see, feel, hear more than he has provided or help him devise a suitable conclusion.

Thus far I have talked about the child at the pre-writing stage; however, much of our concern in schools is about teaching written composition.

By the time a child is ready to learn to write, he can talk very well. If he has had many contacts with good literature and has had many opportunities to talk, both under the carefully planned direction of a teacher, he has begun to understand what a person does when he makes a composition.

Between his skill in telling a story and in writing the story equally well is the necessity for learning to make letters, to put them together in special arrangements, and to design those arrangements in special ways. Learning to manipulate a pencil is a laborious and tension-producing experience. Learning to move the pencil fast enough to catch a thought is impossible. Thoughts have to be slowed down to accommodate the pencil. Perhaps success in accomplishment of writing is sometimes adequate compensation to the child for the loss of the fluency which is his in oral composition; however, the time spent in learning to write (and also learning to read) should not substitute, in the child's experiences, for time spent in talking and in hearing and responding to literature. His ability to think, to organize his thoughts, and to verbalize them should be at the highest level possible when the time comes that he has sufficiently mastered the skills of writing and of reading to use them without having them interfere with his intellectual growth. This means that probably through the first, second, and third grades, and for some children longer, the program in composition must include extensive, well-planned experiences in oral composition through which the child can experiment with organization and vocabulary in ways that let him stretch his intellectual capacities to his limits without the restrictions of handwriting, punctuation, and spelling. Paralleling this are experiences in writing that are leading to the time when the written composition is as satisfying to the child as are his oral compositions.

Teaching Rhetoric in the High School: Some Proposals

RICHARD L. LARSON

The phrase, "Some Proposals," is included in my title[1] to make clear that this discussion is not to be a survey of courses in rhetoric currently being taught in high schools. If I were to attempt such a survey, I fear that it would turn up few such courses. Possibly the major methods now being used to introduce rhetorical principles into high school curricula are the units on rhetoric and composition produced by curriculum study centers such as those at the Universities of Oregon and Nebraska; these units are being tested in the schools in areas surrounding the centers. But these units are new, and they were exposed to teachers outside the immediate vicinity of the study centers for the first time in NDEA institutes held during the summer of 1965; their impact, I think, has yet to be measured.

Instead of presenting a survey of writing courses, then, this paper makes some suggestions about the structure and emphasis of high school courses in composition. (My suggestions apply principally to courses that require expository writing. I leave aside for the present courses in speech or "oral English.") Let me reassure you at once that these suggestions do not include the introduction into the high school curriculum of another course (or even another unit)—this one in the history of rhetoric or in rhetoric as a body of theories about language and communication. Nor do my suggestions include the substitution of Aristotle's *Rhetoric* or Cicero's *De Oratore* or Quintilian's *Institutes* for the texts on composition now in use, although some of the current texts, as we all know, deserve to be replaced. What I am suggesting is that teachers of expository writing in high school look at expository writing from the perspective employed by most classical and many modern writers on rhetoric, and encourage their students to adopt the same perspective. I am urging teachers of composition to view writing not as a process of observing the rules of grammar, or of engaging in "creativity" as an end in itself, or of negotiating the expository "methods" that are regularly

English Journal, vol. 55 (November 1966), pp. 1058–1065.

[1] Based on paper read at the NCTE meetings in Boston, November 1965.

described in standard texts on composition, but rather as an art by which the writer tries to assure that his readers understand what he has to say, respect his opinions, and, if they reasonably can, come to agree with them.

Before developing further the values of the "rhetorical perspective" that I am proposing, I must explain how I am using the term "rhetoric." I have in mind a broader definition of the term than that of Aristotle, who, as you recall, defined rhetoric as "the faculty of discovering in the particular case what are the available means of persuasion." [2] My definition is also broader, I think, than that of Professor Corbett, who more or less adopts Aristotle's definition when he describes classical rhetoric as "the art of persuasive speech," and adds that the end of rhetoric "was to convince or persuade an audience to think in a certain way and act in a certain way." [3] Two of Kenneth Burke's definitions[4] of the term, as "the use of words by human agents to form attitudes or induce actions in other human agents" and as "the use of language as a symbolic means of inducing cooperation in beings that by nature respond to symbols," seem more pertinent for teachers of composition today, if Burke would agree that when a reader desires seriously to entertain and explore the ideas of the writer (the user of words), he has formed an "attitude" and is engaged in a species of "cooperation." I also find Richards' early re-definition of rhetoric as "the study of verbal understanding and misunderstanding" helpful as a guide to teachers of writing, since it focusses on the whole question of how a writer's words are received and understood by his readers.[5]

For my purposes in this paper, however, the most helpful definitions of rhetoric are those offered by Donald Bryant.[6] After noting the superficial meanings ("bombast," "propoganda," and the like) frequently associated with "rhetoric," Bryant reminds us that rhetoric is often concerned with questions of what *probably happened* in a given set of circumstances or what *will probably happen* if proposed action is taken. Observing, then, that rhetoric is often concerned with establishing probabilities, he calls rhetoric the strategy "for deciding best the undecidable questions, for arriving at solutions of the unsolvable problems, for instituting method in those phases of human activity where no method is inherent in the total subject-matter of decision" (p. 11). But Bryant does not limit rhetoric to the art of determining what irrevocable action should be taken in the presence of inadequate information. He finds that what he calls "rhetorical situations" have in common the use of language

[2] *Rhetoric*, 1. 2, trans., Lane Cooper (New York: Appleton-Century-Crofts, 1962), p. 7.
[3] Edward P. J. Corbett, *Classical Rhetoric for the Modern Student* (New York: Oxford University Press, 1965), p. 21.
[4] Kenneth Burke, *A Rhetoric of Motives* (New York: Prentice-Hall, 1950), pp. 41, 43.
[5] I. A. Richards, *The Philosophy of Rhetoric* (New York: Oxford University Press, 1936), p. 23.
[6] Donald Bryant, "Rhetoric: Its Function and Scope," *The Quarterly Journal of Speech*, XXXIX (December 1953). Reprinted in Joseph Schwartz and John Rycenga, editors, *The Province of Rhetoric* (New York: Ronald Press, 1965). Page references are to this reprint.

by human beings "to effect a change in the knowledge, the understanding, the ideas, the attitudes, or the behavior of other human beings" (p. 17). And he describes the rhetorical function as that of "adjusting ideas to people and people to ideas" (p. 19). Rhetoric directs the creative activity by which language is used "for the promulgation of information, ideas, attitudes. . . . Its characteristic is publication, the publicizing, the humanizing, the animating of [ideas and information] for a realized and usually specific audience" (p. 19).

Two features of Bryant's definitions will help teachers to understand the details of my suggestion that they adopt a "rhetorical perspective" in teaching composition. The first, of course, is his focus on the relationship of the writer (or speaker) and his listener. The second is his implicit assumption that rhetoric need not be preoccupied or even principally occupied with persuading or propagandizing, and that the transmitting of any information, the promulgation of any ideas, depends for its success on the adjustment of what is presented to the backgrounds, capacities, and needs of a particular group of receivers (the audience) on a particular occasion. When I speak of "rhetoric," then, I speak of how a writer can most effectively transmit a group of ideas to particular hearers or readers. And I do not insist that the effectiveness of the transmission is measured by the willingness of the audience to believe or act upon what is said. The transmission is effective if the audience understands and respects what has been said, i.e., if the audience is willing to give serious attention to the writer's ideas.

To some who are familiar with Aristotle's painstaking analysis of the interests and dispositions of various kinds of human beings, my insistence that the writer take the needs and interests of his reader into account may seem an unnecessary restatement of the obvious, but recent textbooks that include the term "rhetoric" in their titles suggest that it is not. I am now teaching a course in advanced exposition—with several prospective secondary school teachers of English enrolled—with the aid of a text (I did not help to choose it) whose title proclaims rhetoric as one of its twin subjects. But nowhere in the book do I or my students find significant attention paid to the relationship of writer and reader; nowhere does the author show that he understands the writer's cardinal responsibility to think, before writing, about how best to assure that his message will be received and "respected" by its audience.

Professor Bryant's definitions, then, help us in establishing a rhetorical perspective for teaching exposition in high schools. But even his definition, I think, does not make clear in sufficient detail the responsibilities of a writer whose work is guided by a concern for how his thoughts will be received. We can make the writer's task clearer by recalling the first three of the traditional five parts of the subject of rhetoric: invention (finding ideas), disposition (arranging these ideas in the discourse, and allocating appropriate space to each), and elocution (expressing the ideas in words and sentences).

We can say that rhetoric is the art of adapting the ideas, structure, and style of a piece of writing to the audience, occasion, and purpose for which the discourse is written.

If this definition is accepted, it reminds us of this important fact: that any writing requires the systematic and purposeful making of choices. The principal areas of choice are three: what to say, how to arrange and allocate space to what is to be said, and how to express in words what is to be said. And the major controls on the choices—the forces in consideration of which the writer makes his decisions—are also three: the audience (those who will receive the communication), the occasion (the external circumstances, together with the emotional and intellectual pressures, under which the discourse is composed), and the writer's purpose (what he hopes to accomplish by writing—what he hopes to have his audience know, think, feel, or do as a result of his writing). In identifying these "controls," of course, we recognize that the subject itself and the writer's abilities or personality may also control the ideas, structure, and style. The responsible writer can hardly make statements that his subject or his information will not permit, nor will he, in all probability, adopt a style or a voice in which he feels uncomfortable or at a severe disadvantage.

Rhetoric, then, requires the continued making of decisions as one plans and writes. Viewed from the perspective of rhetoric, writing ceases to be the carrying out of mechanical procedures and becomes, instead, an activity that requires great sensitivity and discretion. Writing is a continuous exercise in the meeting of responsibilities to one's readers.

Now suppose that the teaching of expository writing in a high school were to be designed so that students were required to produce themes directed toward a designated audience, to serve a specific purpose, in response to the demands of a particular occasion. What would result? An example may suggest an answer. The theme of comparison is about as traditional and conventional an assignment in high school courses in writing as any, with the possible exception of assignments in description and narration. But the student is usually asked to write a theme of comparison as if the process of comparing were an end in itself—as if the value lay simply in the completion of the process. Teachers teach comparison because their syllabus tells them to, or they assign comparison papers because such assignments are easy ways of forcing students to talk about two or more literary works or characters that the class has just studied. They trot out the standard methods of organizing a comparison (the last report I heard was that there are seven such methods), remind the student that the comparison must be balanced (corresponding features of both items under examination must be discussed), set the student a subject, and tell him to proceed. If he uses one of the methods of organization consistently (it doesn't usually matter which one), observes the requirement of balance, exhausts the subject (or at least covers the points the teacher has in mind), and preserves the conventions of grammar and usage, he receives an *A* and passes on to the next assignment. But he may have learned nothing of the uses to which he can put comparison as a technique of arriving at or transmitting knowledge.

The teacher with a rhetorical perspective, on the other hand, will ask students to regard comparison as a way of organizing information to achieve a purpose. In fact, students will find that comparison may serve many purposes. By comparing assigned subjects, first of all, students may *discover* important features—ones they had not already seen—of the subjects compared. Comparison, students will find, can also *provide emphasis.* By putting apparently like (or unlike) things together, a writer may discover and give the reader a livelier appreciation of the differences (or similarities) between these things. When the subjects appear side by side, what had earlier been scarcely noted may all of a sudden be sharply observed. Comparison can also *clarify.* The writer may help his reader to understand more fully the properties of an unfamiliar object by reminding the reader of the features of a similar, but more familiar, object. Next, comparison—putting items side by side—can assist a writer in judging each and *ranking* the two. (Comparison thus used is an essential tool in the making of decisions, the resolving of issues, the selecting of courses of action from among alternatives.) Finally, comparison may *argue.* The writer may make his proposition plausible by comparing his subject to another subject about which a similar proposition has already been established. The teacher with a rhetorical perspective, then, helps the student learn how to employ comparison as a method of examining or arranging data when the student's purposes in writing will be best served by that method. Comparison becomes a tool rather than a self-serving exercise. Other traditional expository procedures (definition, enumeration, classification, and the like), when viewed from a rhetorical perspective, will also become tools for a purpose rather than pointless activities in which the students simply get purposeless drill.

One more consequence of adopting this rhetorical perspective will be a re-evaluation of the grouping of writing into four "forms": description, narration, exposition, and argument. The groupings, of course, are supposed to designate different ways of ordering statements within paragraphs and paragraphs within the whole piece. But instead of emphasizing the distinctions among these patterns, the teacher with a rhetorical perspective will show students how they often interpenetrate. On occasion, to be sure, the writer's purpose may be only to "describe," i.e., to realize an object, scene, or person vividly for his reader by pointing out in succession various details of the appearance or constitution of his subject. On occasion, too, the writer's purpose may be served entirely by "narrating," i.e., by relating a sequence of events. But to "describe" an object frequently entails narrating a sequence of events in which the object is involved. To engage in "exposition," i.e., to set forth a group of ideas for the reader according to an orderly plan, frequently requires the describing of persons, places, or objects and the narrating of events. Even to argue a proposition may require the describing of objects, the narrating of events, and the explaining of causes and effects, not to mention the enumerating of grounds of belief and the prediction of the results of action (all of these last three activities would without doubt be regarded as "expository"). A teacher with a rhetorical perspective will encourage students to consider their purposes and the needs of their audiences in deciding what details to give and what kind of order to impose on these details.

Now to say that teachers of exposition in high school should adopt a rhetorical perspective may elicit agreement, but it does little to direct the teacher in employing this perspective in the classroom. Let me make some suggestions about how a teacher can encourage his students consistently to view writing as an effort to put ideas across to an audience so as to win its respect, even if it withholds agreement.

First, in many if not most of his writing assignments, the teacher can stipulate the audience to whom the students should address their papers. He can also suggest the purpose that students should try to achieve in their writing, and he can specify an imagined or an actual occasion for writing. If the designated audience is live and present (school administrators, officers of student government, members of the class just behind or just ahead of those writing), so much the better. If the papers cannot reasonably be addressed to an audience outside the classroom, other members of the class can furnish a live audience for any single student to envisage. A useful variation of the procedure might be to ask students to stipulate their own audience, purpose, and occasion. Still another variation might be to ask students to write on the same subject for different audiences (or for different purposes or on different occasions), and to discuss in class the differences among the papers that result. Students could profitably discuss, even write papers explaining, why they chose one arrangement and style for one audience, another arrangement and style for the second audience.

Second, whatever the audience or purpose for a theme, the teacher can encourage students to approach it with these questions in mind: what procedures ought I to follow in selecting and arranging my material so as to assure that I communicate completely with my reader? Given what I know of my audience and given my purpose, what strategies are available to me and which one will probably work best? Answers to these questions may suggest the amount and kinds of information the student will need to include in his theme, and the pattern of organization best suited to bringing this information together. The answers may even help students to decide how to develop individual paragraphs. To rely on the traditional types of paragraphs (illustration, cause to effect, effect to cause, and so on), students will discover, is grossly to oversimplify the task of arranging material. Quite often several different patterns of movement will have to combine in a single paragraph if that paragraph is to play its proper role in the developing action of the paper.

Third, the teacher can invite students to make rhetorical analyses of contemporary writings and speeches. Students can decide for themselves what selected editorial writers, essayists, political orators, and advertising copy writers are trying to accomplish in their pieces, and can discuss why particular combinations of data, plans of organization, patterns of sentences, levels of language, and figures of speech appear in the pieces under study. Teachers who feel uncertain about carrying on such analyses should find Corbett's *Classical Rhetoric for the Modern Student* especially helpful. Along with samples of spoken and written discourse from Greece and Rome, England, and modern America, Corbett prints extensive rhetorical analyses of many pieces. Particularly instructive for the teacher trying to employ a rhetorical perspective in teaching exposition is Corbett's discussion of President Kennedy's inaugural address. Another book that features extensive rhetorical analyses—this time mostly of essays designed for publication rather than oral delivery—is Israel Kapstein's *Expository Prose: An Analytic Approach* (Harcourt, 1955). Kapstein explores his examples in much greater depth than students or even most teachers will want to follow, but the analyses are nonetheless instructive. For teachers wishing a brief introduction to rhetorical analysis, I suggest the kinescope or the kinescript, entitled "Organization: Rhetorical and Artistic," by George Williams of Duke University, available from the Commission on English of the College Entrance Examination Board.

In asking his students to engage in rhetorical analysis, the teacher should not accept easy generalizations or fuzzy, subjective descriptions of style or argument. To understand the choices made by a speaker or writer, the student needs to identify specifically the role played by each paragraph and sentence.[7] Indeed he should be encouraged to consider why the writer used particular words and phrases—instead of alternatives that come readily to mind—at strategic points in his discourse. The student may need, for example, to decide for himself whether a particular metaphor does indeed accomplish the work of a given sentence more neatly than a plain statement. If the student disagrees with the speaker's choices, he can learn much from defending the organizational plan or figure of speech he prefers in the context. If teacher wishes his students to attempt rhetorical analysis experimentally or on a small scale, following the example set by Williams in the analysis of opening paragraphs will give them good practice—besides telling them something of value about opening paragraphs. One can, to be sure, bear down too heavily on rhetorical analysis (such analysis can produce in students the kind of self-consciousness that paralyzes thought and invention), but when used judiciously, as an instrument to help students learn about writing, rather than as an end in itself, detailed analysis of the

[7] On the rhetorical value of different kinds of sentence structure, teachers may wish to consult Richard Weaver, *The Ethics of Rhetoric* (Chicago: Henry Regnery Company, 1953), Chapter 5.

workings of sentences and paragraphs can teach as much about exposition as any method I know.

The teacher can draw another useful assignment from the rhetorical analysis of prose: he can encourage students to imitate, perhaps better still to parody, the techniques of authors under study. Imitation used to be a commonplace method of teaching writing or learning to write, but it is now out of fashion. Wisely used, however, imitation can help the student learn how it feels to write in other than his normal idiom; the exercise may help free him from inflexible, perhaps tedious, habits of expression, and may help him learn what it means to adapt style to the occasion and purpose of writing. Parody, because it is fun, may be an even more effective learning procedure than direct imitation. To parody a writer's style requires a pretty thorough understanding of that style; the pleasure in recognizing both the likeness and the exaggeration in parody will reward the student for showing that he has understood the distinctive features of that style.

Finally, why not introduce high school students to a few of the "topics," as they are interpreted by modern scholars? Four teachers at the University of Chicago show how definition and classification (argument from *genus*), comparison, analysis of cause and effect, and the use of authority can be taught as methods of *argument* to freshmen in college.[8] Mark Ashin has also shown how these "topics" work in Madison's *Federalist* No. 10.[9] There seems little reason why college preparatory classes in today's high schools cannot profit from similar instruction when they confront assignments in argument. Such assignments appear frequently in high school courses in composition, although often they appear in other guises, as assignments on controversial subjects in the interpretation of literary works, for example. Explicit discussion of a few "topics," as the teachers from Chicago demonstrate, will give students valuable practice in locating and using arguments to support their propositions—including their propositions about literary texts. Attention to the uses of testimony, in addition, will help students develop a discriminating attitude toward ostensibly authoritative statements; they will learn to evaluate the sources of testimony about events and about literary characters. From these studies they will also learn to argue more effectively about propositions that can be no more than "probably" true. Recall that Professor Bryant spoke of rhetoric's concern with deciding "undecidable" questions, with issues of what is more and less "probable."

The procedures suggested here are varied, but they come together in demanding that the student look at writing not as a sterile exercise to be performed at home or in class and shared with the teacher alone, but as a way of getting a message to someone for a purpose. Hopefully they come

[8] Manuel Bilsky and others, "Looking for an Argument," *College English*, 14 (January 1953), pp. 210–218.

[9] Mark Ashin, "The Argument of Madison's Federalist No. 10," *College English*, 15 (October 1953), pp. 37–45.

together, also, in encouraging the student to view writing not merely as a task in achieving correctness or outguessing the teacher, but as a discipline that requires the making of reasonable decisions—plans for verbal action, one might call them—in the face of the many different problems in written communication.

In adopting this view, I echo the comments made by Walker Gibson: that every writer consciously or unconsciously assumes a role and adopts a "voice" when he begins to write, and that he is better off if he chooses deliberately, or at least recognizes, the role he is adopting, than if he is unconscious of how he appears to his reader.[10] I also concur in the observations by Robert Gorrell that were quoted by Gibson.[11] But I think that the choices required of a writer, when his task is viewed from the perspective that modern students of rhetoric have given us, are more numerous than those Gibson described. It is not merely a role and a voice that the writer must choose; he also has the responsibility for selecting the substance, arrangement, and proportioning of his work. (Professor Gibson would probably concur. His discussion was limited to the writer's assumption of role and voice through stylistic choices.) Bringing to bear on the high school composition course the perspectives of rhetoric can help students learn to choose wisely in deciding every feature of their papers, and to bear in mind always the purposes for which they write. One cannot claim that they will always write "better" as a result of adopting this perspective (how hard it is to define "better writing"!), but they may at least write more thoughtfully, responsibly, and convincingly.

[10] Walker Gibson, "An Exercise in Style," unpublished paper delivered at the 1965 convention of the National Council of Teachers of English in Boston, Massachusetts.

[11] Robert Gorrell, *"Very Like a Whale—A Report on Rhetoric,"* *CCC*, 16 (October 1965), p. 142.

Freshman Composition: The Circle of Unbelief

WILLIAM E. COLES, JR.

In 1891 it was possible for J. F. Genung, a professor of English, to introduce a book on rhetoric with the following remarks on general standards of diction:

> Every author has his peculiar diction, and so has every kind of literature. But beyond these individual and class characteristics there is also a general standard of diction, which every writer must regard. That standard, or ideal, is perhaps best expressed by the word PURITY: the writer must see to it he keeps his mother tongue unsullied, and this by observing, in all his choice of language, the laws of derivation, usage, adaptedness, and taste. Transgressions of the standard are owing to want of culture and tact, either in the general knowledge and use of words, or in the special requirements of the discourse in hand.[1]

That is a statement standing for what its speaker is able to take for granted: the fact of uncommon common decency, the existence of belief and faith as shared values, the moral fusion of writing as an action with the standards by which that action is measured. Purity, culture, tact, and taste: these are not words but the terms of a life style made openly invitational. They call for a community of individuals, for self-transcendence as a means of self-realization. They are terms made by and making the syntax which contains them. Genung knew that his students knew what he knew. And in that end were their beginnings.

So much for what was.

That things have changed is no news to anyone. The appeal for writing now is different, and so (perhaps so, therefore) is the situation in which the students and teachers of it find themselves. The following passage will no doubt sound familiar:

> The aim of this text and of the course using it is to teach effective writing. *Ventures in Composition* thus combines compactly a simple,

College English, vol. 31 (November 1969), pp. 134–42.

[1] J. F. Genung, *The Practical Elements of Rhetoric* (Boston, 1891), p. 28.

practical rhetoric with clear-cut writing models. It is arranged so that an inexperienced teacher can start at the beginning and work steadily forward in a systematic manner, and so that a veteran teacher will find a great abundance of materials to use in what way he likes. In making our selections we have sought to bring together interesting, teachable, and challenging essays. [We] have used only complete, current, relatively short, chiefly expository selections and have chosen materials which cover a wide range of subject matter. Such selections as "Undergraduate Kindergarten" and "The Dating Couch" may be directly related to the student's own experience; others, such as "The Negro: Black Peril or Black Pearl?" and "Let's Razz Democracy" are less closely connected but surely will stimulate thought; still others, it is hoped, may provide an occasional shock. Growing out of each essay are exercises that test for the central idea, analyze the organization and the rhetorical principles utilized, improve vocabulary, acquaint the student with some library reference works, provide systematic dictionary study, and suggest subjects for talks and themes. Thus, this material is adaptable for a controlled source paper and also permits the student to go beyond the suggestions included in the essays and to do more independent thinking than is usually possible in projects of this kind.

The first thing a student does in freshman English is attack the problem of theme writing. A major problem for most writers—especially inexperienced ones—is how to transfer thought from mind to paper, how to make the intention and the expression one. Rather than tell the student what not to do, *Ventures in Composition* instructs him in what should be done. We have tried to present teachable principles that apply to student writing rather than to present theoretical rhetorical classifications. Throughout the book generalizations about writing are firmly anchored to detailed consideration of the practice of both professional and student writers. The range of rhetorical approach reflected in the exercises encourages the student to select with discrimination those methods most appropriate to his purpose. The student is addressed directly as one striving to learn principles of clear and vigorous writing of types suitable to his capacities and interests. *Ventures in Composition* is intended essentially to help him face the composition challenge with a measure of ability and confidence.

In hopes of making the task of correcting papers easier for the teacher and more useful for the student, we have provided not only the conventional set of correction symbols, but also a supplementary list of abbreviations which may be used in conjunction with those symbols.

To form the habit of critical reading for rhetorical principles is to begin that lifetime of improvement in reading and writing which a college course on composition should initiate. Learning to think clearly and learning to write correctly, clearly, effectively, appropriately, are worthwhile intellectual processes valuable not only in composition class but in all other outreachings of the mind.

In the sense that that preface does not introduce a specific contemporary handbook or text on rhetoric, and in the sense also that its titles are made up, the paragraphs above are a kind of parody, the preface a kind of trick. But with the exceptions of the dubbed titles and a pronoun change, each of the nineteen sentences of the mock preface is reproduced verbatim from a separate introduction to a different textbook, all of them in print and in use at colleges and universities throughout the United States at the present time.[2] So in another sense there is no trick being played here at all.

From the fact that a trick like that of the portmanteau preface is possible, it is of course possible to conclude too much, but it is possible also to conclude more than that different writers of different composition texts sound alike. For the important thing dramatized here is the way the similarity of tone and manner holding the mock preface together creates an interlocked set of assumptions about what it means to write a sentence in English: how the activity of writing is to be taught, how it is to be learned, how it is to be

---

[2] My sources follow *seriatim:*

First Paragraph

O. B. Hardison, *Practical Rhetoric* (Appleton-Century-Crofts, 1966). Louise E. Rorabacker, *Assignments in Exposition* (third edition, Harper and Brothers, 1959). Sanders, Jordan, and Magoon, *Unified English Composition* (fourth edition, Appleton-Century-Crofts, 1966). Lee and Moynihan, *Using Prose* (Dodd, Mead and Company, 1961). Martha Cox, *A Reading Approach to College Writing* (Chandler Publishing Company, 1966). Cary Graham, *Freshman English Program* (Scott, Foresman and Company, 1960). Morris, Walker, *et al., College English, The First Year* (fourth edition, Harcourt, Brace and World, Inc., 1964). Irmscher and Hagemann, *The Language of Ideas* (Bobbs-Merrill Company, Inc., 1963).

Second Paragraph

Buckler and McAvoy, *American College Handbook* (American Book Company, 1965). Talmadge, Haman, and Bornhauser, *The Rhetoric-Reader* (Scott, Foresman and Company, 1962). Edward P. J. Corbett, *Classical Rhetoric for the Modern Student* (Oxford University Press, 1965). Hulon Willis, *Structure, Style and Usage* (Holt, Rinehart and Winston, 1964). Hans Guth, *A Short New Rhetoric* (Wadsworth Publishing Company, 1964). Richard M. Weaver, *Rhetoric and Composition* (second edition, Holt, Rinehart and Winston, 1967). Harry Shaw, *A Complete Course in Freshman English* (sixth edition, Harper and Row, 1967). J. R. Orgel, *Writing The Composition* (Educators' Publishing Service, 1962).

Third Paragraph

Kane and Peters, *A Practical Rhetoric of Expository Prose* (Oxford University Press, 1966).

Fourth Paragraph

Chittick and Stevick, *Rhetoric For Exposition* (Appleton-Century-Crofts, 1961). Wykoff and Shaw, *The Harper Handbook* (second edition, Harper and Brothers, 1957).

judged and valued. From this perspective, the sentences of the mock preface, no less than the real prefaces from which they are taken, introduce far more than a text on writing. They also describe a course and the expectation of certain patterns of behavior within that course as well. The sentences are both the beginning and the end of a circular process in which text, attitude, and action are dependent to the point of being indistinguishable: the kind of writing taught and learned implies the text which implies the course which implies the activity which implies the kind of writing taught and learned.

This circle is less an emblem of healthy organic wholeness than of one more swing around the prickly pear, not because any author of any textbook on the subject of writing sets out to teach sterility, but because the desire for a universally realizable standard of writing has resulted in demands which may be interpreted as demands for sterility. To split the activities of thinking and writing ("intention and expression") as do the sentences of the mock preface, to suggest that writing involves no more than the "transfer" of thoughts "from mind to paper," is to invite the substitution of a process for an activity, perhaps a product for a process. At any rate, it is to approach what is finally unteachable as though it were teachable, and so to make non-art stand for art.

I wish to underscore the fact that the issue I am addressing is one of interpretation and not one of intent. I think I know what is intended by sentences such as those making up the mock preface. I also know what I understood to be meant by such sentences when I was a student, and what my students for the past seventeen years have shown me that they understand such sentences to mean. And though the difference has never been, nor is it likely to become, a source of seething discontent, it is probably the largest single reason that most students and most teachers of writing at the college freshman level neither like nor believe very much in what it is they are doing. Belief in a system to which belief has been made irrelevant, however undesignedly, is hard to come by. The writers of the prefaces certainly began with a concern for standards, but the assumptions to be inferred from their sentences will not be Genungian. The process of secularization has emerged in what is more readable as a language of standardization than a language of standards, a language which has the effect of turning the activity of writing and everything associated with it into a kind of computerized skill.

The preface, like the text and the course it introduces, will be read not as a demand for writing, but for something like writing, the reasonable facsimile thereof. It will be read as a demand for that kind of non-writing popularly known as Themewriting. Everyone run through the American school system is yawningly familiar with it. Themewriting is a language, a way of experiencing the world. It is used not for the writing of papers, but of Themes. Invented originally by English teachers for use in English classrooms only, it is as closed a language as the Dewey Decimal System, as calculatedly dissociated from the concerns of its user and the world he lives in as it has been possible to make it. But the selling points of it as a commodity are irresistible. For since the skill of Themewriting is based upon the use of language conceived of entirely in terms of communication, the only standard that need be applied to it is whether it succeeds in creating in the reader—that is, in another Themewriter—the desired response. The writer's character, personality, moral nature, convictions, what Genung calls his "culture and tact," it is taken for granted are in no way engaged in forming sentences out of words and paragraphs out of sentences. Language is a tool, it is said. Or just a tool. If the reader buys the product or the idea, believes something, feels certain emotions, votes a particular ticket, etc., then the writing is good. Then the English is good.

The selling points of this commodity are not only irresistible, they are undeniable; and so is the utility of what is being sold. Writing seen as a trick that can be played, a device that can be put into operation, is also a technique that can be taught and learned—just as one can be taught or learn to run an adding machine, or pour concrete. And once equipped with this skill a writer can write a Theme about anything, and at a moment's notice. It is a valuable technique to know, therefore, because like the American dollar it is negotiable anywhere—and its buying power is unlimited. A college student can use the technique of Themewriting not only to write papers but to plan a career or a marriage, to organize a life even. And if the standards of this imitation writing are those to which the dignity of full commitment is unthinkable; if the orders won by it are more sterile than the chaos from which they are won; if the price paid to teach this kind of writing, and to learn it, may be more than the chance to be Lively or Interesting; there are few to say so. For to make Themewriting or non-writing stand for writing in the way that the traditional Freshman English course does, is to make impossible also the conception of, let alone the demand for, writing as writing inside its circle.

To see the truth of this you need only give any college freshman one paragraph of that preface. He will believe he can predict the next. Give him one chapter of *Ventures in Composition*, and he will imagine he can write the rest. And no freshman will be in any doubt of who he thinks is speaking to him in the preface, under what circumstances, or of how he believes it is expected he will respond to what he hears. It is Authority he hears, but Authority of a peculiar sort: a bit uncertain for all its certainty, nervous under the pontification, and devious, above all devious. For though the preface does not exactly promise the student that he *will* be taught to write, it conducts itself as if that were its promise. The preface does not claim to have All the Answers to the problems of composition either, but it behaves as though it did. Nor does the preface describe the activity of writing as if it were a game, but it is written so as to enable a student to interpret it that way. And this is the way he will interpret it, just as it is the way he will interpret his course and everything he does for it. On one side he will place the

Establishment, the System. He is the other. The teacher acts more or less as a referee. That none of this can be acknowledged at the same time it must be clearly understood, is simply a part of what for the student makes the game a game.

In light of the student's educational history, I do not think that such an interpretation on his part is the result of just laziness or cynicism. He has already had a good deal of experience with English courses, after all. He has probably been well-taught. In the root sense of the word he has been well-trained. In fact, although the student would never admit it, on the subject of English courses, particularly on the Themes he has had to write for them, he is something of an expert before he even gets to college. There is not the degree of snoutish illiteracy to contend with in the writing of freshmen that there once was, "he don't go no," and that sort of thing. The writing of most students entering most colleges now is more antiseptic, more brutally correct than it used to be. A modern college student is more than likely to know the difference between a comma and a semicolon, what a run-on sentence is and how to avoid it, about slang and the more popular clichés, their cause and cure. He is likely also to know about topic sentences and transitions, and certain rules for putting paragraphs together—as though they were buildings made of building blocks.

The average freshman in college, quite understandably, wants badly to know who he is supposed to be in relation to what he thinks is wanted of him. It is to be expected then, that in the midst of the threatening unfamiliarity of his freshmen year, the student will shape whatever he can of his academic environment into patterns that he is familiar with. And in this respect the mock preface is peculiarly adaptable. Without very much difficulty it can be made to describe, and so create, a composition course which is no more a new approach to the teaching of writing than prostitution is a new approach to human relations.

The sheer physical circumstances of a freshman student's situation are easy enough for him to twist into support of his assumptions. His English course, for example, is most likely to be required of all freshmen—except those lucky few whose scores on the College Boards have freed them for higher things and nobler thinking. But the majority of the freshman class, broken into malleable units of twenty-five or so, is to experience a training program which will equip it, presumably, to pass into the same Beyond. The student's instructor is young, enthusiastic, somewhat anxious, and most probably a graduate student teaching part time. Even though this graduate student is quite likely to be as good a teacher as those found among the regular faculty, he is carrying a work load that no regular faculty member would think of carrying and being paid less than half as much money to do it. The student may not know this, but he does know that his teacher's name is not listed with those of the regular faculty in the college catalogue, and it is not very hard for him to work out the implications of the fact that the only full-time faculty member associated with his course is someone called The Director of Freshman English, whom he never sees.

Although the emphasis of the course that the student is about to take would seem to be upon writing, because that emphasis is articulated in the way that it is, he can easily manipulate it to confirm his suspicion that this composition course, like every other composition course he has had, is not really going to be a course in composition at all. At least not a course in *his* composition. He will not see himself addressed by the mock preface as someone interested in making *his* writing clear and coherent, but as someone who will be asked to meet the standards of Clarity and Coherence. In the same way he will learn about Organization, Diction, and so on. In class, to be sure, there will be a great deal of analysis of those "challenging essays," and a lot of attention paid to the "teachable principles" to which they can be broken down, but the gap between such "clear-cut writing models" and how exactly the student is to use them "to make [his] intention and [his] expression one" is going to remain as mysterious, but as untroublesome in its unexamined mystery, as it has always been. What he is going to be asked to do in and with his writing, he will imagine, is nothing he has not been asked to do before. He is willing enough, therefore, to haul out his dog-eared credentials once again. He is quite ready to prove himself one of those "striving to learn principles of clear and vigorous writing of types suitable to his capacities and interests" by showing his competence to use "the rhetorical principles" of the essays for the writing of Themes. That is, he will make use of Lead Sentences: "Man, by some it has been contended, is not a rational animal," or develop a Generalization by means of Specific and Relevant Details, or write a Theme of Classification, or Employ the Technique of Comparison and Contrast. To ask the value of this procedure in enabling a writer to develop a voice of his own, or whether indeed the procedure has any value at all, the student will already have decided is simply not part of the game. Nor should things, so far as he is concerned, be otherwise. So long as the student is not asked to do what he does not know how to do already, he is quite content to grant to the Establishment the right to describe the value of what he is doing in whatever terms it chooses.

Besides, in spite of how his course may be described in the preface, or for that matter in the college catalogue, the student is quite sure, both from his experience with English courses in the past and from what he has had to buy for the one he is about to take, that very little time will be devoted to composition whatever the term is understood to mean. For in addition to the "stimulating," up-to-datish essays of *Ventures in Composition*, the student has been made to buy a few other texts. There is the inevitable supplementary anthology containing some more essays, a handful of short stories ("master-pieces"), maybe even a couple of poems. Perhaps there is a play to look forward to toward the end of the term, by Shaw or Arthur Miller; or a timely novel like *The Stranger* or *The Lord of the Flies*. It will not be literature exactly that the student will be studying, but something more like sociological approaches to literature, literature as philosophy or idea. At any rate, the student is quite aware that class discussions will be devoted more to such questions as whether Eliza really loves Henry Higgins than to the ways in which the preposition may be seen as the core of writing.

The composition part of the course, in fact, will be confined to seven or eight writing assignments, most of them spun out of the readings, on which the student knows he will be asked to write Themes. "Is the Government of the United States Liberal or Conservative? Discuss, 450–500 words;" "To what extent may Holden Caulfield be considered a tragic hero?". For each of his seven or eight prescribed writing assignments the student will be given such a prescribed topic along with a prescribed word limit. Approximately one week after the assigning of a subject he will turn in his Theme written in a prescribed form, which he knows without being told must be folded lengthwise down the middle (for filing? as a first step in being wadded for disposal?). These Themes will then be marked and graded on a prescribed scale with a prescribed vocabulary, and returned to the student for prescribed revision about a week after he has handed them in.

This process, it is known as Themerevision, the student will believe is to enable him to prove that he is in fact one of those interested in facing "the composition challenge with a measure of ability and confidence." In the margins of his corrected papers there will appear certain "conventional . . . correction symbols" along with certain "abbreviations . . . used in conjunction with those symbols." These notations he will see as serving notice that one or more of the "principles of clear and vigorous writing" has been violated. In order to demonstrate his intention "to think clearly" and to learn "to write correctly, clearly, effectively" etc., he will use the symbols and abbreviations to correct his papers. This is, as the mock preface suggests, a relatively simple matter. On the inside front cover of *Ventures in Composition*, is a table with a title like *Rhetorical Errors* where all of the rhetorical erors that a student can make are capsulated and symbolized in a list. Some texts on composition even go so far as to include a second table called *Grammatical Errors* or *Mechanical Errors.* Both tables are used in very much the same way. A subheading of the table entitled *Rhetorical Errors*, for instance, may include such a term as WORD CHOICE or DICTION which in turn is broken down into a number of separate errors—*awk, viv, vocab,* etc.; or *23–a, b,* and *c.* In either case, the nomenclature enables a student to move easily from the symbol to the section of *Ventures in Composition* which will correct his error. *Viv* next to "I ran" will thus brighten it to "I loped" or "I shambled," or in the case of a notation like *sub,* the student will be informed that "subordination is needed," a matter that the text explains with something like this:

> A sentence in which the main clause is less important than the subordinate clause exhibits *faulty subordination.* . . .

Faulty: I finished work at five o'clock, and I went to the movies.
Better: When I finished work at five o'clock, I went to the movies.
Best: At five o'clock, when I finished work, I went to the movies.

It is not difficult to see what values the student might attach to the process of Themewriting and Themerevision, particularly when he learns that all of his writing for the course is to be collected at the end of the term and burned. That vague promise of a payoff even more vague (called a "lifetime of improvement in reading and writing") which is claimed to emerge somehow from sportsmanlike obedience to the System, is too easy for him to imagine as just another way in which his course is having its fake and beating it too. Everyone who plays the game according to the rules is promised "a measure of ability and confidence," a share in the collective "outreachings of the mind." But for the student this is likely to mean no more than that everyone can finish work by five o'clock and go to the movies.

The argument here is not that mean or silly assumptions underlie the writing of textbooks on writing, but that such textbooks may be, can be, will be interpreted as meanly assumed no matter what their assumptions—and not because the books are bad ones, but because the books are books. If they do not themselves create a situation of permissive sterility in college Freshman English courses, the situation into which they are introduced creates them as creators of it, no matter what their intentions, no matter how good they may be. Art cannot be taught with the tone and manner of the mock preface and remain art; writing cannot be taught as non-writing and remain writing.

My account of things is hyperbolic, of course, but the argument is not extravagant. Here, for example, is the beginning of an actual preface beginning an actual text on rhetoric:

> Preface: to the Student
>
> The aim of this text and of the course using it is to teach effective writing. Only a few students plan careers in creative writing, but every student eventually finds himself deeply involved in problems of expression. Term papers, essay examinations and reports are regular parts of most of the courses you will take while in college. When you enter professional life, your need for writing skill will probably increase. Business correspondence will have to be answered, projects will have to be "written up," brochures and manuals will have to be composed and speeches delivered. Most of these jobs will have to be done on short notice, usually in the midst of other activities. If you write easily they are opportunities; if you write poorly they are at best unpleasant and at worst, episodes that can jeopardize advancement or threaten the success of an important project. For this reason your writing course is of central importance, both to your success as a student and to later success in your career.

Those are arid, but not stupid sentences. They are meant to be helpful, even inspiriting. But when they are fed into the insidious circularity of the traditional college Freshman English course, they develop a context which makes them mean something quite different from what they seem to say. Although it is "effective writing" and not writing which is being presented here, the manner of the sentences creates the illusion that it *is* writing which is being presented, and that what is being said about it is the most that can possibly be said for it. There is no reasonable demand for writing which cannot be articulated, the tone of the paragraph suggests, nothing about writing which cannot be understood. What is offered in the name of ideals, then, becomes an all too realizable actuality. Writing becomes "effective writing" becomes Themewriting.

Thus "effective writing" is differentiated from another kind of writing called "creative writing," something "only a few students plan careers in." Unlike "creative writing," "effective writing" is something one can learn to do "easily" (the alternative is writing "poorly"), and which once learned will enable a student to write "brochures and manuals" and letters in the same way that he has written "term papers" and "essay examinations"; they can all be seen as just "jobs" that he can learn to do "on short notice" and even "in the midst of other activities." In this way, it is asserted, "effective writing" can be used to take advantage of "opportunities," all opportunities, and is thereby, with a slither of logic, said to be "of central importance" in achieving "success" because "poor" writing can "threaten" it.

This does more than suggest that Themewriting will get one by; it suggests that there is no way of getting on without it. "Effective writing" is being offered not just as useful but as indispensable, in that it is the means by which any opportunity to write, for any student from any college, is converted to an occasion demanding another demonstration of his ability to produce "effective writing." And the chimeras of unrealized opportunity, jeopardized advancement, and aborted success which hover on the rim of failure here, are not simply halloweenish horrors for a college student, particularly for a college freshman. There is no mistaking what is meant by "success" in the context of those sentences, and in spite of what Youth is supposed (and supposes itself) to worship, the American Dream is still the American Dream.

Although nothing in the paragraph specifically prohibits the student from entertaining the question of why he should write to begin with, or for whom, neither is there any gesture made to indicate that these questions might be important or worth asking. It is hard to see how there could be. Such concerns cannot be said to matter because none of what makes possible the use of non-writing to stand for writing would be possible if they were said to matter. No wonder that in both the mock preface and the real one so little is said of the relationship between a writer and what he writes, or between a reader and what he reads. No wonder audience is conceived of as including everyone except the writer who creates it. To suggest that there might be another way of talking about writing, to assume that a student might someday *want* to write a speech or a letter (as opposed to those speeches which "will have to be . . . delivered" and the letters which "will have to be answered"), to attempt to imagine anything like a meaningful relationship between the writer, his writing, and his reader would be at variance with an approach to writing which for each party turns out to be founded on the supposed irrelevance of such concerns to the other.

I do not think that tragic is too strong a word for what this mutual misunderstanding can involve: for students' imagining that writing is conceived of by their teachers as mechanical, sterile, meaningless; for teachers' imagining themselves contained inside the proposition that there is no way of teaching what cannot be taught. It is a misunderstanding which results in a pact made without the realization of either party that it is a party, let alone that it has agreed to anything. And so the sealing is made as it is made possible, not in guilt, or in sorrow, or in shame, or in fear, but unconsciously, with each party's assuming that for the other writing as writing simply doesn't matter. What the student is doing, what the teacher is doing, what gets done, these things are important, but none of them matter for themselves. Writing thus becomes no more than a kind of transcription, a known, not a way of knowing, a way of saying something, not something being said.

And the situation is universal. The juxtaposition of the mock preface with a real one makes clear the paradigmic relation of both to an approach to writing entombed in literally hundreds of handbooks and in thousands of college Freshman English programs. Entombed like Madeline Usher. All the books are being used. Year after year the same freshman programs are rerun from the same worn stencil. And so the circle remains unbroken; the emperor continues his naked parade. Teachers of English Composition go on using methods and materials which were obsolete ten years ago, a hundred years ago, ten centuries ago. Balls go on rolling quietly down inclined planes, while students sit quietly by and watch.

The problem is not just one of better books, a tighter syllabus, more carefully worded assignments, a different personnel. It is not just a problem of abstractions either: more dedication, more purpose, more industry. God knows there is enough of this, or at least enough of this kind of talk, already. The problem is one of developing another way of seeing the activity of writing, of establishing the dignity of collective faith necessary to make possible the learning and teaching of writing as art. To eliminate the composition text as a composition text will not of itself create a conception of writing as writing, but it will at least eliminate the most nameable barrier to it.

What Means? Who Says? Teaching College Freshmen to Write Clearly

ELIZABETH CHRISTMAN

In a small classroom a college freshman has just written a sentence on the blackboard. It is the opening of his paragraph on the importance of a car to a student.

"A car is extremely beneficial to a teen-ager in a social aspect."

The teacher reads the sentence aloud, and the eleven other students scan it with puzzled frowns.

"That sentence is sick," the teacher tells them. "It has a malignant tumor. Ted, will you start surgery?"

Ted goes to the board and, after deep thought, crosses out "extremely." Everybody looks pleased. They remember that adverbs are often expendable.

"What else? That was only a wart," the teacher goads them. Ted wrinkles his brow and chews his lip, but he can't figure out where to put the knife.

"Come on, Ted. If you want to borrow the family car, do you say, 'Dad, it would be beneficial to me in a social aspect to have the car tonight'?"

Ted laughs. "No, I say I need the car for a date."

"Then why not write that way? 'A teen-ager needs a car for dates.' That says it. 'In a social aspect' is a cancerous growth."

The small classroom is in a remodeled apartment building in Jersey City. It is part of the campus of Saint Peter's College. But the teacher, Edward Craig, is not a college professor. His regular job is staff writer for United Press. He comes to Saint Peter's once a week to conduct a two-hour writing laboratory. Along with about thirty other men and women who earn their living by writing and editing, he is on the staff of a program called Operation T.P. Through T.P., which stands for Techniques of Prose, Saint Peter's College is attempting to insure that all its freshmen learn to write clear, readable prose before they go further in college.

The Catholic Educational Review, vol. 66 (March 1969), pp. 774–781. Reprinted by permission of the Catholic University of America Press.

The idea of writers teaching writing is not new. Nearly every campus with any pretense to modernity has a poet—or novelist-in-residence who conducts seminars in creative writing. But the idea of working writers teaching "freshman composition" sprang from the brain of James C. G. Conniff, an associate professor of English at Saint Peter's. A writer himself, Conniff believes that people who write every day for their livelihood can teach writing in a particularly practical way. Three years ago he was discussing—not for the first time—the general ineptitude of students' writing with Father Leo McLaughlin, who was then President of Saint Peter's. Father McLaughlin backed his plan to hire professional writers and editors to staff a writing course which would be required of all freshmen.

T.P. 20, as the catalogue calls it, differs radically from the kind of freshman composition course that most colleges offer. It doesn't even belong to the English Department but is a department by itself, run in free-wheeling fashion by Conniff, whose chief directive to his part-time teachers is: "Make them rewrite every sentence." Revision is the heart of the course. Conniff insists, and the T.P. staff agrees with him heartily, that the only way to teach writing is to analyze every sentence of a student's paper with him, to point out his mistakes, and to make him revise until he gets it right.

The usual freshman composition course is too large to be taught this way. An instructor with forty or fifty students can not do much more than mark obvious misspellings and grammatical errors, add a comment such as "weak in content" or "poorly organized," and assign a grade. The student with a C or D may have little idea how to make his next paper stronger or how to organize his next topic.

Each T.P. section is limited to twelve students. The weekly class is a laboratory where the teacher demonstrates and the students try things out. The student must turn in a paper of 500 or 750 words each week and must rewrite it completely after the teacher has torn it apart. This means that a student has to submit a new paper and a rewritten paper nearly every week for the ten-week term. The teachers spend, on an average, ten or twelve hours a week in the editing and analysis of the papers. Most students have never had close tutoring of this kind before. The real improvement in their writing comes from this massive individual attention.

"You spent more time on it than I did," one student remarked in awe to her teacher as she surveyed her paper, crackling with circled words, underlining, deletions, and brusque comments: What means? Who says? Refers to what? Give details. Fuzzy connection. Faulty logic. Break it up. Simplify. Say it directly.

In the first weeks of their T.P. course the students are baffled by the emphasis on simplicity and directness. They come to college with a noxious assortment of writing faults, and one of the worst is pretentiousness. They reach for the long, fancy word, for the abstraction, for the round-about construction, in the belief that this is the way to sound educated or adult. They are astonished at being urged to write "with common words."

"Everything you say about writing is exactly the opposite of what I was taught in high school," one student burst out in class, and the others all nodded vigorously in corroboration.

Their high school teachers encouraged them to increase their vocabularies by looking up new words and working them into their writing wherever possible. So a student writes: "In the loft, the aroma of fresh hay presides," and feels pleased with himself. "What are you trying to say?" asks his T.P. teacher. "The loft smells of fresh hay," he translates. He is amazed to learn that the teacher considers that a better sentence.

A second literary disease of college writers is verbosity. Faced with the dreadful necessity of producing five hundred words each week, the freshman pads desperately: "We have a situation in our household where it is necessary for my father to do most of the cooking because my mother works at night." The teacher writes this twenty-six-word sentence on the board and then cuts it exactly in half: "My father does most of the cooking because my mother works at night." He turns from the board and sees twelve pairs of eyes regarding him hopelessly.

"I know what you're all thinking," he says. "You squeezed yourselves dry to get five hundred words written, and now I'm telling you to cut out half of them. What's the solution? How are you going to make your length at this rate? The solution is details! Specific details! Show your father in the kitchen—stirring, chopping, frying, tasting. Show him spilling the gravy, burning himself, flipping a pancake."

Students love to line out generalizations with no supporting details. "In the short period of their existence, these diocesan high schools have won overwhelming acclaim in their every field of endeavor," writes a student grandly, feeling that he has wrapped up the subject of diocesan high schools. When he gets his paper back, the teacher's copy pencil has circled "overwhelming acclaim" and "every field of endeavor," and the margin is filled with questions: Who acclaims? Teachers, pupils, parents, educators? What do they say? Quotes? Statistics on pupil performance? What fields of endeavor? Glee club? Athletics? Debating? What honors? Every T.P. teacher hammers away at this lesson: that the way to write five hundred words of meaty prose is to support generalizations with details and examples.

Ambitious freshmen sometimes imitate stylistic conceits that they admire in professional writers. One teacher who assigned a passage of description was overwhelmed by a wave of inept personifications in that week's papers. "A gull swoops into the sea, only to soar towards the sky again, resenting the empty beach," wrote one student. "The stars twinkle impishly," wrote another. A third described church candles "flickering softly for fear they will disturb the silence." The teacher delivered an impassioned sermon against the dangerous practice of imputing human emotions to animals or objects. "Can gulls *resent?* Can candles *fear?* I ask you to consider a star and then to consider an imp. Could anything be more absurd than attributing *impishness* to a star? Leave anthropomorphism to the poets. And God help *them!*"

Director Jim Conniff gives the writer-teachers a free hand in the classroom except for admonishing them not to lecture too much. Most of them have never taught before. Their individual classroom styles vary a good deal.

Arthur F. Lenehan, who directs public relations for the Public Service Electric and Gas Corporation in Newark, gives his students practice in tightening bureaucratic prose. At one class he handed out two versions of a release which his office had issued that day. The final version was about half as long and twice as readable as the early version. The story concerned a new device for tracing the direction of a thunderstorm in order to give electric repairmen advance notice of where the storm might damage wires and poles. One sentence in the original version read: "Although the U. S. Weather Bureau and private weather services give a daily forecast of probability, the approximate time of the arrival of a storm at a given point is not sufficiently accurate for the company's operating purposes."

Lenehan showed his class how to cut this thirty-six-word sentence to twenty words: "U. S. Weather Bureau and private weather services give helpful daily forecasts, but cannot supply the pinpoint accuracy Public Service needs."

"This is the way I earn my salary," he told them, "getting the fat out of these things."

Eugene Murphy, City Editor of the Passaic *Herald-News*, tries to teach his students to be sure of their facts. Before his first class he removes all the candy from a package of Life Savers and puts the reconstructed package on his desk. When class begins he tells his students: "Write a few sentences about that object." After five minutes he asks a student to read what he has written.

"This is a package of mints commonly referred to as Life Savers because the shape of the candy is that of a life-preserver. But these mints also have a symbolic life-saving quality in that they preserve the eater from the Great American Disaster—bad breath."

The student is rather proud of this dig at the American fetish of cleanliness. Other students also note the connection between the shape of the mints and a life-preserver. Some of them mention the price of the package.

"Who'll give me a nickel for it?" Murphy asks, and a student in the front row reaches into his pocket. Murphy crushes the empty package and tosses it to him. "Don't take things for granted. Investigate. A good piece of irony becomes totally ridiculous if it's based on a false assumption," he tells the crestfallen satirist of American hygiene.

Some day an alert student will ruin his act by examining the sham package before starting to describe it. But it hasn't happened yet.

Students love to try irony but they are seldom expert enough to handle it. Stephen C. Rafe of Texaco Public Relations is hard on attempts at sarcasm which turn out coy or "cutesy." One boy ended his piece about some miners trapped underground for several days with this attempt at ironic understatement: "It's an experience one would hope to undergo only a few times in his life."

"You'd hope to undergo this a few times?" Rafe marveled. "Exactly how many times would you hope to be trapped underground for three days without food or water? Five times? Ten?"

The unlucky writer squirmed, but he learned to look harder at the logic of his sentences. Rafe is not enough older than his students to be paternal. He ridicules and berates, shakes his class up by reading out their gaffes and making them laugh at themselves. His students like his class because it is never dull, and because he is hard to please. His offhand praise—"Not bad, Miss Ferguson"—is treasured.

John R. Hayes, Manager of Information at Texaco, Inc., tries to get his students to argue with him, to defend their own wording or to offer alternatives to his editing. "How long did it take you to write that paragraph, Boruski?" he asks. "Half an hour? Look what I did to it. There's only one sentence left of it. Does that make you mad? Do you like it better your way?"

When the students do argue against his changes he sometimes bows to their judgment. One boy began an account of a battle in North Africa like this: "Good Friday, 1943, and 15,000 men of the First Armored Division march on pyramids of sand." At first Hayes objected to "pyramids" as having a meaning too particular for the context. But the class defended it, and finally he conceded that "pyramids of sand" was more vivid than "hills of sand."

"It has a good *sound,*" he admitted, after repeating the sentence out loud. He urges his students to read their papers out loud to themselves before making final copy, in order to spot awkward or repetitious phrasing.

Hayes spends the whole two-hour class on editing one or two papers. His students may work for half an hour on a single sentence, for example: "The Division ordered thirty-two men to die for their country." This sentence bothered the class—they felt there was something amiss but they were all on the wrong track. They thought the flaw was in the word "ordered," and they kept trying alternatives like "commanded," "directed," and "dispatched." Then they tried substituting a human commander for "The Division." The discussion grew hot and every student got into it. Hayes let them worry the sentence until they finally realized that the trouble was not in "ordered" but in "die"—the Division ordered the soldiers to *risk death,* not to die. (And as the account went on, most of the thirty-two did not die.)

Many other T.P. instructors often spend a large chunk of a class period on a single sentence or short paragraph. They believe this shows their students how infinitely hard it is to write clearly. "Easy writing's vile hard reading," said Richard Brinsley Sheridan a century and a half ago. Operation T.P. shows students that a writer must still sweat, pull out his hair, and fill up his wastebasket before he can produce a paragraph that is easy to read. "We teach Saint Peter's College freshmen to write for *readers,*" Jim Conniff says. "Self-expression is important, of course—but a secondary goal."

When these writers and editors arrive at Saint Peter's for their late afternoon classes, they bring a brisk, practical attitude to the classrooms from the offices where they spend their days. Instead of traditional academic terms like "composition" or "theme," they speak of "copy." Instead of saying "Your opening paragraph is dull," they will tell a student to "find a better lead."

Most of them confess that teaching T.P. 20 is much harder than they expected it to be. When they took on the assignment they had no idea of spending ten or twelve hours a week on the papers. "But there's no way of cutting down," says Carroll McGuire, who is Manager of Technical Publications for Walter Kidde and Company. "You've got to show your student on every line what he's done wrong, even if you stay up until three o'clock the night before your class. And I often do."

But in spite of the work, these teachers are solidly enthusiastic about their part-time academic jobs. They believe they are teaching an important skill. Their zeal for clarity in writing and their scorn for verbosity and pretentiousness impress their students and goad them to improve. Entering the course reluctantly, because it is required, most students become interested in spite of themselves. They quickly sense that behind the newsman's dogged search for exactness and the magazine editor's breezy classroom style there is a great seriousness about the power of words in today's—and tomorrow's—world.

From Problem-Solving to a Theory of Imagination

ANN E. BERTHOFF

If "the problem of English" could be solved by those means most often suggested and in the manner most often favored, it wouldn't be much of a problem. The reform of what is known in the schools as "the language arts curriculum" and in the colleges as "Freshman English" or "Introduction to Literary Forms" or "Humanities 101" is a matter immediately pedagogical, but it is nonetheless political and it is ultimately a philosophical matter. Indeed, since nothing short of the reformation of society would adequately do the job, such reform will also be revolutionary. Meanwhile, we must assume that revolution can begin in the classroom rather than in the streets.

There is no chance, however, for fundamental change to be brought about so long as "English" is conceived of as a "problem" for which one or another solution may somehow be discovered or invented. Both the question "What is English?" and the answers it provokes are representative of the kind of inquiry which is undertaken incessantly by a self-conscious society suffering from cultural anxieties and political uncertainty. As it has been posed, "What is English?" is cousin to "What does the national defense require?" "How is higher education to be funded?" "How can we check pollution?" "What are the duties of the Free World?" Such questions are not meant as fundamental challenges but are raised simply as the first step in framing problems which can then be solved by appropriate techniques. The problem-solving approach has the sanction of educational psychologists, systems analysts, defense intellectuals, and other technocrats because it promises guidelines, "structure," models; problem-solving and programming are virtually the same. Certainly, problem-solving is supposed to tell us what to do, but it requires neither fundamental questioning of assumptions nor the study of the solution's implications: problem-solving offers no guarantee that a critical assessment will be undertaken of either the problem or the solution.

Since problem-solving is by definition solution-generating, "English" as a set problem continually generates solutions: one curriculum after

College English, vol. 33 (March 1972), pp. 636–649.

another; a different emphasis in teacher training every few years; a bewildering sequence of approaches in the classroom, from semantics, linguistics, and close reading to rhetoric, role-playing, and T-groups. And teachers of English, following the pattern of these solutions to their problem, move from visionary hopes to self-lacerating despair; from belief that English can reform society to the strongly felt notion that nobody has the right to try to teach anybody anything.

The chief reason for this chaos, I think, is the habit of thinking of English as a problem and of searching, then, for a "solution." Mere solutions are as liable to disintegrate as they are easily formulated. The problem-solving approach actually keeps us from seeing that certain contexts of the "problem" are themselves problematical. The most important context is determined by the account offered of the relationship of society and knowledge, but this kind of philosophical inquiry cannot be turned over to problem-solvers. The problem-solving approach forestalls what we need most which is the development of working concepts. It hampers the dialectic by which questions can generate answers which demand further questions. Those questions raised in the problem-solving approach are directed merely towards narrowing the subject until the "problem area" can be delimited. Subsequent to "What is English?" we therefore have such queries as this: "Is English a subject or an activity?" The curriculum reformer who is solving the problem then proceeds to identify "activity" with the meaningful, relevant, revolutionary things a student can do and "subject" with the dull, authoritarian, pedantic, irrelevant things a teacher can do. The resulting response-oriented, student-centered curriculum may feature "activities" that haven't much to do with "subject," but given the problem-solver's definition of "subject," that will seem all to the good. The possibility of considering English a subject because it is an activity does not arise.

Illogical antitheses and analogies, faulty definitions, unwarranted extrapolations—all the attendant dangers of applying methods of quantification appropriate to the laboratory to matters which need other kinds of evaluation typify problem-solving as it is used as an approach to "English." When a teacher training theorist sets the problem of how to help teachers "radiate" an "atmosphere" compatible with one or another "learning style," he may, without realizing it, effectively institutionalize a non-receptive mode which cannot develop into anything else. He may arrive at a solution whereby lower track students who are thought to prefer "structure" are allowed to take notes on lectures while others whose tests reveal a higher degree of "creativity" are encouraged to follow the "discovery method" in an atmosphere they can "resonate to." The terminology itself and the theory it consolidates will prevent such a problem-solver from realizing that "discovery" in this instance is merely covert programming; that "structure" can be something other than parataxic, linear order; that if cognitive stages can be quantitatively defined, learning styles cannot. The problem-solver will not be aware of the problems his solution has generated.[1]

For those whose concern is reform in the teaching of English, the method of problem-solving has little to offer. Indeed, it is dangerous because it actually requires a conception of language as signal code, a view which precludes an understanding of language as an instrument of knowing; and because it generally is allied with a theory of learning which premises learning as a function of a somewhat modified stimulus-response model. Although the philosophical difficulties of using the methods appropriate to one field of investigation in another are well-known, they do not seem to trouble many of those who have undertaken to ask "What is English?" It will be part of my purpose in this essay to show how a mode of analysis deriving from behaviorist psychology and communication (or information) theory is inappropriate to critical thinking about the teaching of English.

What English teachers need is not solutions to problems but a rediscovery and a recreation of fundamental assumptions about what we are doing. We would do well to accept as a working definition of English "reading and writing anything, especially literature" (Josephine Miles) and go on from there. English teachers should accept the prescription *Begin with where they are,* asking "And where is that?" To answer that question we must have, of course, some understanding of the process of learning, but we will also need a philosophy of knowledge which unhesitatingly proclaims that man is neither an encoding-decoding machine nor a super pigeon but, in Ernst Cassirer's phrase, the *animal symbolicum:* Man is that one creature whose world of behavior is built by language and who makes sense of "reality" by a process of linguistic invention and discrimination. We need to recognize language as "the supreme organ of the mind's self-ordering growth." [2] That, of course, is a philosophical undertaking.

For English teachers, a philosophy of knowledge will be useful insofar as it is, in effect, a theory of the imagination, a theory which could yield continually hopeful assessments of the capacities of students because it would remind us of the natural resources of mind. Without the support and guidance of such a theory, defining the relevance of literature to the lives of the disenchanted and the disadvantaged or deciding what role composition should play in any given syllabus will be virtually impossible. The limits of what we plan, though they may be contingent to an important degree upon budgets and the climate of opinion, are decided finally by how we think of man the language-user; everything we plan—new curricula, new course sequences, schemes for the abolition of English or its reconstitution—follows from what we mean when we say *Begin with where they are.*

---

[1] The references are to D. E. Hunt, *Matching Models in Education: The co-ordination of teaching methods and student characteristics* (Toronto: OISE, 1971).

[2] I. A. Richards, *Speculative Instruments* (New York: Harcourt, 1955), p. 9.

If we accept a cognitive psychology which leaves out of account the very form-finding and form-creating processes and functions and capacities we are in fact concerned with when we address ourselves to the uses of English, we will clearly be unable to formulate a pedagogy based on a theory of imagination. If we are burdened with the rationale for the separation of "intellectual" and "creative" capacities which has been the chief contribution of educational psychology to teachers of English, we will continue to separate learning and knowing, and knowing from reading and writing. If we accept the notion that language is "verbal behavior" which functions in code-like fashion, we will have no way of understanding the role it plays in acts of knowing. Without such understanding of language it will not be possible to make use of the resources of literature, to make it available to students as a form of knowledge. The symbolic nature of language, its power to represent our experience, whether in role-playing, reportage, or lyric, can be the chief working concept in our thinking about the teaching of English. But language as a symbolic form is a concept which is incompatible with a view of thinking as a problem-solving; of communication as a matter of input and feedback; of the intellectual and creative modes as logical opposites. Without an understanding of the symbolic nature of language, there will be an inevitable failure to move from problem-solving to a theory of imagination.

That failure is represented by the deliberations of the Anglo-American Conference on the Teaching of English held at Dartmouth in 1966. There were no philosophers (and no poets) at Dartmouth and, apparently, few to question the propriety of the problem-solving approach. Raising the question "What is English?" the conferees avoided those questions about the purposes of education which are necessarily political and philosophical.[3] Nor did their assumptions about the needs or capacities of students come under questioning. For the Dartmouth Conference, the directive *Begin with where they are* was both a tough-minded appeal to the doctrine of relevance and a soft-hearted recognition of the "creativity" of the human person. But the Conference did not ask *where* students are or how they got there or if they had been there long enough. Accepting unquestioningly the views of language and learning developed by the educational psychologists now in ascendancy, the Conference had no means of asking *how* students know and what it is indeed that they do know.

Of course the Dartmouth Conference realized the importance of a theory of knowledge. The official report declares: "The testing point for a model of English based on experience and language in operation will be its account of knowledge." But the Conference proceeded within a framework which guaranteed misconceptions on this score. Though they were fascinated

[3] See Wayne O'Neil's analysis of the failures of the Dartmouth Conference, *Harvard Educational Review*, Spring, 1969.

by their discovery that the child who comes to school is a "linguistic adult," Conference participants failed to grasp the implications of that important insight because there was no recognition of the vitally important corollary that that linguistic adult is the *animal symbolicum.* Language was defined and discussed as a signal code and learning, effectively separated from knowing, was assumed to be largely a matter of problem-solving. Literature became "literary material"; composition was only creative self-expression. The environment prepared by the psychologists—complete with *task definitions, non-verbalized processes, interaction, search techniques, psychic material, communication situations*—became not the landscape of growth and knowledge but a bog of solved problems.

The shortcomings of the Dartmouth Conference, with respect to a philosophy of knowledge, are representative; otherwise, there would be little point in discussing them five years after the event. There seems to be no respectable rival to the theories of learning and language which were accepted at Dartmouth, and which underlie virtually every assessment, prescription, and exhortation which is formulated by teachers of English. In the remarks which follow, reference will be made to two books closely associated with the Dartmouth Conference—John Dixon's *Growth Through English* (1967), the official Conference report, and *Teaching the Universe of Discourse* (1968) by James Moffett, one of the leading Conference participants. My aim, however, is to question certain assumptions very widely held by those seeking to reform the teaching of English.

The primary and unquestioned assumption of the Dartmouth Conference was that language is a signal code. This conception converts meaning to "information," and form to "medium"; understanding is reduced to "decoding." The Dartmouth Conference answered the question "What is English?" by declaring that "English" is a "symbol system," in contradistinction, that is, to "literature" and "history."[4] Here is James Moffett's explanation: "English, French, and Mathematics are symbol systems, into which the phenomenal data of empirical subjects are cast and by means of which we think about them. Symbol systems are not primarily about themselves; they are about other subjects." Is a "symbol system"—and what is that?—secondarily about itself? What "empirical subject" is cast into mathematical symbols? In what sense is English closer to mathematics than to history? Such questions are not recognized.[5] And they could not be, given

[4] The term *symbol* appears frequently in the papers and reports of the Conference, but it is used loosely and generally stands as a synonym for *sign* or *signal.* The forming and constitutive powers of symbols are not recognized.

[5] There is some recognition in *Growth* that the differentiation of "symbol system" and "empirical subject" may be spurious. Commenting that "English" does not deal with content as "explicit knowledge in systematic order," Dixon goes on to say that "the same may be true for many subjects in their more recent interpretation" (p. 72). No corrective conclusions are drawn.

the theory of knowledge the Conference apparently assembled from bits and pieces of behavioral psychology and the system known as General Semantics.

The curious recrudescence of General Semantics in current discussions of English pedagogy is worth comment. The creation of a Polish nobleman, Alfred Korsybski, and especially popular during the 1940's, General Semantics is a systemization of attitudes which are sometimes given the name *scientism.* Strong approbation is awarded measurement, statistical analysis, operational definitions, etc. One of the principal slogans associated with General Semantics is that language should be "a map for the territory of reality." It is a conception which comes naturally to a problem-solver, but it is a curious one for a teacher of language and literature to adopt. The premises of General Semantics are often either self-evident ("the word is not the thing") or question-begging assertions: "There is no such thing as 'subject matter' in the abstract. [There is no such thing as anything "in the abstract."] 'Subject matter' exists in the minds of perceivers. And what each one thinks it is, is what it is." This solipsism is only the obverse of the scientistic worship of quantification: if you can't measure something, its reality isn't worth arguing about. It leads, logically enough, to the notion "that all problems are merely verbal," the title of Barrows Dunham's refutation of the logic and rhetoric of General Semantics.[6] The way is open, too, for problem-solving that is merely verbal.

With the sanction of quantification there is a concurrent distrust of imagination and all its works.[7] General Semantics offers no theory of metaphor, which is seen, rather, as an aberration of the type that includes the thinking of paranoid schizophrenics. Without accounting for metaphor as a mode of concept formation (not just a way of representing "reality"), there can be no theory of literature. That is why literature in the hands of Korsybski's disciples becomes "literary material." Poetry is scarcely mentioned by James Moffett or Postman and Weingartner *et al.* except insofar as poems can be reduced to "communication situations." "Abstraction" is defined exclusively as an operation of mind that proceeds by way of successive generalizations; those abstractions, therefore, which are exemplified by art—non-discursive forms with symbolic import—remain unaccounted for, except, of course, as magic or therapy. By associating "subjective," "intentional," and "connotative" meanings with all that is irrational and unscientific, General Semanticists manage to make the notion of an "awareness of abstraction" a substitute for the definition of historical, linguistic, and cultural contexts which can determine import in vital ways.[8]

[6] Reprinted in Barrows Dunham, *Man Against Myth* (Boston: Little, Brown, and Co., 1947).

[7] C. S. Lewis' *The Abolition of Man* (New York: Macmillan, 1947) is a passionate denunciation of the political and moral consequences of this philosophy. His point of departure, by the way, is a jolly English textbook for sixth formers.

[8] The Now Generation of curriculum reformers has been troubled neither by the inconsistencies of General Semantics nor by the strong anti-literary character of the system, to say nothing of the

It is interesting to speculate about the effects if I. A. Richards, rather than Count Korsybski, had been the tutelary authority at Dartmouth. What Richards in *Speculative Instruments* observed of the linguistic scientist operating outside the field of his competence would have been an appropriate warning for the Conference: "He does not yet know how to respect the language. He does not yet have a conception of the language which would make it respectable. He thinks of it as a code and has not yet learned that it is an organ—the supreme organ of the mind's self-ordering growth" (p. 9). A useful motto for the Conference would have been Richards' observation that "there is no study which is not a language study, concerned with the speculative instruments it employs" (p. 116). As it was, no one raised the question of what is wrong with communication theory. Here is Richards' answer: "What is wrong with it? This. It stands squarely in the way of our practical understanding and command of language. It hides from us both how we may learn to speak and write better, and how we may learn to comprehend more comprehensively. . . . If anyone is led into a way of thinking—a way of proceeding, rather—as though composing were a sort of catching a nonverbal butterfly in a verbal butterfly net, as though comprehending were a releasing of said butterfly from the net, then he is deprived of the very thing that could help him: exercise in comparing the various equivalences of different words and phrases, their interdependencies in varying situations."[9]

Electronic jargon should be recognized as a symptom of the failure to understand the role of language in building the world we know. But there was no warning at Dartmouth that a receptivity to the notion of molds into which data are poured, scanning devices which "isolate out," coding machines into which raw data are fed—verbal butterfly nets for nonverbal butterflies—necessarily precludes an interest in the symbolic nature of literature and the self-ordering growth of mind.

---

authoritarian, elitist tone, apparent long before Hayakawa donned his Tam o'Shanter. The most economical refutation I know is Susanne K. Langer's memorable disquisition on Stuart Chase's cat, a prime exhibit in *The Tyranny of Words.* (See *Philosophy in a New Key*, Chap. 2.) One well-known linguist, noting that "semantics is concerned with studies of the meaning and changes of meaning of specific language forms," dismisses Korsybski's system as "a kind of linguistic therapy quite unrelated to technical linguistics." I. A. Richards' succinct comment is that "modern attempts to improve the conduct of language should recognize how deep the undertaking must go. It is not enough to be 'non-Aristotelian' while employing the least acceptable tricks of Aristotelian rhetoric, or to pursue propaganda-analysis propagandistically" (*Speculative Instruments,* p. 166).

[9] From "The Future of Poetry," reprinted in *So Much Nearer: Essays Towards a World English* (New York: Harcourt, 1968), p. 175. For those who make a case for the study of literature and who believe that English is a subject precisely because it is the vital human activity, there are no more important books than this collection and *Speculative Instruments.* Yet the NCTE, like the Dartmouth Conference, proceeds as if I. A. Richards had never existed or had never had anything further to say after writing *Practical Criticism.*

A consideration of what has come to be called "drama in the classroom" could perhaps clarify what is at issue when a theory of knowledge deriving from communication theory and behavioral psychology provides the rationale for pedagogical innovation.

The best-known and most important contribution of the Dartmouth Conference has been the emphasis on the notion that "drama" is at the heart of language use. So it is and the idea is a promising one to build on and work with, as Kenneth Burke has been doing for forty years. The importance of stressing the actual and active uses of language in the classroom may strike teachers for whom "discussion" serves such a role as self-evident. But it is an excellent counter-ploy to certain notions now widely regarded as elitist which derive from the theory and practice of New Criticism and it is, of course, a freshening breeze for those becalmed by textbook drill.

"Drama" as entertained by the Dartmouth Conference, however, is a curious concept. In James Moffett's hands, for instance, it becomes subservient to the General Semanticists' notion of the process of abstraction: "drama" is more "real" because it is less "abstract." Here, in a characteristic sentence, is Moffett's definition of drama: "Drama is any raw phenomena as they are being converted to information by the observer." Apparently, Moffett's point is simply that drama can proceed without written symbols and is therefore more "realistic"; the audience is more directly in touch with "reality" in watching a play because they watch it the way they do a street fight. It does not occur to him that our experience in the theater (and our experience of guerrilla theater, or, indeed, of a "dramatic" street fight or of classroom role-playing) is mediated by our perception of pattern and rhythm, of dramaturgical form, by our apprehension of a complex playing off of illusion against one reality or another—mediations which are all logically and aesthetically analogous to the mediations of fiction and poetry. The equation of "real life" and "theater" as "first order abstractions" is contradicted as soon as Moffett needs to talk about selection and order, but he returns to this conception of drama as "what is happening" throughout his book.

The "verbal action" which he takes to be at the heart of drama is at the heart, too, of narrative, whether the teller is Cervantes or Conrad or a third grader. The conception of drama as close-to-what-happens leads axiomatically to the notion that "narrative" stands at a further remove from "real life." Moffett tells us that whereas drama is like going to a football game, narrative is like reading the sports page. How many thousands of college freshmen will there be who will have to be disabused of this idea? The simple truth is, of course, that a visitor from Mars would be as baffled by one as by the other; it takes a good deal of patterned experience to make sense of either. Moffett does not understand that plays and stories and lyrics and novels are all created in the mode called *poiesis*, that all literature—works of imagination—is "poetic" with respect to its symbolic character. Drama provides one form of mediation, stories another, epic another: form is the mediator, no matter what the genre.

What there is to be said of drama must be said of all forms of *poiesis*, that they are dialectical. Experience with drama should enforce the realization that *all knowing is dramatistic*. Such experience should lead not to the narrow literalism that "drama" is primary and more "real," but to the discovery that conversation, essay, argument, reporting are mediating forms too; that all language is dialectical; that in the very notion of linguistic predication, dialectic is born. Drama in the classroom could help us begin with where our students are as knowers; drama could help our students develop conceptions of language as an instrument of knowing. It could help teachers grasp the implications of the fact that knowing in the classroom is a joint enterprise. Creative dramatics, role-playing, enactment can demonstrate the power of language and any experience which can do that is valuable. Drama in the classroom can teach how language works to reveal or hide character; to clarify or obscure a situation or state of affairs; to define and re-define intention. Drama can certainly offer opportunities to learn how narration proceeds, to discover the temporal and spatial constraints of symbolic action. Such experiences can help make explicit what is intuitive; they can be the means of putting the student—that "linguistic adult"—in touch with his native, natural resources; they can help him find out where he is so that his education can begin: self-knowledge is both cause and effect in learning.

It is more than likely, however, that the idea of drama in the classroom will soon fade, having effected very few changes in our ways of thinking about the teaching of English. Given the rationale advanced by the Dartmouth Conference and adopted by the NCTE, there is good reason to hope that this use of "drama" will indeed be short-lived.[10] The philosophy from which it derives trivializes the concept of "language in operation" and actively encourages, if it does not require, the reduction of plays, poems, novels, and stories to "communication situations." The chief heuristic value of literature is thus destroyed, the symbolic means by which it transforms our experience and represents it to us. If literature is only "literary material," there is no reason for it not to disappear from the curriculum.[11]

---

[10] Moffett's discussion of drama has been described by James Hoetker in the NCTE pamphlet "Dramatics in the Classroom" as "the most impressive case yet made by an American for drama as the central activity in the English class." Hoetker accepts the split, philosophically and, I believe, pedagogically disastrous, between what he calls "cognitive understanding" and imagination.

[11] For observations on the anti-literary thrust of Moffett's *Student-Centered Curriculum*, see John Rouse's review, *Harvard Educational Review*, May, 1970. Moffett's comment that English teachers should turn for "curriculum builders" to the new methods now popular in teaching foreign languages is chilling. In French, for instance, "using the symbol system realistically rather than studying it as an object" has come to mean, in effect, (ask a ninth grader) that kids talk, read and

Composition, of course, is already on the way out and no creditable case could be made for keeping it if we argue from the premises of the Dartmouth Conference. Why should anyone in our society learn to write, i.e., to compose written discourse? The simple answer at Dartmouth was that composition serves the purposes of communication and expression. Communication may seem a practical and sober reason for such study, the straightforward application of the criterion of "use" in later life. But who, in fact, actually composes in order to communicate in our society? In commerce and industry, as well as in government, technical writers are hired to handle reports, just as time-motion specialists are consulted. Composition could be taught—and *is* taught—as a skill like typing. Troubled judgments arise, however, when the function of the critical essay, for instance, is considered in this perspective. What does it "communicate" and to whom? "Only one in a hundred thousand will ever do such writing," Paul Diedrich of Educational Testing Service has remarked, and of course if the art of critical analysis is associated merely with what literary critics do, an excellent case for its abolition could be argued.[12] But we should ask Mr. Diedrich how many in a hundred thousand will ever do such writing as is required on the ETS writing sample, an essay on the moral fiber of today's citizenry, for instance. If the case for composition is made in terms of "use" in later life, then the chief models should be the grocery list and the Letter to the Editor.

Educators who accept the antithesis of "intellectual" and "creative" uses of language are no less adept at justifying the cultivation of creative writing skills than they are at explaining the importance of "communication." The rationale stems from the same philosophy: feelings are like problems in that they have shape and meaning which can be encoded in language: the nonverbal butterflies snared by the intellectual nets are iron; those snared by the creativity nets are gossamer. The Dartmouth Conference expressed awe at the powers of creativity, but the actual attitudes represented there remind me of Mrs. Langer's observation about the attitudes of certain aestheticians: "While they speak of poetry as 'creation,' they treat it, by turns, as report, exclamation, and purely phonetic arabesque." [13] If "creative writing" is actually considered as what is left over after language has been seriously at work in solving problems, in communicating, in scientific thinking, then of course it will be merely personal, idiosyncratic—not a matter to be judged or learned from. There will be serious composition and there will be something called "expression" which naturally enough lies

write about trivia. They drone on and on in their aural-oral cubicles about Paul et Danielle and their attempts to buy hamburgers in Paris. Only high-achievers (those who test well) are allowed to "study the symbol system as an object," i.e. to read a book.

[12] *Journal of Higher Education*, February 1964.

[13] *Feeling and Form* (New York: Scribners, 1953), p. 234.

beyond the pale of critical judgment. After all, when writing is something other than problem-solving, then who could possibly judge what goes on?[14]

The identification of the so-called "intellectual uses of language" with "the common sense world" (one of the favorite phrases at Dartmouth) and, at only a slight remove, the world of problems to be solved, is inevitably matched by sentimentalized notion of "feeling" and a concomitant failure to realize the organizing force of awareness. Clearly, nobody at Dartmouth considered beauty a "learning resource." The danger of this false opposition of "intellectual" and "creative" is that both are devalued; that should be a matter of concern not only in the grades but on up through the graduate schools. For when intellectual endeavor is isolated from any experience profounder than that afforded by the common sense world, dissociated from the life of feeling, its assumed irrelevance to what we feel becomes a self-fulfilling prophecy.[15]

Nothing more clearly reveals the faulty epistemology underlying analysis and prescription at Dartmouth than the uncritical dependence on such illogically matched pairs as "awareness of human relations"/"philosophy of life"; interaction/imitation; organization of feelings/organization of knowledge. These dualisms—for they are not true oppositions—are all variations of the supposed antithesis between "creative" and "intellectual." Dixon comments: "When life is felt as immediate and particular, our work in this role [of spectator] is closest to the artist; as it moves towards generality it moves closer to the thinker" (p. 29).[16] Mr. Dixon's second thoughts on this dichotomy do not include a revaluation of the underlying assumption, but

---

[14] This skepticism encourages the institutionalization of a common mistrust of "subjective" judgment. English teachers are used to being told by deans and guidance officers that writing samples cannot be included in a folder along with "hard data" (i.e., test scores racked up by the student as problem solver) because the judgment of "writing" is only personal. Note this observation by an educational psychologist: "In the humanities what is principally involved is appreciation. The reference is entirely personal; the only test of validity is the idiosyncratic, emotional response of the student." (*Learning about Learning*, ed. Jerome Bruner, the report of a government-sponsored conference held the same year as the Dartmouth Conference, 1966.) From such a point of view, the possibility that one aim in the English classroom might be the training of powers of apprehension and the education of taste becomes laughable.

[15] Frederic Crews has recently noted that "some frustrated students deducing that any intellectual effort must be inimical to their neglected feelings, are now turning against 'the mind' and discovering an ally in C. G. Jung—the Jung of numinosity, alchemy, and the vulgarized Mysterious East" (*The New York Review of Books*, Feb. 26, 1970).

[16] Susanne K. Langer comments as follows on a slightly different version of this misconception: "Feeling and form are not logical complements. They are merely associated, respectively, with each other's negatives. Feeling is associated with spontaneity, spontaneity with informality or indifference to form, and thus (by slipshod thinking) with *absence* of form. On the other hand, form connotes formality, regulation, hence repression of feeling, and (by the same slipshodness) *absence* of feeling. The conception of polarity . . . is really an unfortunate metaphor whereby a logical muddle is raised to the dignity of a fundamental principle" (*Feeling and Form*, p. 17).

only a recognition of the consequences of neglecting one "half" for the other. In his Preface to the second edition, he expresses regret that the seminar's emphasis had not been more on the "common sense world" because there then would have been more interest in "the intellectual uses of language which we rather took for granted at Dartmouth." No: when "the intellectual uses of language" are defined in terms imposed by behavioristic conceptions of how the human animal shapes his world, they are not taken for granted; they are not recognized.

The effects of this separation of intellectual and creative modes are not only disastrous pedagogically, but they are also politically suspect.[17] If we have accepted this separation, what do we say, for instance, to the energetic young teacher who wants to make college relevant to blacks and who declares that since "they" are not interested in literature, he has decided to substitute real explorations of the city for "the literary experience"? Or what do we say to the teacher who, as he is personally and professionally dedicated to helping his disadvantaged students gain the skills which will start them off on an equal footing intellectually, scorns the "experience theme" because there is no way of getting from this "fun" thing to the "real" thing, i.e., the critical paper? Each is judging, it seems to me, from faulty premises: that composition is either self-expression or communication; that literature is either immediately "relevant" or a box of puzzles to be solved. And these premises, I would argue, derive from the fundamental misconception which opposes the allegedly creative, personal, emotional charged, intuitively understood experience to the supposedly intellectual, public, abstract, conceptual nonexperience.

What is missing is the understanding of language as an instrument of knowing—our means of knowing our experience, knowing our feelings, knowing our knowledge. When we begin with our students as *knowers,* we must include what happens "inside": "reality" is not something that happens to us from "outside." If there is to be any chance of defining what is "relevant" to our students' lives which will not involve demeaning them or what we aim to teach—"reading and writing anything, especially literature" —then we will have to discard a view of language and a psychology of learning which fosters this notion of reality as "something out there." An old-fashioned pedagogy identifies that "something" with a body of knowledge which the teacher has and must somehow pass on to his students. But a modern student-centered curriculum is just as wrongheaded when it is built

[17] Paulo Freire in *Pedagogy of the Oppressed* (N.Y.: Herder, 1970) has analyzed the political effects of separating "the cognitive, the affective, and the active aspects of the total, indivisible personality." Freire provides the best defense against the counsels of despair of some radical critics because he believes that "naming the world" can become a revolutionary act. I have commented briefly on his importance to us in our thinking about the teaching of English in "The Problem of Problem Solving," *College Composition and Communication*, October 1971.

on the idea that "what is happening" is the reality from which we are successively removed according to the degree of abstraction our language reaches. The speculative instruments we need if we are to encourage the experience of literature, the discovery of the uses of imagination, and the liberating power of language were not forged at the Dartmouth Conference.

Certainly there were helpful points of departure developed at Dartmouth; new programs which have been found very useful got their start there. Do philosophical inadequacies really matter, then, if prescriptions and guidelines deriving from them are in fact encouraging, suggestive, productive? Why shouldn't we willingly tolerate shallow learning theory if inspired teaching comes from it? The point is, I think, that good ideas will have a very short life if they are not well grounded. Just as bad teaching can ruin a good idea, so brilliant and inventive pedagogy can mask false principle and it will be left to the inexperienced or insensitive teacher to prove out the inadequacies. A good teacher's philosophy is of little importance *per se;* it may even be wrongheaded and misguided. But if we do not understand the actual as opposed to the alleged reasons for good teaching it will be very difficult to explain to ourselves and others what works and why. (The teacher who told Kenneth Koch she'd done dreams yesterday and was going to do wishes tomorrow is already legendary.) Without a sound philosophy of knowledge (or an intuitive grasp of the actual functioning of the mind); without an understanding of the way language builds the human world; without a philosophical understanding of the form-creating and form-discovering powers of the imagination, it will be very difficult to decide what is needed or to imagine what is possible.

Without such understanding, teachers are prey to delusion or cynicism, believing that every "innovation" is bound to help or that the "problem of English" is simply intractable. We need philosophy to protect us from problem-solving that is merely verbal, but a sound philosophy of knowledge could also protect us from that unconscious self-righteousness which enables a teacher to decide, for instance, that "they" don't need literature or that instruction is necessarily authoritarian and is therefore to be discarded or that correction is tantamount to an assault on "personhood." What we intend as generosity, the product of an informed and sophisticated understanding of cultural deficiencies, may become little other than a form of condescension. The figure of a radical Lady Bountiful is becoming a commonplace. Most importantly, a philosophy of knowledge which is a theory of imagination could assure us that the choice is not, as the Dartmouth Conference seems to have defined it, between a corruscating discipline and a spiritual and moral freedom. The actual choice, it seems to me, is between a dispiriting regimen, an anti-intellectual manipulation, or a frenetically structured curriculum on the one hand and, on the other, humane instruction claiming as its goal what Coleridge once described as knowing your knowledge.

A philosophy of knowledge will be useful to us, I have suggested, insofar as it provides the means of conceiving of language as an instrument of knowing. We need a theory of imagination and we will find it implicit in the principles of rhetoric which inform our teaching of language and literature, reading and writing. Rhetoric is a formulation of the laws of imagination, that operation of mind by which experience becomes meaningful. The English teacher only needs to use those laws deliberately in thinking about the teaching of English. It is not a matter of introducing rhetoric as a separate discipline; rhetoric is already "there" since we cannot consider structure, function, shape, sound, voice, weight, pace, image, argument, allusion, meaning, intention, interpretation, context without thinking rhetoric. Rhetoric reminds us that the function of language is not only to name but also to *formulate* and to *transform*—to give form to feeling, cogency to argument, shape to memory. Rhetoric leads us again and again to the discovery of that natural capacity for *symbolic transformation,* a capacity which is itself untaught, God-given, universal. The great teachers from Socrates to Montessori have always taught to it and we, I think, must learn why that is so.

To rediscover the form-finding and form-creating power of language, those of us who teach "reading and writing anything, especially literature" should perhaps put ourselves to school to learn from a study of the other arts how form finds form, to rediscover, that is, the relation of perception to conception, the relationship of the primary imagination by which we construe the forms of experience to those symbolic means—kinetic, linguistic, visual, tonal—by which they are articulated. We could begin with Herbert Read's *Education through Art*, Rudolph Arnheim's *Art and Visual Perception* and *Visual Thinking*, E. H. Gombrich's *Art and Illusion*, Susanne K. Langer's *Feeling and Form* and *Mind: An Essay on Human Feeling.* Or we could visit a dance class or a chorus rehearsal or undertake a few drawing lessons—anything which would freshen and sharpen our sense that the resources we need to make language available as a speculative instrument are to be found in a study of literary form. Or we could read Piaget and take seriously Sylvia Ashton-Warner's invitation to visit "the infant room." I have had students in Advanced Composition observe wryly that they hadn't had such assignments as looking at drawings since the fifth grade, only to admit in a week or so that they hadn't really *looked* at anything since the fifth grade. We hear chemistry professors complain that students nowadays may arrive in college classes with a detailed and sophisticated understanding of the concepts of biochemistry but with an almost completely undeveloped capacity for observation and descriptive analysis. Is it not part of our job to teach our students to look and to see all over again? to listen and to hear?

Josephine Miles has defined a composition as "a bundle of parts." [18] Is it not appropriate for courses in English to explore thoroughly the

[18] "What We Compose," *CCC*, XIV (October 1963), pp. 146–154.

implications of the composing process? to teach by means of rhetorical concepts how it is that we distinguish the parts and how we bundle them? In so doing, I think we must learn how to make available for critical use that knowledge which is a natural resource. The discrimination of pattern and design is a capacity to be exercised, not one that must be instilled; space and time are primary categories of human understanding. Experiments in oral composition, for instance, using the rhetorical concept of parallelism can put students in touch with what they already know, namely, that repetition is the primary and most fundamental feature of all form.[19] The concept of *opposition* is surely an important natural resource; it is every human being's birthright. Almost as soon as it is named, *opposition* can become an invaluable speculative instrument for the exploration of how parts are bundled. Its usefulness in ordering and organizing is immediately apparent; the same cannot be said for such a non-rhetorical notion as "meaning." "What is the author trying to say?" is a less useful point of departure than "How is the ending of the story consonant with the beginning?" *Opposition* can clarify the process of abstraction; the development of definitions; the analysis of relationships between characters, between example and precept, cause and effect, *now* and *then,* the I and the Other, etc., etc. Students whose mathematical abilities outshine their "verbal aptitude" find *opposition* a useful bridge from what they know they know to what they don't know that they know. And verbally alert students can enjoy searching out the metaphysical and epistemological depths of a theory of opposition.[20]

In short, a *lexicon rhetoricae* would provide the terms and the central notions for the philosophy of knowledge that we need, for a theory of imagination. *Naming, identifying, differentiating, generalizing, defining, interpreting, evaluating:* these are our working concepts, the ones we are, or ought to be, professionally concerned with, day in and day out, and English teachers, no matter what their individual style, will be on their home ice in employing them. Furthermore, there are fewer hazards in using "our" language than there are in using the language of experimental psychology and information theory. Why should that be so? Why is *meaning* a "better" word for us than *information*? Why is it more useful to an English teacher to think in terms of *interpreting* than *encoding* and *decoding*? of *intention, context, tone, point of view* rather than *input* and *output*? Why is *dialectic* less treacherous than *feedback*? What is to be gained if, in the propaedeutics of a philosophy of knowledge, we discuss linguistic behavior in organic rather than mechanical metaphors? For one thing, words associated with mind rather than machines can prevent those

---

[19] This experiment (and many others which, with some modification, are as appropriate to freshman classes as to the grades) is described in J. W. Patrick Creber's *Sense and Sensitivity: The Philosophy and Practice of English Teaching* (London: Univ. of London Press, 1965; available as a NCTE publication).

[20] C. K. Ogden's fascinating little book is indispensable: *Opposition: A Linguistic and Psychological Analysis* (Bloomington: Indiana Univ. Press, 1967).

short circuits by which mechanical analogies become substantive. The words we use tend to foster one set of assumptions or another. We need to counter the illusion of our mechanistic age that models of human language use derived from engineering can deal with the thing itself; for the full symbolic and creative functions of language cannot be represented by models of signal systems, whether as simple as old-fashioned telephone exchanges or as complex as analog computers. The practical application of rhetorical and logical analysis could enliven that apprehension because it directs our attention to the how as well as the what.[21] No amount of energy expended in celebrating the marvelous powers of poetry, in proclaiming the centrality of "form" in literature can redress the harm done in actually dealing with it as if it were a computer print-out.

The over-arching reason for depending on rhetorical analysis, dialectics, and poetics in our thinking about the teaching of English, that is, in the formulation of the working concepts we will need in approaching our students as knowers, is simply that these instruments put us in touch with the actual forms of human utterance. Rhetoric, dialectics, and poetics cannot do the work of a full philosophy of linguistic form any more than psychoanalysis or radical politics can, but they can remind teachers of the mediating function of language, of its symbolic nature. In this regard, they can do what the problem-solving approach, communication theory and behavioral psychology cannot possibly do; they allow us to conceive of language as an instrument of knowing and to present literature—to invent fresh ways of making it available to our students—as a form of knowledge. They help us to conceive of those uniquely human operations of mind by which the forms of knowing create and discover the substance of knowledge. Thus enabled, we can articulate a theory of imagination, the imagination which creates *poiesis* and the imagination which is "the prime agent of all human perception." Teaching as a revolutionary activity requires nothing less.

[21] See Josephine Miles, "English: A Colloquy: or, How What's What in the Language," *California English Journal*, Winter, 1966.

Part Six

The Uses of Classical Rhetoric

"*When teachers of writing and speaking seek guides for their future, they will find them, I believe, not primarily in grammar, linguistics, and logic, but in the ancient and honorable art of rhetoric.*"

KARL R. WALLACE

The rediscovery of classical rhetoric has more potential for improving the way young people write than any other current movement in education. This should not be taken, though, as a recommendation to rush out to include in the high school curriculum the close reading of Aristotle or an excessive memorization of technical terminology. What it does mean is this: if teachers had a better understanding of classical rhetoric—its history, its techniques, its goals and purposes—then many would be able to translate such understanding into effective classroom practice. Consider for a moment how such knowledge might lead to the improvement of one aspect of student writing, organization. For many years teachers have followed the practice of assigning a topic, asking their students to write on it, marking the papers and returning them. In this sequence, as we have seen, there is often no instruction about the principles of organization, and yet many of the problems in student writing are concerned with organization. If the instructor had an understanding of the principles of classical rhetoric, he would be able to reverse this process; that is, rather than assign the topic and let the students try to find the right organization, he could teach the principles of organization and let the students discover their own topics. This process not only addresses itself to a major problem in student writing, but also permits greater freedom in the choice of what to write about. And what is true of organization is also true of other areas of composition, such as sentence structure, discovery of supporting evidence, balance and symmetry, and consistency in point of view.

In the first essay in this section, "The Relevance of Rhetoric," Barry Ulanov explains the value of rhetoric and reviews its three major divisions: Invention, Arrangement, and Style. These three elements, writes Ulanov, "follow so logical an order, and the kind of analysis and synthesis to which they lead is so unmistakably useful, that rhetoric once again has large numbers of adherents and once again can justify a high place for itself in the high school and college curriculum." Ulanov argues for a view of rhetoric which shows language "*in vivo,* alive and kicking," not sterile or artificial.

Some modern educators reject imitation as a worthwhile teaching method, but according to Edward P. J. Corbett in "The Theory and Practice of Imitation in Classical Rhetoric," such a method not only has a long and honorable history but is still effective. Corbett carefully delineates how ancient rhetoricians successfully used Imitation (along with Theory and Practice) and how the technique flourished in the Tudor schools. He reminds us too that even today many manual, athletic, and intellectual skills are learned by imitation. Why then don't we make more use of the technique? Because of the prevailing mood of the times, answers Corbett, a mood which emphasizes "creativity, self-expression, individuality." But imitation does *not* stultify the creative drive; on the contrary, as Corbett says, it "unlocks our powers and sets us free to be creative, original, and ultimately effective." This essay should assist greatly in reviving a long-neglected but useful technique.

W. Ross Winterowd's excellent article, " 'Topics' and Levels in the Composing Process," shows how some of the new approaches to invention are related to the classical conception. The classification of topics as *content-oriented* or *form-oriented* and as *finite* or *non-finite* is useful both for understanding the theory of topics and for further research. The next essay, Knapp and McCroskey's "The Siamese Twins: Inventio and Dispositio," illustrates how Invention is closely related to, indeed interwoven with, the second division, Arrangement.

Some suggestions for teaching the third major component, Style, appear in Winston Weathers' essay, "Teaching Style: A Possible Anatomy." Weathers insists that style *is* important, for it defines the personality of the writer: ". . . How we choose says something about who we are." The author identifies four aspects of understanding style: (1) recognizing stylistic material, (2) using stylistic material, (3) combining stylistic materials for a consistent point of view, (4) adapting style to a variety of rhetorical situations. The admonition for the student to *recognize, copy, understand,* and then *imitate creatively* agrees strongly with Corbett's position on imitation as a teaching method.

The final selection is taken from a great book written by a remarkable person, *Institutio Oratoria (On the Education of the Orator)* of Marcus Fabius Quintilian. The modern reader will be astonished at the wisdom and freshness of this splendid teacher's insight into the composing process. Quintilian wrote the work about A.D. 93, after he had retired from a highly successful career as teacher of rhetoric in Rome. Even though rhetoric at that time included public speaking and training for the practice of law, and even though the mechanical means of writing were primitive compared to our own, Quintilian nevertheless has the highest praise for the written word: "It is the pen which at once brings the most labor and the most profit. [It is] the best producer and teacher of eloquence." His mind ranged over many topics which still engage composition teachers: What is the relationship between writing well and writing quickly? Is it desirable to dictate? What is the best environment for writing? How does one handle distractions? Even though nineteen centuries separate us, his advice still rings true today. For centuries his grand perspective of rhetoric and education, his thorough scholarship, and his dedication to the highest ideals of teaching have inspired teachers throughout the world.

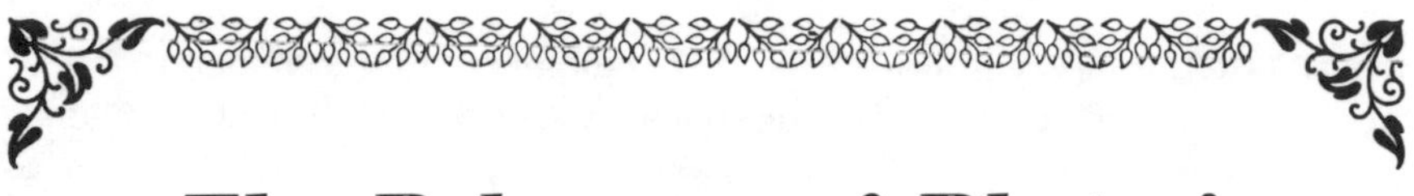

The Relevance of Rhetoric

BARRY ULANOV

We have seen a great deal of the word *rhetoric* in recent years. It has turned up often in speculative treatises about the nature of language and communication. It has been used with increasing frequency by the editors and compilers of English textbooks to describe the methods underlying their editing and compiling. Some of the time, at least, it has been used in accordance with ancient tradition, but more often, I suspect, it has been just a handy term to cover almost anything more or less associated with an apparatus of persuasion. One cannot quarrel with either usage. Both have honorable sanction. Rhetoric is beyond a doubt the generic term that best covers all the arts of verbal persuasion and perhaps other kinds of persuasion as well. But it is not merely a wide word, offering shelter for all sorts of vague maneuvers in the general direction of persuasion. It has a long and richly detailed tradition involving the closest possible analysis of language, not just a description of the way it behaves for the spectators of language. Rhetoric in this sense of the word is the psychology of language. In it, analysis and synthesis are very closely related functions: one takes things apart only to be able to put them together again. One looks at the inner works of a skillful writer with admiration, of course, but the inner works, no matter how elegantly arranged before one, make a fairly sterile object. It is only when they have been put back together again that one can really mark the achievement of the writer and, to the extent that it is relevant to one's own work, perhaps imitiate it as well. Rhetoric in the oldest and deepest sense of the word is dedicated to this double accomplishment. It is determined to show all the inner works of language, but *in vivo,* alive and kicking. It tries to avoid as much as possible a mere presentation of parts, in desiccated disarray. The working example is what counts. That is the sense in which I am concerned with rhetoric in this paper and the sense in which, it seems to me, it has the utmost relevance for the teaching of reading and writing.

English Journal, vol. 55 (April 1966), pp. 403–408.

The ancients who gave rhetoric first place among the subjects of their academies would not have disputed its relevance to reading and writing, but they would have insisted, as we all know, that the primary purpose of rhetoric is to teach the art of speaking well. But speaking well is not merely a fluency of discourse or a sweetness of voice. It is the first term of a sequence of reasoning which ends with human happiness. One speaks well to persuade others but not simply to win victories over their heads or hearts. Persuasion is directed, in this understanding of rhetoric, toward a "right" end, and so a skillful rhetorician such as Isocrates, a generation before Aristotle, saw rhetoricians as men of virtue. Aristotle's *Rhetoric* is less concerned with virtue and human happiness; persuasive speech leading to decision is its express purpose. But the virtues—and the vices—enter one way or another in Aristotle, too, since to affect decisions rhetoricians must understand emotions —"those feelings that so change men as to affect their judgments, and that are also attended by pain or pleasure"—and be able to manipulate them.

It would be hard today to win either willing instructors or willing students for this construction of rhetoric. We have conceded to the advertising agencies and the politicians the rhetoric of emotional manipulation leading to clear decisions in favor of one product or another, human or inhuman or somewhere in-between. We concede to no one the rhetoric that leads to human happiness; we disagree too much about the nature of happiness and have almost no grasp at all of the meaning of virtue, or at least none that we can agree on. And so rhetoric as a form of public instruction in contesting for the human will has been all but discredited, though the contesting goes on and with it the instruction, rather more private than before, if not altogether underground. Public speaking is taught too, but at some distance from the ancients' concern with the virtues, and rarely in any class that is also a class in reading and writing.

Rhetoric survives today, then, in several truncated forms, and for all its inner drive toward completeness and unity, it seems likely to go on that way for many years. Speech as a discipline of learning lives in a separate world. Whatever the original connection between speaking well and reading and writing well, today the association of these functions is at best indirect, except as a few very rare instructors bring them together. As a result, two of the five parts of classical rhetoric, Memory and Delivery, are banished from the realm of readers and writers. And yet, split up as it is, rhetoric continues to exercise an enormous appeal. Its remaining parts, Invention and Arrangement and Style, follow so logical an order, and the kind of analysis and synthesis to which they lead is so unmistakably useful, that rhetoric once again has large numbers of adherents and once again can justify a high place for itself in the high school and college curriculum.

The logic of the classical rhetorical arrangement is, it seems to me, indisputable. Every piece of writing starts with something like *Invention.* One must choose or devise a subject for oneself, or, if the topic has been assigned by an instructor, must invent some individual way of dealing with it. If the term were more in vogue, perhaps the ways of students in dealing with the topics assigned by composition teachers would be more inventive, or even better, perhaps the topics themselves would be chosen with more imagination. For, according to the procedures of the ancients, Invention involved the choice not simply of a subject on which one could discourse, but rather of one for which a convincing case could be made. Just see what this does with such fine old topics as "What I Did Last Summer" or "What Happened to Me on the Way to School Today"!

Inevitably, after Invention comes Arrangement. In modern practice, this is where the emphasis usually lies. Our textbook procedures are essentially exercises in compositional arrangement, and fairly tedious ones at that. The attempt to construct a coherent statement, of whatever length, without convincing subject matter is doomed, and so are all the subsidiary parts of the statement. The instructor stresses the need for a clear beginning, middle, and end—of what? He talks of "significant detail" or paragraph structure or sentence structure—to what purpose? He invokes some of the headier language of literary criticism, such as *tone, tenor, levels of diction,* or *credibility;* he may even, after a rush of T. S. Eliot to the head, bother his students with talk about *objective correlatives* for particular emotions or other experiences. All this must appear at best fragmentary to the student, at worst absolutely meaningless, unless he has been well guided in his Invention, or, by some miracle of self-discovery, has found the resources for a shrewd devising of subject matter. There is no point in an instructor's gathering together all the traditional terms of grammar, syntax, and figurative language and then throwing them at a student without an initial structuring of purpose. If this, the structuring of purpose, is done well, then he can pass to Arrangement, as the classical rhetorician understood the term, with some assurance of clarity in the first line of communication: that between instructor and student.

Arrangement in the ancient sense is carefully distinguished from *Style.* Arrangement does not concern itself with choice of words nor with any of the other minutiae of self-expression. Arrangement is an exercise in order. One looks, under this heading, for some rational sequence of presentation. Persuasion comes here by something like number. That does not mean that there is an appointed order to each argument or that one must approach every idea either forwards or backwards or crabwise or by any other one method in a particular list of alternatives. To the ancients, the categories of movement in writing, as in speech, were strictly limited; they did choose among a specific number. But the number was high and their understanding of the possibilities for variation within different orders of arrangement, as among the huge number of figures of speech which were open to them, was endlessly flexible. Our own choice could, it seems to me, be as flexible or as rigorous as individual temperament dictates, as long as we recognize the precise nature of this stage of the writing process and the need to preserve it, independent of the other large parts of rhetoric, Invention and Style, and yet clearly in sequence with them.

Style is the most elusive of the parts of the rhetorical art. Whether our correlatives are objective or subjective, they must in some measure correspond with a pre-conceived idea or emotion or some experience which we are undergoing as we write. To achieve a style as recognizably one's own as one's handwriting, however inept that may be, is an extraordinary achievement and we should always be quick to acknowledge this fact. This, really, is where the elements of grammar and syntax and figurative language enter. This is where techniques abound. For here, in the jungle of Style, we must somehow guide our students to find appropriate terms for their experiences, appropriate punctuation, appropriate colors and textures, appropriate diction, and having found them to recognize them. And here we must pass well beyond the ancients, for here we have not so much to gather from the past and a very great deal to learn from the explorations of the present.

The data of Style are just beginning to be gathered, if you will allow me to describe the work of two-thirds of a century as a beginning. It is only, really, with the attempts of the anthropologists, the psychologists, the sociologists, and the art historians of this century, that stylistic analysis has become an adult undertaking. And even they sometimes suffer from the narrow limitations of deterministic thinking or from the need to prove a thesis at all costs or from so inflexible a reliance on one particular methodology or another that all other techniques of analysis must be declared inadmissible. Still, the data are now ours, or some of them anyway. We all see how important the social or economic environment of an artist may be. We recognize sexual symbols and religious icons when we see them or hear them described, perhaps, at this point, the sexual rather more easily than the religious, but neither one exclusively. We see close connections between so-called primitive culture and modern urban civilization and see, too, how useful the analysis of one may prove for the understanding of the other. We look hard for symbol systems in a work of art, perhaps too hard at times, for we often find them when they are not there. But in all of this, which I have only described in the roundest of terms, we see the complexity of the creative act and when we talk of Style, we recognize how uncertain our language really is and how far from reducing the processes of art to manageable terms we are.

Thus far, at least, the analysis of Style has not advanced very far in the literary arts. The visual arts have led the way here and some faltering efforts by a few critics and scholars have only suggested adaptations to writing that may be made from the work of the art historians and the psychologists, anthropologists, sociologists and others whose findings they have plundered for their purposes. The best work that has been done in the stylistic analysis of literature is in the medieval period, where the close link between the visual and the verbal arts makes possible something like a dependable identification of symbols and icons and allegorical structures and where there are both universal vocabularies at work in all the arts and contemporary explications, glosses, and commentaries to guide one in interpreting an artist's individual use of the vocabularies. But stylistic analysis of quality has been done in periods later than the medieval, and more is being attempted. In spite of its late arrival on the modern scene, this sort of examination of texts is by now well enough established so that the teacher attempting to bring some examples of it even into the teaching of freshmen and sophomores in high school may find enough evidence of what he wants in the learned journals or scholarly volumes of recent date to get him started. And even if he cannot satisfy himself that he has material lucid or simple enough to bring into his classroom, he can assure himself that he is following a sound rhetorical principle if he distinguishes very clearly between the stages of Arrangement and Style in his presentation of the materials of composition.

Finally, one must go to the texts of the most gifted writers in our language to explain *Style.* The best explanation remains a clear demonstration, and Style has all sorts of clear demonstrations in the performances of English and American writers, of every era, of every genre. There is no need even to attempt to be cumulative about periods or techniques. It is enough to show how remarkably useful and eloquent different styles may be, each in its own way, and with that demonstration to hold out to the student the potentialities of development of his own style, even if what seems to be indicated is a disorderly, ungrammatical mélange in which the identifying marks are no more than his own species of disorder and bad grammar. The mark of the human person—even the disorderly and the ungrammatical mark—is always a precious thing and ought not to be spurned.

Obviously, no one will deliberately encourage disorder and bad grammar, but anyone with a warm respect for and an understanding of rhetorical traditions will be slow to decide just what disorder is and will recognize (and teach) that good grammar is not the pivotal element in the making of a good style, however valuable an aid it may be. The marks of the human person which the analysis of style reveals are so many and so various and so elusive that description must long precede prescription here and, when prescription comes, it can come only as a function of the purpose invented by the writer and the arrangement of parts that has followed the invention. In some cases, as the experimental writing of this century makes abundantly clear, this requires the suspension of many of the rules of grammar and syntax, whether to give a speaker his proper ungrammatical identity or to produce certain levels of meaning that only sentence fragments can provide or simply to underscore the philosophical and psychological muddles and confusions of our era by a matching verbal turmoil. But no matter how much a writer may suspend or condense grammatical and syntactical procedures, he may never dispense with rhetoric altogether, for consciously or unconsciously he always follows the general structure of rhetorical procedure. He chooses a theme. He selects or plans or at least falls into some ordering of his argument, some arrangement of the parts of his writing. And something like a style, however choppy or ill-planned or derivative, must ensue. It is my argument here that enlightened instruction will emphasize these rhetorical elements since, by choice or not, they remain central to all writing and thus to the structure of everything we read as well.

I would go further in my adherence to the terms of rhetoric. I would make use of the ancient orators' categories of questions. For the orators, as we know, there were three kinds of questions, the Demonstrative, the Deliberative, and the Judicial. The Demonstrative dealt with the praise or censure of persons, usually one particular person. The Deliberative question was at the core of rhetorical instruction; it involved a position which the orator hoped to persuade others to agree with or to dissuade others from accepting. As a descriptive name for its category, Judicial suggests, rather more clearly than the other terms, its concern—accusation and defense, as in courts of law.

It is not urgent that we hold on to the ancient names. If one prefers Illustrative to Demonstrative, or perhaps the Category of Proof, that will do. Debate may seem a better term for the second category. Legal Argument or Judgment may attract some people as ways of describing the third. One may prefer the simplest possible descriptions—Praise and Blame, Persuasion and Dissuasion, Accusation and Defense. One may be convinced that these categories do not in any way exhaust the possible topics of rhetoric. Fair enough. As long as one begins with the enormous classes of rhetorical performance which Praise and Blame, Arguments For and Against, and Accusations and Defense represent, that will be enough, I think, to preserve the inherent order and control which the hallowed categories offer.

And after these categories, how far need one go in pursuit of the procedures of classical rhetoric? My own thinking is that it is safest to stick to the roundest terms in the tradition. It is very difficult, if not impossible, to use either the terms or the examples of Aristotle, Cicero, Quintilian, or any of the other ancient authorities once they come to cases chosen from the drama or epic poetry or jurisprudence of their immediate predecessors and contemporaries. But the general principles imbedded in their rhetorical methods remain useful and widely applicable, as do many of the variations and permutations of medieval and Renaissance rhetoricians. Certainly, for example, there is more than a tedious historicism involved in examining the figures of speech of Elizabethan writers. There is great freshness for the present day to be found in their invention. Our reduction of figure to simile and metaphor would have seemed a shocking impoverishment of the language to them, as it should to us as well, and would, if we were more familiar with the devices of a rhetoric-instructed style.

The point of rhetorical instruction is to establish perspective in a student's reading and writing. It insists from the very beginning of any exercise upon that sort of critical examination which will reveal purpose or purposelessness, order or disorder, an identifiable style or a mixture of styles or no style at all, an effort to praise or to blame, to persuade or to dissuade, to accuse or to defend. It takes an almost geometrical approach toward wholes and their parts and yet never reduces anything one reads or writes to simple formulas either of description or of prescription. It is a method so widely open to the divagations of human personality that it goes painstakingly through history looking for more and more devices with which to express human experience but never, at least today, with any one-to-one correspondence between a device and an emotion, a technique and an attitude, a principle of expression and a species of idea. Rhetorical instruction is, in the deepest sense, a vote of confidence on the instructor's part in a student's ability to communicate something, to express something, to describe something he has experienced, however incompletely, and to find some skill and therefore some satisfaction in doing so. It is at the same time a recognition that one must read the same way, looking in the works that move us, whether they are by acknowledged masters or not, for the same indications of theme, and purpose, of coherent structure, of style, of categories of persuasion.

Ultimately, it seems to me, the efficacy of rhetorical method depends upon the matching of reading and writing exercises, at least in the large. Composition classes that do not draw their writing principles from the examination of writing of quality must bog down sooner or later in the dullness and defeatism which afflict almost all young writers. The examples do not have to be of great size. They do not have to roam extensively, though clearly they should touch upon as many kinds of person and style and technique as the make-up of a class seems to require. Short pieces seem to me to be best if they can hold a student's attention as well as demonstrate a substantial variety of rhetorical principles and procedures. The point is to show that the principles and the procedures have a continuing freshness, a freshness that is instinct in the language, but, unfortunately, not a necessary part of our teaching of the language. If rhetoric is shown to have an innate virtuosity, range, and constant openness to the human person, as I am firmly convinced it has, then it will once again become a necessary part of our teaching of the language.

The Theory and Practice of Imitation in Classical Rhetoric

EDWARD P. J. CORBETT

The first point that needs to be made in a paper about the theory and practice of imitation in classical rhetoric is that the term *imitation* had a variety of meanings in antiquity. In his article "Literary Criticism and the Concept of Imitation in Antiquity,"[1] Richard McKeon has carefully and elaborately discriminated five distinct meanings of *imitation* in classical theory. The three meanings of *mimesis* most familiar to teachers of English are (1) the Platonic notion of an image-making faculty which produces extensions of ideal truth in the phenomenal world, (2) the Aristotelian notion of the representation of human actions, and (3) the rhetorical notion of copying, aping, simulating, emulating models. Fascinating as it would be to trace out the evolutions and the interrelationships of these concepts of imitation, I will confine myself in this paper to exploring the theory and practice of imitation in the rhetorician's sense of emulating models.

Curiously enough, Aristotle, who wrote a major work in rhetoric, did not treat of imitation in the sense of emulating successful practitioners of an art. In Chapter 4 of his *Poetics*, he did mention that man is the most imitative of all creatures, that he learns at first by imitation, and that he takes a natural delight in the contemplation of works of imitation. Moreover, as McKeon has reminded us,[2] Aristotle frequently made the distinction in his other works between sciences, which are acquired by learning; virtues, which are acquired by habit; and arts, which are acquired by practice. It was Isocrates who in his *Against the Sophists*[3] first propagated the suggestion about the value of imitating accomplished orators. All of the subsequent major

College Composition and Communication, vol. 22 (October 1971), pp. 243–250.

[1] Reprinted in *Critics and Criticism*, ed. Ronald S. Crane (Chicago: University of Chicago Press, 1952), pp. 147–175. See also Donald L. Clark, "Imitation: Theory and Practice in Roman Rhetoric," *Quarterly Journal of Speech*, 37 (1951), pp. 11–22.

[2] McKeon, p. 168.

[3] *Isocrates*, trans. George Norlin, Loeb Classical Library (Cambridge, Mass.: Harvard University Press, 1962), II, 175.

classical rhetoricians—Dionysius of Halicarnassus, Longinus, Cicero, and Quintilian—recommended the practice of imitation. And there is ample evidence that imitation was fervently recommended and diligently practiced in the medieval and Renaissance schools.

The ancient rhetoricians taught that oratorical skills are acquired by three means—theory, imitation, and practice. These three means are succinctly defined in the *Ad Herennium*:

> By theory *(ars)* is meant a set of rules that provide a definite method and system of speaking. Imitation *(imitatio)* stimulates us to attain, in accordance with a studied method, the effectiveness of certain models in speaking. Practice *(exercitatio)* is assiduous exercises and experience *(usus* and *consuetudo)* in speaking.[4]

A recollection of our own experience is enough to confirm this doctrine that the acquisition of any skill, whether it be a manual skill like knitting or an athletic skill like playing tennis or an intellectual skill like speaking or writing, is effected by one or other or a combination of these three means. There are countless examples of people who learned how to play a musical instrument simply by trial-and-error practice. What usually happens, however, once a person has acquired the rudiments of a skill, is that he yearns to improve that skill. So he observes other practitioners and tries to assimilate their techniques. Eventually, he may feel the urge to study the theory of his art. The most universal instance, of course, of acquiring a skill by these three means is the sequence a child usually follows in learning how to speak his language: first imitation, then practice, ultimately theory or the grammar of the language.

The ancient rhetoricians were not making a very original or profound observation about the learning process when they formulated this triad of theory, imitation, and practice. Anyone who had the faculty to observe and the patience to reflect could have come up with that formula. But it is remarkable how that simple triadic formula provided a structure and a direction for the teaching of the language arts in the schools for over two thousand years. And the roster of famous men who made a contribution to the theoretical and pedagogical development of that triadic orientation constitutes a Who Was Who of the great minds of the Western World. By concentrating in this paper on just one member of that trinity of disciplines, I hope I do not give a distorted picture of how the rhetoricians and the teachers of the past tried to bring their pupils to a functional level of proficiency in the arts of discourse.

One of the words that keeps recurring in all Latin discussions of imitation is *similis*. Apparently, one of the objectives of imitation was to make

[4] *Ad Herennium*, II, ii, 3, trans. Harry Caplan, Loeb Classical Library (Cambridge, Mass.: Harvard University Press, 1954).

someone *similar* to someone else, presumably to someone superior. Quintilian put it this way:

> In fact, we may note that the elementary study of every branch of learning is directed by reference to some definite standard that is placed before the learner. We must, in fact, be either like or unlike *(aut similes aut dissimiles)* those who have proved their excellence. It is rare for nature to produce such resemblance, which is more often the result of imitation.[5]

But in order not to contribute to the unsavory connotation that *imitation* has for many people—namely that imitation succeeds only in producing carbon-copies—I hasten to remind you that *similar* did not mean for Quintilian and the other classical rhetoricians *identical.* Perhaps it was unfortunate that the rhetoricians used the verb *imitate* to designate this activity, because the Latin verb *imitari* does denote "to produce an image of," a meaning which suggests a reproducing of copies of an original. The verb *aemulari,* which is the source of our verb *emulate* and which in Latin has remotely the same roots as *imitari* and *imago,* would have been a more precise word to designate what the rhetoricians hoped to accomplish by imitation, since *aemulari* meant "to try to rival or equal or surpass." The motto of imitation was "Observe and do likewise." Imitation asked the student to observe the manner or pattern or form or means used by a model and then attempt to emulate the model. A friend of mine who coached Little League baseball teams both before and after television sets became a common appliance in the home told me that the big differerence he noted in the boys he worked with over the years is that he rarely had to spend any time showing the TV-conditioned youngsters how to assume a stance in the batter's box or how to hold and swing a bat; imitating the major-league heroes that they had seen on the television screen, they readily assumed classic stances in the box and held a bat as though they had been born with it in their hands. It was that kind of "striving to be like" that the rhetors tried to instill in their pupils. They did not want to reproduce facsimiles of Demosthenes; they wanted to produce orators who could speak *as effectively as* Demosthenes. The ultimate objective of all rhetorical training, imitation included, was well stated by Quintilian: "For what object have we in teaching them but that they may not always require to be taught" *(Institutio Oratoria,* II,v,13).

Since many records of imitative practices in Greek and Roman schools are extant, we must turn to the written accounts of imitative exercises in the English schools of the sixteenth and seventeenth centuries for

[5] *Institutio Oratoria,* X, ii, 2–3, trans. H. E. Butler, 4 vols., Loeb Classical Library (Cambridge, Mass.: Harvard University Press, 1922).

information about specific practices.[6] Imitative exercises involved two steps—Analysis and Genesis. Analysis was the stage in which students, under the guidance of the teacher, made a close study of the model to observe how its excellences followed the precepts of art. Genesis was the stage in which students attempted to produce something or to do something similar to the model that had been analyzed. Donald Lemen Clark has pointed out that Analysis took two forms: "(1) where a literary principle is announced and then illustrated by examples from an author or authors; (2) where the text of an author is given intact and accompanied by an explanation or commentary." [7] Genesis too might be said to have taken two forms: (1) where the schoolboy wrote something closely patterned on the author he had just been studying; (2) where the schoolboy was cut loose from his models and was asked to write something on his own. But when the schoolboy is asked to produce an original composition (like the themes we assign our students to write), he is moving out of the stage of imitation into the stage of *exercitatio* or practice. It is sometimes difficult to tell whether a particular exercise in the Tudor schools should be classified as part of the *genesis* stage of imitation or as part of the *practice* stage of original composition. The criterion for distinguishing imitation from practice should be the length of the tether with the model, but since the length of the tether is a relative matter, it will not always be possible to firmly categorize the exercise as imitation or practice.

A discussion of the *prelection* is a good way to summarize the analysis stage of imitation. *Prelection* is merely the Latinate term for the kind of close analysis of a text that teachers today conduct in the classroom, sometimes with the aid of invited or proferred comments from their students. The elaborate commentary, which sometimes proceeds sentence by sentence and occasionally focuses on units as small as the word, is designed to expose the strengths (and sometimes the weaknesses) in selection, structure, and style to be found in the composed text. Doubting that his students will detect these strengths and weaknesses from a mere exposure to the text, the teacher explicitly points out the excellences, explains how and why they are functioning, and relates them to the rhetorical principles his students have been studying in the abstract. What the prelection is comparable to is the Brooks-and-Warren method of explicating a poem that many of us learned in graduate school right after World War II.

[6] The best primary sources for information about imitative practices in Tudor grammar schools are John Brinsley, *Judus Literarius: or The Grammar Schoole*, ed. E. T. Campagnac (Liverpool: University of Liverpool Press, 1917); Charles Hoole, *A New Discovery of the Old Art of Teaching Schoole*, ed. E. T. Campagnac (Liverpool: University of Liverpool Press, 1913); Roger Ascham, *The Scholemaster*, ed. Edward Arber, English Reprints (Boston: D. C. Heath, 1898). The secondary work that I have relied on heavily for this paper is Donald L. Clark's *John Milton at St. Paul's School: A Study of Ancient Rhetoric in English Renaissance Education* (New York: Columbia University Press, 1948).

[7] *John Milton at St. Paul's School*, p. 158.

Some of those Renaissance prelections must have been brilliantly illuminating, but because those rhetorical analyses were delivered orally and extemporaneously, very few of these classroom performances have been preserved for inspection. Quintilian, however, has elaborately described the classroom procedure in his *Institutio Oratoria* (II,v,6–16), and we have an excellent example of the practice in Plato's *Phaedrus*, where Socrates indulges in an impromptu analysis of a speech by Lysias that has just been read to him from a manuscript.

The prelection was not intended to be a mere display of the teacher's virtuosity in reading a text. It was designed to prepare the student for some imitative exercise that he was subsequently to be assigned to perform. In the lower grades at least, the prelection was not an exhaustive *explication de texte;* instead, it often concentrated on a single rhetorical feature, such as the organization of the discourse or the use of figures of speech—a feature which the student was then expected to imitate in a written assignment. Teachers today who discuss only the ideas in a prose text and neglect to point out the strategies of form are not giving their students the kind of help with their writing problems that the prelection provided. And until teachers are given the kind of training in rhetorical reading that Mortimer Adler is talking about in his book *How to Read a Book,* they are not likely to be able to provide this kind of help for their students.

The three most common species of imitative exercises in the Renaissance schools were *memorizing, translating* and *paraphrasing.* Let me say something about each of these practices.

Roger Ascham in his *The Scholemaster* and John Brinsley in his *Ludus Literarius* both testify that memorizing textbook principles and select passages from esteemed authors was the prevailing method of learning in the Tudor grammar schools.[8] Memorization was one of the five canons of classical rhetoric, along with invention, arrangement, style, and delivery, but after the invention of printing in the fifteenth century, there was less attention paid in the classroom to the memorizing and the oral delivery of a composed discourse, mainly of course because messages could now be transmitted by written or printed copy. Although occasionally English schoolboys were required to memorize their themes and declamations for delivery before a classroom audience, most of the energy of memorizing was expended on the precepts and passages available to everyone in cheaply printed texts. A good deal of this effort of course was just rote memory, which the schoolboys spouted back at the teacher on command and often without really understanding what they were saying. But even at its most mechanical, memorizing paid some dividends to the schoolboys. Quintilian had long ago suggested what some of those dividends might be:

[8] *The Scholemaster*, ed. Arber, p. 88; *Ludus Literarius*, ed. Campagnac, pp. 175, 177.

> [The boys] will form an intimate acquaintance with the best writings, will carry their models with them and unconsciously reproduce the style of the speech which has been impressed upon their memory. They will have a plentiful and choice vocabulary and a command of artistic structure and a supply of figures which will not have to be hunted for, but will offer themselves spontaneously from the treasure-house, if I may so call it, in which they are stored. *(Institutio Oratoria,* II, vii, 3–4)

I call attention especially to the words *unconsciously* and *spontaneously* in the above quotation, because they suggest the chief benefit of saturating one's memory with select passages from admired authors. It is a commonplace that the book which has had the profoundest effect on the styles of English and American authors is the King James version of the Bible. Passages of that magnificent prose were so deeply ingrained in the memory of earlier generations of English and American readers that when they came to write they unconsciously and spontaneously reproduced much of the rhythm, the phraseology, and the structures of the Biblical passages. The practice of memorizing passages of poetry and prose seems to have disappeared from American classrooms at about the time that the elocution contest disappeared, and the only thing that young people memorize today is the lyrics of their favorite songs. But anyone who has had the experience while writing of having a phrase or a structure come back to him unbidden from the deep well of the subconscious might be willing to concede that the restoration of the practice of memorizing might be a good thing.

An imitative exercise that can serve as a substitute for memorizing and that can pay much the same dividends is the practice of copying verbatim select passages from accomplished writers. A variation of this practice is the daily stint of taking down a dictated passage, a discipline that Rollo Walter Brown, in his book *How the French Boy Learns to Write*, tells us was once widely practiced in French schools. And recently we learned from Chapter XI of his Autobiography that Malcolm X acquired his command of language by laboriously copying out the entire dictionary.

The second most common imitative exercise in the Tudor schools was the practice of double translation. Until well into the seventeenth century the English schoolboy had to be at least bilingual to survive in school. Latin was the language of most of his textbooks and the language in which he did most of his reading and writing. Many of the schoolboys also had a smattering of Greek, and a few of them, like John Milton at St. Paul's School, were even introduced to Hebrew. The schoolboy then was language-oriented to a degree that he has never been since. Accordingly, he was expected to be able to turn a Latin passage into idiomatic if not elegant English, and then perhaps to turn his English version back into a semblance of classical Latin.

Sometimes the translation went through three versions: from Greek to Latin to English. The themes he composed in English often had to be later rendered into Ciceronian Latin.

Since Latin and Greek are inflected languages, it may be difficult for us to imagine what benefit there could be in this practice of double translation for the schoolboy when he wrote in English, which is essentially a word-order language. Perhaps the chief benefit was that this incessant activity made the Tudor schoolboy extremely language-conscious. But I dare say that the English schoolboy also realized some of the benefits that Cicero and Quintilian confessed they had reaped from translating Greek into their native language. Cicero said that in rendering into Latin what he had read in Greek he "not only used the best words, and yet such as were of common occurrence, but also formed some words by imitation, which would be new to our countrymen, taking care, however, that they were appropriate."[9] Quintilian recognized something of the same value in this practice but also pointed out some others:

> The purpose of this form of exercise is obvious. For Greek authors are conspicuous for the variety of their matter, and there is much art in all their eloquence, while, when we translate them, we are at liberty to use the best words available, since all that we use are our very own. As regards figures, too, which are the chief ornament of oratory, it is necessary to think out a great number and variety for ourselves, since in this respect the Roman idiom differs largely from the Greek. (*Institutio Oratoria*, X, v, 2–3)

Since most of our students are functionally monolingual and since we rarely have available in any one class a group of students who are in command of another common modern language—except perhaps in certain Puerto Rican sections of large cities like Chicago and New York or in certain Mexican-American communities in the Southwest—we cannot make use in our classrooms of the imitative exercise of translation. But we can make use of the third kind of imitative exercise widely practiced in the English Renaissance schools—the practice of paraphrasing. The precedent for teaching paraphrase was established by Erasmus, when he recommended for the curriculum of St. Paul's School the practice of turning poetry into prose and of turning prose into poetry. Those Renaissance humanists who believed in the inviolable relationship between matter and form objected vehemently to this practice. Roger Ascham stated the reason for the objection in these words: ". . . because the author, either orator or poet, had chosen out before, the fittest words and aptest composition for the matter, and so he, in

[9] Cicero, *De Oratore*, I, xxxix, 155, trans. E. W. Sutton, Loeb Classical Library (Cambridge, Mass.: Harvard University Press, 1959).

seeking other, was driven to use the worse" (*The Scholemaster*, ed. Arber, p. 93). But the schoolmaster who persisted in the practice had the authority of Quintilian behind him. Quintilian defended the practice in these terms:

> For if there were only one way in which anything could be satisfactorily expressed, we should be justified in thinking the path to success had been sealed to us by our predecessors. But, as a matter of fact, the methods of expression still left us are innumerable, and many roads lead us to the same goal. Brevity and copiousness each have their own peculiar grace, the merits of metaphor are one thing and of literalness another, and, while direct expression is most effective in one case, in another the best result is gained by a use of figures. (*Institutio Oratoria,* X, v, 7–8)

Those who view style as a matter of choices made from the available lexical and syntactical resources of a language can easily salve their consciences about subjecting their students to the discipline of the paraphrase. And, indeed, of all the Renaissance imitative exercises, the paraphrase, in a variety of forms, is the one most often practiced in our schools today. Some teachers give their students a sentence and ask them to phrase the same idea in two or three different ways. Those teachers are probably not aware that Erasmus also set the precedent for that practice, when in his *De copia verborum ac rerum* he turned the simple sentence "Your letter pleased me greatly" into 150 different versions—in some instances by substituting different words, in other instances by altering the word-order, and in still other instances by rendering the literal statement into figurative language. Students who have some acquaintance with transformational grammar are especially amenable to this kind of exercise. Another variation on paraphrase is what is now called "pattern practice." The teacher presents a sentence to the students, analyzes the structure of the sentence with them, and then asks them to write a sentence of their own on the pattern of the model. A recently published book called *Copy and Compose* (Englewood Cliffs, N. J.: Prentice-Hall, 1969) by Winston Weathers and Otis Winchester exposes students to a series of progressively more sophisticated sentence patterns. I have heard of some teachers who engage their students in a periphrastic exercise that Benjamin Franklin confessed he had practiced as a young man and that Hugh Blair recommended to the students in his rhetoric class at the University of Edinburg in the eighteenth century. The student takes a passage of prose that he especially admires, reads it over and over again in order to absorb the sense and structure of it, then puts the passage aside and tries to render the thought of the passage in his own words. Précis-writing is another form of paraphrase, but I have not seen much evidence lately that his kind of reductive writing is much practiced now in the schools. Another periphrastic exercise that some of us may have inflicted on our students is the assignment to render the "thought" of a poem into prose, but we may have been persuaded to abandon that practice by Cleanth Brook's cry about the "heresy of paraphrase."

I could go on to talk about the Renaissance practice of keeping commonplace books and of exercising students in the writing of the graded series of fourteen elementary theme-forms set forth in Aphthonius's widely used textbook *Progymnasmata.* But the commonplace book was less an aid for the learning of form than a resource for the finding of subject-matter, and the formulary exercises in Aphthonius's textbook very soon moved the student from close observance of theme-forms into the writing of original themes, and thus moved him out of the realm of Imitation into the realm of Practice. But I hope I have said enough to give you some idea of the rationale of imitation as a learning device and of specific imitative exercises.

Although there is no question that students still learn their writing skill, as well as other skills, largely through imitation, I seriously doubt that formal exercises in imitation will make much of a comeback in our schools during the coming decade. For one thing, the present mood of education theorists is against such structured, fettered training. The emphasis now is on creativity, self-expression, individuality. Then too there is the suspicion among us that imitation stultifies and inhibits the writer rather than empowers and liberates him. The nineteenth-century Samuel Butler expressed that attitude when he said, "I never knew a writer yet who took the smallest pain with his style and was at the same time readable. . . . I cannot conceive how any man can take thought for his style without loss to himself and his readers." [10]

But the number of creative and expository writers who would testify to the value of imitation to them during their apprenticeship years is legion. We can let Robert Louis Stevenson, the classic example of the "sedulous ape," speak for this group of grateful writers:

> But enough has been said to show by what arts of impersonation, and in what purely ventriloquial efforts, I first saw my words on paper. That, like it or not, is the way to learn to write; whether I have profited or not, that is the way. It was so Keats learned, and there was never a finer temperament for literature than Keats's; it was so, if we could trace it out, that all men have learned; and that is why a revival of letters is always accompanied or heralded by a cast back to earlier and fresher models.[11]

More recently, in an article in the *Quarterly Journal of Speech*, W. Ross Winterowd went right to the heart of the value of imitative exercises:

[10] Samuel Butler, *Notebooks*, ed. Geoffrey Keynes and Brian Hill (London: Jonathan Cape, 1951), pp. 290–1.

[11] "A College Magazine," *The Works of Robert Louis Stevenson* (New York: Charles Scribner's Sons, 1902), XIII, pp. 213–214.

> In this sense, stylistic exercises enable. That is, "mere" exercises in style allow the student to internalize structures that make his own grammar a more flexible instrument for combining and hence enable the student to take experience apart and put it together again in new ways, which is, after all, the generative function of language. . . . Such imitation is not slavish, for it brings about a mix that equals individuality: the resources of the language per se and the individual sensibility that will use them.[12]

The phrase "to internalize structures" hits the nail right on the old bong. For it is that internalization of structures that unlocks our powers and sets us free to be creative, original, and ultimately effective. *Imitate that you may be different.*

[12] "Style: A Matter of Manner," *QJS*, 56 (1970), pp. 164, 167.

"Topics" and Levels in the Composing Process

W. ROSS WINTEROWD

One of the most interesting (and certainly one of the most neglected) aspects of rhetoric is the notion of topics or places of invention. Throughout the more recent history of rhetoric, the importance of topics for invention or creativity has been either minimized or overlooked, and the prevailing attitude was never more unequivocally stated than by Bernard Lamy, whose *De l'Art de Parler* appeared in English translation in 1676:

> Those who reject these Topicks, do not deny their Fecundity; they grant that they supply us with infinite numbers of things; but they alledg that that Fecundity is inconvenient; That the things are trivial, and by consequent the Art of *Topicks* furnishes nothing that is fit for us to say. If an Orator (say they) understands the subject of which he treats; if he be full of incontestable Maxims that may inable him to resolve all Difficulties arising upon that subject; If it be a question in Divinity, and he be well read in the Fathers, Councils, Scriptures, &c. He will quickly perceive whether the question propos'd be Orthodox, or otherwise. It is not necessary that he runs to his Topicks, or passes from one common place to another, which are unable to supply him with necessary knowledg for decision of his Question. If on the other side an Orator be ignorant, and understands not the bottom of what he Treats, he can speak but superficially, he cannot come to the point; and after he has talk'd and argued a long time, his adversary will have reason to admonish him to leave his tedious talk that signifies nothing; to interrupt him in this manner, Speak to the purpose; oppose Reason against my Reason, and coming to the Point, do what you can to subvert the Foundations upon which I sustain my self.[1]

Lamy might well have been paraphrasing remarks that typify discussions of rhetoric in both English and speech departments of modern universities.

College English, vol. 34, No. 5 (February 1973), pp. 701–709.

[1] Quoted in Wilbur Samuel Howell, *Eighteenth-Century British Logic and Rhetoric* (Princeton University Press, 1971), p. 92.

But topics need to be reconsidered from both the theoretical and the pedagogical points of view. The purpose of this discussion will be (a) to point out that all topics fall into one of four categories, according to the nature of their operation, and (b) to attempt to revitalize the concept of topics in rhetorical theory and in pedagogy. The first purpose of the discussion will clarify the nature of all topics, and among the expert witnesses who would testify concerning the desirability of the second purpose is Richard McKeon:

> We need a new art of invention and discovery in which places are used as means by which to light up modes and meanings of works of art and natural occurrences and to open up aspects and connections in existence and possibility. The data and qualifications of existence are made by attention and interest; and discoveries made in a book or a work of art should provide places by which to perceive creatively what might otherwise not be experienced in the existent world we constitute. It is a long time since topics have been used as an art of invention in rhetoric. . . . A reconstituted verbal art of invention, adapted to our circumstances and arts, might be used to shadow forth the methods and principles of an architectonic productive art generalized from invention in language to discovery in existence.[2]

With at least one school of modern linguistics, I assume that the composing process involves putting meanings into structures or saturating structures with meanings, though, to be sure, the mechanisms whereby this process takes place are not known, and, in fact, the assumption that something of the kind takes place is really just an explanatory metaphor adopted to get theorists over the barricades of some extremely difficult questions. What I am saying—though I do not intend to argue the point—is that in some sense, there is both form and meaning, even though separating the two is next to impossible if one holds as a criterion the complete satisfaction of every opinion concerning what is form and what is content.[3]

Central to the composing process is what rhetoric traditionally has called "invention," the means whereby the writer discovers subject matter. And the concept of "topics" or "commonplaces" was the very heart of invention in the classical theory of Aristotle. It will be recalled that topics are,

---

[2] "The Uses of Rhetoric in a Technological Age," *The Prospect of Rhetoric*, ed. Lloyd F. Bitzer and Edwin Black (Englewood Cliffs, N.J.: Prentice-Hall, 1971), p. 55.

[3] Roland Barthes goes so far as to say, ". . . we can no longer see a text as a binary structure of Content and Form; the text is not double but multiple; within it there are only forms, or more exactly, the text in its entirety is only a multiplicity of forms without content. We can say metaphorically that the literary text is a stereography: neither melody, nor harmony (or at least not unrelieved harmony), it is resolutely contrapuntal; it mixes voices in a volume, not in a line, not even a double line." "Style and Image," *Literary Style: A Symposium*, ed. Seymour Chatman (London and New York: Oxford University Press, 1971), p. 6.

in effect, probes or a series of questions that one might ask about a subject in order to discover things to say about that subject. They are general and apply to all subject matter; they are not, as it were, subject-specific. So that Aristotle's topics can generate arguments for, say, negotiating any peace, not just peace in Viet Nam.

For example, the first of the twenty-eight demonstrative topics that Aristotle lists is the argument from opposites:

> If, now, it is not fair to grow enraged when evil doers injure us unwittingly, then neither do we owe a grain of thanks to him who does us good when forced to do it.

Another of the topics is *a fortiori* (from degrees of more and less):

> If it behooves each citizen among you to care for the reputation of your city, it behooves you all as a city to care for the glory of Greece.[4]

There is no better comment on the topics than Kenneth Burke's: "The so-called 'commonplaces' or 'topics' in Aristotle's *Art of Rhetoric* . . . are a quick survey of opinion. . . ."[5] Burke goes on to say that in the topics, Aristotle "catalogues" the available means of persuasion, and it will be the kinds of cataloguing that interest us first, and then the sorts of things that are catalogued. In fact, it will become apparent that, classed according to system of cataloguing and things catalogued, there are only four possible kinds of topics.

First, simply but significantly, it is apparent that topics can be either *finite or non-finite lists.*

Perhaps the most common sort of topics that one encounters (and in many ways the least interesting, though useful) are what are generally called "methods of paragraph development." These are so commonly encountered that I will not here go into detail concerning them, but typically such a list would contain items like the following: data, enumeration, analogy, anecdote, cause and effect, comparison and contrast, definition, description, metaphor, restatement, and so on.[6] Now it is perfectly obvious that this list could be extended almost indefinitely, for it might contain all of the sorts of things that can go into paragraphs, which ultimately implies classification in some way of all the sorts of things in the universe. That is, methods of paragraph development as topics are characteristically non-finite lists. Aristotle's topics are also just as obviously a non-finite list.

[4] *The Rhetoric of Aristotle*, trans. Lane Cooper (New York: Appleton-Century-Crofts, 1960). The twenty-eight demonstrative topics are on pp. 159–72.

[5] *A Rhetoric of Motives, A Grammar of Motives and A Rhetoric of Motives* (New York: World Publishing Company, 1962), p. 580.

[6] In fact, this is the list in *Structure, Language, and Style*, a rhetoric handbook that I wrote three or four years ago.

But we can conceive of, find in great abundance, and invent for ourselves topics which constitute finite lists. Burke's Pentad is nothing more than a finite set of topics, as Burke himself avows:

> What is involved, when we say what people are doing and why they are doing it? An answer to that question is the subject of this book. The book is concerned with the basic forms of thought which, in accordance with the nature of the world as all men necessarily experience it, are exemplified in the attributing of motives. . . . any complete statement about motives will offer *some kind of* answers to these five questions: what was done (act), where or when it was done (scene), who did it (agent), how he did it (agency), and why (purpose).[7]

(The Pentad is particularly useful, of course, in generating subject matter concerning any piece of discourse, either written or spoken, either literary or nonliterary. But my purpose at the moment is not to demonstrate the usefulness—or lack thereof—of any set of topics.)

It follows from the nature of a finite list of topics that it must not allow for any questions that are not "covered" by the items in the set. That is, if one can ask questions, *within the terms set down for the Pentad,* which cannot be classed under one of the items of the Pentad, then the Pentad is *faulty* as a finite set of topics. (I personally do not feel that the Pentad is faulty, but that question is beside the point of this discussion.)

A faulty set of topics, used here as an example, will clarify the problem that we are getting at.

A five-item set emerged from the National Developmental Project on Rhetoric.[8] In a severely abbreviated (but not, I think, unfair) form, this is the set:

1. The social reality of the present moment may be viewed in terms of the resources for innovation or the defense of tradition. . . . what are the social conditions and resources available to the inventing person?
2. A second set of questions: What are the materials and perspectives upon facts out of which invention may be fashioned? What technologies may be harnessed in making a car, what facts or interpretations of facts may be spoken. . . ?
3. What about the *persons* who will participate in the invention—and the drives which make them vital or retarding factors in the process. . . ?
4. What is the *deep structure* of the invention. . . ?

---

[7] *A Grammar of Motives*, p. xvii.

[8] *The Prospect of Rhetoric*, pp. 228–236.

5. Finally, what *presentational form* is adopted for the thing invented. . . ?

For this provocative and useful set of topics, the authors[9] make the following unfortunate claim: "These five aspects may be considered as a generative frame, *an ordering of all the relevant aspects of any invented, innovative, or novel creation.* As such they provide a place of places, a frame of frames, an account of the origin or creation of all things novel, including rhetorical artifacts." [10] One question generated by another set of topics that we will be dealing with shortly[11] demonstrates the faultiness of the above as a finite set. "How is the subject under consideration changing?" This question does not fit any of the topics in the set (and one can find other questions that do not fit); therefore, the set is faulty.

If rhetorical theory is to have the integrity that only precision and logical consistency can bring to it, then non-finite sets of topics must not masquerade as finite sets. We have here something of the dilemma faced by grammarians who worked under the assumption that "A noun is the name of a person, place or thing" or that "A sentence is the expression of a complete idea." These definitions were theoretically destructive and had only marginal value—if any—in pedagogy, since they precipitated the whole logomachy of what a "thing" or a "complete idea" is.

Sets of topics can be, then, either finite or non-finite lists. They can also be *content-oriented* or *form-oriented.*

For one example of a set of form-oriented topics, I refer to my own "The Grammar of Coherence," [12] a set that, according to my claim, will generate structures at the paragraph level and beyond. (In brief, my argument is that six and only six relationships prevail in coherent discourse beyond the sentence, or, more precisely, beyond the transformational unit. If this is indeed the case, as I believe it is, then these relationships will serve as topics that will "automatically" generate paragraphs or, for that matter, essays.)

A further example: in an article that has received far too little attention, Alton L. Becker[13] developed a schema to analyze and describe the structure of paragraphs. What has not been generally recognized is that this schema can be used as a finite set of form-oriented topics. It happens that the schema is brief enough to serve as an example in the present context.

Becker claims that empirical investigation reveals that expository paragraphs invariably have the elements

---

[9] Robert L. Scott, James R. Andrews, Howard H. Martin, J. Richard McNally, William F. Nelson, Michael M. Osborn, Arthur L. Smith, Harold Zyskind.

[10] *The Prospect of Rhetoric*, pp. 232–233. Italics mine.

[11] That developed by Young, Becker, and Pike.

[12] *College English*, 31 (May 1970), p. 828–835.

[13] "A Tagmemic Approach to Paragraph Analysis," *The Sentence and the Paragraph* (Champaign, Ill.: National Council of Teachers of English, 1966), p. 33.

Topic
Restriction
Illustration

Problem
Solution

Question
Answer

in various combinations and permutations, the details of which I will ignore. (That is, TRIPSQA will describe the form of any expository paragraph.) A paragraph that Becker analyzes will serve as an example of what he is getting at.

> (P) How obsolete is Hearn's judgment? (S_1) (T) On the surface the five gentlemen of Japan do not themselves seem to be throttled by this rigid society of their ancestors. (R) Their world is in fact far looser in its demands upon them than it once was. (I) Industrialization and the influence of the West have progressively softened the texture of the web. Defeat in war badly strained it. A military occupation, committed to producing a democratic Japan, pulled and tore at it. (S_2) (T) But it has not disappeared. (R) It is still the invisible adhesive that seals that nationhood of the Japanese. (I) Shimizu, Sanada, Yamazaki, Kisel, and Hirohito were all born within its bonds. Despite their individual work, surroundings and opinions, they have lived most of their lives as cogs geared into a group society. . . .[14]

It is easy to see how TRIQAPS—and note that I have acronymized the system—can serve as a set of form-oriented topics.

Write a topic sentence.
As one ages, one learns that all vices are pleasant.

Restrict it.
But some vices are unhealthy.

Illustrate.
Smoking causes cancer.
Drinking causes cirrhosis.
Even the caffeine in coffee has been found to increase the process of aging.

Admittedly, depending on one's vantage point, TRIQAPS can be viewed as either a form-oriented or a content-oriented set of topics. Perhaps

[14] From Frank Gibney, *Five Gentlemen of Japan*, quoted in Becker.

the best known example of a set of *purely* form-oriented topics is the set that constitutes what Francis Christensen called "free modifiers." Christensen did not view his modifiers as topics, but, in effect, they are precisely that, for they can be used to generate sentences. That is, to a sentence base, one can add a variety of structures (noun clusters, verb clusters, absolutes, and so on). In deciding to add a structure, one must search for subject matter to "fill" that structure. I will illustrate the process.

Write a base.
The little girl skated.

Add an absolute.
Her pigtails flying, the little girl skated.

Add a verb cluster.
Her pigtails flying, the little girl skated, effortlessly gliding down the sidewalk.

Add a relative clause.
Her pigtails flying, the little girl, who every Saturday morning came to my house for popcorn, skated, effortlessly gliding down the sidewalk.

And so on. Note that the instructions specify the addition of structures, not of content. Adding a structure must generate content for the structure.

In my opinion, the most interesting and productive set of content-oriented topics is that developed by Richard E. Young, Alton L. Becker, and Kenneth L. Pike.[15] To summarize it here would distort its complexity, but what Young, Becker, and Pike claim is (a) that to know anything, we must know how it differs from everything else, how much it can change and still be itself, and how it fits into hierarchies of larger systems; and (b) that we can view anything from three perspectives, that of particle, that of wave, and that of field. The juxtaposition of these two concepts creates a nine-item finite set of content-oriented topics that I personally find to be most exciting.

Now then, we can recapitulate and systematize.

Content-oriented non-finite sets of topics
(Aristotle's topics; methods of paragraph development, etc.)

Content-oriented finite sets of topics
(Young, Becker, and Pike's topics; from one point of view, TRIQAPS; Burke's Pentad; the parts of the classical oration, etc.)

Form-oriented finite sets of topics
(from one point of view, TRIQAPS; the set outlined in "The Grammar of Coherence"; Christensen's free modifiers, etc.)

[15] *Rhetoric: Discovery and Change* (New York: Harcourt, Brace & World, 1970).

Regarding the fourth category, *form-oriented non-finite sets of topics,* a theoretical problem of considerable dimensions arises. It is this: any set of topics that is non-finite and form-oriented must be faulty (according to the definition of "faulty" developed in this essay), for it is impossible that formal relationships regarding any level of discourse can be infinite in number. The same argument that demonstrates the finite nature of a grammar can be applied to demonstrate the finite nature of relationships beyond those handled by the grammar of a language. The validity of this argument seems self-evident. Therefore, a form-oriented set of topics that is non-finite must be merely incomplete and hence faulty. Nonetheless, there are such lists. One example is lists of figures of grammar—from Peacham to Lanham[16]—for lists of figures of grammar are sets of topics; another example is methods of organization discussed in rhetorics.

The conceptual framework for theories of topics is, then, clearcut, but what of topics in pedagogy?

One way of conceptualizing the process of composition is to assume that it involves a three-level hierarchy.

The first level is that of the proposition. Following the model developed by Charles Fillmore, I would argue that a "core" or "kernel" sentence is made up of a modality plus a proposition.[17] The modality contains such elements as auxiliary, yes/no question, negation, and so on. The proposition is a predicate and a variety of "roles" or cases that relate to it and to one another. Thus, schematically:

Modality	*Proposition*
Present tense	Predicate (kiss): Agent (George), Patient (Mary)

George kisses Mary.
Mary is kissed by George.

The teacher cannot, it seems to me, intervene at this level. If the student, of whatever age, is incapable of generating these core sentences, there is obviously some dysfunction that is beyond the reach of mere pedagogy.

The next level is that of inter-propositional connections, which might be called the level of *syntax.*

George, who is a neurotic, chews gum.
George, a neurotic, chews gum.
A neurotic, George chews gum. (ambiguous?)

In his work, Francis Christensen demonstrates that the teacher can intervene at this level in the composing process, indeed with dramatic results. In *Transformational Sentence-Combining,*[18] John Mellon also demonstrates that the

[16] *A Handlist of Rhetorical Terms* (Berkeley and Los Angeles: University of California Press, 1968).
[17] "The Case for Case," *Universals in Linguistic Theory*, ed. Emmon Bach and Robert Harms (New York: Holt, Rinehart and Winston, 1968), pp. 1–88.
[18] (Champaign, Ill.: National Council of Teachers of English, 1969).

teacher can help the student at the level of syntax. Since one of the great intellectual powers that one can attain is the ability to combine predications, the work of Christensen and Mellon is not to be ignored or to be written off lightly.

But in this discussion of topics, we are most concerned with the third level in the composing process, which I shall call the level of the *transition* since it has to do with units such as paragraphs and essays. It is at this level that the concept of topics becomes tremendously important.

To refer back to Lamy, who was quoted at the beginning of this discussion: surely he—and virtually everyone else who in the last three hundred years has written about topics—must have missed a significant point concerning the theory of topics. The purpose of topics is not to supply verbiage in lieu of real subject matter, but to generate ideas concerning the subject. In this sense, topics are devices for problem-solving; they are heuristics. Young, Becker, and Pike explain heuristics and, in the process, give an admirable explanation of how topics function:

> A heuristic procedure . . . provides a series of questions or operations that guides inquiry and increases the chances of discovering a workable solution. More specifically, it serves three functions:
>
> 1. It aids the investigator in retrieving relevant information that he has stored in his mind. (When we have a problem, we generally know more that is relevant to it than we think we do, but we often have difficulty in retrieving the relevant information and bringing it to bear on the problem.)
> 2. It draws attention to important information that the investigator does not possess but can acquire by direct observation, reading, experimentation, and so on.
> 3. It prepares the investigator's mind for the intuition of an ordering principle or hypothesis.[19]

In this sense, everyone uses "topics" more or less systematically all the time; most of us unconsciously have developed a variety of sets of topics that we apply quite automatically in all kinds of circumstances. (It occurs to me that I have developed a set of topics for planning fishing trips, and my adherence to the procedure that they imply never varies. Of course, in the last three years my success at fishing has been minimal!)

The concept of topics, then, is not trivial, though, to be sure, there are trivial or faulty sets of topics. But what about topics in the classroom as a pedagogical device?

The future of the profession holds a great deal of promise; we are well into the era of "technical breakthrough"; we are at the point where we have the "software" and the "hardware" to do a much more effective job

[19] *Rhetoric: Discovery and Change*, p. 120.

than we have in the past. As briefly as possible, I would like to explain why it is conceivable that instruction in writing can now be more effective than it ever was in the past.

First—an important point that is connected with my thesis, but that would take us far afield if we pursued it—we are at the point where we can say, with the eloquence and passion of James Sledd, "Leave your language alone!" We are ready to allow youngsters to function in their own dialects, and hence we will not wreak the spiritual devastation that a "purist" attitude inevitably brings about.

At the level of syntax, we are beginning to get theories and materials—such as those of Francis Christensen and John Mellon—that enable the teacher to be of significant help in the student's quest for the ability to put idea within idea within idea. . . . That is, for the first time, we now have the means actually to help students systematically attain syntactic fluency, and surely that fluency is one of the significant intellectual accomplishments.

Finally, it is time to revitalize the concept of topics. The reasons for this are clear enough to anyone who has ever taught writing at any level. As Charlie Brown learned when his teacher said, "Write a five-hundred word essay on what you did during your summer vacation," one of the most intransigent problems for inexperienced (and experienced!) writers is invention, and what I am suggesting is that topics as they have developed and as they are developing provide the best devices of invention.

This is not to say that students are robots, who automatically turn to this or that set of topics before they write, but that they are alert and aware, and that they know what sort of help is available to them when they must solve the problem implied by the question "What can I say about this subject?" I am also claiming that some work with sets of topics will introduce students to techniques that they can use to develop their own problem-solving devices, their own heuristics.

I must plead guilty to the charge that I sound unhumanistic, for I *am* profoundly unhumanistic in the normal English department sense of that word, but I do avow that I am not suggesting students should be deprived of their marvelous, chaotic freedom, for I love both chaos and freedom. But what I am suggesting is that there are more efficient "programs" for enabling students to gain the *freedom* to express themselves than the old by-guess-and-by-golly method that is so tremendously humanistic. The object is not syntax for its own sake or random ideas to fill empty egg crates; rather, the quest of the English teacher should be for every means whereby the student can most efficiently gain the liberation that self-expression gives him.

Now my final comment about the theory of topics can be made. Composition is obviously a total process, a whole fabric, that can be "taken apart" only schematically and for theoretical purposes, so that when I claim there are three levels in the process of composition, I do not mean to imply that in practice the writer works first on one level and then on the other. (In fact, I know just as little about the act of composition as anyone else.) And viewing the compositional process from the standpoint of topics allows us to conceptualize it in a more unified way than the *points d'appui* taken by most theories. What I mean is this: if one views theories of form and theories of style merely as sets of topics—which in most instances they are—then the whole process of composition is unified under the auspices of invention, generally conceived to be the least mechanical and most "creative" of the departments of rhetoric.

And this viewpoint is a healthy corrective to the tendency that creeps into textbooks and classrooms: namely, to "do" a "unit" on the sentence and then a unit on the paragraph, and so on. Thus, the theory developed in this discussion could, ultimately, lead to a change in classroom practice, and it seems to me that change is badly needed.

Topics should not shackle the mind. They should liberate.

The Siamese Twins: Inventio and Dispositio

MARK L. KNAPP and JAMES C. McCROSKEY

Traditionally rhetorical literature has reflected a distinct separation of inventio and dispositio. One of the earliest statements supporting this view is found in Book I of *De Inventione.* Cicero tells us that

> . . . when the point for decision and the arguments which must be devised for the purpose of reaching a decision have been diligently discovered by the rules of art, and studied with careful thought, then, and not until then, the other parts of the oration are to be arranged in proper order.

This assumption, which is also frequently made today, suggests that the inventive process should continue until the speaker amasses a large number of arguments, and then dispositio should ensue.

This separation, however, does not seem to be as distinct as one might be led to believe. In audience-centered rhetoric there is substantial interaction of inventional and dispositional thought processes. It is our purpose to specify this interaction and to suggest that for persuasive communication a complete dichotomization of inventio and dispositio is theoretically unsound and pedagogically impractical.

First, let us review some of the mental activities usually considered to be components of inventio and dispositio. Then we will be able to specify more clearly the interrelationships involved.

Our discussion will utilize terminology based on the model of argument developed by the British logician, Stephen Toulmin. Three of these terms need to be explained briefly: (1) data—informational statements believed by an audience and employed by a speaker to secure belief in another statement; (2) claim—an explicit conclusion that a speaker wants an audience to accept; and (3) warrant—an inferential statement which links the data to the claim.

Today's Speech, vol. 14 (Spring 1966), pp. 17–18, 44. Reprinted by permission of the Speech Association of the Eastern States.

Inventio and Dispositio

A speaker's first concern in inventio is to determine what reaction he wants to evoke from his audience. In short, what claim does he desire them to accept? All inventio must be based upon his answer to that question. He must discover data and warrants that will enable him to invent arguments that will secure audience acceptance of his central idea. In essence, his first concern is to determine his central argument. This is the argument that culminates in the claim which represents his specific purpose for speaking. In most cases the speaker will find it necessary to develop a series of interrelated arguments in order to gain acceptance of this ultimate claim. These will develop as branches from the basic argument and the need to invent them will become apparent through audience analysis and hypothesizing audience reaction to arguments or portions of arguments. It must be stressed that all inventio must be based on continuing analysis of the audience. Each argument and each datum, warrant, and claim should be checked against an hypothesized reaction to that argument or portion of an argument by the specific audience for whom it is being invented. The importance of this point will be considered later, but now let us take an example to further clarify what we mean:

The speaker is a superintendent of schools. His audience is the local school board. His purpose, his ultimate claim, is that the board should purchase television equipment for the classrooms in the local high school. His invention process must begin from here. He must ask, "What data and warrants can be used to establish this claim?" He could possibly base his argument on his own ethos. Such an argument might go something like this: "I say that TV equipment should be purchased for the local high school (data), and since I am a credible source (warrant) therefore, we should purchase the equipment (claim)." He must then analyze his audience to determine whether they would be likely to accept such a claim based exclusively on his ethos. If he hypothesizes that they would not, he must strive to invent another argument. He may conclude that the audience is primarily motivated by two factors—how education in the school can be upgraded and how costs can be kept down. If he determines this, he will have found two possible warrants of a motivational nature which can be used. His basic arguments then might be something like this: "TV will improve education (data) and since we are motivated by our desire to improve education (warrant) we should buy the TV (claim)," and "TV will cut costs (data) and since we are motivated by our desire to cut costs (warrant) we should buy the TV (claim)."

From here we can see how the rest of the inventio process would proceed. The speaker would look at the data in the above arguments as claims and proceed to invent arguments to establish them. In each case, every part of the argument is selected or rejected on the basis of an hypothesized audience response.

Dispositio. The mental operations involved in dispositio are not as easily described in isolation. However, reasoning from the desired results of dispositio, it seems that these ends can be met through three Ciceronian operations: (1) *selecting*—the choosing of the materials to be included in the speech; (2) *arranging*—the strategic maneuvering of arguments to produce the desired effect; and (3) *apportioning*—the weighing of the relative importance of materials to determine the amount of stress they should receive in the speech.

Interrelation of the Two

With the above mental operations of inventio and dispositio in mind, let us examine that part of dispositional thinking which is closely interwoven with inventio.

Selecting. One can readily see that this dispositional process is also a vital part of inventio. In fact, much of inventio is simply a matter of selection, based on audience analysis. Each datum and each warrant is selected on the basis of an hypothesized audience reaction to it and further data and warrants are selected as validation and/or support for those selected previously. In short, when inventio is complete, few problems of selection remain to be considered. Only if we treat inventio as being divorced from audience considerations can it be otherwise. If inventio is the creation of arguments in a vacuum, then selection can follow it. However, if inventio is based on the audience, selection is an integral part of the process.

Arranging. The mental process of arranging is also partially completed during inventio. The main factor determining the strategic importance of an argument is where the argument leads. If an argument is invented to validate data, then it must be presented in the speech in such a manner as to lead to that end. This rhetorical process is similar to that of an engineer building a bridge over a river. The engineer must know the nature of both banks and then plan a bridge which will lead from one to the other. Similarly, the speaker must know what his audience's present position is on the issue to be considered and what he wants it to be. Then he builds a speech that will lead to that end. The wisdom of an engineer would be doubtful indeed if he were to build six spans and ninety-six supports for a bridge and then try to figure out how to arrange them for functional use. Each span of a bridge is planned and built to fit in a certain place so as to connect properly with the spans on either end of it, as are the supports for the structure. The arguments of a speech need to be planned and built in the same way.

Apportioning. To understand how this dispositional process interrelates with inventio we must remember that inventio is predicated on the *need* for argument to gain acceptance of claims. The speaker must hypothesize the probable audience response to an idea to determine how far to go in the invention of argument leading to that idea. This is actually an apportioning decision. He is deciding whether, with this particular audience, he will need one, two or seven arguments to gain acceptance of the idea; or whether he will need one, two or twenty pieces of data in a given argument. If the speaker wishes to leave all apportioning until the completion of inventio, he may never determine that he is ready to conclude inventio—at best he will have no accurate guide upon which to base a decision to terminate at a given point. He will probably find he has invented either too many or too few arguments or materials when he decides to apportion.

Thus the lines seem to be far from sharply drawn between how one thinks during inventio and how one thinks during dispositio. Rather than being two separate processes, inventio and dispositio are complementary parts of the same process—the process of analyzing the audience and developing a speech to evoke a predetermined reaction from that audience. If one chooses to consider inventio and dispositio as two completely separate and distinct rhetorical functions, he chooses to consider rhetoric apart from audience.

Although, as we have noted above, we cannot completely dichotomize these functions, we can make some distinctions. Barrett Wendell, a 19th Century professor of English at Harvard, made a distinction between "preview" and "review" dispositional thought processes. Thus far, we have been discussing primarily the "preview" operations—those inextricably bound to inventio.

Although one is still concerned with selecting, arranging and apportioning as he "reviews" the products of his original or inventional thoughts, we must note that the mind is now functioning with these processes at a different level. The reviewing process provides a more definitive focus for dispositional thought. There are obvious differences in what one has to select, apportion and arrange. For instance, a question of arrangement might now take this form: "Should the claim be stated before the data are presented or after?" A question of selection might now be: "Since this speech is too long for the time allowed, which evidence can I omit?" The mind is now manipulating information already derived from similar processes at an inventional level.

The most important thing to remember is that dispositional thought occurs at two points in the development of audience-centered rhetoric. It may take place during inventio as a "preview" process and again as a distinguishably separate process in the "review" stage. While dispositio has a function outside inventio, if the discourse is to be audience-centered, the function of dispositio within inventio must not be overlooked.

Teaching the Interrelation

The fact that dispositio cannot be divorced from inventio has pedagogical as well as theoretical implications. For instance, one of the tasks of the speech pedagogue is to evaluate the dispositional aspects of a speech. Although the point is conspicuously simple, it seems worthwhile to point out that what often appears to be a poor job of organization may actually be a manifestation of an insufficient grasp of inventional processes. A failure to correctly identify the audience's role in relation to a particular type of speech; the perfunctory use of a Topic System; a nonspecific purpose; all these inventional operations may be manifested as poor organization. Thus, in some cases, the critical comment "poor organization" ignores the real problem.

Another facet of criticizing dispositio in student speeches is concerned with the thought processes involved. If we are to assume that dispositio includes selecting, arranging, and apportioning, is it not likely that a student may be deficient in one or perhaps two of these while performing the other(s) satisfactorily? He may select the proper arguments and apportion them correctly, but make a gross error in arrangement. Or, as happens more frequently, he may select the proper arguments and arrange them correctly, but over stress the problem to the detriment of the solution. In such cases, the "poor organization" comment does not accurately specify the student's problem. The instructor must determine the specific thought process that is faulty and bring it to the student's attention.

It seems tenable that the primary pedagogical focus should be on the "preview" aspects of dispositio. It is neither practical nor desirable to de-emphasize the dispositional processes of selecting, arranging and apportioning in audience-centered inventio. One might suggest that telling students to gather their ideas and materials and then organize their speeches retards their rhetorical growth. At the very least, the instructor must be cognizant of the fact that treating dispositio as a purely "review" process fosters material-centered rather than audience-centered rhetoric. Whether we consider our rhetoric to be "Aristotelian," "Ciceronian," or "Modern," there are few among us who would prefer material-centered rhetoric to that which is audience-centered.

Teaching Style: A Possible Anatomy

WINSTON WEATHERS

A general approach to the teaching of style can embrace any number of pedagogical tasks and obligations. There are three tasks, however, that seem obligatory: (1) making the teaching of style significant and relevant for our students, (2) revealing style as a measurable and viable subject matter, and (3) making style believable and real as a result of our own stylistic practices. These are all *sine qua non,* and to neglect them, one or all, is to do our discipline a disservice. They are not the only tasks involved in teaching style, of course, but they are the underlying concerns in all our particular classroom procedures. A discussion of these three tasks—the questing for relevance, viability, and credibility—may possibly serve as a kind of mapping of our pedagogical territory.

First, making style significant for our students. To teach style well, to reach the final goals we have in mind for the written page, we must confront our students not only with its justification. F. L. Lucas, the Cambridge professor, said that after forty years of trying, he had come to the conclusion that it was impossible to teach students to write well. "To write well," Professor Lucas said, "is a gift inborn; those who have it teach themselves; one can only try to help and hasten the process." But surely one of the best ways to "hasten the process" is to make it seem important. It is difficult to imagine any successful technical approach being made in teaching style if students are not aware of the great values involved. Surely many a student needs, at least in the context of freshman English, relevance pointed out to him, for otherwise he may think of style as a kind of aesthetic luxury, if not beyond his grasp at least beyond his interests.

I fear, though, that we often neglect to explain the significance of the discipline. In teaching *literature* we seem much more inclined to indicate relevance; in teaching *language,* once we have made the pitch about better communication we have a tendency, don't we, to drop the task of relevance altogether.

College Composition and Communication, vol. 21 (May 1970), pp. 144–149.

I think we should confirm for our students that style has something to do with better communication, adding as it does a certain technicolor to otherwise black-and-white language. But going beyond this "better communication" approach, we should also say that style is the proof of a human being's individuality; that style is a writer's revelation of himself; that through style, attitudes and values are communicated; that indeed our manner is a part of our message. We can remind students of Aristotle's observation, "character is the making of choices," and point out that since style, by its very nature, is the art of selection, how we choose says something about who we are.

In addition, we can tell students that style is a gesture of personal freedom against inflexible states of mind; that in a very real way—because it is the art of choice and option—style has something to do with freedom; that as systems—rhetorical or political—become rigid and dictatorial, style is reduced, unable as it is to exist in totalitarian environments. We can reveal to students the connection between democracy and style, saying that the study of style is a part of our democratic and free experience. And finally we can point out that with the acquisition of a plurality of styles (and we are after pluralities, aren't we? not *just* the plain style?) the student is equipping himself for a more adaptive way of life within a society increasingly complex and multifaceted.

To some, this "publicizing" task may seem beside the point in our discussion of approaches to style. Yet if we perform this task well, no student of ours will ever assume that we are teaching some dainty humanistic pastime; our students will know that we are playing the game for real. And I am convinced that it's this preparatory task that makes any other approach meaningful. Many students write poorly and with deplorable styles simply because they do not care; their failures are less the result of incapacity than the lack of will.

Now if this first approach, à la propaganda, can be successfully made, we can move on to the task of revealing style as a viable subject matter. Certainly we must keep rescuing style from what Professor Louis Milic has called the metaphysical approach—elevated descriptions that finally prove terribly nebulous—for if we find style unteachable because students see no relevance, we can also find style unteachable because students never get their fingers on it, never see it in measurable, quantitative terms.

To make style viable, we must teach students some rather specific skills—(1) how to recognize stylistic material, (2) how to master this stylistic material and make it a part of a compositional technique, (3) how to combine stylistic materials into particular stylistic modes, and (4) how to adapt particular stylistic modes to particular rhetorical situations. In teaching these four "how to's" we are providing students with a *modus operandi* for learning style and an overall strategy for using it. It is in these ways that style becomes a reality, a true discipline and a true art.

To begin, we do well to emphasize the concept of stylistic material; to explain to students that in the art of choosing, one *can* and must choose *from something*. We need to explain that certain real materials exist in style—measurable, identifiable, describable: Demetrius's "phrases, members, and periods," or Professor Josephine Miles' "linear units" (the terms do not really matter): but real material that serves as the substantive foundation of style, this material being of three general kinds: individual words; collections of words into phrases, sentences, and paragraphs; and larger architectural units of composition.

A certain amount of stylistic material is already a part of the student's repertoire when he comes to college, of course; the simple sentence, after all, is an ingredient of stylistic material, and any given word in a vocabulary is an element of style. But now, in college, the student must enlarge his collection of usable stylistic materials. The student learned a compound sentence in high school; he will now learn a periodic sentence. He learned a simile in high school; he will now learn reification. And it becomes our task to lead students to the storehouses of material from which they can make acquisition, to help students encounter the sources of stylistic materials and to draw from them.

There is certainly the traditional source—the established schemes and tropes, the established arrangements and procedures of writing. A metaphor, an oxymoron, an inductive paragraph. The student can draw upon the wealth of materials in classical and subsequent rhetorics. In addition, the student can draw upon materials that are not a part of tradition, but are the results of current achievements in the study of style. In the past decade or so, the great interest in rhetoric and style has effected new identifications of materials—such elements as serial sentences, patterned paragraphs, and the like are being analyzed and described in our professional literature. And finally—through the creative analysis of literary texts—the student can himself discover new materials. If, for instance, a student observes a writer habitually using a construction of "opening prepositional phrase, a subject, a compound predicate, a closing prepositional phrase" the student may note that sequence as a usable stylistic element. Admittedly, the student may be discovering material already discovered by Longinus—but that's fine; the student has the pleasure of confirming established knowledge. And if the student makes a discovery of material not heretofore identified, so much the better. Let the student name it: the D. H. Lawrence construction, the Hemingway verb, the Faulkner paragraph. The ingredients of style are that much more a reality. Indeed, this seems to me—this inductive approach—one of the great values in the stylistic analysis of a text; it is a chance to make discoveries about style that have not, amazingly enough, already been made.

Teaching the recognition of stylistic material, old or new, brings us to an interesting juncture, however, for it is easy to assume that with recognition and identification of an adequate supply of material, the student somehow has mastered style itself. But recognition of stylistic material is not the same as the practice of it; the knowledge must be converted into performance.

One widespread approach to the task of moving stylistic material from the depot of the student's mind to the front line of his writing fingers is, alas, the contemplative approach. If we use the contemplative approach, we tell students that by looking at style long enough they will finally find themselves practicing style—by a kind of osmosis. We say "read a lot of good literature, make a lot of good stylistic analyses, and someday you'll wake up a writer." But can one learn to drive a car simply by taking a lot of car rides as a passenger? Surely one needs, in addition to contemplation, a great deal of involvement. One learns metaphor, not just by analysis, but by writing metaphors.

Some of us would advocate, therefore, a definite exercise system. We would advocate setting up recognized stylistic material as models; the models to be copied until the student can create similar but original versions of his own. It is a process of creative imitation that works like this: If we are going to teach a tricolon, an established bit of stylistic material, we first locate a tricolon in a text and point it out to our student; let us say the tricolon "of the people, by the people, for the people." The student learns to identify and recognize the tricolon. But our second step is to isolate the tricolon sentence from the text, set it up as a model, and ask the student to make an exact copy of it in his own hand—word for word, comma for comma. After the student has made his perfect copy and we have checked it for accuracy, we then ask the student to discuss with us—or at least learn *from* us—the nature of the model tricolon, its use in the text in which it occurred, and the use of such tricola in general. Finally, we ask the student to compose a sentence of his own containing a tricolon—on some subject far removed from that which Lincoln was discussing. We ask the student to write a sentence on a topic of his own choosing, but following the "model" he has just studied.

In this process, the student is asked to *recognize, copy, understand,* then *imitate creatively.* And this process can be used to master all possible stylistic materials: from the use of particular words to the more complex combinations of materials found in long passages. Creative imitation or generative copying is not new, of course; we all know the famous essay by Rollo Walter Brown on "How the French Boy Learns to Write" and certainly Professor Edward P. J. Corbett has given great support to this method in his *Classical Rhetoric for the Modern Student.*

Teaching viability of style does not end here, however. The student must not be left in the lurch at this point either; he must not be left with the ability to recognize and imitate stylistic materials without having a rationale for using them. A student has the legitimate right to ask, "Now what do I do? I know how to recognize and compose a tricolon, but what do I do with one?"

What students are actually asking for at this point is a strategy of style—and we can establish such a strategy by doing two primary things: (1)

identifying the categories of style, and (2) describing the constituency of those categories in terms of stylistic material.

First, a word about categories. The categories of style we choose to identify will depend upon our own individual way of seeing things: some of us may still use the four levels of style acknowledged by Demetrius; some of us may use the fairly conventional levels of usage—formal, informal, colloquial; some of us may prefer more elaborate categories combining both levels and intensities of language into a complex of rhetorical profiles; some of us may prefer such new categories as the styles of certitude, judiciousness, emotion, and absurdity, or "tough, sweet, and stuffy"; or some of us may even be so reductive as to prefer a simple two-category system of plain and literary style. But whatever our preferences, we must identify some *set of categories,* some *system* of categories, to serve as a framework in which various styles can be achieved.

Second, the constituency of these categories. Having established a system of diverse styles, we must establish recipes for achieving individual styles within the system. We must teach our students that certain stylistic material goes here; certain material goes there; that a certain combination and sequence of stylistic material creates one style; a certain combination and sequence creates another. Though given enough time a student might, by induction, discover the constituency of given categories himself, the burden of the description falls upon the teacher who is obligated to list the observable characteristics of the various styles. Indeed, I suspect that a good deal of our homework as teachers is, or should be, spent in discovering, in as great a detail as possible, these characteristics and pointing them out to our classes.

If we are able to effect for our classes these primary conditions of strategy—identification and description of categories—then we can exercise our students in the following ways:

Exercise One—We call for a student to write down all the possible verbalizations he can think of for any given message. How many ways can he say, "It's a beautiful day"? How many ways can he say, "Space exploration is too expensive"? Having made a list of all the possible ways, the student is then asked to allocate the various verbalizations on his list, placing them in the categories of style we have taught him. That is, given the recipes for a number of different styles—which verbalizations go where. Practicing this exercise over a period of time, the student—under our guidance—comes to realize that nearly any verbalization he can think of per given message can play its part in a total system of style; he stops seeking one eternally correct verbalization, but seeks rather to place all verbalizations in their appropriate communities.

Exercise Two—We ask a student to write a paragraph—on any topic—and to identify the particular style he has used in that paragraph. Having done so, the student next transforms the paragraph into another style. If he has written about campus revolution in a militant style, we ask him to transform his composition—with the same facts, observations, data, and opinions—into the judicious style. If he has written about his flower garden in an elegant style, we ask him now to write about it in a plain style. If in a colloquial style, now in a formal style. The point of the exercise is to teach the student how to add or subtract or substitute particular stylistic materials so as to change one style to another. Ultimately by means of this transformational exercise, the student will be able to decline—as it were—any sentence, paragraph, or essay through all possible styles.

Finally, of course, after the exercises, we ask students to write complete compositions. Though in teaching viability perhaps we err too often by beginning with whole compositions, by plunging the student into the middle of stylistic performance without making it truly viable for him, step by step, we do not err by asking the student to make the final effort of demonstrating all that we have been talking about—to demonstrate a knowledge of stylistic material, piece by piece, and a capacity for its strategic incorporation into stylistic wholeness.

The third task in our general approach to style—after the tasks of relevance and viability—is that of making the practice of style tremendously believable as the result of our performances in front of students. Robert Zoellner recently wrote in *College English* that he had "never, repeat never, seen a composition instructor, whether full professor or graduate student, walk into a composition classroom cold-turkey, with no preparation, ask the class for a specific theme-topic . . . and then—off the top of his head—actually compose a paragraph which illustrates the rhetorical principles that are the current concern of the class."

Professor Zoellner was surely exaggerating with the "never, repeat never" but I suspect that in general his charge is valid. We are an amazing lot of piano players refusing to play the piano. Yet should not the student's most significant model, so far as style is concerned, be the teacher himself? Isocrates, that ancient member of the profession, did not, as Werner Jaeger points out in *Paideia*, "merely discuss the technique of language and composition—the final inspiration was derived from the art of the master himself." And surely this is so: what the teacher writes on the blackboard in front of the student, or even what the teacher writes outside of class and brings to read to his students, is the teacher's commitment to the style he is urging his students to learn. Perhaps some of the difficulties in teaching style arise because of teacher failure: not failure in sincerity or industry or knowledge, but failure in demonstrating an art and a skill. Teacher failure ever to write and perform as a master stylist creates an amazing credibility gap.

I would propose a definite incorporation of teacher performance into our approach to style. Such a program would entail original composition by the teacher, at the blackboard, at least three to five minutes each class—or at least a five-to-ten minute performance once a week. We are limited by the physical circumstances of the classroom and by the pressures of time, but every blackboard is large enough for five or six sentences or a short paragraph, and every class period is long enough for a few minutes of teacher composition. Even if our demonstration of style is faulty and less than excellent, the fact that the teacher "did something" *for all to see* is noteworthy. And I have found that students actually learn a great deal from watching a teacher put in a word, take out a word, rewrite a sentence, even misspell and then correct a spelling, ponder over the use of a comma or a semicolon. Believe me: the teacher's struggle amidst the chalk dust can become the student's education.

And to prove to our class that we are not conning them, we can have one student call out a noun, another call out a verb—then using the noun and verb, we can write without prearrangement what needs to be written that day: a balanced sentence, a serial sentence, a circular paragraph. We may be reluctant to do this sort of impromptu writing—yet we are obligated. We are supposed to be professionals, and we should know enough about style to do a passing job, if not a brilliant job, and do the job "on call."

Teacher performance can go beyond the blackboard even. I think a certain amount of talk—modest and judicious, but enthusiastic—about the writing we do outside the class is important in the teaching of style. And I wonder if we shouldn't write some of the essays we ask our students to write—or write something comparable at least—and on occasion read to our classes what we have written. We could risk offending students with our vanity in an attempt to convince them that composition, rhetoric, and style are things we really do, that they are a part of our lives, that *we* are involved.

Such are the three obligations that must be met, three important tasks that must be performed in a general approach to teaching style. Our decisions how best to make style relevant, viable, and credible in the classroom may indeed vary; you and I may not agree about the details; we may use different syllabi and different textbooks. But I hope we will agree concerning the obligations themselves. At least I offer this anatomy for teaching as a possibility.

from

Institutio Oratoria

MARCUS FABIUS QUINTILIAN
(Book X, iii–iv)

Such are the aids which we may derive from external sources; as regards those which we must supply for ourselves, it is the pen which brings at once the most labour and the most profit. Cicero is fully justified in describing it as the best producer and teacher of eloquence, and it may be noted that in the *de Oratore* he supports his own judgment by the authority of Lucius Crassus, in whose mouth he places this remark. We must therefore write as much as possible and with the utmost care. For as deep ploughing makes the soil more fertile for the production and support of crops, so, if we improve our minds by something more than mere superficial study, we shall produce a richer growth of knowledge and shall retain it with greater accuracy. For without the consciousness of such preliminary study our powers of speaking extempore will give us nothing but an empty flow of words, springing from the lips and not from the brain. It is in writing that eloquence has its roots and foundations, it is writing that provides that holy of holies where the wealth of oratory is stored, and whence it is produced to meet the demands of sudden emergencies. It is of the first importance that we should develop such strength as will not faint under the toil of forensic strife nor be exhausted by continual use. For it is an ordinance of nature that nothing great can be achieved in a moment, and that all the fairest tasks are attended with difficulty, while on births as well she has imposed this law, that the larger the animal, the longer should be the period of gestation.

There are, however, two questions which present themselves in this connexion, namely, what should be our method and what the subjects on which we write, and I propose to treat them in this order. At first, our pen must be slow yet sure: we must search for what is best and refuse to give a joyful welcome to every thought the moment that it presents itself; we must first criticise the fruits of our imagination, and then, once approved, arrange them with care. For we must select both thoughts and words and weigh them one by one. This done, we must consider the order in which they should be placed, and must examine all the possible varieties of rhythm, refusing

Reprinted by permission of the publishers and the Loeb Classical Library from Quintilian, *Institutio Oratoria*, H. E. Butler, tr., Cambridge, Mass.: Harvard University Press, 1922.

necessarily to place each word in the order in which it occurs to us. In order to do this with the utmost care, we must frequently revise what we have just written. For beside the fact that thus we secure a better connexion between what follows and what precedes, the warmth of thought which has cooled down while we were writing is revived anew, and gathers fresh impetus from going over the ground again. We may compare this processs with what occurs in jumping matches. The competitors take a longer run and go at full speed to clear the distance which they aim at covering; similarly, in throwing the javelin, we draw back our arms, and in archery pull back the bow-string to propel the shaft. At times, however, we may spread our sails before the favouring breeze, but we must beware that this indulgence does not lead us into error. For we love all the offspring of our thought at the moment of their birth; were that not so, we should never commit them to writing. But we must give them a critical revision, and go carefully over any passage where we have reason to regard our fluency with suspicion. It is thus, we are told, that Sallust wrote, and certainly his works give clear evidence of the labour which he expended on them. Again, we learn from Varius that Virgil composed but a very small number of verses every day. It is true that with orators the case is somewhat different, and it is for this reason that I enjoin such lowness of speed and such anxious care at the outset. For the first aim which we must fix in our minds and insist on carrying into execution is to write as well as possible; speed will come with practice. Gradually thoughts will suggest themselves with increasing readiness, the words will answer to our call and rhythmical arrangement will follow, till everything will be found fulfilling its proper function as in a well-ordered household. The sum of the whole matter is this: write quickly and you will never write well, write well and you will soon write quickly. But it is just when we have acquired this facility that we must pause awhile to look ahead and, if I may use the metaphor, curb the horses that would run away with us. This will not delay our progress so much as lend us fresh vigour. For I do not think that those who have acquired a certain power in writing should be condemned to the barren pains of false self-criticism. How can anyone fulfil his duties as an advocate if he wastes his time in putting unnecessary finish on each portion of his pleadings? There are some who are never satisfied. They wish to change everything they have written and to put it in other words. They are a diffident folk, and deserve but ill of their own talents, who think it a mark of precision to cast obstacles in the way of their own writing. Nor is it easy to say which are the most serious offenders, those who are satisfied with everything or those who are satisfied with nothing that they write. For it is of common occurrence with young men, however talented they may be, to waste their gifts by superfluous elaboration, and to sink into silence through an excessive desire to speak well. I remember in this connexion a story that Julius Secundus, my contemporary, and, as is well known, my very dear friend, a man with remarkable powers of eloquence, but with an infinite passion for precision, told me of the words once used to him by his uncle, Julius Florus, the leading orator of Gaul, for it was there that he practised, a man eloquent as but few have ever been, and worthy of his nephew. He once noticed that Secundus, who was still a student, was looking depressed, and asked him the meaning of his frowns. The youth made no concealment of the reason: he had been working for three days, and had been unable, in spite of all his efforts, to devise an exordium for the theme which he had been given to write, with the result that he was not only vexed over his immediate difficulty, but had lost all hope of future success. Florus smiled and said, "Do you really want to speak better than you can?" There lies the truth of the whole matter. We must aim at speaking as well as we can, but must not try to speak better than our nature will permit. For to make any real advance we need study, not self-accusation. And it is not merely practice that will enable us to write at greater length and with increased fluency, although doubtless practice is most important. We need judgement as well. So long as we do not lie back with eyes turned up to the ceiling, trying to fire our imagination by muttering to ourselves, in the hope that something will present itself, but turn our thoughts to consider what the circumstances of the case demand, what suits the characters involved, what is the nature of the occasion and the temper of the judge, we shall acquire the power of writing by rational means. It is thus that nature herself bids us begin and pursue our studies once well begun. For most points are of a definite character and, if we keep our eyes open, will spontaneously present themselves. That is the reason why peasants and uneducated persons do not beat about the bush to discover with what they should begin, and our hesitation is all the more shameful if it is simply the result of education. We must not, therefore, persist in thinking that what is hard to find is necessarily best; for, if it seems to us that there is nothing to be said except that which we are unable to find, we must say nothing at all. On the other hand, there is a fault which is precisely the opposite of this, into which those fall who insist on first making a rapid draft of their subject with the utmost speed of which their pen is capable, and write in the heat and impulse of the moment. They call this their rough copy. They then revise what they have written, and arrange their hasty outpourings. But while the words and the rhythm may be corrected, the matter is still marked by the superficiality resulting from the speed with which it was thrown together. The more correct method is, therefore, to exercise care from the very beginning, and to form the work from the outset in such a manner that it merely requires to be chiselled into shape, not fashioned anew. Sometimes, however, we must follow the stream of our emotions, since their warmth will give us more than any diligence can secure.

The condemnation which I have passed on such carelessness in writing will make it pretty clear what my views are on the luxury of dictation which is now so fashionable. For, when we write, however great our speed, the fact that the hand cannot follow the rapidity of our thoughts gives us time to think, whereas the presence of our amanuensis hurries us on, and at times we feel ashamed to hesitate or pause, or make some alteration, as though we were afraid to display such weakness before a witness. As a result our language tends not merely to be haphazard and formless, but in our desire to produce a continuous flow we let slip positive improprieties of diction, which show neither the precision of the writer nor the impetuosity of the speaker. Again, if the amanuensis is a slow writer, or lacking in intelligence, he becomes a stumbling-block, our speed is checked, and the thread of our ideas is interrupted by the delay or even perhaps by the loss of temper to which it gives rise. Moreover, the gestures which accompany strong feeling, and sometimes even serve to stimulate the mind, the waving of the hand, the contraction of the brow, the occasional striking of forehead or side, and those which Persius notes when he describes a trivial style as one that

> "Thumps not the desk nor smacks of bitten nails,"

all these become ridiculous, unless we are alone, Finally, we come to the most important consideration of all, that the advantages of privacy are lost when we dictate. Everyone, however, will agree that the absence of company and deep silence are most conducive to writing, though I would not go so far as to concur in the opinion of those who think woods and groves the most suitable localities for the purpose, on the ground that the freedom of the sky and the charm of the surroundings produce sublimity of thought and wealth of inspiration. Personally I regard such an environment as a pleasant luxury rather than a stimulus to study. For whatever causes us delight, must necessarily distract us from the concentration due to our work. The mind cannot devote its undivided and sincere attention to a number of things at the same time, and wherever it turns its gaze it must cease to contemplate its appointed task. Therefore, the charm of the woods, the gliding of the stream, the breeze that murmurs in the branches, the song of birds, and the very freedom with which our eyes may range, are mere distractions, and in my opinion the pleasure which they excite is more likely to relax than to concentrate our attention. Demosthenes took a wiser view; for he would retire to a place[1] where no voice was to be heard, and no prospect greeted the sight, for fear that his eyes might force his mind to neglect its duty. Therefore, let the burner of the midnight oil seclude himself in the silence of night, within closed doors, with but a solitary lamp to light his labours. But for every kind of study, and more especially for night work, good health and its chief source, simple living, are essential; for we have fallen into the habit of devoting to relentless labour the hour which nature has appointed for rest and relaxation. From those hours we must take only such time as is superfluous for sleep, and will not be missed. For fatigue will make us careless in writing, and the hours of daylight are amply sufficient for one who has no other distractions. It is only the busy man who is driven to encroach on the hours of darkness.

[1] An underground room.

Nevertheless, night work, so long as we come to it fresh and untired, provides by far the best form of privacy.

But although silence and seclusion and absolute freedom of mind are devoutly to be desired, they are not always within our power to attain. Consequently we must not fling aside our book at once, if disturbed by some noise, and lament that we have lost a day: on the contrary, we must make a firm stand against such inconveniences, and train ourselves so to concentrate our thoughts as to rise superior to all impediments to study. If only you direct all your attention to the work which you have in hand, no sight or sound will ever penetrate to your mind. If even casual thoughts often occupy us to such an extent that we do not see passers-by, or even stray from our path, surely we can obtain the same result by the exercise of our will. We must not give way to pretexts for sloth. For unless we make up our mind that we must be fresh, cheerful and free from all other care when we approach our studies, we shall always find some excuse for idleness. Therefore, whether we be in a crowd, on a journey, or even at some festive gathering, our thoughts should always have some inner sanctuary of their own to which they may retire. Otherwise what shall we do when we are suddenly called upon to deliver a set speech in the midst of the forum, with lawsuits in progress on every side, and with the sound of quarrels and even casual outcries in our ears, if we need absolute privacy to discover the thoughts which we jot down upon our tablets? It was for this reason that Demosthenes, the passionate lover of seclusion, used to study on the seashore amid the roar of the breakers that they might teach him not to be unnerved by the uproar of the public assembly.

There are also certain minor details which deserve our attention, for there is nothing too minute for the student. It is best to write on wax owing to the facility which it offers for erasure, though weak sight may make it desirable to employ parchment by preference. The latter, however, although of assistance to the eye, delays the hand and interrupts the stream of thought owing to the frequency with which the pen has to be supplied with ink. But whichever we employ, we must leave blank pages that we may be free to make additions when we will. For lack of space at times gives rise to a reluctance to make corrections, or, at any rate, is liable to cause confusion when new matter is inserted. The wax tablets should not be unduly wide; for I have known a young and over-zealous student write his compositions at undue length, because he measured them by the number of lines, a fault which persisted, in spite of frequent admonition, until his tablets were changed, when it disappeared. Space must also be left for jotting down the thoughts which occur to the writer out of due order, that is to say, which refer to subjects other than those in hand. For sometimes the most admirable thoughts break in upon us which cannot be inserted in what we are writing, but which, on the other hand, it is unsafe to put by, since they are at times forgotten, and at times cling to the memory so persistently as to divert us from some other line of thought. They are, therefore, best kept in store.

The next point which we have to consider is the correction of our work, which is by far the most useful portion of our study: for there is good reason for the view that erasure is quite as important a function of the pen as actual writing. Correction takes the form of addition, excision and alteration. But it is a comparatively simple and easy task to decide what is to be added or excised. On the other hand, to prune what is turgid, to elevate what is mean, to repress exuberance, arrange what is disorderly, introduce rhythm where it is lacking, and modify it where it is too emphatic, involves a twofold labour. For we have to condemn what had previously satisfied us and discover what had escaped our notice. There can be no doubt that the best method of correction is to put aside what we have written for a certain time, so that when we return to it after an interval it will have the air of novelty and of being another's handiwork; for thus we may prevent ourselves from regarding our writings with all the affection that we lavish on a newborn child. But this is not always possible, especially in the case of an orator who most frequently has to write for immediate use, while some limit, after all, must be set to correction. For there are some who return to everything they write with the presumption that it is full of faults and, assuming that a first draft must necessarily be incorrect, think every change an improvement and make some alteration as often as they have the manuscript in their hands: they are, in fact, like doctors who use the knife even where the flesh is perfectly healthy. The result of their critical activities is that the finished work is full of scars, bloodless, and all the worse for their anxious care. No! let there be something in all our writing which, if it does not actually please us, at least passes muster, so that the file may only polish our work, not wear it away. There must also be a limit to the time which we spend on its revision. For the fact that Cinna[2] took nine years to write his Smyrna, and that Isocrates required ten years, at the lowest estimate, to complete his Panegyric does not concern the orator, whose assistance will be of no use, if it is so long delayed.

[2] C. Helvius Cinna, the friend of Catullus. The Smyrna was a short but exceptionally obscure and learned epic.